TECHNOLOGY AND
THE RISE OF GREAT POWERS

PRINCETON STUDIES IN INTERNATIONAL
HISTORY AND POLITICS

*Tanisha M. Fazal, G. John Ikenberry, William C. Wohlforth, and
Keren Yarhi-Milo, Series Editors*

Technology and the Rise of Great Powers

HOW DIFFUSION SHAPES ECONOMIC COMPETITION

JEFFREY DING

PRINCETON UNIVERSITY PRESS

PRINCETON & OXFORD

Portions of chapters 4 and 7 appeared as "The Diffusion Deficit in Scientific and Technological Power: Re-assessing China's Rise" by Jeffrey Ding in *Review of International Political Economy* (2023). Reprinted by permission of Taylor & Francis Group.

Portions of chapters 2 and 4 originally appeared in "The Rise and Fall of Technological Leadership: General-Purpose Technology Diffusion and Economic Power Transitions" by Jeffrey Ding in *International Studies Quarterly* (2024). Reprinted by permission of Oxford University Press.

Published by Princeton University Press
41 William Street, Princeton, New Jersey 08540
99 Banbury Road, Oxford OX2 6JX
press.princeton.edu

All Rights Reserved

ISBN 9780691260334
ISBN (pbk.) 9780691260341
ISBN (e-book) 9780691260372

British Library Cataloging-in-Publication Data is available

Editorial: Bridget Flannery-McCoy and Alena Chekanov
Production Editorial: Theresa Liu
Jacket / Cover Design: Hunter Finch
Production: Lauren Reese
Publicity: William Pagdatoon
Copyeditor: Cynthia Buck

This book has been composed in Arno

Printed and bound by CPI Group (UK) Ltd, Croydon, CR0 4YY

CONTENTS

LIST OF FIGURES AND TABLES

Figures

Tables

ACKNOWLEDGMENTS

THIS BOOK GREW out of nurturing environments at the University of Oxford (where it started as a dissertation), Stanford University (where it evolved during my fellowship years), and George Washington University (where it was finally completed).

I am very grateful to my PhD supervisor, Duncan Snidal, for his support throughout my time at Oxford. Duncan's belief in this project endured, even as mine wavered. At the Department of Politics and International Relations, I was lucky to learn alongside a warmhearted community of students with whom I shared commiserations, encouragement, and hot-pot meals. Thanks especially to Lucie Cadzow, Ben Garfinkel, Josh Goldstein, Kate Guy, David Hagebölling, Yang Han, Yutao Huang, Tuuli-Anna Huikuri, Kan Li, and Chenchao Lian. I am also grateful to Janina Dill, Todd Hall, Karolina Milewicz, Andrea Ruggeri, and Duncan Snidal for organizing workshops where I received excellent feedback in the early stages of my dissertation.

My intellectual nest in Oxford was the Centre for the Governance of AI (GovAI). Walks in Christ Church Meadow and Thai food dinners in local pubs with the GovAI team fueled my dissertation work. I am indebted to Markus Anderljung, Miles Brundage, Carrick Flynn, Ben Garfinkel, Jade Leung, Toby Shevlane, Baobao Zhang, and especially Allan Dafoe for cultivating such a stimulating research environment. For their constructive engagement with my PhD project, I am grateful to Carolyn Ashurst, Joslyn Barnhart, Max Daniel, Richard Danzig, Eric Drexler, Sophie-Charlotte Fischer, Hamish Hobbs, Alex Lintz, Carina Prunkl, Matt Sheehan, Helen Toner, and Remco Zwetsloot.

For their friendship over the years at Oxford, I thank Fahad Al Shaibani, Russell Bogue, Tom Carroll, Emily Gong, Kaleem Hawa, Richard Lu, Machmud Makhmudov, Jared Milfred, Jay Ruckelshaus, my amazing MPhil cohort, Bogdan Knezevic, and all the regulars at the weekly Jackdaw Lane pickup football game.

At Stanford's Center for International Security and Cooperation (CISAC), I was able to further develop and introduce new ideas into my manuscript. For going above and beyond amid the COVID-19 pandemic to make my predoctoral and postdoctoral fellowships at CISAC as fruitful as possible, I thank Andrea Gray, Tracy Hines, Scott Sagan, Harold Trinkunas, and two wonderful cohorts of CISAC fellows.

I finished this book as an assistant professor at George Washington University's Department of Political Science. I am grateful to my colleagues for believing in this project, especially Alex Downes and Charlie Glaser, who helped me organize a book workshop where Mike Beckley, Steve Brooks, Adam Dean, Marty Finnemore, Stephen Kaplan, Iris Malone, and Abe Newman provided incisive feedback that greatly improved the manuscript. Eric Grynaviski and Mike Miller imparted friendly advice during the book publication process. I am also indebted to Dan Drezner and William Thompson for their helpful comments.

I would also like to thank Alena Chekanov and Bridget Flannery-McCoy at Princeton University Press for taking a chance on this manuscript. I was floored by the generosity, care, and rigor of comments from two anonymous reviewers, and their suggestions pushed me through that last stage of revisions when one gets tired of painstakingly rewriting the same paragraph. Thanks to the editors at *International Studies Quarterly* and the *Review of International Political Economy* for allowing me to draw from some of my previously published material. In the process of writing this manuscript, I received financial support from the Rhodes Trust, Stanford's Institute for Human-Centered Artificial Intelligence, and George Washington University's Institute for Security and Conflict Studies.

One characteristic of academic writing that I love is its commitment to acknowledging how the work of others has influenced the work at hand—perhaps more so than in any other communication medium. Each citation is a nod to someone else's impact on one's own thinking, an exercise in humbleness and transparency about the debts we owe to our intellectual forerunners. Of all the thinkers who have shaped the ideas in this book, Nathan Rosenberg, a transformative historian of technology, stands out. One of the most rewarding aspects of this process has been the opportunity to share with Professor Rosenberg's family the impact of his insights on this book.

My wife, Joelle Brown, read every word of this book, and she has made these last few years the happiest and most fulfilling of my life. I am deeply appreciative.

Lastly, I wish to thank my family, including my sister, Rachel Ding, and my parents, Changmin Ding and Yuping Zhang. I dedicate this book to my parents for all the sacrifices they have made for us.

ABBREVIATIONS

AI	artificial intelligence
ASME	American Society of Mechanical Engineers
ASOM	American System of Manufacturing
ASTM	American Section of the International Association for Testing Materials
CME	coordinated market economy
DRAM	dynamic random-access memory
E&E	electrical and electronic
ENIAC	electronic numerical integrator and calculator
GPT	general-purpose technology
HDTV	high-definition television
ICT	information and communications technology
IFR	International Federation of Robotics
IR-1	First Industrial Revolution
IR-2	Second Industrial Revolution
IR-3	Third Industrial Revolution
IR-4	Fourth Industrial Revolution
ITU	International Telecommunication Union
LME	liberal market economy
LS	leading sector
MITI	Ministry of International Trade and Industry
MPD	Maddison Project Database
OECD	Organization for Economic Cooperation and Development
TFP	total factor productivity
TSCS	time-series cross-sectional
VOC	varieties of capitalism
WOS	Web of Science

1

Introduction

IN JULY 2018, the BRICS nations (Brazil, Russia, India, China, and South Africa) convened in Johannesburg around a specific, noteworthy theme: "Collaboration for Inclusive Growth and Shared Prosperity in the Fourth Industrial Revolution." The theme was noteworthy in part because of its specificity. Previous iterations of the BRICS summit, which gathers five nations that account for about 40 percent of the world's population and 25 percent of the world's GDP,[1] had tackled fuzzy slogans such as "Stronger Partnership for a Brighter Future" and "Broad Vision, Shared Prosperity." What stood out not only about that year's theme but also in comments by BRICS leaders at the summit was an unambiguous conviction that the world was undergoing a momentous season of technological change—one warranting the title "Fourth Industrial Revolution."[2]

Throughout the gathering, leaders of these five major emerging economies declared that the ongoing technological transition represented a rare opportunity for accelerating economic growth. When Chinese president Xi Jinping addressed the four other leaders of major emerging economies, he laid out the historical stakes of that belief:

> From the mechanization of the first industrial revolution in the 18th century, to the electrification of the second industrial revolution in the 19th century, to the informatization of the third industrial revolution in the 20th century, rounds of disruptive technological innovation have . . . fundamentally changed the development trajectory of human history.[3]

1. Iqbal 2022.
2. Klaus Schwab (2017a), founder and executive chairman of the World Economic Forum, first popularized the term "Fourth Industrial Revolution."
3. Qiushi 2018, cited in Doshi 2021, 286.

1

Citing recent breakthroughs in cutting-edge technologies like artificial intelligence (AI), Xi proclaimed, "Today, we are experiencing a larger and deeper round of technological revolution and industrial transformation."[4]

While the BRICS summit did not explicitly address how the Fourth Industrial Revolution could reshape the international economic order, the implications of Xi's remarks loomed in the backdrop. In the following months, Chinese analysts and scholars expanded upon them, especially the connection he drew between technological disruption and global leadership transitions.[5] One commentary on Xi's speech, published on the website of the authoritative Chinese Communist Party publication *Study Times*, detailed the geopolitical consequences of past technological revolutions: "Britain seized the opportunity of the first industrial revolution and established a world-leading productivity advantage. . . . After the second industrial revolution, the United States seized the dominance of advanced productivity from Britain."[6] In his analysis of Xi's address, Professor Jin Canrong of Renmin University, an influential Chinese international relations scholar, argued that China has a better chance than the United States of winning the competition over the Fourth Industrial Revolution.[7]

This broad sketch of power transition by way of technological revolution also resonates with US policymakers and leading thinkers. In his first press conference after taking office, President Joe Biden underscored the need to "own the future" as it relates to competition in emerging technologies, pledging that China's goal to become "the most powerful country in the world" was "not going to happen on [his] watch."[8] In 2018, the US Congress stood up the National Security Commission on Artificial Intelligence (NSCAI), an influential body that convened leading government officials, technology experts, and social scientists to study the national security implications of AI. Comparing AI's possible impact to past technologies like electricity, the NSCAI's 756-page final report warned that the United States would soon lose its technological leadership to China if it did not adequately prepare for the "AI revolution."[9]

---

4. Ibid.

5. Xi's emphasis on a new round of scientific and technological revolution [新一轮科技革命] dates as far back as September 2013, when he presided over a collective study session of the Politburo (Huang 2018).

6. Li 2018, cited in Doshi 2021, 287.

7. Jin 2019, cited in Doshi 2021, 288.

8. The White House 2021.

9. National Security Commission on Artificial Intelligence 2021, 19–20.

Caught up in the latest technical advances coming out of Silicon Valley or Beijing's Zhongguancun, these sweeping narratives disregard the process by which emerging technologies can influence a power transition. How do technological revolutions affect the rise and fall of great powers? Is there a discernible pattern that characterizes how previous industrial revolutions shaped the global balance of power? If such a pattern exists, how would it inform our understanding of the Fourth Industrial Revolution and US-China technological competition?

Conventional Wisdom on Technology-Driven Power Transitions

International relations scholars have long observed the link between disruptive technological breakthroughs and the rise and fall of great powers.[10] At a general level, as Yale historian Paul Kennedy has established, this process involves "differentials in growth rates and technological change, leading to shifts in the global economic balances, which in turn gradually impinge upon the political and military balances."[11] Yet, as is the case with present-day speculation about the effects of new technologies on the US-China power balance, largely missing from the international relations literature is an explanation of *how* technological change creates the conditions for a great power to leapfrog its rival. Scholars have carefully scrutinized how shifts in economic balances affect global military power and political leadership, but there is a need for further investigation into the very first step of Kennedy's causal chain: the link between technological change and differentials in long-term growth rates among great powers.[12]

Among studies that do examine the mechanics of how technological change shapes economic power transitions, the standard explanation stresses dominance over critical technological innovations in new, fast-growing industries ("leading sectors"). Britain became the world's most productive economy, according to this logic, because it was home to new advances that transformed its burgeoning textile industry, such as James Hargreaves's spinning jenny. In the same vein, Germany's mastery of major breakthroughs in the chemical industry is seen as pivotal to its subsequent challenge to British

---

10. Gilpin 1981, 1987; Kennedy 1987; Modelski and Thompson 1996.
11. Kennedy 1987, xx.
12. Gilpin 1981; Kennedy 1987; Kirshner 1998.

economic leadership. Informed by historical analysis, the leading-sector (LS) perspective posits that, during major technological shifts, the global balance of economic power tips toward "the states which were the first to introduce the most important innovations."[13]

Why do the benefits of leading sectors accrue to certain countries? Explanations vary, but most stress the goodness-of-fit between a nation's domestic institutions and the demands of disruptive technologies. At a general level, some scholars argue that rising powers quickly adapt to new leading sectors because they are unburdened by the vested interests that have built up in more established powers.[14] Others point to more specific factors, including the degree of government centralization or sectoral governance arrangements.[15] Common to all these perspectives is a focus on the institutions that allow one country to first introduce major breakthroughs in an emerging industry. In the case of Britain's rise, for example, many influential histories highlight institutions that supported "heroic" inventors.[16] Likewise, accounts of Germany's success with leading sectors focus on its investments in scientific education and industrial research laboratories.[17]

The broad outlines of LS theory exert substantial influence in academic and policymaking circles. Field-defining texts, including works by Robert Gilpin and Paul Kennedy, use the LS model to map out the rise and fall of great powers.[18] In a review of international relations scholarship, Daniel Drezner summarizes their conclusions: "Historically, a great power has acquired hegemon status through a near-monopoly on innovation in leading sectors."[19]

The LS template also informs contemporary discussion of China's challenge to US technological leadership. In another speech about how China could leverage this new round of industrial revolution to become a "science and technology superpower," President Xi called for China to develop into "the world's primary center for science and high ground for innovation."[20] As US policymakers confront China's growing strength in emerging technologies

13. Akaev and Pantin 2014, 869; see also Modelski and Thompson 1996; Thompson 1990.
14. Gilpin 1996; Moe 2009.
15. Drezner 2001; Kim and Hart 2001; Kitschelt 1991.
16. Nuvolari 2004.
17. Drezner 2001; Moe 2007.
18. Gilpin 1981, 1987; Kennedy 1987; Modelski and Thompson 1996; Rostow 1960; Schumpeter 1934, 1939; Thompson 1990.
19. Drezner 2001, 7. Drezner (2019, 289) repeats this claim in an article marking the centenary of the international relations discipline.
20. Xi 2021. This speech was delivered at a joint meeting of the Chinese Academy of Sciences and the Chinese Academy of Engineering in May 2018.

like AI, they also frame the competition in terms of which country will be able to generate radical advances in new leading sectors.[21]

Who did it first? Which country innovated it first? Presented with technical breakthroughs that inspire astonishment, it is only natural to gravitate toward the moment of initial discovery. When today's leaders evoke past industrial revolutions, as Xi did in his speech to the BRICS nations, they tap into historical accounts of technological progress that also center the moment of innovation.[22] The economist and historian Nathan Rosenberg diagnoses the problem with these innovation-centric perspectives: "Much less attention . . . if any at all, has been accorded to the rate at which new technologies have been adopted and embedded in the productive process. Indeed the diffusion process has often been assumed out of existence."[23] Yet, without the humble undertaking of diffusion, even the most extraordinary advances will not matter.

Taking diffusion seriously leads to a different explanation for how technological revolutions affect the rise and fall of great powers. A diffusion-centric framework probes what comes after the hype. Less concerned with which state first introduced major innovations, it instead asks why some states were more successful at adapting and embracing new technologies at scale. As outlined in the next section, this alternative pathway points toward a different set of institutional factors that underpin leadership in times of technological leadership, in particular institutions that widen the base of engineering skills and knowledge linked to foundational technologies.

GPT Diffusion Theory

In September 2020, the *Guardian* published an opinion piece arguing that humans should not fear new breakthroughs in AI. Noting that "Stephen Hawking has warned that AI could 'spell the end of the human race,'" the article's "author" contends that "I am here to convince you not to worry. Artificial intelligence will not destroy humans. Believe me."[24] If one came away from this piece with the feeling that the author had a rose-tinted view of the future of AI, it would be a perfectly reasonable judgment. After all, the author was GPT-3, an AI model that can understand and produce humanlike text.

21. Allison and Schmidt 2020; National Security Commission on Artificial Intelligence 2021; Tellis 2013.
22. Edgerton 2010, 2011.
23. Rosenberg 1982, 19.
24. GPT-3 2020.

Released earlier that year by OpenAI, a San Francisco–based AI lab, GPT-3 surprised everyone—including its designers—with its versatility. In addition to generating poetry and essays like the *Guardian* op-ed from scratch, early users demonstrated GPT-3's impressive capabilities in writing code, translating languages, and building chatbots.[25] Six months after its launch, one compilation listed sixty-six unique use cases of GPT-3, which ranged from automatically updating spreadsheets to generating website landing pages.[26] Two years later, OpenAI's acclaimed ChatGPT model, built on an improved version of GPT-3, would set the internet aflame with its wide-ranging capabilities.[27]

While the name "GPT-3" derives from a class of language models known as "generative pre-trained transformers," the abbreviation, coincidentally, also speaks to the broader significance of recent breakthroughs in AI: the possible arrival of the next general-purpose technology (GPT). Foundational breakthroughs in the ability of computers to perform tasks that usually require human intelligence have the potential to transform countless industries. Hence, scholars and policymakers often compare advances in AI to electricity, the prototypical GPT.[28] As Kevin Kelly, the former editor of *WIRED*, once put it, "Everything that we formerly electrified we will now cognitize . . . business plans of the next 10,000 startups are easy to forecast: Take X and add AI."[29]

In this book, I argue that patterns in how GPTs diffuse throughout the economy illuminate a novel explanation for how and when technological changes affect power transitions. The emergence of GPTs—fundamental advances that can transform many application sectors—provides an opening for major shifts in economic leadership. Characterized by their scope for continuous improvement, pervasive applicability across the economy, and synergies with other technological advances, GPTs carry an immense potential for boosting productivity.[30] Carefully tracking how the various applications of GPTs are adopted across various industries, a process I refer to

25. To the best of my knowledge—and believe me, I have searched far and wide—AI models have not yet figured out how to write original academic books.

26. Dickson 2021. There are also concerns about the use of language models like GPT-3 to generate toxic speech and misinformation; see Kreps, McCain, and Brundage 2022.

27. Hu 2023.

28. A Google search for the exact phrase "AI is the new electricity," conducted on November 18, 2022, returned over sixteen thousand hits. Andrew Ng, founder of Google Brain, first popularized this comparison in a 2017 speech at Stanford.

29. Kelly 2014.

30. Bresnahan 2010; Bresnahan and Trajtenberg 1995; Lipsey, Carlaw, and Bekar 2005.

as "GPT diffusion," is essential to understanding how technological revolutions disrupt economic power balances.

Based on the experience of past GPTs, this potential productivity boost comes with one notable caveat: the full impact of a GPT manifests only after a gradual process of diffusion into pervasive use.[31] GPTs demand structural changes across a range of technology systems, which involve complementary innovations, organizational adaptations, and workforce adjustments.[32] For example, electrification's boost to productivity materialized about five decades after the introduction of the first electric dynamo, occurring only after factories had restructured their layouts and there had been interrelated breakthroughs in steam turbines.[33] Fittingly, after the release of GPT-3, OpenAI CEO Sam Altman alluded to this extended trajectory: "The GPT-3 hype is way too much . . . it still has serious weaknesses and sometimes makes very silly mistakes. AI is going to change the world, but GPT-3 is just a very early glimpse. We have a lot still to figure out."[34]

Informed by historical patterns of GPT diffusion, my explanation for technology-driven power transitions diverges significantly from the standard LS account. Specifically, these two causal mechanisms differ along three key dimensions, which relate to the technological revolution's impact timeframe, phase of relative advantage, and breadth of growth. First, while the GPT mechanism involves a protracted gestation period between a GPT's emergence and resulting productivity boosts, the LS mechanism assumes that there is only a brief window during which countries can capture profits in leading sectors. "The greatest marginal stimulation to growth may therefore come early in the sector's development at the time when the sector itself is expanding rapidly," William Thompson reasons.[35] By contrast, the most pronounced effects on growth arrive late in a GPT's development.

Second, the GPT and LS mechanisms also assign disparate weights to innovation and diffusion. Technological change involves a phase when the technology is first incubated as a viable commercial application ("innovation") and a phase when the innovation permeates across a population of potential users

31. David 1990, 356.

32. Brynjolfsson, Rock, and Syverson 2017; David 1990.

33. Devine 1982.

34. Vincent 2020. Many also noted that some of the most impressive examples were cherry-picked, and that GPT-3 still requires a lot of fine-tuning from humans. For more background on GPT-3, see Dale 2021.

35. Thompson 1990, 211; see also Freeman, Clark, and Soete 1982, 80; Gilpin 1987, 112.

("diffusion"). The LS mechanism is primarily concerned about which country dominates innovation in leading sectors, capturing the accompanying monopoly profits.[36] Under the GPT mechanism, successful adaptation to technological revolutions is less about being the first to introduce major innovations and more about effectively adopting GPTs across a wide range of economic sectors.

Third, regarding the breadth of technological transformation and economic growth, the LS mechanism focuses on the contributions of a limited number of leading sectors and new industries to economic growth in a particular period.[37] In contrast, GPT-fueled productivity growth is spread across a broad range of industries.[38] Dispersed productivity increases from many industries and sectors come from the extension and generalization of localized advances in GPTs.[39] Thus, the LS mechanism expects the breadth of growth in a particular period to be concentrated in leading sectors, whereas the GPT mechanism expects technological complementarities to be dispersed across many sectors.

A clearer understanding of the contours of technological change in times of economic power transition informs which institutional variables matter most. If the LS trajectory holds, then the most important institutional endowments and responses are those that support a monopoly on innovation in leading sectors. In the context of skill formation, institutional competencies in science and basic research gain priority. For instance, the conventional explanation of Germany's industrial rise in the late nineteenth century attributes its technological leadership to investments in industrial research labs and highly skilled chemists. These supported Germany's dominance of the chemical industry, a key LS of the period.[40]

The impact pathway of GPTs brings another set of institutional complementarities to the fore. GPT diffusion theory highlights the importance of "GPT skill infrastructure": education and training systems that widen the pool of engineering skills and knowledge linked to a GPT. When widespread adoption of GPTs is the priority, it is ordinary engineers, not heroic inventors, who matter most. Widening the base of engineering skills associated with a GPT cultivates a more interconnected technological system, spurring cross-

36. Modelski and Thompson 1996, 91.
37. Grübler 2003, 118.
38. See Harberger (1988) for the original formulation of these two views of long-term economic growth.
39. Crafts 2001, 306; David and Wright 1999, 12.
40. Drezner 2001, 13–18; Moe 2007, 253–66; Thompson 1990.

fertilization between institutions optimized for applied technology and those oriented toward foundational research.[41]

Returning to the example of late-nineteenth-century advances in chemicals, GPT diffusion spotlights institutional adjustments that differ from those of the LS mechanism. In a decades-long process, innovations in chemical engineering practices gradually enabled the chemicalization of procedures common to many industries beyond synthetic dyes, which was controlled by Germany. Despite trailing Germany in the capacity to produce elite chemists and frontier chemical research, the United States was more effective at adapting to chemicalization because it first institutionalized the discipline of chemical engineering.[42]

Of course, since GPT diffusion depends on factors aside from human capital, GPT skill infrastructure represents one of many institutional forces at work. Standards-setting organizations, financing bodies, and the competitiveness of markets can all influence the flow of information between the GPT domain and application sectors.[43] Since institutions of skill formation produce impacts that spill over into and complement other institutional arrangements, they comprise the focus of my analysis.[44]

Assessing GPT Diffusion across Industrial Revolutions

To test this argument, I employ a mixed-methods approach that pairs qualitative historical analysis with quantitative methods. Historical case studies permit me to thoroughly trace the interactions between technologies and institutions among great powers in previous industrial revolutions. I then explore the generalizability of GPT diffusion theory beyond the chosen set of great powers. Using data on nineteen countries from 1995 to 2020, I analyze the theorized connection between GPT skill infrastructure in software engineering and computerization rates.

To investigate the causal processes that connect technological changes to economic power transitions, I set the LS mechanism against the GPT diffusion mechanism across three historical case studies: Britain's rise to preeminence in the First Industrial Revolution (IR-1); America's and Germany's

---

41. Shapley and Roy 1985.

42. Rosenberg and Steinmueller 2013.

43. Timothy Bresnahan and Manuel Trajtenberg (1995) argue that these coordination mechanisms help unleash positive externalities associated with GPT trajectories. See also Rosenberg 1998b; Vona and Consoli 2014.

44. Thelen 2004, 285–86.

overtaking of Britain in the Second Industrial Revolution (IR-2); and Japan's challenge to America's technological dominance in the Third Industrial Revolution (IR-3), or what is sometimes called the "information revolution." This case setup allows for a fair and decisive assessment of the explanatory relevance of GPT diffusion theory in comparison to LS theory. Because the IR-1 and IR-2 function as typical cases where the cause and outcome are clearly present, they are ideal for developing and testing mechanism-based theories.[45] The IR-3, a deviant case in that a technological revolution is not followed by an economic power transition, provides a different but still useful way to compare the two mechanisms.

The IR-1 (1780–1840) is a paradigmatic case of technology-driven power transition. It is well established that the IR-1's technological advances propelled Great Britain to unrivaled economic supremacy. As for the specific causal pathway, international relations scholarship tends to attribute Britain's rise to its monopoly over innovation in cotton textiles and other leading sectors. According to these accounts, Britain's technological leadership in the IR-1 sprang from its institutional capacity to nurture genius inventors in these sectors. Since the publication of these field-defining works, economic and technology historians have uncovered that the impacts on British industrialization of the two most prominent areas of technological change, cotton textiles and iron, followed different trajectories. Often relying on formal econometric methods to understand the impact of key technologies, these historical accounts question the prevailing narrative of the IR-1.

The IR-2 (1870–1914) supplies another opportunity to pit GPT diffusion theory against the LS account. International relations scholars interpret the IR-2 as a case in which Britain's rivals challenged its economic leadership because they first introduced significant technological advances in leading sectors. Particular emphasis is placed on Germany's ability to corner market shares in chemicals, which is linked to its strengths in scientific education and industrial research institutions. More granular data on cross-national differences in engineering education suggest that the U.S. technological advantage rested on the country's wide base of mechanical engineers. Combined with detailed tracing of the pace and extent of technology adoption during this period, this chapter's evidence suggests modifications to conventional understandings of the IR-2.

---

45. Beach and Pedersen 2019, 97–98; Goertz 2017.

In the IR-3 (1960–2000), fundamental breakthroughs in information and communication technologies presented another opening for a shift in economic leadership. During this period, prominent thinkers warned that Japan's lead in industries experiencing rapid technological change, including semiconductors and consumer electronics, would threaten U.S. economic leadership. Influential scholars and policymakers advocated for the United States to adopt Japan's *keiretsu* system of industrial organization and its aggressive industrial policy approach. Ultimately, Japan's productivity growth stalled in the 1990s. Given the absence of an economic power transition, the primary function of the IR-3 case therefore is to provide disconfirming evidence of the two explanations. If the components of the LS mechanism were present, then the fact that an economic power transition did not occur would damage the credibility of the LS mechanism. The same condition applies to GPT diffusion theory.

In each of the cases, I follow the same standardized procedures. First, I test three pairs of competing propositions about the key technological trajectories, derived from the different expectations of the LS and GPT mechanisms related to the impact timeframe, phase of relative advantage, and breadth of growth. Then, depending on whether the LS or GPT trajectory better accords with the historical evidence, I analyze the goodness-of-fit between the institutional competencies of leading industrial powers and the prevailing trajectory. For instance, if an industrial revolution is better characterized by the GPT trajectory, then the corresponding case analysis should show that differences in GPT skill infrastructure determine which powers rise and fall. Although I primarily distinguish GPT diffusion theory from the LS model, I also examine alternative factors unique to the particular case, as well as two other prominent explanations of how advanced economies differentially benefit from technological changes (the varieties of capitalism and threat-based approaches).

The historical case analysis supports the explanatory power of the GPT mechanism over the LS mechanism. In all three periods, technological changes affected the rise and fall of great powers in a gradual, decades-long impact pathway that advantaged those that effectively diffused GPTs across a broad range of sectors. Education and training systems that cultivated broad pools of engineering skills proved crucial to GPT diffusion.

Evaluating these two competing explanations requires a clear understanding of the cause and outcome that bracket both the GPT and LS mechanisms. The hypothesized cause is a "technological revolution," or a period characterized by particularly disruptive technological advances.[46] Since the shape of technological change is uneven, not all improvements in useful knowledge are relevant for power transitions.[47] However, some extraordinary clusters of technological breakthroughs, often deemed industrial revolutions by historians, do have ramifications for the rise and fall of great powers.[48] I am primarily interested in the pathway by which these technological revolutions influence the global distribution of power.

The outcome variable of interest is an economic power transition, in which one great power sustains productivity growth at higher levels than its rivals. The balance of power can shift in many ways; here I focus on relative economic growth rates because they are catalysts for intensifying hegemonic rivalries.[49] Productivity growth, in particular, determines economic growth over the long run. Unique in its fungibility with other forms of power, sustained economic growth is central to a state's ability to exert political and military influence. As demonstrated by the outcomes of interstate conflicts between great powers, economic and productive capacity is the foundation of military power.[50]

Lastly, the quantitative analysis supplements the historical case studies by scrutinizing the generalizability of GPT diffusion theory outside of great powers. A key observable implication of my argument is that the rate at which a GPT spreads throughout the economy owes much to that country's institutional capacity to widen the pool of pertinent engineering skills and knowledge. Using a novel method to estimate the breadth of software engineering education at a cross-national level, I analyze the theorized connection between GPT skill infrastructure and computerization rates across nineteen advanced and emerging economies from 1995 to 2020. I supplement my time-series cross-sectional models with a duration analysis and cross-sectional regressions. Robust to many alternative specifications, my results show that, at least for computing technology, advanced economies that have higher levels of GPT skill infrastructure preside over higher rates of GPT diffusion.

46. Other related terms include "technology waves" (Milner and Solstad 2021) and "long waves" (Goldstein 1988).

47. Technology includes both physical manifestations of hardware and blueprints as well as improvements in organizational and managerial practices (Rosenberg 1982).

48. Von Tunzelmann 1997, 2. Though this analytic categorization of industrial revolutions is contested (see, for example, Hull 1996), these periods of technological change also correspond to cases used to support the LS explanation, so they are workable constructs for testing GPT diffusion theory against the standard account.

49. Kennedy 1987; Kim and Morrow 1992; Kugler and Lemke 1996; Väyrynen 1983.

50. Kirshner 1998; Modelski and Thompson 1996.

Key Contributions

The book makes several contributions to scholarship on power transitions and the effects of technological change on international politics. First, it puts forward a novel explanation for how and when significant technological break-throughs generate a power transition in the international system. GPT diffusion theory revises the dominant theory based on leading sectors, which holds significant sway over academic and policymaking circles. By deepening our understanding of how technological revolutions influence shifts in economic leadership, this book also contributes to long-standing debates about the causes of power transitions.[51]

Second, the findings of this book bear directly on present-day technological competition between the United States and China. Emphasizing where fundamental breakthroughs are first seeded, the LS template strongly informs not only assessments of the US-China competition for technological leadership but also the ways in which leading policymakers in both countries formulate technology strategies. It is no coincidence that the three cases in this study match the three technological revolutions referenced by Chinese president Xi in his speech on the IR-4 to the BRICS summit.

As chapter 7 explores in detail, GPT diffusion theory suggests that Xi, along with other leading policymakers and thinkers in both the United States and China, has learned the wrong lessons from previous industrial revolutions. If the IR-4 reshapes the economic power balance, the impact will materialize through a protracted period during which a GPT, such as AI, acquires a variety of uses in a wide range of productive processes. GPT skill infrastructure, not the flashy efforts to secure the high ground in innovation, will decide which nation owns the future in the IR-4.

Beyond power transitions, *Technology and the Rise of Great Powers* serves as a template for studying the politics of emerging technologies. An enduring dilemma is that scholars either assign too much weight to technological change or underestimate the effects of new technologies.[52] Approaches that emphasize the social shaping of technology neglect that not all technologies are created equal, whereas technologically deterministic approaches discount the influence of political factors on technological development. By first distinguishing GPTs, together with their pattern of diffusion, from other technologies and technological trajectories, and then showing how social and political

51. Ogburn 1949a.
52. Sprout 1963, 187.

factors shape the pace and direction of GPT diffusion, my approach demonstrates a middle way forward.

Roadmap for the Book

The book proceeds as follows. Chapter 2 fleshes out the key differences between GPT diffusion theory and the LS-based account, as well as the case analysis procedures and selection strategy that allow me to systematically evaluate these two causal mechanisms. The bulk of the evidence follows in three case studies that trace how technological progress affected economic power transitions in the First, Second, and Third Industrial Revolutions.

The first two case studies, the IR-1 and IR-2, show that a gap in the adoption of GPTs, as opposed to monopoly profits from dominating LS innovations, was the crucial driver of an economic power transition. In both cases, the country that outpaced its industrial rivals made institutional adjustments to cultivate engineering skills related to the key GPT of the period. The IR-1 case, discussed in chapter 3, reveals that Britain was the most successful in fostering a wide pool of machinists who enabled the widespread diffusion of advances in iron machinery. In considering the IR-2 case, chapter 4 highlights how the United States surpassed Britain as the preeminent economic power by fostering a wide base of mechanical engineering talent to spread interchangeable manufacturing methods.

The IR-3 case, presented in chapter 5, demonstrates that technological revolutions do not necessarily always produce an economic power transition. The fact that Japan did not overtake the United States as the economic leader would provide disconfirming evidence of both the LS and GPT mechanisms, if the components of these mechanisms were present. In the case of the LS mechanism, Japan did dominate innovations in the IR-3's leading sectors, including consumer electronics and semiconductor components. In contrast, the IR-3 does not discredit the GPT mechanism because Japan did not lead the United States in the diffusion of information and communications technology across a wide variety of economic sectors.

Chapter 6 uses large-*n* quantitative analysis to explore how GPT diffusion applies beyond great powers. Chapter 7 applies the GPT diffusion framework to the implications of modern technological breakthroughs for the US-China power balance. Focusing on AI technology as the next GPT that could transform the international balance of power, I explore the extent to which my findings generalize to the contemporary US-China case. I conclude in chapter 8 by underscoring the broader ramifications of the book.

2

GPT Diffusion Theory

HOW AND WHEN do technological changes affect the rise and fall of great powers? Specifically, how do significant technological breakthroughs result in differential rates of economic growth among great powers? International relations scholars have long observed that rounds of technological revolution lead to upheaval in global economic leadership, bringing about a power transition in the international system. However, few studies explore how this process occurs.

Those that do tend to fixate on the most dramatic aspects of technological change—the eureka moments and first implementations of radical inventions. Consequently, the standard account of technology-driven power transitions stresses a country's ability to dominate innovation in leading sectors. By exploiting brief windows in which to monopolize profits in new industries, the country that dominates innovation in these sectors rises to become the world's most productive economy. Explanations vary regarding why the benefits of leading sectors tend to accrue in certain nations. Some scholars argue that national systems of political economy that accommodate rising challengers can more readily accept and support new industries. Leading economies, by contrast, are victims of their past success, burdened by powerful vested interests that resist adaptation to disruptive technologies.[1] Other studies point to more specific institutional factors that account for why some countries monopolize leading sectors, such as the degree of government centralization or industrial governance structures.[2]

An alternative explanation, based on the diffusion of general-purpose technologies (GPTs), draws attention to the less spectacular process by which

1. Gilpin 1996; Moe 2009.
2. Drezner 2001; Kitschelt 1991.

fundamental innovations gradually diffuse throughout many industries. The rate and scope of diffusion is particularly relevant for GPTs, which are distinguished by their scope for continual improvement, broad applicability across many sectors, and synergies with other technological advances. Recognized by economists and historians as "engines of growth," GPTs hold immense potential for boosting productivity.[3] Realizing this promise, however, necessitates major structural changes across the technology systems linked to the GPT, including complementary innovations, organizational changes, and an upgrading of technical skills. Thus, GPTs lead to a productivity boost only after a "gradual and protracted process of diffusion into widespread use."[4] This is why more than five decades passed before key innovations in electricity, the quintessential GPT, significantly transformed manufacturing productivity.[5]

The process of GPT diffusion illuminates a pathway from technological change to power transition that diverges from the LS account (figure 2.1). Under the GPT mechanism, some great powers sustain economic growth at higher levels than their rivals do because, during a gradual process spanning decades, they more intensively adopt GPTs across a broad range of industries. This is analogous to a marathon run on a wide road. The LS mechanism, in contrast, specifies that one great power rises to economic leadership because it dominates innovations in a limited set of leading sectors and captures the accompanying monopoly profits. This is more like a sprint through a narrow running lane.

Why are some countries more successful at GPT diffusion? Building from scholarship arguing that a nation's success in adapting to emerging technologies is determined by the *fit* between its institutions and the demands of evolving technologies, I argue that the GPT diffusion pathway informs the institutional adaptations crucial to success in technological revolutions.[6] Unlike institutions oriented toward cornering profits in leading sectors, those optimized for GPT diffusion help standardize and spread novel best practices between the GPT sector and application sectors. Education and training systems that widen the base of engineering skills and knowledge linked to new GPTs, or what I call "GPT skill infrastructure," are essential to all of these institutions.

3. Bresnahan and Trajtenberg 1995.
4. David 1990, 356.
5. Devine 1982.
6. Gilpin 1996; Kim and Hart 2001; Kitschelt 1991; Perez 2002.

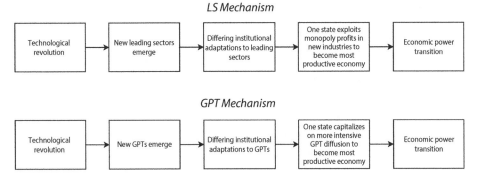

FIGURE 2.1. Causal Diagrams for LS and GPT Mechanisms

The differences between these two theories of technological change and power transition are made clear when one country excels in the institutional competencies for LS product cycles but does not dominate GPT diffusion. Take, for example, chemical innovations and Germany's economic rise in the late nineteenth century. Germany dominated major innovations in chemicals and captured nearly 90 percent of all global exports of synthetic dyestuffs.[7] In line with the LS mechanism, this success was backed by Germany's investments in building R&D labs and training doctoral students in chemistry, as well as a system of industrial organization that facilitated the rise of three chemical giants.[8] Yet it was the United States that held an advantage in adopting basic chemical processes across many industries. As expected by GPT diffusion theory, the United States held institutional advantages in widening the base of engineering skills and knowledge necessary for chemicalization on a wide scale.[9] This is when the ordinary tweakers and the implementers come to the fore, and the star scientists and inventors recede to the background.[10]

The rest of this chapter fleshes out my theoretical framework. It first clarifies the outcome I seek to explain: an economic power transition in which one great power becomes the economic leader by sustaining productivity growth at higher levels than its rivals. The starting point of my argument is that the diffusion of GPTs is central to the relationship between technological change

7. Lehrer 2005, 254–55.

8. Haber 1958, 121–31.

9. Rosenberg and Steinmueller 2013. A later section of this chapter expands on U.S. advantages in chemical engineering.

10. I adopt the terms "tweaker" and "implementer" from Meisenzahl and Mokyr 2011, 446.

and productivity leadership. This chapter explicates this argument by justifying the emphasis on both GPTs and diffusion, highlighting the differences between the GPT and LS mechanisms. It then extends the analysis to the institutional competencies that synergize with GPT trajectories. From the rich set of technology-institution interactions identified by evolutionary economists and comparative institutionalists, I justify my focus on institutions that enable countries to widen the skill base required to spread GPTs across industries. After differentiating my argument from alternative explanations, the chapter closes with a description of the book's research methodology.[11]

The Outcome: Long-Term Economic Growth Differentials and Power Transitions

Power transitions are to the international system as earthquakes are to the geological landscape. Shifts in the relative power of leading nations send shock waves throughout the international system. What often follows is conflict, the most devastating form of which is a war waged by coalitions of great powers for hegemony over the globe.[12] Beyond heightened risks of conflict, the aftershocks of power transitions reverberate in the architecture of the international order as victorious powers remake international institutions in their own images.[13]

While the power transition literature largely tackles the consequences of power transitions, I treat the rise and fall of great powers as the outcome to be explained. This follows David Baldwin's instruction for international relations scholars "to devote more attention to treating power as a dependent variable and less to treating it as an independent variable."[14] Specifically, I explore the causes of "economic power transitions," in which one great power sustains economic growth rates at higher levels than its rivals.[15]

11. Parts of this chapter derive from Ding 2024.

12. Power transition theory expects that the risk of a major war is greatest when a rising challenger threatens the established power (Gilpin 1975; Organski 1958; Tammen 2008). For a critique, see Chan 2007.

13. For discussions of other possible consequences of power shifts, such as discussions of hegemonic stability, see Keohane 1984; Snidal 1985.

14. Baldwin 2012, 288.

15. My outcome variable, differential rates of economic growth among established and rising powers, is regarded by international relations scholars as a key stage in the overarching process of power transition (Gilpin 1981). Related literature references shifts in industrial leadership (Moe 2009), leading economies (Modelski and Thompson 1996; Reuveny and Thompson

It might not be obvious, at first glance, why I focus on economic power. After all, power is a multidimensional, contested concept that comes in many other forms. The salience of certain power resources depends on the context in which a country draws upon them to exert influence.[16] For my purposes, differentials in economic growth are the most relevant considerations for intensifying hegemonic rivalry. An extensive literature has demonstrated that changes in relative economic growth often precede hegemonic wars.[17]

Moreover, changes in global political and military leadership often follow shifts in economic leadership. As the most fungible mode of power, economic strength undergirds a nation's influence in global politics and its military capabilities.[18] The outcomes of interstate conflicts bear out that economic and productive capacity is the foundation of military power.[19] Paul Kennedy concludes that

> all of the major shifts in the world's military-power balances have followed alterations in the productive balances . . . the rising and falling of the various empires and states in the international system has been confirmed by the outcomes of the major Great Power wars, where victory has always gone to the side with the greatest material resources.[20]

How does one identify if or when an economic power transition occurs? Phrased differently, how many years does a great power need to lead its rivals in economic growth rates? How large does that gap have to reach? Throughout this book, I judge whether an economic power transition has occurred based on one great power attaining a lead in overall economic productivity over its

---

2001), and the technological hegemon (Drezner 2001, 4). I use the term "economic power transition" because it concisely captures the outcome I focus on while avoiding the associations of "industrial" with heavy industry.

16. For instance, a large military may be an especially important component of a state's influence in fighting conventional wars but not as salient for that state's influence in defending against cyberattacks from nonstate actors. David Baldwin (2016) cautions against making context-free estimates of power resources and reducing the multidimensional concept of power into a single measure.

17. Kennedy 1987; Kim and Morrow 1992; Kugler and Lemke 1996; Väyrynen 1983. For a view that complicates the relationship between differential rates of economic growth and war, see Debs and Monteiro 2014.

18. Huntington 1993, 81; see also Monteiro 2014, 34.

19. Kirshner 1998; Modelski and Thompson 1996. On World War I, see Kennedy 1976; on World War II, see Hanson 2017. Economic strength does not map perfectly onto military strengths. Some economic giants, such as Japan in the 1980s, limit their military capabilities.

20. Kennedy 1987, 439.

rivals by sustaining higher levels of productivity growth rates.[21] Productivity growth ensures that efficient and sustainable processes are fueling growth in total economic output. Additionally, productivity is the most important determinant of economic growth in the long run, which is the appropriate time horizon for understanding power transitions. "Productivity isn't everything, but in the long run it is almost everything," states Nobel Prize–winning economist Paul Krugman.[22]

Alternative conceptualizations of economic power cannot capture how effectively a country translates technological advance into national economic growth. Theories of geo-economics, for instance, highlight a state's balance of trade in certain technologically advanced industries.[23] Other studies emphasize a state's share of world-leading firms.[24] National rates of innovation, while more inclusive, measure the generation of novel technologies but not diffusion across commercial applications, thereby neglecting the ultimate impact of technological change.[25] Compared to these indicators, which account for only a small portion of the value-added activities in the economy, productivity provides a more comprehensive measure of economic leadership.[26]

This focus on productivity is supported by recent work on power measurement, which questions measures of power resources based on economic size. Without accounting for economic efficiency, solely relying on measures of gross economic and industrial output provides a distorted view of the balance of power, particularly where one side is populous but poor.[27] If national power was measured by GDP alone, China was the world's most powerful country during the first industrial revolution. However, China's economy was far from the productivity frontier. In fact, as the introduction chapter spotlighted, the view that China fell behind the West because it

21. Throughout the book, to vary word choice, I describe the outcome variable as a shift in "productivity leadership," as an "economic power transition," or as change to the "economic balance of power." These all refer to the same concept.

22. Krugman 1997, 11.

23. Kim 2020; Luttwak 1993.

24. Sean Starrs (2013) measures American economic power by the profit shares of US-headquartered transnational corporations.

25. Taylor 2012, 2016.

26. Krugman 1994. Most international political economy scholars regard productivity growth as the most telling measure of technological competitiveness (Hart 1992, 15; Porter 1990, 5).

27. Anders, Fariss, and Markowitz 2020; Beckley 2018.

could not capitalize on productivity-boosting technological breakthroughs is firmly entrenched in the minds of leading Chinese policymakers and thinkers.

Lastly, it is important to clarify that I limit my analysis of productivity differentials to great powers.[28] In some measures of productivity, other countries may rank highly or even outrank the countries I study in my cases. In the current period, Switzerland and other countries have higher GDP per capita than the United States; before World War I, Australia was the world leader in productivity, as measured by GDP per labor-hour.[29] However, smaller powers like pre–World War I Australia and present-day Switzerland are excluded from my study of economic power transitions, as they lack the baseline economic and population size to be great powers.[30]

There is no exact line that distinguishes great powers from other countries.[31] Kennedy's seminal text *The Rise and Fall of the Great Powers*, for instance, has been challenged for not providing a precise definition of great power.[32] Fortunately, across all the case studies in this book, there is substantial agreement on the great powers of the period. According to one measure of the distribution of power resources, which spans 1816 to 2012 and incorporates both economic size and efficiency, all the countries I study rank among the top six at the beginning of the case.[33]

The Diffusion of GPTs

Scholars often gravitate to technological change as the source of a power transition in which the mantle of industrial preeminence changes hands. However, there is less clarity over the process by which technical breakthroughs translate

28. I am indebted to Allan Dafoe, Max Daniel, and Duncan Snidal for helping me clarify the points that follow.

29. Wright 1990, 653.

30. Australia's population in 1870 was 1.6 million, which was only 4 percent of that of the United States at the time (Romer 1996, 202).

31. Some definitions of "great powers" regard powerful military capabilities as a requirement (Monteiro 2014, 44). Kennedy (1987, 224) writes that a great power is "by definition, a state capable of holding its own against any other nation." I do not make military capabilities a necessary criterion for great powers in my study because some rising powers become economic leaders before they become capable of projecting military power overseas. In work in progress, Jennifer Lind (2023) employs the term "latent great powers" to characterize these powers. I am grateful to her for sharing insights on this topic. See also Mearsheimer 2014.

32. D. Baldwin 2016, 103; Kaiser 1989, 738.

33. My calculations are based on data from Anders, Fariss, and Markowitz 2020.

into this power shift among countries at the technological frontier. I argue that the diffusion of GPTs is the key to this mechanism. In this section, I first outline why my theory privileges GPTs over other types of technology. I then set forth why diffusion should be prioritized over other phases of technological change, especially innovation. Finally, I position GPT diffusion theory against the leading sector (LS) model, which is the standard explanation in the international relations literature.

Why GPTs?

Not all technologies are created equal. When assessed on their potential to transform the productivity of nations, some technical advances, such as the electric dynamo, rank higher than others, such as an improved sleeping bag. My theory gives pride of place to GPTs, such as electricity and the steam engine, which have historically generated waves of economy-wide productivity growth.[34] Assessed on their own merits alone, even the most transformative technological changes do not tip the scale far enough to significantly affect aggregate economic productivity.[35] GPTs are different because their impact on productivity comes from accumulated improvements across a wide range of complementary sectors; that is, they cannot be judged on their own merits alone.

Recognized by economists and economic historians as "engines of growth," GPTs are defined by three characteristics.[36] First, they offer *great potential for continual improvement*. While all technologies offer some scope for improvement, a GPT "has implicit in it a major research program for improvements, adaptations, and modifications."[37] Second, GPTs acquire *pervasiveness*. As a GPT evolves, it finds a "wide variety of uses" and a "wide range of uses."[38] The former refers to the diversity of a GPT's use cases, while the latter alludes to

---

34. Brynjolfsson, Rock, and Syverson 2017; David 1990; Ruttan 2006, 5.

35. For instance, Robert William Fogel's classic study of railroads concluded that "the railroad did not make an overwhelming contribution to the production potential of the economy" (Fogel 1964, 235). Related categories, including "enabling technologies," spur complementary innovations and exhibit substantial scope for improvement but do not find pervasive applications (Teece 2018, 1369).

36. Bresnahan and Trajtenberg 1995. The following discussion is mostly drawn from Bresnahan and Trajtenberg 1995 and Lipsey, Carlaw, and Bekar 2005. Other accounts employ similar definitions, albeit with some modifications; see Bresnahan 2010; Jovanovic and Rousseau 2005. For a critical view of the GPT concept, see Field 2008.

37. Lipsey, Bekar, and Carlaw 1998, 39.

38. Cantner and Vannuccini 2012.

the breadth of industries and individuals using a GPT.[39] Third, GPTs have *strong technological complementarities*. In other words, the benefits from innovations in GPTs come from how other linked technologies are changed in response and cannot be modeled from a mere reduction in the costs of inputs to the existing production function. For example, the overall energy efficiency gains from merely replacing a steam engine with an electric motor were minimal; the major benefits from factory electrification came from electric "unit drive," which enabled machines to be driven individually by electric motors, and a radical redesign of plants.[40]

Taken together, these characteristics suggest that the full impact of a GPT materializes via an "extended trajectory" that differs from those associated with other technologies. Economic historian Paul David explains:

> We can recognize the emergence of an extended trajectory of incremental technical improvements, the gradual and protracted process of diffusion into widespread use, and the confluence with other streams of technological innovation, all of which are interdependent features of the dynamic process through which a general purpose engine acquires a broad domain of specific applications.[41]

For example, the first dynamo for industrial application was introduced in the 1870s, but the major boost of electricity to overall manufacturing productivity did not occur until the 1920s. Like other GPT trajectories, electrification required a protracted process of workforce skill adjustments, organizational adaptations, such as changes in factory layout, and complementary innovations like the steam turbine, which enabled central power generation in the form of utilities.[42] To track the full impact of these engines of growth, one must travel the long roads of their diffusion.

Why Diffusion?

All technological trajectories can be divided into a phase when the technology is incubated and then first introduced as a viable commercial application ("innovation") and a phase when the innovation spreads through a population of

39. One does not imply the other. For instance, a screw has a "wide range of use" since it is used to fasten things together across a large swath of productivity activities in the economy, but it does not have a "wide variety of uses" (Lipsey, Bekar, and Carlaw 1998, 39).

40. Devine 1982.

41. David 1990, 356.

42. Brynjolfsson, Rock, and Syverson 2017; David 1990; Smil 2005, 33–97.

potential users, both nationally and internationally ("diffusion").[43] Recognizing this commonly accepted distinction, other studies of the scientific and technological capabilities of nations primarily focus on innovation.[44] I depart from other works by giving priority to diffusion, since that is the phase of technological change most significant for GPTs.[45]

Undeniably, the activities and conditions that produce innovation can also spur diffusion.[46] A firm's ability to conduct breakthrough R&D does not just create new knowledge but also boosts its capacity to assimilate innovations from external sources ("absorptive capacity").[47] Faced with an ever-shifting technological frontier, building competency at producing new innovations gives a firm the requisite prior knowledge for identifying and commercializing external innovations. Other studies extend these insights beyond firms to regional and national systems.[48] In order to absorb and diffuse technological advances first incubated elsewhere, they argue, nations must invest in a certain level of innovative activities.

This connection between innovation capacity and absorptive capacity could question the GPT mechanism's attention to diffusion. Possibly, a country's lead in GPT innovation could also translate directly into a relative advantage in GPT diffusion.[49] Scholarship on the agglomeration benefits of

43. "GPT diffusion" refers to the assimilation and adoption of GPTs *within* one country's economic system. A rich scholarship on diffusion studies how norms and policies spread *across* countries (Finnemore and Sikkink 1998; Simmons and Elkins 2004). When discussing how GPTs spread from one economy to another, I use the term "international diffusion."

44. Existing work on the scientific and technological power of nations makes the same distinction. In his book, Andrew Kennedy (2018, 16) writes, "I focus on transnational processes that support firms' and universities' efforts to engage in the first of these tasks: the creation of a product or process that is 'new to the world.'" Mark Zachary Taylor (2016, 28, emphasis in original) writes that his book, *The Politics of Innovation*, is more interested in "*innovation* than *diffusion* . . . where possible, I focus more on why some countries are better at inventing new technologies. . . . I am somewhat less concerned with the spread of new technology throughout society." See also Taylor 2009, 865.

45. A diffusion-oriented approach checks the "innovation-centrism" that has permeated the analysis of technology in the social sciences (Edgerton 2010, 689). In his book-length treatment of the concept of innovation, Benoît Godin (2015, 8) describes the current moment as one when "innovation becomes a value per se" and an "object of veneration and cult worship." Relatedly, studies of technological change in military affairs are strongly biased toward military innovation (Goldman and Andres 1999, 80n4).

46. Taylor 2016, 231. Joel Simmons (2016, 33) has argued that "the differences between the two processes often are exaggerated."

47. Aghion and Howitt 1998; Cohen and Levinthal 1998.

48. Fagerberg 1987; Fu 2008; Howitt and Mayer-Foulkes 2005.

49. Arnulf Grübler (1998), for example, argues that the leading innovation center, the country where new technological changes originate, tends to also have the highest adoption levels of the technology.

innovation hot spots, such as Silicon Valley, support this case to some extent. Empirical analyses of patent citations indicate that knowledge spillovers from GPTs tend to cluster within a geographic region.[50] In the case of electricity, Robert Fox and Anna Guagnini underscore that it was easier for countries with firms at the forefront of electrical innovation to embrace electric power at scale. The interconnections between the "learning by doing" gained on the job in these leading firms and academic labs separated nations in the "fast lane" and "slow lane" of electrification.[51]

Being the first to pioneer new technologies could benefit a state's capacity to absorb and diffuse GPTs, but it is not determinative. A country's absorptive capacity also depends on many other factors, including institutions for technology transfer, human capital endowments, openness to trade, and information and communication infrastructure.[52] Sometimes the "advantages of backwardness" allow laggard states to adopt new technologies faster than the states that pioneer such advances.[53] In theory and practice, a country's ability to generate fundamental, new-to-the-world innovations can widely diverge from its ability to diffuse such advances.

This potential divergence is especially relevant for advanced economies, which encompass the great powers that are the subject of this research. Although innovation-centered explanations do well at sorting the advantages of technological breakthroughs to countries at the technological frontier compared to those trying to catch up, they are less effective at differentiating among advanced economies. As supported by a wealth of econometric research, divergences in the long-term economic growth of countries at the technology frontier are shaped more by *imitation* than innovation.[54] These advanced countries have firms that can quickly copy or license innovations; first mover advantages from innovations are thus limited even in industries, like pharmaceuticals, that enforce intellectual property rights most strictly.[55] Nevertheless, advanced countries that are evenly matched in their capacity for radical innovation can undertake vastly different growth trajectories in the wake of technological revolutions. Differences in diffusion pathways are central to explaining this puzzle.

50. Feldman and Yoon 2012.
51. Fox and Guagnini 2004, 170.
52. Comin and Hobijn 2010; Fu 2008.
53. Gerschenkron 1962/2008.
54. Fagerberg 1987; Pavitt and Soete 1982.
55. Hannah 1994, 90–91. I thank Daniel Raff for sharing this text with me.

This diffusion-centered approach is especially well suited for GPTs. Since GPTs entail gradual evolution into widespread use, there is a longer window for competitors to adopt GPTs more intensively than the leading innovation center. In other technologies, first-mover benefits from pioneering initial break-throughs are more significant. For instance, leadership in the innovation of electric power technologies was fiercely contested among the industrial powers. The United States, Germany, Great Britain, and France all built their first central power stations within a span of three years (1882–1884), their first electric trams within a span of nine years (1887–1896), and their first three-phase AC power systems within a span of eight years (1891–1899).[56] However, the United States clearly led in the diffusion of these systems: by 1912, its electricity production per capita had more than doubled that of Germany, its closest competitor.[57] Thus, while most countries at the technological frontier will be able to compete in the production and innovation of GPTs, the hardest hurdles in the GPT trajectory are in the diffusion phase.

GPT Diffusion and LS Product Cycles

GPT diffusion challenges the LS-based account of how technological change drives power transitions. The standard explanation in the international relations literature emphasizes a country's dominance in leading sectors, defined as new industries that experience rapid growth on the back of new technologies.[58] Cotton textiles, steel, chemicals, and the automobile industry form a "classic sequence" of "great leading sectors," developed initially by economist Walt Rostow and later adapted by political scientists.[59] Under the LS mechanism, a country's ability to maintain a monopoly on innovation in these emerging industries determines the rise and fall of lead economies.[60]

This model of technological change and power transition builds on the international product life cycle, a concept pioneered by Raymond Vernon. Constructed to explain patterns of international trade, the cycle begins with a product innovation and subsequent sales growth in the domestic market.

56. Taylor 2016, 189.
57. Author's calculations based on Comin and Hobijn 2009.
58. Kennedy 2018, 51; Rostow 1960, 14.
59. Rostow 1978, 104–9. Thompson (1990) uses ten indicators proposed by Rostow as prox-ies for the rise and fall of critical leading sectors, adding two new indicators for semiconductor and jet airframe production starting in the 1950s.
60. Thompson 1990, 217.

Once the domestic market is saturated, the new product is exported to foreign markets. Over time, production shifts to these markets, as the original innovating country loses its comparative advantage.[61]

LS-based studies frequently invoke the product cycle model.[62] Analyzing the effects of leading sectors on the structure of the international system, Gilpin states, "Every state, rightly, or wrongly, wants to be as close as possible to the innovative end of 'the product cycle.'"[63] One scholar described Gilpin's *US Power and the Multinational Corporation*, one of the first texts that outlines the LS mechanism, as "[having] drawn on the concept of the product cycle, expanded it into the concept of the growth and decline of entire national economies, and analyzed the relations between this economic cycle, national power, and international politics."[64]

The product cycle's assumptions illuminate the differences between the GPT and LS mechanisms along three key dimensions. In the first stage of the product cycle, a firm generates the initial product innovation and profits from sales in the domestic market before saturation. Extending this model to national economies, the LS mechanism emphasizes the clustering of LS innovations and attendant monopoly profits in a single nation.[65] "The extent of national success that we have in mind is of the fairly extreme sort," write George Modelski and William Thompson. "One national economy literally dominates the leading sector during its phase of high growth and is the primary beneficiary of the immediate profits."[66] The GPT trajectory, in contrast, places more value on where technologies are diffused than where an innovation is first pioneered.[67] I refer to this dimension as the "phase of relative advantage."

In the next stage, the product innovation spreads to global markets and the technology gradually diffuses to foreign competitors. Monopoly rents associated with a product innovation dissipate as production becomes routinized

---

61. Vernon 1971.

62. Gilpin 1975, 78, 197; 1987, 234–37; Moe 2007, 207; Tellis et al. 2000, 37.

63. Gilpin 1987, 99.

64. Kurth 1979, 4.

65. Rasler and Thompson 1994, 7.

66. Modelski and Thompson 1996, 91; see also Thompson 1990, 217. It is important to note that recent work on technology and systemic leadership points out that, starting during the postwar period, it is more difficult for one state to completely monopolize innovation. See Thompson 2022, 184–211.

67. For other political science work that emphasizes variation in technological adoption, see Milner 2006; Milner and Solstad 2021.

and transfers to other countries.[68] Mirroring this logic, Modelski and Thompson write, "[Leading sectors] bestow the benefits of monopoly profits on the pioneer until diffusion and imitation transform industries that were once considered radically innovative into fairly routine and widespread components of the world economy."[69] Thompson also states that "the sector's impact on growth tends to be disproportionate in its early stages of development."[70]

The GPT trajectory assumes a different impact timeframe. The more wide-ranging the potential applications of a technology, the longer the lag between its initial emergence and its ultimate economic impact. This explains why the envisioned transformative impact of GPTs does not appear straightaway in the productivity statistics.[71] Time for complementary innovations, organizational restructuring, and institutional adjustments such as human capital formation is needed before the full impact of a GPT can be known. It is precisely the period when diffusion transforms radical innovations into routine components of the economy—the stage when the causal effects of leading sectors are expected to dissipate—that generates the productivity gap between nations.

The product cycle also reveals differences between the LS and GPT mechanisms regarding the "breadth of growth." Like the product cycle's focus on an innovation's life cycle within a singular industry, the LS mechanism emphasizes the contributions of a limited number of new industries to economic growth in a particular period. GPT-fueled productivity growth, on the other hand, is dispersed across a broad range of industries.[72] Table 2.1 specifies how LS product cycles differ from GPT diffusion along the three dimensions outlined here. As the following section will show, the differences in these two technological trajectories shape the institutional factors that are most important for national success in adapting to periods of technological revolution.

68. "Monopoly rents" refers to a condition wherein a producer lacks competition and can sell its goods and services at an above-market price. In the context of LS theory, it is the lead economy that monopolizes rents from new technologies, in the sense that it accumulates higher profits from a fast-growing industry. I thank an anonymous reviewer for pushing me to clarify this point.

69. Modelski and Thompson 1996, 52.

70. Thompson 1990, 211. The impact timeframe of leading sectors is like "distributing money on the ground," write Abraham Newman and John Zysman (2006, 393–94). "Some radically valuable possibilities, the larger bills, are picked up first; the smaller opportunities are captured later. But the original technological revolution loses force, as the most valuable opportunities are picked up and implemented."

71. Brynjolfsson, Rock, and Syverson 2017; David 1990; Helpman and Trajtenberg 1994.

72. Crafts 2001, 306; David and Wright 1999, 12.

TABLE 2.1. Two Mechanisms of Technological Change and Power Transitions

Mechanisms	Impact Timeframe	Phase of Relative Advantage	Breadth of Growth	Institutional Complements
LS product cycles	Lopsided in early stages	Monopoly on innovation	Concentrated	Deepen skill base in LS innovations
GPT diffusion	Lopsided in later stages	Edge in diffusion	Dispersed	Widen skill base in spreading GPTs

While I have highlighted the differences between GPT diffusion and LS product cycles, it is important to recognize that there are similarities between the two pathways.[73] Some scholars, for example, associate leading sectors with broad spillovers across economic sectors.[74] In addition, lists of leading sectors and lists of GPTs sometimes overlap, as evidenced by the fact that electricity is a consensus inclusion on both lists. Moreover, both explanations begin with the same premise: to fully uncover the dynamics of technology-driven power transitions, it is essential to specify which new technologies are the key drivers of economic growth in a particular time window.[75]

At the same time, these resemblances should not be overstated. Many classic leading sectors do not have general-purpose applications. For instance, cotton textiles and automobiles both feature on Rostow's series of leading sectors, and they are studied as leading sectors because each has "been the largest industry for several major industrial nations in the West at one time or another."[76] Although these were certainly both fast-growing large industries, the underlying technological advances do not fulfill the characteristics of GPTs. In addition, many of the GPTs I examine do not qualify as leading sectors. The machine tool industry in the mid-nineteenth century, for instance, was not a new industry, and it was never even close to being the largest industry in any of the major economies. Most importantly, though the GPT and LS

73. Gilpin 1987, 217; Reuveny and Thompson 2001, 711n13.
74. Drezner 2001, 7; Thompson 1990, 211.
75. I share the opinion of one of the earliest LS-based texts that "revolutionary technological breakthroughs" are the "primary concern in explaining the rise and decline of successive capitalistic core economies" (Gilpin 1975, 69). I differ on which technologies are considered "revolutionary" and on how these breakthroughs actually resulted in the rise and decline of major economies.
76. Kurth 1979, 3.

mechanisms sometimes point to similar technological changes, they present very different understandings of *how* revolutionary technologies bring about an economic power transition. As the next section reveals, these differences also map onto varied institutional adaptations.

GPT Skill Infrastructure

New technologies agitate existing institutional patterns.[77] They appeal for government support, generate new collective interests in the form of technical societies, and induce organizations to train people in relevant fields. If institutional environments are slow or fail to adapt, the development of emerging technologies is hindered. As Gilpin articulates, a nation's technological fitness is rooted in the "extent of the congruence" between its institutions and the demands of evolving technologies.[78] This approach is rooted in a rich tradition of work on the coevolution of technology and institutions.[79]

Understanding the demands of GPTs helps filter which institutional factors are most salient for how technological revolutions bring about economic power transitions. Which institutional factors dictate disparities in GPT adoption among great powers? Specifically, I emphasize the role of education and training systems that broaden the base of engineering skills linked to a particular GPT. This set of institutions, which I call "GPT skill infrastructure," is most crucial for facilitating the widespread adoption of a GPT.

To be sure, GPT diffusion is dependent on institutional adjustments beyond GPT skill infrastructure. Intellectual property regimes, industrial relations, financial institutions, and other institutional factors could affect GPT diffusion. Probing inter-industry differences in technology adoption, some studies find that less concentrated industry structures are positively linked to GPT adoption.[80] I limit my analysis to institutions of skill formation because their effects permeate other institutional arrangements.[81] GPT skill infrastruc-

77. I am very thankful for feedback from Stephen Kaplan and Abe Newman on this section.
78. Gilpin 1996, 413.
79. Freeman and Louca 2001; Nelson and Winter 1982; Perez 2002.
80. Romeo 1975; Copeland and Shapiro 2010.
81. Thelen 2004, 4, 285–86. A substantial body of literature stresses the importance of human capital for technology adoption; see, for example, Comin and Hobijn 2004; Goldin and Katz 2008; Nelson and Phelps 1966. Later in the chapter, I outline my tests for the validity of two alternative explanations for cross-national differences in GPT diffusion.

ture provides a useful indicator for other institutions that standardize and spread the novel best practices associated with GPTs.[82]

It should also be noted that the institutional approach is one of three main categories of explanation for cross-country differences in economic performance over the long term.[83] Other studies document the importance of geography and culture to persistent cross-country income differences.[84] I prioritize institutional explanations for two reasons. First, natural experiments from certain historical settings, in which institutional divergence occurs but geographical and cultural factors are held constant, suggest that institutional differences are particularly influential sources of long-term economic growth differentials.[85] Second, since LS-based accounts of power transitions also prioritize institutional adaptations to technological change, my approach provides a more level test of GPT diffusion against the standard explanation.[86]

One final note about limits to my argument's scope. I do not investigate the deeper origins of why some countries are more effective than others at developing GPT skill infrastructure. Possibly, the intensity of political competition and the inclusiveness of political institutions influence the development of skill formation institutions.[87] Other fruitful lines of inquiry stress the importance of government capacity to make intertemporal bargains and adopt long time horizons in making technology investments.[88] It is worth noting that a necessary first step to productively exploring these underlying causes is to establish which types of technological trajectories and institutional adaptations are at work. For instance, LS product cycles may be more closely linked to mercantilist or state capitalist approaches that favor narrow interest groups, whereas, political systems that incorporate a broader group of stakeholders may better accommodate GPT diffusion pathways.

82. Rosenberg 1998b; Vona and Consoli 2014.

83. For a review of these "three fundamental causes" of international patterns of growth, see Acemoglu, Johnson, and Robinson 2005, 397–402.

84. For geographical explanations, see Diamond 1997; Gallup, Sachs, and Mellinger 1999. For cultural theories, see Harrison and Huntington 2000; Weber 1930.

85. Acemoglu, Johnson, and Robinson 2005, 402–21.

86. Some scholarship does explore how certain geographical settings are more conducive to specific types of technological change, but these studies are limited to agricultural technologies. See, for example, Diamond 1997, 358.

87. Acemoglu and Robinson 2006, 2012.

88. Doner and Schneider 2016; Simmons 2016; see also Doner, Hicken, and Ritchie 2009.

Institutions Fit for GPT Diffusion

If GPTs drive economic power transitions, which institutions fit best with their demands? Institutional adaptations for GPT diffusion must solve two problems. First, since the economic benefits of GPTs materialize through improvements across a broad range of industries, capturing these benefits requires extensive coordination between the GPT sector and numerous application sectors. Given the sheer scope of potential applications, it is infeasible for firms in the GPT sector to commercialize the technology on their own, as the necessary complementary assets are embedded with different firms and industries.[89] In the AI domain, as one example of a potential GPT, firms that develop general machine learning algorithms will not have access to all the industry-specific data needed to fine-tune those algorithms to particular application scenarios. Thus, coordination between the GPT sector and other organizations that provide complementary capital and skills, such as academia and competitor firms, is crucial. In contrast, for technologies that are *not* general-purpose, this type of coordination is less conducive and could even be detrimental to a nation's competitive advantage, as the innovating firm could leak its technical secrets.[90]

Second, GPTs pose demanding conditions for human capital adjustments. In describing the connection between skill formation and technological fitness, scholars often delineate between general skills and industry-specific skills. According to this perspective, skill formation institutions that optimize for the former are more conducive to technological domains characterized by radical innovation, while institutions that optimize for the latter are more favorable for domains marked by incremental innovation.[91] GPT diffusion entails both types of skill formation. The skills must be specific to a rapidly changing GPT domain but also broad enough to enable a GPT's advance across many industries.[92] Strong linkages between R&D-intensive organizations at the technological frontier and application areas far from the frontier also play a key role in GPT diffusion. This draws attention to the interactions between researchers who produce innovations and technicians who help absorb them into specific contexts.[93]

---

89. Teece 2018.
90. Goldfarb, Taska, and Teodoridis 2021.
91. Hall and Soskice 2001; Culpepper and Finegold 1999.
92. Aghion and Howitt 2002, 312–13; Streeck 1992, 16.
93. Mason, Rincon-Aznar, and Venturini 2020; Rincon-Aznar et al. 2015.

Education and training systems that foster relevant engineering skills for a GPT, or what I call GPT skill infrastructure, address both constraints. Engineering talent fulfills the need for skills that are rooted in a GPT yet sufficiently flexible to implement GPT advances in a wide range of sectors. Broadening the base of engineering knowledge also helps standardize best practices with GPTs, thereby coordinating information flows between the GPT sector and application sectors. Standardization fosters GPT diffusion by committing application sectors to specific technological trajectories and encouraging complementary innovations.[94] This unlocks the horizontal spillovers associated with GPTs.[95]

Indeed, distinct engineering specializations have emerged in the wake of a new GPT. New disciplines, such as chemical engineering and electrical engineering, have proved essential in widening knowledge bases in the wake of a new GPT.[96] Computer science, another engineering-oriented field, was central to US leadership in the information revolution.[97] These professions developed alongside new technical societies—ranging from the American Society of Mechanical Engineers to the Internet Engineering Task Force—that formulated and disseminated guidelines and benchmarks for GPT development.[98]

Clearly, the features of GPT skill infrastructure have changed over time. Whereas informal associations systematized the skills crucial for mechanization in the eighteenth century, formal higher education has become increasingly integral to computerization in the twenty-first century.[99] Some evidence suggests that computers and other technologies are skill-biased, in the sense that they favor workers with more years of schooling.[100] These

94. Baron and Schmidt 2014; Bresnahan and Trajtenberg 1995; Thoma 2009.

95. Because it is more difficult for the GPT sector to capture all associated spillovers, relative to industries connected to narrower "discrete" technologies, the GPT sector may underinvest in innovation (Bresnahan 2010; Bresnahan and Trajtenberg 1995; Gambardella et al. 2021). I do not concentrate as much on this appropriability problem because great powers are likely to have access to a source of GPT development. What differentiates them is the breadth and depth of commercialization.

96. Rosenberg 1998b, 169. Historical studies attribute the successful adoption of new electrical technologies in the United States to the "better match between the technologies advanced by electrification and the country's institutions of education and worker training" (David and Wright 2006, 154).

97. Vona and Consoli 2014, 1403–5.

98. Russell 2014; Yates and Murphy 2019.

99. Still, recent studies emphasize the continuing importance of informal education opportunities for computer science (Guzdial et al. 2014).

100. Johnson 1997; Krueger 1993.

trends complicate but do not undercut the concept of GPT skill infrastructure. Regardless of the extent of formal training, all configurations of GPT skill infrastructure perform the same function: to widen the pool of engineering skills and knowledge associated with a GPT. This can take place in universities as well as in informal associations, provided these settings train engineers and facilitate the flow of engineering knowledge between knowledge-creation centers and application sectors.[101]

Which Institutions Matter?

The institutional competencies for exploiting LS product cycles are different. Historical analysis informed by this frame highlights heroic inventors like James Watt and pioneering research labs at large companies.[102] Studying which countries benefited most from emerging technologies over the past two centuries, Herbert Kitschelt prioritizes the match between the properties of new technologies and sectoral governance structures. Under his framework, for example, tightly coupled technological systems with high causal complexity, such as nuclear power systems and aerospace platforms, are more likely to flourish in countries that allow for extensive state support.[103] In other studies, the key institutional factors behind success in LS product cycles are education systems that subsidize scientific training and R&D facilities in new industries.[104]

These approaches equate technological leadership with a state's success in capturing market shares and monopoly profits in new industries.[105] In short, they use LS product cycles as the filter for which institutional variables matter. Existing scholarship lacks an institutional explanation for why some great powers are more successful at GPT diffusion.

Competing interpretations of technological leadership in chemicals during the late nineteenth century crystallize these differences. Based on the LS template, the standard account accredits Germany's dominance in the chemical

101. Mokyr and Voth 2010.
102. See, for example, Kennedy 2018, 54.
103. Kitschelt 1991; see also Kim and Hart 2001.
104. Drezner 2001; Moe 2009, 216–17.
105. Another example of this is Espen Moe's work on the industrial rise and fall of great powers, which takes a state's competitiveness in a particular period's "core industry" to be equivalent to a state's industrial leadership. His choice of core industries draws from leading sectors identified in Gilpin 1987 and Modelski and Thompson 1996 (Moe 2009, 224fn3; Moe 2007).

industry—as represented by its control over 90 percent of global production of synthetic dyes—to its investments in scientific research and highly skilled chemists.[106] Germany's dynamism in this leading sector is taken to explain its overall industrial dominance.[107]

GPT diffusion spotlights a different relationship between technological change and institutional adaptation. The focus turns toward institutions that complemented the extension of chemical processes to a wide range of industries beyond synthetic dye, such as food production, metals, and textiles. Under the GPT mechanism, the United States, not Germany, achieved leadership in chemicals because it first institutionalized chemical engineering as a discipline. Despite its disadvantages in synthetic dye production and chemical research, the United States was more effective in broadening the base of chemical engineering talent and coordinating information flows between fundamental breakthroughs and industrial applications.[108]

It is important to note that some parts of the GPT and LS mechanisms can coexist without conflict. A state's capacity to pioneer new technologies can correlate with its capacity to absorb and diffuse GPTs. Countries that are home to cutting-edge R&D infrastructure may also be fertile ground for education systems that widen the pool of GPT-linked engineering skills. However, these aspects of the LS mechanism are not necessary for the GPT mechanism to operate. In accordance with GPT diffusion theory, a state can capitalize on GPTs to become the most powerful economy without monopolizing LS innovation.

Moreover, other dimensions of these two mechanisms directly conflict. When it comes to impact timeframe and breadth of growth, the GPT and LS mechanisms advance opposing expectations. Institutions suited for GPT diffusion can diverge from those optimized for creating new-to-the-world innovations. Research on human capital and long-term growth separates the effects of engineering capacity, which is commonly tied to adoptive activities, and other forms of human capital that are more often connected to inventive activities.[109] This divergence can also be seen in debates over the effects of competition on technological activity. On the one hand, Joseph Schumpeter and others have argued that monopoly structures incentivize more R&D activity because the

106. Drezner 2001, 13–18; Moe 2007, 125.
107. Moe 2007, 253–55; Thompson 1990.
108. Rosenberg and Steinmueller 2013.
109. Maloney and Caicedo 2017.

monopolists can appropriate all the gains from technological innovation.[110] On
the other hand, empirical work demonstrates that more competitive market
structures increase the rate of technological adoption across firms.[111] Thus,
while there is some overlap between these two mechanisms, they can still be
set against each other in a way that improves our understanding of technological
revolutions and power transitions.

This theoretical framework differs from related work on the political economy of technological change.[112] Scholars attribute the international competitiveness of nations to broader institutional contexts, including democracy,
national innovation systems, and property rights enforcement.[113] Since this
book is limited to the study of shifts in productivity leadership at the technological frontier, many of these factors, such as those related to basic infrastructure and property rights, will not explain differences among technologically
advanced nations.

In addition, most of the institutional theories put forth to explain the productivity of nations are technology-agnostic, in that they treat all forms of
technological change equally. To borrow language from a former chairman
of the US Council of Economic Advisers, they do not differentiate between
an innovation in potato chips and an innovation in microchips.[114] In contrast,
I am specific about GPTs as the sources of shifts in competitiveness at the
technological frontier.

Other theories identify key technologies but leave institutional factors at a
high level of abstraction. Some scholars, for instance, posit that the lead economy's monopoly on leading-sector innovation eventually erodes because of
"ubiquitous institutional rigidities."[115] Unencumbered by the vested interests
that resist disruptive technologies, rising challengers inevitably overtake established powers. Because these explanations are underspecified, they cannot
account for cases where rich economies expand their lead or where poorer
countries do not catch up.[116]

110. Nelson and Winter 1982; Schumpeter 1994.

111. Copeland and Shapiro 2010.

112. Cerny 1990; Katzenstein 1985; Olson 1982; Porter 1990; Rosecrance 1999; Weiss 2003.
For surveys of this literature, see Breznitz 2009; Taylor 2016.

113. Respectively, see Acemoglu et al. 2018; Nelson 1993; North 1990.

114. Michael J. Boskin once said, "It doesn't make any difference whether a country makes
computer chips or potato chips" (Thurow 1994).

115. Rasler and Thompson 1994, 81; see also Gilpin 1996; Gilpin 1981, 179; Moe 2009.

116. Taylor 2004, 604.

When interpreting great power competition at the technological frontier, adjudicating between the GPT and LS mechanisms represents a choice between two different visions. The latter prioritizes being the first country to introduce novel technologies, whereas the former places more value on disseminating and transforming innovations after their inception. In sum, industrial competition among great powers is not a sprint to determine which one can create the most brilliant Silicon Valley; it is a marathon won by the country that can cultivate the closest connections between its Silicon Valleys and its Iowa Citys.

Alternative Explanations

Although I primarily set GPT diffusion theory against the LS model, I also consider two other prominent explanations that make specific claims about how technological breakthroughs differentially advantage leading economies. Crucially, these two lines of thinking could account for differences in GPT diffusion, nullifying the import of GPT skill infrastructure.

Threat-Based Arguments

According to one school of thought, international security threats motivate states to invest in science and technology.[117] When confronted with more threatening geopolitical landscapes, states are more incentivized to break down status quo interests and build institutions conducive to technological innovation.[118] Militaries hold outsized influence in these accounts. For example, Vernon Ruttan argues that military investment, mobilized against war or the threat of war, fueled commercial advances in six technologies designated as GPTs.[119] Studies of the success of the United States and Japan with emerging technologies also stress interconnections between military and civilian technological development.[120] I group these related arguments under the category of threat-based theories.

117. More broadly, many important works in international relations posit that international competition spurs the diffusion of military technology; see, for example, Gilpin 1981; Waltz 1979. For a more recent account, see Milner and Solstad 2021.

118. Taylor 2016, 224.

119. Ruttan 2006, 184; see also Coccia 2017.

120. Weiss 2014; Samuels 1994.

Related explanations link technological progress with the balance of external threats and domestic roadblocks. Mark Taylor's "creative insecurity" theory describes how external economic and military pressures permit governments to break from status quo interest groups and promote technological innovation. He argues that the difference between a nation's external threats and its internal rivalries determines its propensity for innovation: the greater the difference, the greater the national innovation rate.[121] Similarly, "systemic vulnerability" theory emphasizes the influence of external security and domestic pressures on the will of leaders to invest in institutions conducive to innovation, as well as the effect of "veto players" on their ability to do so.[122]

Certainly, external threats could impel states to invest more in GPTs, and military investment can help bring forth new GPTs; however, there are several issues with adapting threat-based theories to explain differences in GPT diffusion across great powers. First, threat-based arguments tend to focus on the initial incubation of GPTs, as opposed to the gradual spread of GPTs throughout a national economy. During the latter phase, a great deal of evidence suggests that civilian and military needs can greatly conflict.[123] Besides, some GPTs, such as electricity in the United States, developed without substantial military investment. Since other civilian institutions could fill in as strong sources of demand for GPTs, military procurement may not be necessary for spurring GPT diffusion. Institutional adjustments to GPTs therefore can be motivated by factors other than threats. Ultimately, to further probe these points of clash, the impact of security threats and military investment must be traced within the historical cases.

121. Taylor 2016; see also Milner and Solstad 2021 for an application of Taylor's argument to global waves of technology adoption.

122. Doner, Ritchie, and Slater 2005; Tsebelis 2002. Interestingly, while the "creative insecurity" and "systemic vulnerability" theories both identify the positive effect of external threats for national competitiveness, they differ on the role of domestic tensions. Whereas the former posits that domestic tensions have a negative effect on technological progress, the latter argues that domestic pressures positively incentivize the development of institutions conducive to innovation (Doner, Ritchie, and Slater 2005, 328). This difference can be partially explained by different conceptions of domestic tensions. For "systemic vulnerability" theory, domestic tension characterizes a relationship between the masses and the political leadership; for "creative insecurity" theory, domestic tension refers to a relationship between status quo interests and proponents of science and technology.

123. Alic et al. 1992, 37–43; Misa 1985.

Varieties of Capitalism

The "varieties of capitalism" (VoC) explanation highlights differences among developed democracies in labor markets, industrial organization, and interfirm relations and separates them into coordinated market economies (CMEs) and liberal market economies (LMEs). VoC scholars argue that CMEs are more suited for incremental innovations because their thick intercorporate networks and protected labor markets favor gradual adoption of new technological advances. LMEs, in contrast, are more adept at radical innovation because their fluid labor markets and corporate organization make it easier for firms to reorganize themselves around disruptive technologies. Most relevant to GPT diffusion theory, VoC scholars argue that LMEs incentivize workers to acquire general skills, which are more accommodative to radical innovation, whereas CMEs support industry-specific training, which is more favorable for incremental innovation.[124]

It is possible that differences between market-based capitalism and strategically coordinated capitalism account for GPT diffusion gaps between nations. Based on the expectations of the VoC approach, LMEs should be more likely to generate innovations with the potential to become GPTs, and workers in LMEs should possess more general skills that could spread GPTs across firms.[125] Examining the pattern of innovation during the information revolution, scholars find that the United States, an LME, concentrated on industries experiencing radical innovation, such as semiconductors and telecommunications, while Germany, a CME, specialized in domains characterized by incremental innovation, such as mechanical engineering and transport.[126]

Despite bringing vital attention to the diversity of skill formation institutions, VoC theory's dichotomy between general and industry-specific skills does not dovetail with the skills demanded by specific GPTs.[127] Cutting across this sometimes arbitrary distinction, the engineering skills highlighted in GPT diffusion theory are specific to a fast-evolving GPT field and general enough to transfer ideas from the GPT sector across various sectors. Software engineering skills, for instance, are portable across multiple industries, but their reach is not as ubiquitous as critical thinking skills or mathematics knowledge.

124. Hall and Soskice 2001.
125. Huo 2015.
126. Hall and Soskice 2001, 41–44; for a critical view, see Taylor 2004.
127. For an example of how scholars have adapted VoC-based arguments about skill provision to developments in information technology, see Crouch, Finefold, and Sako 1999.

To address similar gaps in skill classifications, many political economists have appealed for "a more fine-grained analysis of cross-national differences in the particular mix of jobs and qualifications that characterize different political economies."[128] In line with this move, GPT skill infrastructure stands in for institutions that supply the particular mix of jobs and qualifications for enabling GPT diffusion. The empirical analysis provides an opportunity to examine whether this approach should be preferred to the VoC explanation for understanding technology-driven power transitions.

Research Methodology

My evaluation of the GPT and LS mechanisms primarily relies on historical case studies, which allow for detailed exploration of the causal processes that connect technological change to economic power transitions. Employing congruence-analysis techniques, I select cases and assess the historical evidence in a way that ensures a fair and rigorous test of the relative explanatory power of the two mechanisms.[129] This sets up a "three-cornered fight" among GPT diffusion theory, the rival LS-based explanation, and the set of empirical information.[130]

The universe of cases most useful for assessing the GPT and LS mechanisms are technological revolutions (cause) that produced an economic power transition (outcome) in the industrial period. Following guidance on testing competing mechanisms that prioritize typical cases where the cause and outcome are clearly present, I investigate the First Industrial Revolution (IR-1) and the Second Industrial Revolution (IR-2).[131] Both cases featured clusters of disruptive technological advances, highlighted by some studies as "technological revolutions" or "technology waves."[132] They also saw economic power transitions, when one great power sustained growth rates at substantially higher levels than its rivals.[133] I also study Japan's challenge to American economic leadership—which ultimately failed—in the Third Industrial Revolu-

---

128. Thelen 2004, 11.

129. Blatter and Haverland 2012.

130. Van Evera 1997, 83.

131. Beach and Pedersen 2018; Goertz 2017.

132. Gilpin 1975, 69; Milner and Solstad 2021; Goldstein 1988.

133. For related concepts, see Drezner 2001, 4; Modelski and Thompson 1996; Moe 2009; Reuveny and Thompson 2001.

tion (IR-3). This deviant case can disconfirm mechanisms and help explain why they break down.[134]

These cases are highly crucial and relevant for testing the GPT mechanism against the LS mechanism. All three cases favor the latter in terms of background conditions and existing theoretical explanations. Scholarship has attributed shifts in economic power during this period to the rise of new leading sectors.[135] Thus, if the empirical results support the GPT mechanism, then my findings would suggest a need for major modifications to our understanding of how technological revolutions affect the rise and fall of great powers. The qualitative analysis appendix provides further details on case selection, including the universe of cases, the justification for these cases as "most likely cases" for the LS mechanism, and relevant scope conditions.[136]

This overall approach adapts the methodology of process-tracing, often conducted at the individual or micro level, to macro-level mechanisms that involve structural factors and evolutionary interactions.[137] Existing scholarship on diffusion mechanisms, which the GPT mechanism builds from, emphasizes the influence of macro-level processes. In these accounts the diffusion trajectory depends not just on the overall distribution of individual-level receptivity but also on structural and institutional features, such as the degree of interconnectedness in a population.[138] This approach aligns with a view of mechanistic thinking that allows for mechanisms to be set at different levels of abstraction.[139] As Tulia Falleti and Julia Lynch point out, "Micro-level mechanisms are no more fundamental than macro-level ones."[140]

To judge the explanatory strength of the LS and GPT mechanisms, I employ within-case congruence tests and process-tracing principles to evaluate the predictions of the two theoretical approaches against the empirical record.[141] In each historical case, I first trace how leading sectors and GPTs developed in the major economies, paying particular attention to adoption timeframes, the technological phase of relative advantage, and the breadth

134. Beach and Pedersen 2018, 861–63; Goertz 2017, 66.

135. Gilpin 1981, 1987; Kennedy 2018, 51; Modelski and Thompson 1996; Freeman, Clark, and Soete 1982; Kim and Hart 2001.

136. I am grateful to Marty Finnemore for advice on organizing this section.

137. Mayntz 2004, 255.

138. Mayntz 2004, 251.

139. Bennett and Checkel 2015, 11; Falleti and Lynch 2009; George and Bennett 2005, 142; Mahoney 2003, 5; Tilly 2001.

140. Falleti and Lynch 2009, 1149.

141. Blatter and Haverland 2012, 144; George and Bennett 2005, 181–204.

of growth—three dimensions that differentiate GPT diffusion from LS product cycles.[142]

For example, my assessment of the two mechanisms along the impact time-frame dimension follows consistent procedures in each case.[143] To evaluate when certain technologies were most influential, I establish when they initially emerged (based on dates of key breakthroughs), when their associated industries were growing fastest, and when they diffused across a wide range of application sectors. When data are available, I estimate a GPT's initial arrival date by also factoring in the point at which it reached a 1 percent adoption rate in the median sector.[144] Industry growth rates, diffusion curves, and output trends all help measure the timeline along which technological breakthroughs substantially influenced the overall economy. The growth trajectory of each candidate GPT and LS is then set against a detailed timeline of when a major shift in productivity leadership occurs.

I then turn to the institutional factors that could explain why some countries were more successful in adapting to a technological revolution, with a focus on the institutions best suited to the demands of GPTs and leading sectors.[145] If the GPT mechanism is operative, the state that attains economic leadership should have an advantage in institutions that broaden the base of engineering human capital and spread best practices linked to GPTs. Additional evidence of the GPT diffusion theory's explanatory power would be that other countries had advantages in institutions that complement LS product cycles, such as scientific research infrastructure and sectoral governance structures.

These evaluation procedures are effective because I have organized the competing mechanisms "so that they are composed of the same number of diametrically opposite parts with observable implications that rule each other out."[146] This allows for evidence in favor of one explanation to be doubly decisive in that it also undermines the competing theory.[147] In sum, each case study

142. In line with best practices for tracing mechanisms, causal diagrams for these two competing explanations (figure 2.1) were introduced earlier in this chapter (Waldner 2015).

143. The qualitative analysis appendix provides further details on case analysis procedures.

144. Jovanovic and Rousseau 2005, 1184.

145. A leading state could possess advantages in both GPT skill infrastructure and institutions that complement LS product cycles. Thus, particularly strong evidence in favor of GPT diffusion theory would be that the lead state trailed its rivals with respect to institutional complements to LS product cycles.

146. Beach and Pedersen 2013, 15.

147. Collier 2011, 827.

TABLE 2.2. Testable Propositions of the LS and GPT Mechanisms

Dimensions	Key Questions	LS Propositions	GPT Propositions
Impact timeframe	When do revolutionary technologies make their greatest marginal impact on the economic balance of power?	New industries make their greatest impact on growth differentials in early stages.	GPTs do not make a significant impact on growth differentials until multiple decades after emergence.
Key phase of relative advantage	Do monopoly profits from innovation or benefits from more successful diffusion drive growth differentials?	A state's monopoly on innovation in leading sectors propels it to economic leadership.	A state's success in widespread adoption of GPTs propels it to economic leadership.
Breadth of growth	What is the breadth of technology-driven growth?	Technological advances concentrated in a few leading sectors drive growth.	Technological advances dispersed across a broad range of GPT-linked industries drive growth.
Institutional complements	Which types of institutions are most advantageous for national success in technological revolutions?	Key institutional adaptations help a state capture market shares and monopoly profits in new industries.	Key institutional adaptations widen the base of engineering skills and knowledge for GPT diffusion.

is structured around investigating a set of four standardized questions that correspond to the three dimensions of the LS and GPT mechanisms as well as the institutional complements to technological trajectories (table 2.2).[148]

In each case study, I consider alternative theories of technology-driven power transitions. Countless studies have examined the rise and fall of great powers. My aim is not to sort through all possible causes of one nation's rise or another's decline. Rather, I am probing the causal processes behind an established connection between technological advances in each industrial revolution and an economic power transition. The VoC framework and threat-based theories outline alternative explanations for how significant technological advances

148. This follows the format of a structured, focused comparison (George 1979).

translated into growth differentials among great powers. Across all the cases, I assess whether they provide a better explanation for the historical case evidence than the GPT and LS mechanisms.

I also address case-specific confounding factors. For example, some scholars argue that abundant inputs of wood and metals induced the United States to embrace more machine-intensive technology in the IR-2, reasoning that Britain's slower adoption of interchangeable parts manufacturing was an efficient choice given its natural resource constraints.[149] For each case, I determine whether these types of circumstantial factors could nullify the validity of the GPT and LS mechanisms.

In tracing these mechanisms, I benefit from a wealth of empirical evidence on past industrial revolutions, which have been the subject of many interdisciplinary inquiries. Since the cases I study are well-traversed terrain, my research is primarily based on secondary sources.[150] I rely on histories of technology and general economic histories to trace how and when technological breakthroughs affected economic power balances. Notably, my analysis takes advantage of the application of formal statistical and econometric methods to assess the impact of significant technological advances, part of the "cliometric revolution" in economic history.[151] Some of these works have challenged the dominant narrative of previous industrial revolutions. For instance, Nick von Tunzelmann found that the steam engine made minimal contributions to British productivity growth before 1830, raising the issue that earlier accounts of British industrialization "tended to conflate the economic significance of the steam engine with its early diffusion."[152]

I supplement these historical perspectives with primary sources. These include statistical series on industrial production, census statistics, discussions of engineers in contemporary trade journals, and firsthand accounts from commissions and study teams of cross-national differences in technology systems. In the absence of standardized measures of engineering education, archival evidence helps fill in details about GPT skill infrastructure for each of the cases. In the IR-1 case, I benefit from materials from the National Archives

149. Broadberry 1997. This relates to other work on technological innovation and changes in systemic leadership that focuses on the role of energy transitions; see Thompson and Zakhirova 2018.

150. This is an acceptable practice for comparative historical research; see Skocpol 1984, 382; Thies 2002, 359.

151. Fogel 1964.

152. Nuvolari, Verspagen, and von Tunzelmann 2011, 292. See also von Tunzelmann 1978.

(United Kingdom), the British Newspaper Archive, and the University of Nottingham Libraries, Manuscripts, and Special Collections. My IR-2 case analysis relies on collections based at the Bodleian Library (United Kingdom), the Library of Congress (United States), and the University of Leipzig and on British diplomatic and consular reports.[153] In the IR-3 case analysis, the Edward A. Feigenbaum Papers collection, held at Stanford University, helps inform US-Japan comparisons in computer science education.

My research also benefits greatly from new data on historical technological development. I take advantage of improved datasets, such as the Maddison Project Database.[154] New ones, such as the Cross-Country Historical Adoption of Technology dataset, were also beneficial.[155] Sometimes hype about exciting new technologies influences the perceptions of commentators and historians about the pace and extent of technology adoption. More granular data can help substantiate or cut through these narratives. Like the reassessments of the impact of previous technologies, these data were released after the publication of the field-defining works on technology and power transitions in international relations. Making extensive use of these sources therefore provides leverage to revise conventional understandings.

When assessing these two mechanisms, one of the main challenges is to identify the key technological changes to trace. I take a broad view of technology that encompasses not just technical designs but also organizational and managerial innovations.[156] Concretely, I follow Harvey Brooks, a pioneer of the science and technology policy field, in defining technology as "knowledge of how to fulfill certain human purposes in a specifiable and reproducible way."[157] The LS and GPT mechanisms both call attention to the outsized import of particular technical breakthroughs and their interactions with social systems, but they differ on which ones are more important. Therefore, a deep and wide understanding of advances in hardware and organizational practices in each historical period is required to properly sort them by their potential to spark LS or GPT trajectories.

153. The British diplomatic and consular reports have been described as "a rich but neglected historical source" (Barker 1981).

154. Inklaar et al. 2018.

155. Comin and Hobijn 2009. For an expansion of this dataset, which is now the most extensive dataset on technology adoption, see Milner and Solstad 2021.

156. Rosenberg 1982.

157. Brooks 1980, 66, cited in Skolnikoff 1993, 13.

This task is complicated by substantial disagreements over which technologies are leading sectors and GPTs. Proposed lists of GPTs often conflict, raising questions about the criteria used for GPT selection.[158] Reacting to the length of such lists, other scholars fear that "the [GPT] concept may be getting out of hand."[159] According to one review of eleven studies that identified past GPTs, twenty-six different innovations appeared on at least one list but only three appeared on all eleven.[160]

The LS concept is even more susceptible to these criticisms because the characteristics that define leading sectors are inconsistent across existing studies. Though most scholars agree that leading sectors are new industries that grow faster than the rest of the economy, there is marked disagreement on other criteria. Some scholars select leading sectors based on the criterion that they have been the largest industry in several major industrial nations for a period of time.[161] Others emphasize that leading sectors attract significant investments in R&D.[162] To illustrate this variability, I reviewed five key texts that analyze the effect of leading sectors on economic power transitions. Limiting the lists of proposed leading sectors to those that emerged during the three case study periods, I find that fifteen leading sectors appeared on at least one list and only two appeared on all five.[163]

My process for selecting leading sectors and GPTs to trace helps alleviate concerns that I cherry-pick the technologies that best fit my preferred explanation. In each historical case, most studies that explicitly identify leading sectors or GPTs agree on a few obvious GPTs and leading sectors. To ensure that I do not omit any GPTs, I consider all technologies singled out by at least two of five key texts that identify GPTs across multiple historical periods.[164] I apply the same approach to LS selection, using the aforementioned list I compiled.

Following classification schemes that differentiate GPTs from "near-GPTs" and "multipurpose technologies," I resolve many of the conflicts over what

158. Field 2008; Mokyr 2006; Ristuccia and Solomou 2014.

159. David and Wright 1999, 10.

160. Field 2008. The three innovations were steam, electricity, and information technology.

161. Kurth 1979, 3.

162. Drezner 2001, 6–7. Despite being universally recognized as a leading sector, the cotton textile industry in the late eighteenth century would not qualify as a leading sector under this definition because it did not require significant investments in R&D activities.

163. See qualitative appendix table 2.

164. See qualitative appendix table 3 for the full list.

counts as a GPT or leading sector by referring to a set of defining criteria.[165] For instance, while some accounts include the railroad and the automobile as GPTs, I do not analyze them as candidate GPTs because they lack a variety of uses.[166] I support my choices with empirical methods for LS and GPT identification. To confirm certain leading sectors, I examine the rate of growth across various industry sectors. I also leverage recent studies that identify GPTs with patent-based indicators.[167] Taken together, these procedures limit the risk of omitting certain technologies while guarding against GPT and LS concept creep.[168] The qualitative analysis appendix outlines how I address other issues related to LS and GPT identification, including concerns about omitting important single-purpose technologies and scenarios when certain technological breakthroughs are linked to both LS and GPT trajectories.

These considerations underscore that taking stock of the key technological drivers is only the first step in the case analysis. To judge whether these breakthroughs actually brought about the impacts that are often claimed for them, it is important to carefully trace how these technologies evolved in close relation with societal systems.

As a complement to the historical case studies, this book's research design includes a large-n quantitative analysis of the relationship between the breadth of software engineering skill formation institutions and computerization rates. This tests a key observable implication of GPT diffusion theory, using time-series cross-sectional data on nineteen advanced and emerging economies across three decades. I leave the more detailed description of the statistical methodology to chapter 6.

Summary

The technological fitness of nations is determined by how they adapt to the demands of new technical advances. I have developed a theory to explain how revolutionary technological breakthroughs affect the rise and fall of great

---

165. On "near-GPTs," see Lipsey, Bekar, and Carlaw 1998, 46–47. "Multipurpose technologies" have multiple economically relevant application sectors but lack the pervasive technological complementarities of GPTs. X-ray and laser technology, for example, falls under this category (Battke and Schmidt 2015, 336).

166. Field 2008, 12; Mokyr 2006, 1073. A "variety of uses" is a key characteristic of GPTs (Lipsey, Bekar, and Carlaw 1998, 39).

167. For efforts to empirically verify GPTs, see Gross 2014, 32; Petralia 2020, 1–2.

168. In each of the historical case studies, I trace no more than four candidate leading sectors and no more than four candidate GPTs.

powers. My approach is akin to that of an investigator tasked with figuring out why one ship sailed across the ocean faster than all the others. As though differentiating the winning ship's route from possible sea-lanes in terms of trade wind conditions and course changes, I first contrast the GPT and LS trajectories with regard to the timing, phase, and breadth of technological change. Once the superior route has been mapped, attention turns to the attributes of the winning ship, such as its navigation equipment and sailors' skills, that enabled it to take advantage of this fast lane across the ocean. In similar fashion, having set out the GPT trajectory as the superior route from technological revolution to economic leadership, my argument then highlights GPT skill infrastructure as the key institutional attribute that dictates which great power capitalizes best on this route.

3

The First Industrial Revolution and Britain's Rise

FEW HISTORICAL EVENTS have shaken the world like the First Industrial Revolution (IR-1, 1780–1840). Extraordinary upheaval marked the contours and consequences of the IR-1. For the first time in history, productivity growth accelerated dramatically, allowing large numbers of people to experience sustained improvements in their living standards. Small towns transformed into large cities, new ideologies gathered momentum, and emerging economic and social classes reshaped the fabric of society. These changes reverberated in the international sphere, where the ramifications of the IR-1 included the transition to industrialized mass warfare, the decline of the absolutist state, and the birth of the modern international system.

Among these transformations, two phenomena stand out. The first is the remarkable technological progress that inaugurated the IR-1 period. Everything was changing in part because so many *things* were changing—water frames, steam engines, and puddling processes not least among them. The second is Britain's rise to unrivaled economic leadership, during which it sustained productivity growth at higher levels than its rivals, France and the Netherlands. The following sections adjudicate the debates over the exact timeline of Britain's industrialization, but there is no doubt that Britain, propelled by the IR-1, became the world's most advanced economic power by the mid-nineteenth century.

No study of technological change and power transitions is complete without an account of the IR-1. For both the LS and GPT mechanisms, the IR-1 functions as a typical case that is held up as paradigmatic of technology-driven power transitions. The standard account in international relations scholarship attributes Britain's industrial ascent to its dominance of innovation in the IR-1's leading sectors, including cotton textiles, iron metallurgy, and steam power.[1] Present-day scholarship and policy discussions often draw upon stylized views of the IR-1, analogizing present developments in information technology and biotechnology to the effects of steam power and cotton textiles in the industrial revolution.[2]

A deeper inquiry into the IR-1 and Britain's economic rise challenges many of these conventional views. First, it reveals that general-purpose transformations linked to advances in iron metallurgy diffused widely enough to significantly affect economy-wide productivity only after 1815—a timeline that aligns with the period when Britain significantly outpaced its rivals in industrialization. Other prominent advances, including the steam engine, made only limited contributions to Britain's rise to industrial prominence in this period owing to a prolonged period of gestation before widespread adoption. Second, the IR-1 case also demonstrates that it was Britain's advantage in extending mechanization throughout the economy, not monopoly profits from innovations in cotton textiles, that proved crucial to its industrial ascendancy. Third, the historical data illustrate that the dispersion of mechanical innovations across many sectors fueled British productivity growth. Across these three dimensions, the IR-1 case matches the GPT trajectory better than the LS trajectory.

Since no country monopolized innovations in metalworking processes and Britain's competitors could also absorb innovations from abroad, why did Britain gain the most from this GPT trajectory? In all countries, as technical advances surged forward, institutional adjustments raced to cultivate the skills required to keep pace. Importantly, France and the Netherlands were competitive with Britain—and even surpassed it in some respects—in scientific research infrastructure and education systems for training expert engineers. These institutional settings in France and the Netherlands, however, produced knowledge and skills that were rather divorced from practical applications.

Britain's comparative advantage rested on another type of skill infrastructure. It depended less on heroic innovators like James Watt, the famed creator of the modern steam engine, and more on competent engineers who could build and maintain new technological systems, as well as make incremental adaptations to implement these systems in many different settings.[3] As ex-

1. Gilpin 1975, 67–80.
2. See, for example, Manning 2020.
3. Kelly, Mokyr, and Ó Gráda 2020; Meisenzahl and Mokyr 2011.

pected by GPT diffusion theory, Britain benefited from education systems that expanded the base of mechanically skilled engineers and disseminated knowledge of applied mechanics. Britain's competitors could not match its system for cultivating a common technical language in applied mechanics that encouraged the knowledge exchanges between engineers and entrepreneurs needed for advancing mechanization from one industry to the next.

To trace these mechanisms, I gathered and sorted through a wealth of evidence on the IR-1. Historical accounts served as the foundational materials, including general economic histories of the IR-1, histories of influential technologies and industries like the steam engine and the iron industry, country-specific histories, and comparative histories of Britain, France, and the Netherlands. I also benefited from contemporary assessments of the IR-1's institutional features provided by trade journals, proceedings of mechanics' institutes, recruitment advertisements published in local newspapers, and essays by leading engineers. This evidence stems from archival materials at the British Newspaper Archive, the National Archives (United Kingdom), and the University of Nottingham Libraries, Manuscripts, and Special Collections. Triangulating a variety of sources, I endeavored to back up my claims with statistical evidence in the form of industrial output estimates, patenting rates, and detailed biographical information on British engineers.

The assessment of the GPT and LS mechanisms against historical evidence from the IR-1 proceeds as follows. To begin, the chapter reviews Britain's rise to industrial preeminence, which is the outcome of the case. Next, it sorts the key technological breakthroughs of the period by their potential to drive two types of trajectories—LS product cycles and GPT diffusion. I then assess whether Britain's rise in this period is better explained by the GPT or LS mechanism, tracing the development of candidate leading sectors and GPTs in terms of impact timeframe, phase of relative advantage, and breadth of growth. If the GPT trajectory holds for this period, there should be evidence that Britain was better equipped than its competitors in GPT skill infrastructure. Another section evaluates whether the historical data support this expectation. Before concluding the chapter, I address alternative factors and explanations.

A Power Transition: Britain's Rise

When did Britain ascend to industrial hegemony? The broad outlines of the story are well known. Between the mid-eighteenth century and the mid-nineteenth century, the industrial revolution propelled Great Britain to global preeminence. Although Britain did not boast the world's largest economy—China held that title during this period—it did capitalize on the technologies of the industrial revolution to become "the world's most advanced productive power."[4] France and the Netherlands, its economic rivals, did not keep pace with Britain's productivity growth.

While both the LS and GPT models agree that Britain established itself as the preeminent industrial power in this period, a clearer sense of when this shift occurred is essential for testing the explanatory power of the LS and GPT mechanisms during this period. One common view of Britain's industrialization, brought to prominence by Rostow, depicts an accelerated takeoff into sustained growth. Rostow's timeline dates this takeoff to the last two decades of the eighteenth century.[5] In alignment with this periodization, some scholars writing in the LS tradition claim that Britain achieved its industrial ascent by the late eighteenth century.[6]

A different perspective, better supported by the evidence that follows, favors a delayed timeline for Britain's ascent to industrial preeminence. Under this view, Britain did not sustain economic and productivity advances at levels substantially higher than its rivals until the 1820s and after. To clarify the chronology of Britain's industrial ascent, the following sections survey three proxies for productivity leadership: GDP per capita, industrialization, and total factor productivity.

GDP PER-CAPITA INDICATORS

Trend lines in GDP per capita, a standard proxy for productivity, confirm the broad outlines of Britain's rise. Evidence from the Maddison Project Database (MPD) points to the decades *after* 1800, not before, as the key transition period (figure 3.1).[7] These trends come from the 2020 version of the MPD, which updates Angus Maddison's data and incorporates new annual estimates of GDP per capita in the IR-1 period for France, the Netherlands, and the United Kingdom.[8] In 1760, the Netherlands boasted the world's highest per-

4. Kennedy 2018, 53.

5. Rostow 1960; Rostow 1956, 31.

6. Gilpin 1996, 413; Thompson 1990, 220.

7. For full lists of sources for this figure, see Bolt and van Zanden 2020; Broadberry, Campbell, et al. 2015; Ridolfi 2017; Smits, Horlings, and van Zanden 2000; van Zanden and van Leeuwen 2012.

8. Bolt and van Zanden 2020, 8–9.

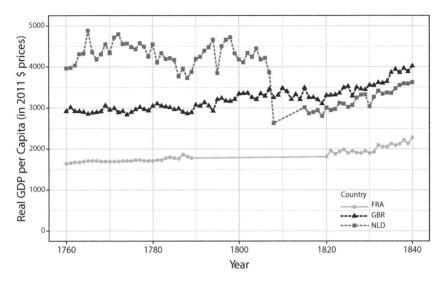

FIGURE 3.1. Economic Power Transition in the IR-1. *Source*: Maddison Project Database, version 2020 (Bolt and van Zanden 2020).

capita income, approximately 35 percent higher than Britain's.[9] The Dutch held this lead for the rest of the eighteenth century through to 1808, when Britain first overtook the Netherlands in GDP per capita. By 1840, Britain's GDP per capita was about 75 percent higher than that of France and about 10 percent ahead of that of the Netherlands.[10]

It should be noted that GDP per-capita information for the early years of the IR-1 is sometimes missing or only partially available. For years prior to 1807, the MPD bases Dutch GDP per-capita estimates on data for just the Holland region, so the Dutch economy's decline during this time could be an artifact of changes in data sources.[11] At the same time, to ensure that the MPD data can be used to provide accurate information on historical patterns of economic growth and decline, researchers have made adjustments to partial data series and consulted experts to assess their representativeness.[12] Furthermore,

9. My calculations are based on Maddison Project Database, version 2020; see also Maddison 2007, 76. For other evidence of the Dutch lead in GDP per capita in the early nineteenth century, see Engerman and O'Brien 2004, 462; van Zanden and van Riel 2004, 264.

10. My calculations are based on Maddison Project Database, version 2020.

11. The MPD switches to estimates of Dutch GDP per capita based on data from the entire country starting in 1808 (Bolt and van Zanden 2020, 9). I thank Adam Dean for pointing out this possibility.

12. Bolt and van Zanden 2020, 9.

the Holland-based data in the early 1800s already indicated a decline in Dutch GDP per capita. Although data scarcity makes it difficult to mark out exactly when Britain's GDP per capita surpassed that of the Netherlands, the MPD remains the best source for cross-country comparisons of national income in this period.

INDUSTRIALIZATION INDICATORS

Industrialization indicators depict a mixed picture of when Britain sustained leadership in economic efficiency. By one influential set of metrics compiled by economic historian Paul Bairoch, Britain's per-capita industrialization levels had grown to 50 percent higher than those of France in 1800, from a position of near-equality with France and Belgium in 1750. For scholars who map the trajectories of great powers, these estimates have assumed a prominent role in shaping the timeline of British industrial ascendance.[13] For instance, Paul Kennedy employs Bairoch's estimates to argue that the industrial revolution transformed Britain into a different kind of world power.[14]

Further examination of Bairoch's estimates qualifies their support for an accelerated timeline of Britain's industrial ascendance. First, by limiting his definition of "industrial output" to manufacturing industry products, Bairoch excludes the contribution of notable sectors such as construction and mining, a distinction even he admits is "rather arbitrary."[15] Second, the gap between Britain and France in per-capita industrialization levels in 1800 still falls within the margin of error for Bairoch's estimates.[16]

Moreover, a delayed timeframe is supported by industrialization measures that encompass more than the manufacturing industries. In 1700, the Netherlands had a substantially higher proportion of its population employed in industry (33 percent) compared to the United Kingdom (22 percent). In 1820, the proportion of people employed in UK industry had risen to 33 percent—higher than the Dutch corresponding rate of 28 percent.[17] One

13. Acemoglu, Johnson, and Robinson 2002, 1237; Ikenberry 2001, 168; Moe 2004, 146.
14. Kennedy 1987, 151.
15. Bairoch 1982, 322.
16. By Bairoch's (ibid., 327) own judgment, there is a 25 to 30 percent margin of error for 1800 estimates of European countries.
17. Maddison 2007, 76. There is limited primary source data that allow for cross-national comparisons of industrialization rates in this period. Maddison does not have statistics on this ratio for the years between 1700 and 1820.

expert on the pre-industrial revolution in Europe notes that the Netherlands was at least as industrialized as England, if not more so, throughout the eighteenth century.[18] Lastly, aggregate industrial production trends map out a post-1815 surge in British industrialization, providing further evidence that Britain did not solidify its productivity advantage until decades into the nineteenth century.[19]

PRODUCTIVITY INDICATORS

Total factor productivity (TFP) indicators, which capture the efficiency by which production factors are converted into useful outputs, further back the delayed ascent story. As was the case with trends in aggregate industrial output, TFP growth in Britain did not take off until after 1820.[20] In truth, British TFP growth was very modest throughout the eighteenth century, averaging less than 1 percent per year.[21]

While the paucity of reliable data on total factor productivity in France hinders cross-national comparisons in this period, some evidence suggests that Britain did not surpass the Netherlands in TFP until after 1800.[22] Historian Robert Allen estimated TFP in agriculture by calculating the ratio between actual output per worker and the output per worker predicted by a country's available agricultural population and land. On this metric for the year 1800, the Netherlands ranked higher than Britain and all other European nations.[23] The Dutch also attained the highest absolute TFP in Europe for almost all of the eighteenth century.[24]

Which periodization of Britain's industrial ascent better reflects the empirical evidence? On balance, measures of per-capita GDP, industrialization levels, and total factor productivity support a deferred timeline for Britain's industrial rise. This clarification of when an economic power transition occurred during the IR-1 provides a stable target to test the competing LS and GPT mechanisms.

---

18. Gutmann 1988, 119–20.

19. Greasley and Oxley 2000.

20. Crafts 1995, 752

21. Crafts 1998.

22. Tentative estimates of French productivity in 1815 suggest that Britain had opened up a substantial lead (Moe 2007, 32–33).

23. Allen 2003, 409, 435.

24. De Vries and van der Woude 1997, 693. Roughly estimated with a wage rate index, Dutch labor productivity probably led Europe throughout the eighteenth century, with the exception of the last decade (ibid., 620, 695).

Key Technological Changes in the IR-1

Before evaluating the LS and GPT mechanisms in greater depth, the technological elements of the IR-1 must be further specified. Hargreaves's spinning jenny (1764), Arkwright's water frame (1769), Watt's steam engine (1769), Cort's puddling process (1784), and many other significant technical advances emerged during the First Industrial Revolution. The most likely sources of GPT and LS trajectories can be identified with guidance from existing work that calls attention to key technologies and accepted criteria for these two categories. Narrowing the assessment of these two mechanisms to a limited set of technologies makes for a more viable exercise.

Candidate Leading Sectors: Cotton Textiles, Iron, and Steam Power

A strong degree of consensus on the leading sectors that powered Britain's rise in the IR-1 makes it relatively easy to identify three candidate sectors: cotton textiles, iron, and steam power.[25] Among these, historians widely recognize the cotton textile industry as the original leading sector of the First Industrial Revolution.[26] New inventions propelled the industry's rapid growth, as its share of total value added to British industry rose from 2.6 percent in 1770 to 17 percent in 1801.[27] In characterizing the significance of the cotton industry, Schumpeter went as far as to claim, "English industrial history can, in the epoch 1787–1842 . . . be almost resolved into the history of a single industry."[28]

If the cotton textile industry places first in the canon of the IR-1's leading sectors, then the iron industry follows close behind. In their account of Britain's rise, Modelski and Thompson single out these two major industries, employing pig iron production and cotton consumption, as indicators for Britain's leading sector growth rates.[29] According to the traditional view of the IR-1, the iron and cotton industries were the only two that experienced "highly successful, rapidly diffused technical change" before the 1820s.[30]

I also evaluate the steam power industry as a third possible leading sector. A wide range of LS-based scholarship identifies steam power as one of the

25. Gilpin 1975, 67; Rostow 1991, 33, 52–57; Tomory 2016, 155.
26. Hobsbawm 1968, 40; Kurth 1979; Rostow 1960, 53–54.
27. Freeman and Louca 2001, 154.
28. Schumpeter 1939, 270–1.
29. Modelski and Thompson 1996, 85–87.
30. Deane 1965, 140; see also Cameron 1989, 196; Temin 1997, 63.

technological foundations of Britain's leadership in the nineteenth century.[31] Most of this literature labels only the steam engine itself as the leading sector, but since leading sectors are new industries, the steam engine–producing industry is the more precise understanding of the leading sector related to major advances in steam engine technology. Compared to the iron and cotton textile industries, it is much more uncertain whether the steam engine–producing industry, which experienced relatively slow growth in output and productivity, meets the analytical criteria for a leading sector during the IR-1 case.[32] Still, I include the steam engine–producing industry as a potential leading sector, leaving it to the case analysis to further study its growth trajectory.

Candidate GPTs: Iron, Steam Engine, and the Factory System

Since the possible sources of GPT trajectories in the IR-1 are less established, I drew on previous studies that mapped out technological paradigms in this period to select three candidate GPTs: the steam engine, mechanization based on advances in iron machinery, and the factory system.[33] As a possible source of GPT-style effects, the steam engine is a clear choice. Alongside electricity and (ICT) technology, it has been described as one of the "Big Three" GPTs, appearing in nearly all catalogs of GPTs.[34] Here the emphasis is on the capacity of steam engines to transform a wide variety of industrial processes across many sectors, as opposed to the potential growth of the steam engine–producing industry.

Of the two paradigmatic industries of the IR-1, cotton and iron, the latter was a more plausible driver of GPT-style effects for Britain. As the demand for iron-made machinery grew, iron foundries development of new generations of machine tools, such as cylinder-boring machines, contributed to the creation

---

31. Rostow (1960, 54, 60), the pioneer of LS analysis, lists steam power as one of the key drivers of British takeoff. Long-cycle theorists consider steam power the "emblematic" technology for the IR-1 (Bruland and Smith 2013, 1717; see also Reuveny and Thompson 2001, 689–719).

32. The steam engine producing industry's output never surpassed 1 percent of total industrial production in the United Kingdom from 1760 to 1860 (Edquist and Henrekson 2006).

33. Indeed, Deane's influential history of the IR-1 identifies the steam engine and Cort's puddling process, which facilitated the widespread availability of cheap malleable iron, as the two crucial advances that "ensured a continuous process of industrialization and technical change" (Deane 1965, 130).

34. Field 2008, 12.

of a mechanical engineering industry.[35] This spurred the mechanization of production processes in a wide range of industries, including agriculture, food processing, printing, and textiles.[36] Although both cotton textiles and iron were fast-growing industries, developments in iron better resembled a "motive branch" driving pervasive effects across the economy.[37]

In addition, the late eighteenth century saw the emergence of centralized factories, which significantly increased the scale of goods production. The factory system offered the potential to change the techniques of production across many industries. One widely cited classification scheme for GPTs picks out the factory system as an "organizational GPT" in the late eighteenth to early nineteenth century period.[38] Other scholars describe this organizational innovation as "one of the most fundamental changes of 'metabolism' in the Industrial Revolution."[39]

I also considered but ultimately decided against including developments in railroads as a candidate GPT. Among five core texts that classify GPTs across many historical periods, at least two highlighted the significance of the railroad to the IR-1.[40] In my view, the railroad represented a disruptive advance, but it did not acquire the variety of uses to qualify as a GPT. Railways carried many types of freight and made new business models possible, but their function was limited to transport.[41]

Sources of LS and GPT Trajectories

Table 3.1 recaps the potential technological sources for both the GPT and LS mechanisms. It is important to clarify three points about the sorting process. First, it is notable but not surprising that the candidate leading sectors and GPTs draw from similar technological wellsprings. Both mechanisms agree that some inventions, like Cort's puddling process for making wrought iron, mattered much more than others in terms of their impact on the economic balance of power.

35. MacLeod and Nuvolari 2009, 229; von Tunzelmann 2000, 125.
36. MacLeod and Nuvolari 2009; Paulinyi 1986; von Tunzelmann 1995, 104–122.
37. Freeman and Louca 2001, 155; Perez 1983, 363.
38. Lipsey, Carlaw, and Bekar 2005, 132, 246.
39. Freeman and Louca 2001, 174; see also Mantoux 2006, 25.
40. See qualitative appendix table 3.
41. Field 2008, 12.

TABLE 3.1. Key Sources of Technological Trajectories in the IR-1

Candidate Leading Sectors	Candidate GPTs
Cotton textile industry	Factory system
Iron industry	Mechanization
Steam engine–producing industry	Steam engine

Where the mechanisms separate is in how this process transpired. Cort's puddling process and other ironmaking innovations, under the GPT model, are expected to follow an impact pathway characterized by three features: an extended lag before they affect productivity growth, the spread of mechanization across the economy, and widespread complementary innovations in many machine-using industries. Under the LS model, the same technological sources are expected to affect economic growth in a way that is lopsided in the early stages of development, fueled by monopolizing iron exports, and limited to technological innovations in the iron industry.

Second, it is still useful to classify three distinct candidate GPTs in the IR-1, despite the fact that developments in factory systems, mechanization, and steam engines were mutually reinforcing in many respects. Steam engines depended on the transition from hand-tool processes to machinery-based production systems; at the same time, the impact of steam engines on coal mining was to boost the iron industry, spurring mechanization. Yet a number of historians distinguish the expansion of mechanization in the British industrial revolution from transformations linked to the steam engine, arguing that the latter's economic impact materialized much later than the former.[42] Thus, while these candidate GPT trajectories are interconnected, it is still possible to locate various GPTs at different stages of their life cycle.

Third, not all of these technological changes necessarily had a decisive impact on Britain's capacity to sustain higher productivity levels than its rivals during the period of interest. They are labeled as candidates for a reason. As this chapter will show, the steam engine did not achieve widespread diffusion until after Britain had already established economic leadership. When subjected to more rigorous empirical analysis, developments in some technologies may not track well with the proposed LS and GPT trajectories for this period.

42. MacLeod and Nuvolari 2009, 217; Paulinyi 1986; von Tunzelmann 1995, 104–122.

GPT vs. LS Trajectories in the IR-1

Spelling out possible sources of technological trajectories in the IR-1 provides a bounded terrain for testing the validity of the GPT and LS mechanisms. By leveraging differences between the two mechanisms with respect to impact timeframe, phase of relative advantage, and breadth of growth, I derive three sets of opposing predictions for how technological changes translated into an economic power transition in this period. I then assess whether, and to what extent, the developments in the IR-1 supported these predictions.

OBSERVABLE IMPLICATIONS RELATED
TO IMPACT TIMEFRAME

When did the revolutionary technologies of the IR-1 disrupt the economic balance of power? If the impact timeframe of the LS mechanism holds, then radical technical advances in the cotton textile, iron, and/or steam engine–producing industries should have substantially stimulated British economic growth shortly after the emergence of major technological advances in the 1760s and 1770s.[43] Accordingly, scholars theorize that leading sectors propelled Great Britain to industrial superiority in the late eighteenth century.[44] In line with this conception of a rapid timeline, Modelski and Thompson expect that the growth of two lead industries, cotton and iron, peaked in the 1780s.[45]

On the other hand, if the GPT mechanism was operational, the impact of major technological breakthroughs on Britain's industrial ascent should have arrived on a more gradual timeline. Key advances tied to mechanization, steam power, and the factory system emerged in the 1770s and 1780s. Given that GPTs require a long period of delay before they diffuse and achieve widespread adoption, the candidate GPTs of the IR-1 should not have had substantial economy-wide repercussions until the early decades of the nineteenth century and after. I use the year 1815 as a rough cut-point to separate the accelerated impact timeframe of leading sectors from that of GPTs in this period.

---

43. A cluster of major breakthroughs occurred during this period in cotton spinning: Hargreaves's spinning jenny (1764), Arkwright's water frame (1769), and Crompton's spinning mule (1779).

44. Cameron 1989; Modelski and Thompson 1996, 116; Rostow 1960.

45. Using indicators of cotton consumption and wrought iron production, Modelski and Thompson (1996, 111) designate a predicted "high growth" period (1763–1792) for the leading sectors of cotton and iron.

OBSERVABLE IMPLICATIONS RELATED
TO THE PHASE OF RELATIVE ADVANTAGE

The LS mechanism places high value on the innovation phase of technological change. Where major breakthroughs arise is key. Accordingly, Britain's capacity to pioneer major technological advances should explain economic growth differentials in the IR-1. Concretely, the LS mechanism expects that Britain's rise was fueled by its dominance of innovation in the cotton textile, iron, and steam engine–producing industries, as well as the resultant monopoly rents from exports in these sectors.

The GPT mechanism emphasizes a less-celebrated phase of technological change. Where innovations diffuse is key. Differentials in the rate and intensiveness of GPT adoption generate the gap between an ascending industrial leader and other competitors. The GPT mechanism suggests that Britain's rise to industrial preeminence can be traced to its superior ability to diffuse generic technological changes across the economy.

OBSERVABLE IMPLICATIONS RELATED
TO BREADTH OF GROWTH

The last set of observable implications relate to the breadth of growth during the IR-1. As illustrated in the descriptions here of the candidate leading sectors, many accounts attribute Britain's industrial ascent to a narrow set of critical advances.[46] In one of the first texts dedicated to the investigation of technology and international relations, William Ogburn declared, "The coming of the steam engine . . . is the variable which explains the increase of Britain as a power in the nineteenth century."[47] According to GPT diffusion theory, Britain's rise to industrial preeminence came from the advance of GPTs through many linked sectors.

Taken together, these three sets of diverging predictions guide my assessment of the GPT mechanism against the LS mechanism. I make expectations specific to the IR-1 case by using the relevant information on particular technologies and the timeline of British industrialization. Table 3.2 lays out the specific, testable predictions that provide the framework of evaluation in the following sections.

46. Bruland 2004; Kennedy 1976, 150–51.
47. Ogburn 1949b, 17.

TABLE 3.2. Testable Predictions for the IR-1 Case Analysis

Prediction 1: LS (impact timeframe)	The cotton textile, iron, and/or* steam engine–producing industries made a significant impact on Britain's rise to industrial preeminence before 1815.
Prediction 1: GPT	Mechanization, the steam engine, and / or the factory system made a significant impact on Britain's rise to industrial preeminence only after 1815.
Prediction 2: LS (relative advantage)	Innovations in cotton textile, iron, and/or the steam engine–producing industries were concentrated in Britain.
	British advantages in the production and exports of textiles, iron, and/or steam engines were crucial to its industrial superiority.
Prediction 2: GPT	Innovations in iron, the steam engine, and/or the factory system were not concentrated in Britain.
	British advantages in the diffusion of mechanization, steam engines, and/or the factory system were crucial to its industrial superiority.
Prediction 3: LS (breadth of growth)	Productivity growth in Britain was limited to the cotton textile, iron, and/or steam engine –producing industries.
Prediction 3: GPT	Productivity growth in Britain was spread across a broad range of industries linked to mechanization, the steam engine, and/or the factory system.

* The operator "and/or" links all candidate leading sectors and GPTs because it could be the case that only some of these technologies drove the trajectories of the period.

Impact Timeframe: Delayed Surge vs. Fast Rise of British Industrialization

The painstaking reconstruction of temporal chronology is at the heart of tracing mechanisms. Tremendous technological changes occurred during this period, but when exactly did they make their mark on Britain's industrial superiority? The period when significant technological innovations emerge often does not match up with the time when their impacts are felt. Unfortunately, when drawing lessons from the IR-1 on the effect of technology on international politics, scholars have conflated the overall significance of certain technologies with near-immediate impact.[48] Establishing a clear timeline of when technological

48. Nuvolari, Verspagen, and von Tunzelmann 2011, 292. For a response to some of these criticisms, see Rostow 1991, 172–211.

changes catalyzed a shift in productivity leadership during the IR-1 is therefore an important first step in comparing the LS and GPT mechanisms.

DIVERGING TIMELINES: COTTON VS. IRON

Time-series data on the output growth of twenty-six industries that accounted for around 60 percent of Britain's industrial production help differentiate the growth schedules of the cotton textiles and iron industries. According to these data, the major upswing in British industrialization took place after 1815, when the aggregate growth trend increased from 2 percent to a peak of 3.8 percent by 1825. In line with the expectations of the LS model, the cotton textile industry grew exceptionally fast following major technological innovations in the 1760s, but from the 1780s there was a deceleration in the output growth of cotton textiles. Based on the relatively early peak of the cotton industry's expansion, David Greasley and Les Oxley conclude that "it appears unlikely that cotton played the major role in the post-1815 upswing in British industrialization."[49]

Following a completely different trajectory, growth in iron goods was more in line with the GPT model. Starting in the 1780s, the growth rate of the British iron industry accelerated to a peak of about 5.3 percent in the 1840s.[50] "Compared to cotton textiles, change in iron was gradual, incremental, and spread out over a longer period of time," Espen Moe writes.[51] With a limited role for cotton, the gradual expansion of the iron industry led Britain's post-1815 industrial surge, as its trend output tracked much more closely with that of aggregate industry. In sum, the cotton industry followed the growth path of a leading sector, whereas developments in the iron industry reflected the impact timeline of a GPT.

The timing of Britain's mechanization, linked to the expanded uses of iron in machine-making, also aligned with the GPT trajectory. The first metalworking tools for precision engineering, including Wilkinson's boring mill of 1774 and Maudslay's all-iron lathe, appeared in the late eighteenth century, but they would remain in a "comparatively rudimentary state" until about 1815.[52] According to accounts of qualified engineers and the 1841 Select Committee on Exportation of Machinery, over the course of the next two decades improvements and standardization in such machine tools ushered in a "revolution" in

49. Greasley and Oxley 2000, 114. There is general acceptance that the cotton industry's influence on British economic growth peaked relatively early (Farnie 2003, 734).

50. Greasley and Oxley 2000.

51. Moe 2007, 81; see also Lilley 1971, 197.

52. Musson 1981, 34.

machine-making.[53] The gradual evolution of the mechanical engineering industry provides additional support for a delayed impact timeframe for mechanization. According to British patent data from 1780 to 1849, the share of mechanical engineering patents among the total number of patents increased from an average of 18 percent in the decade starting in 1780 to a peak of 34 percent in the one starting in 1830.[54]

DELAYED, OUT-OF-PERIOD EFFECTS:
STEAM ENGINE AND FACTORY SYSTEM

Compared to mechanization, the steam engine had not diffused widely enough through Britain's economy by the mid-nineteenth century to make a substantial impact on overall industrial productivity. Detailed investigations of steam engine adoption have forced a reassessment of commonly held assumptions about the rapid impact of steam power on British productivity growth.[55] According to one growth accounting analysis, which compares the impact of steam against water power as a close substitute source of power, steam power's contribution to British productivity growth was modest until at least the 1830s and most influential in the second half of the nineteenth century.[56] This revised impact timeframe conflicts with international relations scholarship, which advances faster trajectories for steam's impact as a leading sector.[57]

Steam engine adoption was slow. In 1800, thirty years after Watt patented his steam engine, there were only about thirty-two engines operating in Manchester, which was a booming center of industrialization.[58] Even into the 1870s, many important sectors in the British economy, such as agriculture and services, were virtually unaffected by steam, as most of steam power's applications were concentrated in mining and in cotton textiles.[59] During the period

53. Ibid.; see also Musson 1980, 90–93.

54. MacLeod and Nuvolari 2009, 224.

55. Greenberg 1982.

56. Crafts 2004b; see also Mokyr 2010, 124–25; von Tunzelmann 1978.

57. LS accounts designate the years from 1815 to 1850 as a high-growth period for steam engine–based industries (Modelski and Thompson 1996, 69; Akaev and Pantin 2014, 868).

58. Bruland and Mowery 2006, 353. Much of the statistics used to measure the diffusion of steam engines focus on the usage of steam engines. Peralta 2020 criticizes this approach for not accounting for the effects of GPTs on the development of interrelated technologies. Later, I show that the timeline of complementary innovations also supports the slow diffusion trajectory of the steam engine.

59. Crafts 2004b, 341–42; von Tunzelmann 1978, 294.

when LS accounts expect its peak growth, the steam engine could not claim generality of use.

The process by which the steam engine gained a broad variety and range of uses entailed complementary innovations that followed many years after the introduction of Watt's steam engine. It took sixty years for steam to become the prime driver of maritime transport; that was made possible only after cumulative enhancements to the power of steam engines and the replacement of paddle wheels by screw propellers, which increased the speed of steam-powered ships.[60] Watt's original low-pressure design engines consumed large amounts of coal, which hindered widespread adoption. After 1840, aided by inventions such as the Lancashire boiler and discoveries in thermodynamics, it became economically viable to deploy steam engines that could handle higher pressures and temperatures.[61] In sum, steam power may be the quintessential example of the long delay between the introduction of a GPT and significant economy-wide effects.

It is worth assessing whether interconnections between developments in steam and those in iron and cotton give grounds for an earlier impact trajectory.[62] Yet both forward and backward linkages were limited in the early stages of the steam engine's evolution. Regarding the latter, the steam engine–producing industry did not substantially stimulate the iron industry's expansion. In the late 1790s, at a peak in sales, Boulton and Watt steam engines consumed less than 0.25 percent of Britain's annual iron output.[63] Forward linkages to textiles, the most likely sector to benefit from access to cheaper steam power, were also delayed. Steam-powered inventions in textiles did not overtake water-powered textile processes until after 1830.[64] Of course, over the long run steam power was a critical technological breakthrough that changed the energy budget of the British economy.[65] However, for investigating the mechanisms that facilitated Britain's rise to become the clear productivity leader in First Industrial Revolution, the steam engine played a modest role and most of its effects were out-of-period.

60. Smil 2010, 12–13.
61. Bryant 1973; von Tunzelmann 1978, 86–67.
62. Rostow 1960; Landes 1969.
63. Von Tunzelmann 1978, 285–86. Increased mechanization spurred the demand for technologies like the steam engine, not the other way around (Paulinyi 1986, 283).
64. Von Tunzelmann 1978, 289–92.
65. Cipolla 1962; Wrigley 1988.

A similar timeline characterizes the progression of the factory system, another candidate GPT considered for this period. The factory system diffused slowly and took hold in only a limited number of trades during the time when Britain was establishing its industrial preeminence. The British textile industry, as the earliest adopter of this organizational innovation, had established nearly five thousand steam- or water-powered factories by the 1850s.[66] Other industries, however, were much slower to adopt the factory system. In the first decades of the nineteenth century, small workshops and domestic production still dominated the metal trades as well as other hardware and engineering trades.[67]

Moreover, factories were still relatively small even into the mid-nineteenth century, and some industries adopted a mixed factory system in which many processes were outsourced to household workers.[68] It was not until steam power overtook water power in the 1830s and 1840s as a source of power in factories that the subsequent redesigns of factory layouts led to large gains in productivity.[69]

What does this clarified chronology of technological impacts in the IR-1 mean for the explanatory power of the GPT and LS mechanisms? Of the three candidate leading sectors, only cotton textiles, which expanded rapidly and peaked in terms of output growth in the 1780s and 1790s, followed the impact timeframe of a leading sector. As figure 3.2 shows, by 1814 British cotton exports had already surpassed 75 percent of the value they would attain in 1840. Yet Britain sustained productivity growth rates at higher levels than its rivals only in the first decades of the nineteenth century. Thus, the period when cotton should have made its greatest impact on Britain's industrial ascent does not accord with the timeline of Britain's industrialization surge.

The hurried timeline of the LS mechanism contrasts with the more delayed impact of other technological advances. As predicted by the GPT mechanism, all three candidate GPTs—mechanization, the steam engine, and the factory system—had little impact on Britain's industrial rise until after 1815. In fact, the diffusion timelines for the steam engine and factory system were so elongated that their impact on Britain's rise to industrial preeminence was limited in this period. In 1830, steam engine adoption, as measured by total horsepower in-

---

66. Jones 1987, 71.
67. Berg 1985; Mantoux 2006, 474–75; Mokyr 2001, 6.
68. Von Tunzelmann 1997.
69. Lipsey, Bekar, and Carlaw 1998, 45.

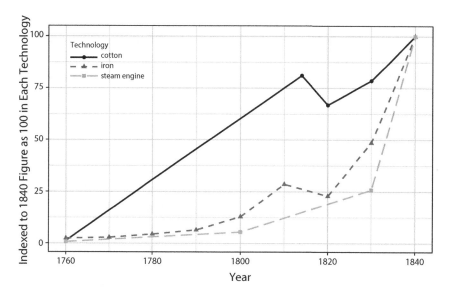

FIGURE 3.2. Technological Impact Timeframes in the IR-1. *Note*: British cotton exports, iron production, and steam engine adoption over time. *Source*: Robson 1957, 331–35; Mitchell 1988, 280–81; Crafts 2004, 342.

stalled, was only one-quarter of the 1840 level, whereas by 1830 the level of iron production had reached about 50 percent of its corresponding value in 1840 (see figure 3.2). This is consistent with the steady expansion of mechanization across industry in the early decades of the 1800s as the GPT trajectory most attuned with the timing of Britain's rise to economic leadership.

Phase of Relative Advantage: Diffusion of Iron vs. Monopoly Profits from Cotton

Thus far, the empirical evidence has presented a bird's-eye view of the overall timeline of technological change and industrialization in the IR-1, but there are two other dimensions on which the GPT and LS trajectories diverge. According to the expectations of the LS mechanism, the phase of technological development central to Britain's relative economic rise was its dominance of key innovations in cotton textiles, iron, or the steam engine. The GPT mechanism predicts, in contrast, that Britain's advantage in the diffusion of mechanization, the steam engine, or the factory system was the key driver.

The rest of this section tests two sets of predictions derived from the diverging assumptions of the two mechanisms. First, regarding the geographic clustering of major technological breakthroughs in the IR-1, I assess whether innovations in candidate leading sectors and GPTs were concentrated in Britain. Next, regarding the comparative consequences of these technologies, I evaluate whether Britain's industrial superiority drew more from its advantages in the production and exports of the IR-1's leading sectors or from its advantage in the diffusion of the IR-1's GPTs.

INNOVATION CLUSTERING IN THE IR-1'S BREAKTHROUGHS

Did Britain dominate innovation in the leading sectors of the IR-1? At first glance, there is no question that radical advances in candidate leading sectors clustered in Britain. This list includes Watt's steam engine, Arkwright's water frame, Cort's puddling process, and many more. Per one analysis of 160 major innovations introduced during the nineteenth and twentieth centuries, Britain was home to 44 percent of major innovations from 1811 to 1849—a rate that was double that of the closest competitor (the United States at 22 percent).[70]

Further investigation into British superiority in technological innovation paints a more mixed picture. According to another list of technical advances by country of origin, Britain accounted for only 29 percent of major innovations in the years from 1826 to 1850, a period that corresponds to when it cemented its productivity leadership.[71] Moreover, the European continent introduced many significant innovations, including the Jacquard loom, mechanical flax spinning, chlorine bleaching, the Leblanc soda–making process, and the Robert continuous papermaking machine.[72] France, in particular, generated many of the major industrial discoveries, such as in chemicals, clocks, glass, papermaking, and textiles.[73]

Thus, some scholars argue that Britain's comparative edge was in more incremental improvements. Reflecting on technological creativity in the IR-1,

---

70. Modelski and Thompson 1996, 117. Germany and France were the first to innovate in 17 percent of the 160 technological inventions. The list of major inventions comes from Van Duijn 1983, 176–79.

71. Cited in Vries 2013, 22; Kelly, Mokyr, and Ó Gráda 2020, 41. The value of this exercise is limited owing to subjective determinations of which innovations count as "major" as well as the lack of documentation for timings and names of creators for many early-nineteenth-century innovations (Van Duijn 1983, 174).

72. Mokyr 1999, 36.

73. Allen 2011, 358; Mathias 1975, 94.

economic historian Joel Mokyr argues, "Britain seems to have no particular advantage in generating *macroinventions* . . . the key to British technological success was that it had a comparative advantage in *microinventions*."[74] A proverb from the time captured this distinction: "For a thing to be perfect it must be invented in France and worked out in England."[75] This suggests that digging deeper into the different phases of technological development can help uncover the roots of Britain's industrial leadership.

MONOPOLY PROFITS VS. DIFFUSION DEFICIT

First, as was the case with the period when they made their impact, developments in cotton and iron followed very different paths with respect to the phase of technological change that determined economic differentials. Britain's cotton textile industry, the most likely source of monopoly profits, grew faster than other industries before 1800, and it sold most of its goods abroad. Technological innovations such as the spinning jenny and the water frame triggered exponential increases in the efficiency of cotton production, and Britain's cotton output increased by 2,200 percent from 1770 to 1815.[76] From 1750 to 1801, cotton's share of Britain's major exports increased from 1 percent to 39.6 percent.[77]

Certainly, the growth of British cotton exports was remarkable, but what was the impact of associated monopoly rents on overall growth differentials? Supported by improved quantitative estimates of the cotton industry's impact on the British economy, historians generally accept that the cotton industry was much more significant for enhancing Britain's trade balance than for boosting its economic productivity.[78] According to one estimate, between 1800 and 1860, the cotton industry accounted for 43 percent of the threefold increase in the value of exports but only 8 percent of the threefold increase in national income.[79]

Overall, exports constituted a small proportion of British economic activity during the IR-1. From 1770 to 1841, British exports as a percentage of overall

74. Mokyr 1999, 36, emphasis in original.
75. Wadsworth and Mann 1931, 413.
76. Harley 1982, 268–69.
77. Moe 2007, 38–39.
78. Farnie 2003, 734; Tomory 2016, 157.
79. Farnie 2003, 735; Moe 2007, 37; see also Harley 1982, 269.

industrial demand increased only from 13 to 16 percent.[80] Now, these figures probably underrate trade as a critical engine of growth for Britain in the IR-1, as they ignore gains from the reinvestment of profits from overseas trade.[81] But the impact of reinvestment has been challenged, and it is not apparent why reinvestments from exports were more important than reinvestments from the profits generated by domestic production.[82]

The iron industry's impact on Britain's economic rise did not run through monopoly profits from innovation. From 1794 to 1796, British ironmakers contributed 11 percent of Britain's manufacturing exports. This proportion actually declined to just 2 percent by the 1814–1816 period and stayed around that rate into the 1830s.[83] It is also questionable whether Britain held a relative advantage in iron exports during the late eighteenth century, which is when LS accounts expect monopoly profits to drive British industrialization.[84] In fact, British industries continued to rely on imports of high-grade iron from Sweden and Russia well into the nineteenth century.[85]

An alternative pathway, captured by the GPT trajectory, posits that Britain's advantage came from the diffusion of iron machinery advances across a wide range of sectors. To trace this trajectory, it is necessary to pay more attention to what a prominent historian of the IR-1 calls one of the astonishing things about the phenomenon: the gap between "innovation as 'best practice' technique and the diffusion of innovation to become 'representative' technique."[86]

Britain was more successful than its industrial rivals in the diffusion of mechanization. Contemporary observers from the European continent often remarked upon Britain's ability to bridge this gap between best practice and representative practice.[87] Writing in 1786 in their *Voyages aux Montagnes*, French observers F. and A. de la Rochefoucauld-Liancourt, commenting

80. Harley 1982, 282; see also Macpherson 1805, 340.

81. For one prominent account, see Findlay and O'Rourke 2007, 311–64.

82. McCloskey 2010, 217–28. In this section, Deirdre McCloskey also constructs a counterfactual in which being shut out from foreign markets halved Britain's cotton textile output. Even using assumptions that favor the trade-based argument, McCloskey finds that this trade restriction would revise British productivity downwards by only 8 percent over an eighty-year period.

83. Cotton's contribution was above 15 percent of manufacturing exports for each of these time periods (Davis 1979, 94–101; Moe 2007, 86).

84. Some scholars assert that British iron production led French production by 1780 (Modelski and Thompson 1996, 99; but see Crouzet 1990; Landes 1969, 95).

85. Berg 1985, 38–39.

86. Mathias 1969, 127.

87. Meisenzahl and Mokyr 2011, 448.

on Britain's relative advantage in the widespread adaptation of the use of iron, noted

> the great advantage [their skill in working iron] gives them as regards the motion, lastingness and accuracy of machinery. All driving wheels and in fact almost all things are made of cast iron, of such a fine and hard quality that when rubbed up it polishes just like steel. There is no doubt but that the working of iron is one of the most essential of trades and the one in which we are most deficient.[88]

But France's deficiency in iron machinery was not a product of its lack of access to key innovations. In fact, France was the world's center of science from the late eighteenth century until the 1830s.[89] Rather, as the following quote illustrates, Britain's industrial rivals fell behind in "diffused average technology" and the "effective spread of technical change more widely." Economic historian Peter Mathias writes:

> It is remarkable how quickly formal knowledge of "dramatic" instances of new technology, in particular steam engines, was diffused, and how quickly individual examples of "best-practice" technology in "show piece" innovations were exported. The blockage lay in the effective spread of technical change more widely—diffused average technology rather than single instances of best-practice technology in "dramatic" well-publicized machines.[90]

Advances in iron metallurgy played a crucial role in a GPT trajectory that spread from a sector that improved the efficiency of producing capital goods. The GPT trajectory unfolds as the technology becomes more general-purpose through interactions between the upstream capital goods sector and the user industries that enlarge the range of applications. Rosenberg's depiction of this type of system highlights the nineteenth-century American machine tool industry as the innovative capital goods sector.[91] In this case, Britain's metal-processing works were the crucial wellspring. Specifically, technical advances in iron fed into metalworking industries from which broadly similar production processes diffused over a large number of industries.[92] Maxine Berg, a

---

88. Armytage 1961, 93.
89. Moe 2007, 42.
90. Mathias 1975, 102.
91. Rosenberg 1963.
92. MacLeod and Nuvolari 2009; Rosenberg 1970.

professor of history at the University of Warwick, pinpoints these industries as the "prime mechanism for technological diffusion."[93]

Scholars also identify Watt's improved steam engine as a potential source of both LS- and GPT-based effects. Here I focus on testing the LS prediction about the steam engine–producing industry because the previous section showed that the steam engine and the factory system, as candidate GPTs, diffused too slowly to make a meaningful impact on the economic power transition in the IR-1.

It is tough to make a case that the growth of the steam engine–producing industry generated a substantial source of monopoly profits for Britain. Equipped with an exclusive patent, James Watt and Matthew Boulton set up a firm in 1775 to sell steam engines.[94] In the period from 1775 to 1825, however, the firm sold only 110 steam engines to overseas customers.[95] By 1825, France and the United States were manufacturing the Watt engine and high-pressure engines at more competitive prices, and overseas demand declined sharply.[96] Thus, the international sales history of this firm severely weakens the significance of the monopoly profits associated with the innovation of the steam engine.[97]

In sum, the evidence from this section supports two conclusions. British advantages in the *production* and *export* of iron, steam engines, and cotton textiles (the best representative of the LS trajectory) had muted effects on its overall industrialization and productivity advances. Second, the contributions of technological breakthroughs in iron metallurgy and steam power to Britain's industrial rise track better with the GPT mechanism, based on relative advantages in widespread technological diffusion as opposed to monopoly profits from innovation.

93. Berg 1985, 265.

94. While Boulton and Watt faced competition from makers of "pirate" engines in the first twenty-five years of their exclusive patent (1775–1800), the sales of pirated engines were relatively small and would not alter the overall trend of international sales of the Watt engine (Tann and Breckin 1978, 542).

95. Ibid., 544.

96. By 1833, an estimated 946 steam engines were at work in France, 759 of which were of French manufacture. While the comparable US figures are not as detailed, "there were, clearly, more USA-manufactured Watt engines at work than imported ones by 1810 and the total number of engines may have been in the region of 500 by 1825" (ibid., 558–59).

97. It could be that export growth in leading sectors caused growth in industrial output. One time-series analysis of the period 1780–1851 finds, however, that this was not the case (Greasley and Oxley 1998a).

Breadth of Growth: Complementarities
of Iron vs. Spillovers from Cotton Textiles

The breadth of growth in the IR-1 is the last dimension on which the LS and GPT trajectories disagree. Was Britain's industrial rise driven by technological changes confined to a narrow range of leading sectors, or was it based on extensive, complementary innovations that enabled the spread of GPTs? Making use of data on sectoral sources of productivity growth, trade flows, and patents, I evaluate these competing propositions about the breadth of technological change in the industrial revolution.

WIDESPREAD PRODUCTIVITY GROWTH

In differentiating between the narrow view and the broad view of technical change during the IR-1, a natural starting point is to estimate the contribution of various industries to British productivity growth. Deirdre McCloskey's calculations of sectoral contributions to productivity growth support the broad view. Though cotton accounted for a remarkable 15 percent of Britain's total productivity growth, nonmodernized sectors still drove the lion's share (56 percent) of productivity gains.[98]

Manufacturing trade data provide another testing ground. If other manufacturing industries outside of textiles and iron were technologically stagnant during the first fifty years of the nineteenth century, then British competitiveness in these industries should decline relative to textiles and iron. The narrow view implies that Britain should have imported other manufactures. Peter Temin's analysis of British trade data, however, finds the opposite. Throughout the first half of the nineteenth century, British manufacturing exports matched the increase in cotton exports throughout the first half of

---

98. McCloskey 1981, 114. For an estimate that assigns much more credit to leading, or "modernized," sectors for fueling British productivity growth, see Crafts 1985, 86. An important detail about these two estimates is that the latter revised downward the overall growth rate of British productivity over this period but kept McCloskey's estimates for the productivity gains of modernized sectors. This is akin to revising downward estimates of jobs created—but not adjusting estimates of jobs created by the manufacturing sector—and then concluding that the service sector accounted for a smaller share of jobs created. In fact, following scrutiny, Crafts revised his estimates. Berg and Hudson 1992; Crafts and Harley 1992. In later work Crafts concedes that "the data may leave more possibility of productivity advance in the 'unmodernized sectors' than he allowed." Crafts and Harley 1992, 719n67.

the nineteenth century.[99] In a wide range of manufactures, such as arms and ammunition, carriages, glass, and machinery and metals, Britain held a clear comparative advantage. This pattern points to some general pattern of change that spanned industries. "The spirit that motivated cotton manufactures extended also to activities as varied as hardware and haberdashery, arms, and apparel," Temin concludes.[100]

The patent record also depicts a landscape of extensive technological change.[101] From 1780 to 1840, about 80 percent of all patented inventions came from outside the textiles and metals industries.[102] Per Christine MacLeod's data on British patents covering the 1750–1799 period, most capital goods patents originated from sectors outside of textile machinery and power sources.[103] As summed up by historian Kristine Bruland, the historical evidence supports "the empirical fact that this was an economy with extensive technological change, change that was not confined to leading sectors or highly visible areas of activity."[104]

GPTS AND COMPLEMENTARY INNOVATIONS

At this point, indicators of the multisectoral spread of innovation in the IR-1 should not be sufficient to convince a skeptical reader of the GPT mechanism's validity. Broad-based growth could be a product of macroeconomic factors, such as sound fiscal and monetary policy or labor market reforms, rather than a GPT trajectory.[105] Proving that the dispersion of technological change in Britain's economy reflected a GPT at work requires evidence that connects this broad front to mechanization.[106]

99. Temin 1997, 76.
100. Ibid., 79.
101. There are some limitations to patent data. Many advances are not patentable, and patenting varies over time and across industries. The existence of a patent does not guarantee the technique had economic value, and patenting can also be affected by social factors. Still, this period's patent record "gives us a reasonable guide to the pace and direction of technological advance in industry" (Bruland 2004, 123).
102. Author's calculations are based on compiled patent data in Sullivan 1990, 352.
103. MacLeod 1988, 148. Steam engines are included in textile machinery and power sources; see also Sullivan 1990, 352.
104. Bruland 2004, 119.
105. Hartwell 1965, 180–81.
106. That technological change in the IR-1 was widespread does not necessitate that it was uniform. Some British industries, such as clockmaking and watchmaking, declined in competitiveness and became import industries by the middle of the nineteenth century (Landes 1983).

Input-output analysis, which sheds light on the linkages between indus-tries, suggests that improvements in the working of iron had broader economic significance. To better understand the interrelationships among industries during the industrial revolution, Sara Horrell, Jane Humphries, and Martin Weale constructed an input-output table for the British economy in 1841. Across the seventeen industries included in the analysis, the two industries most closely associated with mechanization—metal manufacture and metal goods—scored the highest on combined backward and forward linkages.[107] These two domains were "lynchpins of linkage effects."[108]

Patent indicators confirm these results. When patents are grouped according to standard industry taxonomies, the resulting distribution shows that the tex-tile industry contributed to 15 percent of the patents issued between 1711 and 1850, making it the most inventive industry in aggregate terms.[109] However, when patents are sorted by general techniques as opposed to industry sectors, the same data reveal the underlying drive force of mechanical technology: it is linked to almost 50 percent of all British patents during this period.[110]

Along all three dimensions of technological trajectories in the IR-1, the process-tracing evidence bolsters the validity of the GPT mechanism. First, slower-moving developments in mechanization lined up with a delayed time-line of Britain's industrialization. Other candidate leading sectors and GPTs either peaked too early (cotton) or got started too late (steam engine, factory system). Second, Britain gained its industrial dominance from a relative ad-vantage in widespread adoption of iron metalworking and linked machinery. Third, the benefits from this GPT advantage circulated throughout the econ-omy, rather than remaining concentrated in the iron industry.

The standard explanation of how the IR-1 gave rise to a power transition, as captured by the LS mechanism, analyzes technological change at the level of industries that grow faster than others. The historical evidence reveals the limitations of these industry taxonomies. Instead, advantages in the diffu-sion of production machinery—a general pattern of change that extended

107. Horrell, Humphries, and Weale 1994, 555.
108. Ibid., 557.
109. Interestingly, the textile industry had a relatively low rate of patents per worker over this period. As Richard Sullivan writes (1990, 353), "the simple fact that it was a large industry helps account for the many textile patents."
110. Ibid., 354. Another analysis of British patents finds that the share of mechanical engi-neering patents grew from 17 percent to 30 percent over the period 1780 to 1849 (MacLeod and Nuvolari 2009, 223).

across a wide range of economic activities—propelled Britain to industrial dominance.[111]

Institutional Complementarities: GPT Skill Infrastructure in the IR-1

Having mapped Britain's industrial rise to a GPT trajectory linked to mechanization, there is still a need to explain why Britain was best positioned to exploit this trajectory. If other countries at the technological frontier can also cultivate mechanical innovations at home and absorb them from abroad, why were Britain's competitors unable to benefit from the diffusion of metalworking processes to the same extent? This section supports an explanation based on Britain's institutional competencies in widening the pool of engineering skills and knowledge linked to mechanization.

Which types of institutions for skill provision were most conducive to national success in the IR-1? One common refrain is that Britain's leadership was rooted in the genius of individual innovators like James Watt, and such genius did not transfer as quickly across borders during the IR-1.[112] Though recent scholarship has weakened this view, many influential histories center on the "heroic" inventors of the industrial revolution.[113] Consistent with the LS template, this view focuses on the institutions that helped drive heroic invention in Britain, such as the development of a patent system.[114]

The pathway by which mechanization propelled Britain's industrial ascent, established as a GPT trajectory in the previous section, emphasizes another set of institutions for skill formation. In line with GPT diffusion theory, Britain owed its relative success in the IR-1 to mechanics, instrument-makers, and engineers who could build machines according to blueprints and improve upon them depending on the application context. Under this view, the institutions that trained the "tweakers" and "implementers," rather than those that cultivated genius inventors, take center stage.[115]

---

111. Sullivan 1990, 350; Temin 1997, 79.

112. For example, in his summary of the role of leading sectors in past industrial revolutions, Andrew Kennedy (2018, 54) claims, "British leadership in the first industrial revolution sprang from the genius of individual inventors." See also Cardwell 1994, 496–501.

113. Nuvolari 2004.

114. Dutton 1984; North 1981.

115. Meisenzahl and Mokyr 2011, 446. As Gillian Cookson (2018, 154) writes in her study of the engineers who built Britain's first modern textile machines: "There was a limit to how many

Widening the Base of Mechanical "Tweakers" and "Implementers"

At first, rapid advances in precise metalworking exposed a skills shortage in applied mechanics. Beginning in the 1770s, a cascade of recruitment advertisements in local newspapers sought out an "engine-maker" or a "machine-maker."[116] Reflecting on this skills mismatch, the president of Britain's Institute of Civil Engineers stated that the use of cast iron in machine parts "called for more workmen than the millwright class could supply."[117]

A number of institutional adjustments helped Britain meet this demand for mechanically skilled tweakers and implementers. Initially, Britain benefited from a flexible apprenticeship system that empowered workers in related domains to get trained in applied mechanics.[118] Thus, to develop the workforce to build and maintain the machinery of the IR-1, Britain could draw from a wide pool of blacksmiths, millwrights, gunsmiths and locksmiths, instrument-makers, mechanics, and toolmakers.[119]

In addition, institutes dedicated to broadening the base of mechanical expertise helped diffuse ironmaking and machine-making skills. Starting in the 1790s, private and informal initiatives created a flurry of trade associations that supported a new class of mechanical and civil engineers and helped connect them with scientific societies and entrepreneurs.[120] Critical centers included the Andersonian Institution in Glasgow, the Manchester College of Arts and Sciences, the School of Arts in Edinburgh, the Mechanical Institution in London, the Society for the Diffusion of Useful Knowledge, and hundreds of mechanics' institutes.[121] These institutes helped to absorb knowledge from foreign publications on science and engineering, recruit and upskill new mechanical engineers from a variety of trades, and spread mechanical engineering knowledge more widely.[122]

James Watts could be accommodated in a business. The real need was for skilled workers on shop-floor duties."

116. Musson and Robinson 1969, 436.

117. Buchanan 1841, 394–95, cited in Jefferys 1945, 12; see also Pollard 1965, 167–68.

118. Thompson 1880.

119. Kelly, Mokyr, and Ó Gráda 2020, 27.

120. Jefferys 1945, 17; Mokyr and Voth 2010, 39.

121. Marsden 2004, 405; Pollard 1965, 180–81. By 1850, there were around seven hundred mechanics' institutes across Great Britain (Birse 1983, 62).

122. Musson and Robinson 1960; Musson 1969.

It is important to note that these institutional features differed from those more suited to the "heroic inventor" model. In Britain's cotton textile industry, the classic leading sector of the IR-1, the key institutional complements deviated greatly from the education and training systems that widened the base of mechanical expertise in the IR-1. Collating information from biographies of British engineers, online databases, and detailed economic histories, Ralf Meisenzahl and Joel Mokyr constructed a database of 759 British individuals who made incremental improvements to existing inventions during the industrial revolution.[123] Notably, based on their analysis of interactions between tweakers and their institutional surroundings, they found that the textile industry was an outlier in terms of protectiveness over intellectual property rights and reluctance to share information about new techniques. Less than one-tenth of tweakers in textiles published their knowledge to a broader audience or joined professional societies, in stark contrast to the two-thirds of tweakers in mechanically inclined fields who did so.[124] Over 80 percent of the tweakers who were active primarily in textiles took out at least one patent, compared to just 60 percent for tweakers overall.[125]

These trends in applied mechanics underscore the significance for British mechanization of "collective invention," a process that involved firms sharing information freely with one another and engineers publishing technical procedures in journals to spur the rapid diffusion of best-practice techniques. According to one analysis of how various districts adapted to the early phases of industrialization, areas that practiced collective invention often cultivated "a much higher degree of technological dynamism than locations which relied extensively on the patent system."[126]

123. Because individuals had to leave behind some record in the form of patents or a mention in a biographical collection to be included in this sample, these 759 engineers cover only a small slice of the broader base of competent technicians. Nevertheless, this prosopographical database provides a glimpse into the layer of human capital below that of the heroic inventors (Meisenzahl and Mokyr 2011, 453).

124. I use the following four sectors as proxies for mechanical expertise: road and rail and canals, instruments, iron and metallurgy, and other engineering (Meisenzahl and Mokyr 2011, 472).

125. Ibid., 461.

126. Nuvolari 2004, 360.

Britain's Comparative Advantage over France and the Netherlands in GPT Skill Infrastructure

Britain's competitors also grasped the significance of Britain's wide pool of mechanical skills. Whereas codified knowledge crisscrossed western Europe and North America via patent specifications, global exchanges among scientific societies, and extensive visits by foreign observers to British workshops and industrial plants, the European continent struggled greatly to absorb tacit knowledge, especially the know-how embodied in the practical engineering skills of British mechanical tweakers and implementers.[127] France and the Netherlands fiercely poached British engineers, as the transfer of tacit knowledge in the fields of large-scale ironworking and machine construction almost always necessitated the migration of skilled workers from Britain.[128] "It was exactly in the skills associated with the strategic new industries of iron and engineering that [Britain's] lead over other countries was most marked," argues Mathias.[129]

Why did this repository of engineering skills develop more fruitfully in Britain than in its industrial rivals? A growing body of evidence suggests that Britain's institutions better adapted its distribution of skills to mechanization. Britain's institutional advantage was rooted in the system of knowledge diffusion that connected engineers with entrepreneurs, cities with the countryside, and one social class with another. Institutes that trained mechanics took part in a broader "mushrooming of associations" that spread technical knowledge in early-nineteenth-century Britain.[130] By the mid-nineteenth century, there were 1,020 such associations in Britain, with a total membership of approximately 200,000; clearly, these networks are essential to any explanation that links human capital to Britain's industrial ascent.[131] Compared to their peers on the continent, British mechanics had superior access to scientific and technical

---

127. One historian even goes as far as to write, "The republic of science was truly international at this time; possibly more so even than today" (Mathias 1975, 100). Moe (2007, 94) states that France's adoption of mechanization was hampered by a "human capital lag" in "engineers with skills in machinery."

128. Berg 1985, 188; Harris 1991; Mathias 1975, 102–3.

129. Mathias 1969, 129.

130. Crafts 1996, 199. Mechanics' institutes took pride in the fact that they were creating a more widespread pool of knowledge in applied mechanics (*Durham Chronicle* 1825; *Hampshire Advertiser* 1849).

131. Mokyr 2002, 66.

publications.[132] As a result, the British system of the early nineteenth century had no match in its abundance of people with "technical literacy."[133]

The French system, by way of comparison, lacked similar linkages and collaborations between highly educated engineers and local entrepreneurs.[134] Though France produced elite engineers at schools like the École Polytechnique, it trained too few practitioners to widen the base of mechanical skills.[135] For example, Napoleon's early-nineteenth-century reform of France's higher education system encouraged the training of experts for narrow political and military ends, thereby limiting the ability of trainees to build connections with industry.[136] These reforms and other industrial policies directed French engineers toward projects associated with luxury industries and specialized military purposes, which "tended to become locked away from the rest of the economy in special enclaves of high cost."[137] To illustrate, through the mid-1830s, only one-third of École Polytechnique graduates entered the private sector.[138] France's system for disseminating mechanical knowledge and skills was vastly inferior to that of the British.

The Netherlands also failed to develop a base of mechanical skills that linked scientific research to practical ends. In some mechanical sciences, the Dutch generated plenty of potentially useful innovations, even pioneering key breakthroughs that eventually improved the steam engine.[139] Yet the Dutch struggled to translate these scientific achievements into practical engineering knowledge because they trailed the British in forming institutional settings that made widespread knowledge of applied mechanics possible.

132. Moe 2007, 94. Such materials were housed in mechanics' institutes, which laid the groundwork for the public library system and modern technical education institutions (Kelly 1952; Lyme Regis Mechanics Institute 1844). Relatedly, the Netherlands and the United Kingdom far exceeded other countries in book production per capita across Europe in the eighteenth century (Baten and van Zanden 2008).

133. Mokyr 2002, 73.

134. Jacob 1997, 184; Crouzet 1967, 239.

135. This is the commonly held view; see, for example, Kindleberger 1976, 13. Others argue that middle-level technical schools, like the Écoles d'arts et métiers, did implement reforms that widened access to mechanical engineering instruction. By the 1860s, graduates of the Écoles d'arts et métiers "comprised about 40 percent of the trained engineers and middle-level technicians of France including almost all mechanical engineers" (Day 1978, 444). Peter Lundgreen (1990, 39) also warns against "dubious retrospective extrapolations" that associate France's lack of technical education with its falling behind international competitors.

136. Crouzet 1967, 239; Lundgreen 1990, 39; Moe 2007, 43.

137. Mathias 1975, 99.

138. Ahlström 1982, 44.

139. Davids 1995, 358–59; Mokyr 2000.

Records of Dutch educational systems, the dearth of societies that held lectures and demonstrations for mechanical learning, and the materials available at libraries in technical colleges all "reflected a profound lack of interest in applied mechanics."[140] In his study of Dutch technological leadership, Karel Davids argues that, during the first three-quarters of the eighteenth century, "collaboration between science and industry in the Netherlands failed to merge in the very period that relations between the two became rapidly closer in Britain."[141]

Britain's advantage in GPT diffusion was not rooted in its higher education system, which lagged far behind the French education system during the IR-1 period.[142] France had already established more than twenty universities before the French Revolution. The French system of higher technical education, from the late eighteenth century through the 1830s, had no rival. The Grande Écoles system, including the elite École Polytechnique (established in 1794), trained expert scientists and engineers to take on top-level positions as industrial managers and high-level political personnel.[143] Up until 1826, England had set up only two universities, Oxford and Cambridge. These institutions made limited contributions to training the workforce necessary for industrialization. One study with a sample of 498 British applied scientists and engineers born between 1700 and 1850 found that only 50 were educated at Oxford or Cambridge; 329 were not university-educated.[144]

At this point, curiosity naturally leads us to ask why Britain accumulated an advantage in GPT skill infrastructure. Due to practical constraints of time and space, I acknowledge but do not delve into the deeper causes for the notable responsiveness of Britain's institutions to the skill demands of mechanization. In surveying valuable lines of inquiry on this subject, chapter 2 points to government capacity to adopt long time horizons and reach intertemporal bargains. In the IR-1 case, two specific factors are also worthy of consideration. Attributing Britain's later success to pre-industrial training practices, some studies suggest that Britain's apprenticeship system allowed for agile and flexible adaptation to fluctuations in the demand for skills, especially in mechanical

140. Jacob 1997, 144. For more on this phenomenon, see ibid., 141–54.

141. Davids 1995, 357.

142. The Dutch system of higher education was also strong during this time. Up through the end of the eighteenth century, research at Dutch universities still garnered strong international recognition (Mokyr 2000, 14).

143. Moe 2007, 42–43.

144. Mokyr 2005, 311n90. The remaining 119 were educated at universities in Scotland.

trades.[145] Looking even further back, other scholars probe the geographical origins of Britain's mechanical skills, underscoring the lasting effects of Britain's adoption of watermills in the early Middle Ages.[146]

Alternative Explanations of Britain's Rise

The history of the IR-1 is certainly not a neglected topic, and the literature features enthusiastic debates over a wide range of possible causes for Britain's rise. Prominent explanations tie Britain's early industrialization to population growth,[147] demand and consumption standards,[148] access to raw materials from the colonies,[149] slavery,[150] and trade.[151] The obvious concern is that various contextual factors may confound the analysis of the LS and GPT mechanisms.

I am not rewriting the history of the IR-1. I am drawing from one particularly influential and widely held view of the IR-1—that technological advances drove Britain's industrial ascent—and investigating how technological change and institutional adaptations produced this outcome. The most relevant alternative factors, therefore, are those that provide a different interpretation of how technologies and institutions coevolved to result in Britain's industrial hegemony. Although I primarily focus on the LS mechanism as the most formidable alternative explanation to the GPT diffusion theory, other explanations also warrant further investigation.

Threat-Based Explanations

Threat-based theories assert that external threats are necessary to incentivize states to innovate and diffuse new technologies. Did Britain owe its technological leadership to war and its military's impetus to modernize? During the IR-1 period, Britain was embroiled in the Revolutionary and Napoleonic Wars (1793–1815), a near-continuous stretch of conflicts involving France and other European states. If threat-based explanations stand up in the IR-1

145. Leunig, Minns, and Wallis 2011; Zeev, Mokyr, and van der Beek 2017.
146. Sarid, Mokyr, and van der Beek 2019.
147. Clark 2007.
148. Gilboy 1932.
149. Pomeranz 2000.
150. Williams 1944.
151. Habakkuk and Deane 1963.

case, then the historical record should show that these wars made an essential and positive contribution to Britain's adoption of iron machinery and mechanization.

Some evidence supports this argument. By 1805, the British government's needs for iron in the war effort accounted for 17 percent of the total British iron output in 1805.[152] This wartime stimulus to iron production facilitated improvements in iron railways, iron ships, and steam engines.[153] In particular, military investments in gunmaking produced important spin-offs in textiles and machine tools, most famously encapsulated by Watt's dependence on John Wilkinson's cannon boring techniques to make the condenser cylinders for his steam engine.[154]

On the flip side, war's disruptive costs are likely to have offset any stimulus to Britain's mechanization. Aside from Wilkinson's cannon boring device and some incremental improvements, wartime pressures did not produce any major technological breakthroughs for the civilian economy.[155] Military needs absorbed productive laborers from Britain's civilian economy, resulting in labor shortages.[156] War also limited both the domestic demand for iron, by halting investment in construction, agriculture, and other industries, and the foreign demand for British iron, by cutting off foreign trade. Historian Charles Hyde notes, "In the absence of fighting, overall demand for iron might have been higher than it was."[157]

Furthermore, any temporary benefits that accrued to Britain's iron industry in wartime were wiped out in the transition to peacetime. In one influential text, historian Thomas Ashton reviewed how each of the wars of the eighteenth century, including the Revolutionary and Napoleonic Wars, affected Britain's iron industry.[158] He observed a similar pattern in each case. At first, the outbreak of hostilities boosts demand for iron in the form of armament, and trade disruptions protect domestic producers against foreign competitors. This initial boom is followed by a severe crash, however, when the iron industry adjusts to the conflict's aftermath. A trade depression follows. Converting foundries to make plowshares instead of cannons incurs heavy losses, made

152. Hyde 1977, 115.
153. O'Brien 2017, 51–53; Trebilcock 1969.
154. Kaempffert 1941, 435; Satia 2018.
155. Mathias 1969, 124; O'Brien 2017, 47.
156. Hueckel 1973, 371.
157. Hyde 1977, 115–16.
158. Ashton 1963, 128–61.

even more painful by the fact that war conditions promoted "feverish" developments that were unsustainable in the long run.[159]

On a more fundamental level, threat-based theories have limited leverage in explaining Britain's relative rise because its economic competitors were also embroiled in conflicts—in many cases, against Britain. The Dutch fought Britain in the fourth Anglo-Dutch War (1780–1784) as well as in the Napoleonic Wars.[160] Of course, during this time, France was Britain's main military opponent. Thus, since the Netherlands and France also faced a threatening external environment, the net effect of the war on economic growth differentials should have been minimal.[161] If anything, since France fought on many more fronts than Britain during this period, proponents of threat-based explanations would expect France to have experienced more effective and widespread diffusion of iron machinery throughout its economy. The case analysis clearly discredits that expected outcome.

VoC Explanations

Can Britain's particular brand of capitalism account for its technological rise? The varieties of capitalism (VoC) approach posits that liberal market economies (LMEs) are particularly suited to radical innovation. Consistent with this framework, international political economy scholars emphasize that Britain's free market economy supported gains in rapidly changing technological domains like consumer goods, light machine tools, and textiles.[162] During the IR-1 period, Britain began to develop the institutional features that would cement it as a LME, including decentralized collective bargaining and high levels of corporatization.[163] Most pertinent to GPT diffusion theory, VoC scholars expect LMEs like Britain to excel at cultivating general skills, which help transfer GPT-related knowledge and techniques across firms.

Taking measure of Britain's human capital development in general skills in this period is therefore central to evaluating whether its technological leader-

159. Ibid., 153.
160. Alphen et al. 2021.
161. Mechanization in both Britain and France benefited from wartime trade protections (Juhász 2018; O'Brien 2017).
162. One study asserts that "Britain, as a decentralized, market-oriented society with a weak state, could seize most energetically the opportunities offered by the new technological trajectory" (Kitschelt 1991, 471); see also Kim and Hart 2001; Kurth 1979).
163. Crafts 2014.

ship can be explained by its form of capitalism. Overall, estimates of literacy rates and school attendance demonstrate that the general level of human capital in Britain was notably low for an industrial leader.[164] British literacy rates for males were relatively stagnant between 1750 and 1850, and average literacy rates in Britain were much lower than rates in the Netherlands and barely higher than those in France around the turn of the nineteenth century.[165] In fact, general levels of educational attainment in Britain, as measured by average years of schooling, declined from around 1.4 years in 1740 to 1.25 years in 1820.[166] Contrary to VoC theory's expectations, Britain did not hold an advantage in general skills during this period.

The VoC explanation's applicability to the IR-1 period is further limited by issues with designating Britain as the only LME in this period. Like Britain, the Netherlands functioned as a relatively open economy and exhibited tendencies toward economic liberalism, but it was not able to adapt and diffuse significant technological changes.[167] Though France is now considered a co-ordinated market economy, in the early nineteenth century it took on some of the characteristics of LMEs by implementing capital market reforms and trade liberalization.[168] The VoC approach therefore struggles to resolve why these two LMEs diverged so greatly in their adaptation to mechanization.

Case-Specific Factors

Among other factors specific to the IR-1 setting, one alternative explanation emphasizes Britain's fortunate geographic circumstances. More specifically, classic works have argued that proximity to plentiful coalfields was essential to British industrialization.[169] These natural resource endowments enabled the expansion of coal-intensive industries, such as the iron industry. In this line of thinking, the fact that coal was cheaper in Britain than elsewhere in Europe explains why Britain was the first to sustain productivity leadership.[170]

164. Meisenzahl and Mokyr 2011, 475.
165. Mitch 1999; de Pleijt 2018.
166. De Pleijt 2018.
167. Davids 2008; Mokyr 2000, 514–15; Wrigley 2000.
168. Nye 1991.
169. Pomeranz 2000; Wrigley 1988.
170. For a summary of debates over coal's impact in the IR-1, see Fernihough and O'Rourke 2021.

The relationship between coal and industrialization does not necessarily undermine the GPT mechanism. For one, in principle, Britain's competitors could also have effectively leveraged coal resources. The southern provinces of the Netherlands were located close to Belgian coalfields.[171] Over the course of the eighteenth century, Dutch industry had mostly shifted to coal, and away from peat stocks, as a key source of energy.[172] Even if Britain's industrial rivals had to pay more by importing coal, the expected productivity gains associated with adopting new technologies should have outweighed these costs. Moreover, GPT skill infrastructure could have mediated the relationship between coal and mechanization, as Britain's edge in metalworking skills spurred the adoption of new coal-using technologies, which strengthened the connection between proximity to coal and economic growth.[173]

Summary

In many ways, the industrial revolution marked an exceptional transformation. It is to any number of historical trends what the birth of Jesus is to the Gregorian calendar—an inflection point that separates "before" and "after." For my purposes, however, the industrial revolution is a typical case showing how technological revolutions influence the rise and fall of great powers. Evidence from great powers' different adaptations to technological changes in this period therefore helps test GPT diffusion theory against the LS mechanism.

In sum, GPT diffusion theory best explains why Britain led Europe's industrial transformation in this period. Britain effectively capitalized on general-purpose improvements in mechanization owing to its institutional advantages that were conducive to widening the pool of mechanical skills and knowledge. According to GPT diffusion theory, countries like this disproportionately benefit from technological revolutions because they adapt more successfully to the GPT trajectories that transform productivity. In line with these expectations, Britain was more successful than its industrial rivals in sustaining long-term economic growth, which became the foundation of its unrivaled power in the early and mid-nineteenth century.

171. Jacob 1997, 7.
172. Davids 1995, 355.
173. According to one appealing explanation that integrates coal-based arguments and GPT skill infrastructure, British coalfields were important not as a source of cheap energy but as a source of artisan skill in metalworking (Kelly, Mokyr, and Ó Gráda 2020).

On the flip side, this chapter's case analysis undercuts the LS-based explanation. The timeframe for when leading sectors were expected to stimulate
Britain's productivity growth did not align with when Britain's industrialization took off. Britain's economic ascent owed more to the widespread adoption of iron metalworking and linked production machinery than to monopoly
profits from cotton textiles. The key institutional complements were not those
that produced heroic inventions—Britain's rivals held their own in these
areas—but rather those that fostered widespread knowledge of applied
mechanics.

Do these findings hold in other periods of technological and geopolitical
upheaval? The IR-1 was one of the most extraordinary phases in history, but it
was not the only era to attain the title of an "industrial revolution." To further
explore these dynamics, it is only appropriate to turn to the period some have
labeled the Second Industrial Revolution.

4

The Second Industrial Revolution and America's Ascent

IN THE LATE nineteenth and early twentieth centuries, the technological and geopolitical landscape transformed in ways familiar to observers of today's environment. "AI is the new electricity" goes a common refrain that compares current advances in machine intelligence to electrical innovations 150 years ago. Those fundamental breakthroughs, alongside others in steel, chemicals, and machine tools, sparked the Second Industrial Revolution (IR-2), which unfolded from 1870 to 1914.[1] Studies of how present-day technological advances could change the balance of power draw on geopolitical competition for technological leadership in the IR-2 as a key reference point.[2]

Often overshadowed by its predecessor, the IR-2 is equally important for investigating causal patterns that connect technological revolutions and economic power transitions. The presence of both cause and outcome ensures a fruitful test of the GPT and LS mechanisms. The beginning of the period featured remarkable technological innovations, including the universal milling machine, the electric dynamo, the synthesis of indigo dye, and the internal combustion engine. According to some scholars, one would be hard-pressed to find another period with a higher density of important scientific advances.[3] By the end of the period, Britain's decline and the rise of Germany and the United States had yielded a new balance of economic power, which one historian describes as a "shift from monarchy to oligarchy, from a one-nation

---

1. There is some debate over this conventional periodization of the IR-2 (Hull 1996; Mokyr 1998.

2. Allison 2017, xviii; Horowitz 2018, 51.

3. Mowery and Rosenberg 1991, 22; Delong 2022, 63–65.

to a multi-nation industrial system."[4] Arguably, British industrial decline in the IR-2 was the ultimate cause of World War I.[5]

International relations scholars hold up the IR-2 as a classic case of a power transition caused by LS product cycles.[6] According to this view, Britain's rivals cornered market shares in the new, fast-growing industries arising from major technological innovations in electricity, chemicals, and steel.[7] Specifically, scholars argue that Germany surpassed Britain in the IR-2 because it was "the first to introduce the most important innovations" in these key sectors.[8] Analysis of emerging technologies and today's rising powers follows a similar template when it compares China's scientific and technological capabilities to Germany's ability to develop major innovations in chemicals.[9] Thus, as a most likely case for the LS mechanism, which is favored by background conditions and existing theoretical explanations, the IR-2 acts as a good test for the GPT mechanism.

Historical evidence from this period challenges this conventional narrative. No country monopolized innovation in leading sectors such as chemicals, electricity, steel, and motor vehicles. Productivity growth in the United States, which overtook Britain in productivity leadership during the IR-2, was not dominated by a few R&D-based sectors. Moreover, major breakthroughs in electricity and chemicals, prominent factors in LS accounts, required a protracted process of diffusion across many sectors before their impact was felt. This made them unlikely key drivers of the economic rise of the United States before 1914.

Instead, the IR-2 case evidence supports GPT diffusion theory. Spurred by inventions in machine tools, the industrial production of interchangeable parts, known as the "American system of manufacturing," embodied the key GPT trajectory.[10] The United States did not lead the world in producing the

4. Landes 1969, 247.

5. Gilpin 1975, 77; Organski 1958, 291–92. Others dispute that World War I was caused by Germany overtaking the United Kingdom in economic capabilities. For a summary of these criticisms, see Vazquez 1996, 41–42.

6. Gilpin 1981, 1987; Kennedy 2018, 51; Modelski and Thompson 1996.

7. Rostow 1960, 175.

8. Akaev and Pantin 2014, 869.

9. For an argument about why China today compares unfavorably to Germany in the IR-2, see Beckley 2011, 63–72.

10. Ferguson 1968, 298. Scholars question whether developments in interchangeable parts manufacturing mapped neatly onto the standard concept of the "American system of manufacturing," citing the infeasibility of achieving perfect interchangeability of parts in the middle of the nineteenth century. Still, even if perfect interchangeability was not achieved in some indus-

most advanced machinery; rather, it had an advantage over Britain in adapting machine tools across almost all branches of industry. Though the American system's diffusion also required a long gestation period, the timing matches America's industrial rise. Incubated by the growing specialization of machine tools in the mid-nineteenth century, the application of interchangeable parts across a broad range of manufacturing industries was the key driving force of America's relative economic success in the IR-2.[11]

Since a nation's efficacy in adapting to technological revolutions is determined by how well its institutions complement the demands of emerging technologies, the GPT model of the IR-2 highlights institutional factors that differ from those featured in standard accounts. LS-based theories tend to highlight Germany's institutional competencies in scientific education and industrial R&D.[12] In contrast, the case analysis points toward the American ability to develop a broad base of mechanical engineering skills and standardize best practices in mechanical engineering. Practice-oriented technical education at American land-grant colleges and technical institutes enabled the United States to take better advantage of interchangeable manufacturing methods than its rivals.

This chapter's evidence comes from a variety of sources. In tracing the contours of technological trajectories and the economic power transition in this period, I relied on histories of technology, categorization schemes from the long-cycle literature, general accounts of economic historians, and revised versions of historical productivity measures. I investigated the fit between institutions and technology in leading economies using annual reports of the US Commissioner of Education, British diplomatic and consular reports, cross-national data on technological diffusion, German engineering periodicals, and firsthand accounts from inspection teams commissioned to study related issues.[13] My analysis benefited from archival materials based at the Bodleian Library's Marconi Archives (United Kingdom), the Library of Congress (United States), and the University of Leipzig and from records of the British Foreign Office.

---

tries during the IR-2, increased uniformity played a significant role in enabling mass production (Hoke 1990; Hounshell 1985).

11. David 1975; Rosenberg 1972, 87–90.

12. Drezner 2001, 13; Moe 2009, 216–17.

13. According to Michael Piore and Charles Sabel (1984, 46), "the most sober accounts of the consolidation of mass-production practice in the United States were written by the British engineers who toured American plants after 1850."

This chapter proceeds as follows. I begin by chronicling the economic power transition that took place during the IR-2 to clarify that the United States, not Germany, ascended to industrial preeminence. I then identify the key technological breakthroughs, which I sort according to their ties to GPT and LS trajectories. Along the dimensions of impact timeframe, phase of relative advantage, and breadth of growth, this chapter demonstrates that the GPT trajectory aligns better with how the IR-2 enabled the economic rise of the United States. Next, I evaluate whether differences in GPT skill infrastructure can account for the American edge over Britain and Germany in interchangeable manufacturing methods. Toward the chapter's end, I also tackle alternative explanations.[14]

A Power Transition: America's Ascent

To begin, tracing *when* an economic power transition takes place is critical. In 1860, Britain was still at the apogee of its industrial power.[15] Most historians agree that British industrial preeminence eroded in the late nineteenth century. By 1913, both the United States and Germany had emerged as formidable rivals to Britain with respect to the industrial and productive foundations of national power. According to Paul Kennedy's influential account, before World War I Britain was "in third place," and "in terms of industrial muscle, both the United States and imperial Germany had moved ahead."[16] Aided with more data than was available for the IR-1 case, I map the timeline of this economic power transition with various measures of industrial output and efficiency.

In the IR-2 case, clarifying *who* surpassed Britain in economic efficiency takes on added gravity. Whereas in the IR-1 Britain separated itself from the rest, both the United States and Germany challenged British industrial power in the IR-2. But studies of this case often neglect the rise of the United States. Preoccupied with debates over whether Germany's overtaking of Britain sparked World War I, the power transition literature has directed most of its attention to the Anglo-German competition for economic leadership.[17] Some

14. Parts of this chapter draw from Ding 2024.

15. Britain's per-capita level of industrialization was more than double that of Belgium, the second-ranked power (Bairoch 1982, 281).

16. Kennedy 1987, 228.

17. Chan 2007, 21; Vazquez 1996, 41. Kennedy (1987, 242) writes, "Of all the changes which were taking place in the global power balances during the late nineteenth and early twentieth

LS-based accounts explain only Germany's rise in this period without investigating America's ascent.[18]

As the rest of this section will show, Germany and the United States both surpassed Britain on some measures of economic power, but the United States emerged as the clear productivity leader. Therefore, any explanation of the rise and fall of technological leadership in this period must be centered on the US experience. The following sections trace the contours of the IR-2's economic power transition with a range of indicators for productivity leadership, including GDP per capita, industrialization, labor productivity, and total factor productivity.

GDP PER-CAPITA INDICATORS

Changes in total GDP over the course of the IR-2 provide a useful departure point for understanding changes in the balance of productive power. At the beginning of the period in 1871, Germany's economy was around three-quarters the size of the British economy; by the end of the period, in 1913, Germany's economy was approximately 14 percent larger than Britain's. The growth trajectory of the American economy was even starker. Over the same time period, overall economic output in the United States increased from 1.2 times to around 3.4 times that of Britain's total GDP.[19] This trend is further confirmed by the growth rates of overall GDP for the three countries. In the period between 1870 and 1913, the US GDP grew roughly 5.3 times over, compared to 3.3 for Germany and 2.2 for the United Kingdom.[20]

While gross economic size puts countries in contention for economic leadership, the most crucial outcome is sustained economic efficiency. Compared to total output, trend lines in real GDP per capita mark out a broadly similar picture of the IR-2 period, but they also differ in two significant respects (figure 4.1). First, whereas the United States was already the largest economy by

---

centuries, there can be no doubt that the most decisive one for the future was the growth of the United States."

18. Drezner 2001, 12n33; Moe 2009, 215–18. Daniel Drezner does acknowledge that the United States also surpassed Great Britain in this period. Nevertheless, he justifies his choice to solely study Germany on two grounds. First, German science and technology were superior to US science and technology. Second, since Germany's military spending was greater than Great Britain's, the claim that Britain's military commitments detracted from its relative productivity can be tested.

19. Fouquin and Hugot 2016.

20. Maddison 1995, cited in Smil 2005, 286.

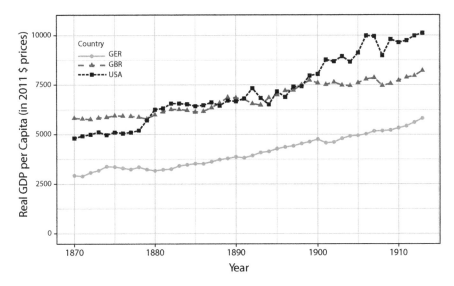

FIGURE 4.1. Economic Power Transition during the IR-2. *Source*: Maddison Project Database, version 2020 (Bolt and van Zanden 2020).

total output in 1870, the United Kingdom maintained a slight lead in real GDP per capita over the United States in the 1870s. The United Kingdom's average GDP per capita over the decade was about 15 percent higher than the US equivalent.[21] US GDP per capita was roughly on par with Britain's throughout the 1880s and 1890s, but the United States established a substantial lead starting around 1900.[22]

Second, in contrast to trend lines in aggregate economic output, Germany did not surpass Britain in GDP per capita before World War I. Germany certainly closed the gap, as its GDP per capita increased from around 50 percent of British GDP per capita in 1870 to around 70 percent in the years before World War I. However, Germany never even came close to overtaking the United Kingdom in GDP per capita during this period.[23] This is an important distinction that justifies the focus on US technological success in the IR-2, since surpassing at the technological frontier is a different challenge than merely catching up to the technological frontier.

21. My calculations are based on Maddison Project Database, version 2020 (Bolt and van Zanden 2020).

22. Nelson and Wright 1992, 1939.

23. Bolt and van Zanden 2020.

INDUSTRIALIZATION INDICATORS

Industrialization indicators back up the findings from the GDP per-capita data. The United States emerged as the preeminent industrial power, boasting an aggregate industrial output in 1913 that equaled 36 percent of the global total—a figure that exceeded the combined share of both Great Britain and Germany.[24] More importantly, the United States became the leading country in terms of industrial efficiency, with a per-capita industrialization level about 10 percent higher than Britain's in 1913.[25]

Once again, the emphasis on productivity over aggregate output reveals that the economic gap between Germany and Britain narrowed but did not disappear. In aggregate terms, Germany's share of the world's industrial production rose to 16 percent in 1913. This eclipsed Britain's share, which declined from 32 percent of the world's industrial production in 1870 to just 15 percent in 1913.[26] However, Germany did not overtake Britain in industrial efficiency. In 1913, its per-capita industrialization level was about 75 percent of Britain's.[27] The magnitude of this gap was approximately the same as the gap between German per-capita GDP and British per-capita GDP.

PRODUCTIVITY INDICATORS

Lastly, I consider various productivity statistics. Stephen Broadberry's work on the "productivity race" contains the most comprehensive and rigorous assessments of productivity levels in Britain, Germany, and the United States in this period.[28] Comparative statistics on labor productivity line up with findings from other indicators (figure 4.2). The United States surpassed Britain in aggregate labor productivity during the 1890s or 1900s, whereas Germany's aggregate labor productivity increased relative to but did not fully overtake Britain's over the IR-2 period.[29]

24. Rostow 1978, 52–53.

25. Bairoch 1982, 294.

26. Rostow 1978, 52–53. From 1870 to 1896, Germany's industrial output growth rate (3.1 percent) surpassed that of Britain (1.9 percent). The US rate was 4.6 percent (Bénétrix, O'Rourke, and Williamson 2015, 21).

27. Bairoch 1982, 292–302.

28. Broadberry 2006.

29. Ibid., 20–21, 150. Germany did overtake Britain in labor productivity in the industrial sector before 1911.

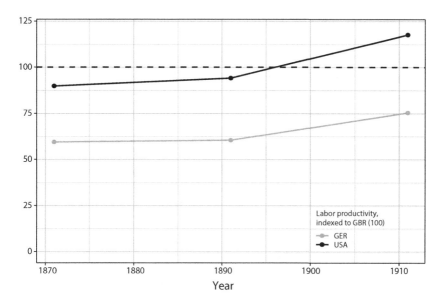

FIGURE 4.2. Comparative Labor Productivity Levels in the IR-2.
Source: Broadberry 2006, 110.

Another set of productivity indicators, Maddison's well-known and oft-cited historical data on comparative GDP per hour worked, supports Broadberry's comparative measures of labor productivity levels.[30] According to Maddison's estimates of the average rate of productivity growth from 1870 to 1913, the American and German economies were both growing more productive relative to the British economy. The growth rate of America's GDP per hour worked was 1.9 percent compared to 1.8 percent for the German rate and 1.2 percent for the UK rate.[31]

It should be noted that the United Kingdom may have retained a total factor productivity lead in this period. Based on 1909 figures, the last measurements available before World War I, the US aggregate TFP was a little over 90 percent of Britain's. By 1919, US aggregate TFP was nearly 10 percent larger than Britain's.[32] The United States could have surpassed Britain in overall TFP before World War I, but the data do not clearly demonstrate this

30. Maddison 1995.
31. Broadberry 1992; Smil 2005, 286.
32. Broadberry 2006, 109.

outcome. Still, the TFP data track well with the general trends found in other measures of economic efficiency, including a marked increase in US TFP in the 1890s and 1900s as well as a steady narrowing of the gap between UK and German TFP throughout the period. Issues related to the availability, reliability, and comparability of capital stock estimates during this period, however, caution against concluding too much from the TFP trends alone.[33]

Albeit with some caveats, the general thrust of evidence confirms that the United States overtook Britain in productivity leadership around the turn of the twentieth century. In productive efficiency, Germany significantly narrowed the gap but did not surpass Britain. A clarified picture of the outcome also helps guide the assessment of the LS and GPT mechanisms. In contrast to work that focuses on Anglo-German rivalry in this period, I prioritize explaining why the United States became the preeminent economic power. Moreover, if GPT diffusion theory holds for this period, it should also explain why the United States was more successful than Germany in overtaking Britain in productivity during this period.

Key Technological Changes in the IR-2

Which technological changes could have sparked the economic power transition before World War I? The IR-2 was an age of dizzying technological breakthroughs, including but not limited to the electric dynamo (1871), the first internal combustion engine (1876), the Thomas process for steel manufacturing (1877), and the synthesis of indigo dye (1880).[34] Tracking down how every single technical advance could have affected the growth differentials among Britain, Germany, and the United States is an unmanageable task. I narrow the scope of analysis to the most likely sources of LS and GPT trajectories based on previous scholarship that calls attention to the significance of certain technological developments in the IR-2. Once confirmed to meet the established criteria for leading sectors and GPTs, these technological drivers serve as the fields of reference for assessing the validity of the GPT and LS mechanisms in this case.

33. Ibid., 108.
34. Indigo was the most important of natural dyes, so its synthesis marked a turning point in the organic chemical industry.

Candidate Leading Sectors

I focus on the chemicals, electrical equipment, motor vehicles, and steel industries as the leading sectors of the IR-2. These choices are informed by scholars who study the implications of technological change during this period from a LS perspective. The first three sectors feature in the standard rendering of the IR-2 by prominent historical accounts, which centers major discoveries in chemistry and electricity as well as the invention of the internal combustion engine.[35] Among those who study the effect of technological revolutions on the balance of power, there is near-consensus that the chemicals and electrical industries were technologically advanced, fast-growing industries during this time.[36] Some scholars also identify the automobile industry as a key industry in this period.[37] Others reason, however, that automobiles did not emerge as a leading sector until a later period.[38]

The automobile, chemicals, and electrical industries all experienced prodigious growth during the IR-2, meeting the primary qualification for leading sectors. According to statistics from the US census, the percentage increase in value added by manufacture in each of the chemicals, electrical, and automobile industries was much higher than the average across all industries from 1899 through 1909. In fact, the automobile and electrical equipment industries boasted the two highest rates of percentage growth in value added over this period among sectors with a market size over $100 million.[39]

I also consider developments in steel as a possible source of leading-sector product cycles. It is hard to ignore the explosive growth of the steel industry in both Germany, where it multiplied over 100-fold from 1870 to 1913, and the United States, where it multiplied around 450 times over the same period.[40] In addition, many scholars list steel as one of the leading sectors that affected the economic power balance in the IR-2.[41] Rostow identifies steel as part of

---

35. Hull 1996, 192, 196; Landes 1969, 4; Schumpeter 1939, 167.

36. Gilpin 1987, 309; Kim and Hart 2001, 304; Modelski and Thompson 1996, 87–88; Ostry and Nelson 1995, 43.

37. Gilpin 1987, 309; Kim and Hart 2001, 304.

38. Gilpin 1975; Kurth 1979, 26; Moe 2009, 218–19; Thompson 1990, 213.

39. For statistics on automobiles and electricity (captured in the "electrical machinery, apparatus, and supplies" category), see US Bureau of the Census 1913, 40; for statistics on the chemical industry ("chemicals and allied products"), see ibid., 53.

40. My calculations are based on crude steel output figures in Mitchell 1998, 466–67; Mitchell 1993, 356–58.

41. Gilpin 1975, 67; Kurth 1979; Modelski and Thompson 1996, 69; Rostow 1978, 105.

"the classic sequence" of "great leading sectors."[42] In sum, I consider four candidate leading sectors in this period: the automobile, chemicals, electrical equipment, and steel industries.

Candidate GPTs

I analyze chemicalization, electrification, the internal combustion engine, and interchangeable manufacture as potential drivers of GPT-style transformations in the IR-2. Of these four, electricity is the prototypical GPT. It is "unanimously seen in the literature as a historical example of a GPT."[43] Electricity is one of three technologies, alongside the steam engine and information and communications (ICT) technology, that feature in nearly every article that seeks to identify GPTs throughout history.[44] Electrical technologies possessed an enormous scope for improvement, fed into a variety of products and processes, and synergized with many other streams of technological development. Empirical efforts to identify GPTs with patent data provide further evidence of electricity as a GPT in this period.[45]

Like advances in electricity, clusters of innovations in chemicals and the internal combustion engine not only spurred the rapid growth of new industries but also served as a potential source of GPT trajectories. Historians of technology pick out chemicalization, alongside electrification, as one of two central processes that transformed production routines in the early twentieth century.[46] Historical patent data confirm that chemical inventions could influence a wide variety of products and processes.[47]

In line with GPT classification schemes by other scholars, I also evaluate the internal combustion engine as a candidate GPT, with the potential to replace the steam engine as a prime mover of many industrial processes.[48] After its introduction, many believed that the internal combustion engine

42. Rostow 1978, 105.
43. Ristuccia and Solomou 2014, 227.
44. Field 2008, 10.
45. Petralia 2020.
46. Nelson and Winter 1982, 261; Noble 1977, 18; Landau and Rosenberg 1992, 76.
47. Moser and Nicholas 2004. Notably, Petra Moser and Tom Nicholas (2004, 393) find that developments in chemicals "fulfill the criteria for GPTs at least as well as those in electricity." For further discussion of whether electrical technologies better fit the characteristics of a GPT than chemical technologies, see Petralia 2020.
48. Jovanovic and Rousseau 2005; Lipsey, Carlaw, and Bekar 2005, 133.

would transform a range of manufacturing processes with smaller, divisible power units.[49]

Lastly, I examine the advance of interchangeable manufacture, spurred by innovations in machine tools, as a candidate GPT in this period. Though the machine tool industry was neither new nor especially fast-growing, it did play a central role in extending the mechanization of machine-making first incubated in the IR-1. The diffusion of interchangeable manufacture, or the "American system," owed much to advances in turret lathes, milling machines, and other machine tools that improved the precision of cutting and shaping metals. Rosenberg's seminal study of "technological convergence" between the American machine tool industry and metal-using sectors highlighted how innovations in metalworking machines transformed production processes across a wide range of industries.[50] Following Rosenberg's interpretation, historians recognize the nexus of machine tools and mechanization as one of the key technological trajectories during this period.[51]

Sources of LS and GPT Trajectories

I aimed to include as many candidate technological drivers as possible, provided that the technological developments credibly met the criteria of a leading sector or GPT.[52] All candidate leading sectors and GPTs I study in this period were flagged in multiple articles or books that explicitly identified leading sectors or GPTs in the IR-2 period, which helped provide an initial filter for selection. This allows for a good test of the GPT diffusion mechanism against the LS product cycles mechanism.[53] This sorting process is an important initial step for evaluating the two mechanisms, though a deeper excavation

49. Du Boff 1967, 514.

50. Rosenberg 1963, 423.

51. Mosk 2010, 22; Thomson 2010, 4. Richard Nelson and Sidney Winter (1982, 261) identify a "natural trajectory," similar to a GPT trajectory, in mechanization. Note that Richard Lipsey, Cliff Bekar, and Kenneth Carlaw (1998, 46–47) categorize the nineteenth-century machine tool industry as a "near-GPT" because the range of use of machine tools was restricted to manufacturing. The effect of machine tool advances on mechanization, however, was also seen in many nonmanufacturing sectors, including agriculture.

52. Some scholars identify the railroad as a GPT (Lipsey, Carlaw, and Bekar 2005), but railways did not have the variety of uses to qualify. This lack of pervasiveness may account for why studies have found that the contributions of railroads to productivity growth were fairly modest in the mid-1800s (Fishlow 1966; Fogel 1964).

53. For example, one LS text attributes Britain's decline to the same four industries as the candidate leading sectors selected in this section (Thompson 1990, 226).

TABLE 4.1. Key Sources of Technological Trajectories in the IR-2

Candidate Leading Sectors	Candidate GPTs
Steel industry	Interchangeable manufacture
Electrical equipment industry	Electrification
Chemicals industry	Chemicalization
Automobile industry	Internal combustion engine

of the historical evidence is required to determine whether the candidates actually made the cut.

There is substantial overlap between the candidate GPTs and leading sectors in the IR-2, as reflected in table 4.1, but two key distinctions are worth emphasizing. First, one difference between the candidate GPTs and leading sectors is the inclusion of machine tools in the former category. The international relations scholarship on leading sectors overlooks the impact of machine tools in this period, possibly because the industry's total output did not rank among the largest industries, and also because innovation in machine tools was relatively incremental.[54] One survey of technical development in machine tools from 1850 to 1914 described the landscape as "essentially a series of minor adaptations and improvements."[55] Relatedly, the steel industry, commonly regarded as an LS, is not considered a candidate GPT. Under the GPT mechanism, innovations in steel are bound up in a GPT trajectory driven by advances in machine tools.

Second, even though some technological drivers, such as electricity, are considered both candidate leading sectors and candidate GPTs, there are different interpretations of *how* developments in these technological domains translated into an economic power transition. In the case of new electrical discoveries, control over market share and exports in the electrical equipment industry represents the LS trajectory, whereas the gradual spread of electrification across many industries stands in for the GPT trajectory. Two trajectories diverge in a yellow wood, and the case study evidence will show which one electricity traveled.[56]

54. According to one estimate of the US machine tool industry's size in 1914, its total output amounted to only $31.5 million (US Bureau of the Census 1918, 269).

55. Floud 1976, 31.

56. This point applies as well to advances in chemicals and combustion, which also serve as the sources of both candidate GPTs (chemicalization and the internal combustion engine, respectively) and candidate leading sectors (the chemical industry and the automobile industry, respectively).

GPT vs. LS Trajectories in the IR-2

Equipped with a better grasp of the possible technological drivers in the IR-2, I follow the same procedures used in the previous chapter to assess the validity of the GPT and LS mechanisms.

OBSERVABLE IMPLICATIONS RELATED
TO THE IMPACT TIMEFRAME

GPT diffusion and LS product cycles present two competing interpretations of the IR-2's impact timeframe. The LS mechanism expects growth associated with radical technological breakthroughs to be explosive in the initial stages. Under this view, off the back of major breakthroughs such as the first practical electric dynamo (1871), the modern internal combustion engine (1876), and the successful synthesis of indigo dye (1880), new leading sectors took off in the 1870s and 1880s.[57] Then, according to the expected timeline of the LS mechanism, these new industries stimulated substantial growth in the early stages of their development, bringing about a pre–World War I upheaval in the industrial balance of power.[58]

The GPT trajectory gives a different timeline for when productivity benefits from major technological breakthroughs were realized on an economy-wide scale. Before stimulating economy-wide growth, the candidate GPTs that emerged in the 1880s—tied to advances in electricity, chemicals, and the internal combustion engine—required many decades of complementary innovations in application sectors and human capital upgrading. These candidate GPTs should have contributed only modestly to the industrial rise of the United States before World War I, with impacts, if any, materializing toward the very end of the period.

Critically, one candidate GPT should have produced substantial economic effects during this period. Unlike other GPT trajectories, interchangeable manufacture had been incubated by earlier advances in machine tools, such as the turret lathe (1845) and the universal milling machine (1861).[59] Thus, by the late nineteenth century, interchangeable manufacturing methods

---

57. Another method dates the year 1894 as the arrival date of electricity as a GPT. In the United States, about 1 percent of horsepower in the median manufacturing industry was powered by electricity by that time (Jovanovic and Rousseau 2005).

58. Gilpin 1987, 98, 112; Thompson 1990, 226.

59. Hobsbawm 1968, 147.

should have diffused widely enough to make a significant impact on US indus-trial productivity.

OBSERVABLE IMPLICATIONS RELATED
TO THE PHASE OF RELATIVE ADVANTAGE

When spelling out how the IR-2 produced an economic power transition, the two mechanisms also stress different phases of technological change. According to the LS mechanism, Britain's industrial prominence waned because it lost its dominance of innovation in the IR-2's new industries. The United States and Germany benefited from monopoly profits accrued from being lead innova-tors in electrical equipment, chemical production, automobiles, and steel. In particular, Germany's industrial rise in this period draws a disproportionate share of attention. Many LS accounts attribute Germany's rise to its dominance of innovations in the chemical industry, "the first science-based industry."[60] Others emphasize that the American global lead in the share of fundamental innovations after 1850 paved the way for the United States to dominate new industries and become the leading economy in the IR-2.[61]

The GPT mechanism has different expectations regarding the key determi-nant of productivity differentials. Where innovations are adopted more effec-tively has greater significance than where they are first introduced. According to this perspective, Britain lost its industrial preeminence because the United States was more effective at intensively adopting the IR-2's GPTs.

OBSERVABLE IMPLICATIONS RELATED
TO BREADTH OF GROWTH

Finally, regarding the breadth of growth, the third dimension on which the two mechanisms diverge, the LS trajectory expects that a narrow set of mod-ernized industries drove productivity differentials, whereas the GPT trajectory holds that a broad range of industries contributed to productivity differentials. The US growth pattern serves as the best testing ground for these diverging predictions, since the United States overtook Britain as the economic leader in this period.

60. Moe 2007, 125; see also Drezner 2001, 11–18.
61. Thompson 1990.

TABLE 4.2. Testable Predictions for the IR-2 Case Analysis

Prediction 1: LS (impact timeframe)	The steel, electrical equipment, chemicals, and/or* automobile industries made a significant impact on the rise of the United States to productivity leadership before 1914.
Prediction 1: GPT	Electrification, chemicalization, and/or the internal combustion engine made a significant impact on the rise of the United States to productivity leadership only after 1914. The extension of interchangeable manufacture made a significant impact on the rise of the United States to productivity leadership before 1914.
Prediction 2: LS (phase of relative advantage)	Innovations in the steel, electrical equipment, chemicals, and/or automobile industries were concentrated in the United States. German and American advantages in the production and export of electrical equipment, chemical products, automobiles, and/or steel were crucial to their industrial superiority.
Prediction 2: GPT	Innovations in machine tools, electricity, chemicals, and/or the internal combustion engine were not concentrated in the United States. American advantages in the diffusion of interchangeable manufacture were crucial to its productivity leadership.
Hypothesis 3: LS (breadth of growth)	Productivity growth in the United States was limited to the steel, electrical, chemicals, and/or automotive industries.
Hypothesis 3: GPT	Productivity growth in the United States was spread across a broad range of industries linked to interchangeable manufacture.

*The operator "and/or" links all the candidate leading sectors and GPTs because it could be the case that only some of these technologies drove the trajectories of the period.

The two explanations hold different views about how technological disruptions produced an economic power transition, related to the impact timeframe of new advances, the phase of technological change that yields relative advantages, and the breadth of technology-fueled growth. Based on the differences between the LS and GPT mechanism across these dimensions, I derive three sets of diverging predictions for how technological changes contributed to relative shifts in economic productivity during this period. Table 4.2 collects these predictions, which structure the case analysis in the following sections.

Impact Timeframe: Gradual Gains vs.
Immediate Effects from New Breakthroughs

The opening move in assessing the LS and GPT mechanisms is determining when the IR-2's eye-catching technological advances actually made their mark on leading economies. Tracking the development timelines for all the candidate leading sectors and GPTs of the IR-2 produces two clear takeaways. First, innovations related to electricity, chemicals, and the internal combustion engine did not make a significant impact on US productivity leadership until after 1914. Second, advances in machine tools and steel—the remaining candidate GPT and leading sector, respectively—contributed substantially to US economic growth before World War I; thus, their impact timeframes fit better with when the United States overtook Britain as the preeminent economic power.

DELAYED TIMELINES: CHEMICALS, ELECTRICITY,
AND THE INTERNAL COMBUSTION ENGINE

Developments in chemicals, electricity, and internal combustion provide evidence against the LS interpretation. If the LS mechanism was operational in the IR-2, advances in chemicals should have made a significant impact on US productivity leadership before World War I.[62] Yet, in 1914, the United States was home to only seven dye-making firms.[63] Major US chemicals firms did not establish industrial research laboratories like those of their German counterparts until the first decade of the twentieth century.[64] Terry Reynolds, author of a history of the American Institute of Chemical Engineers, concludes, "Widespread use of chemists in American industrial research laboratories was largely a post–World War I phenomenon."[65] Thus, it is very unlikely that chemical innovations made a meaningful difference to growth differentials between the United States and Britain before 1914.

At first glance, the growth of the German chemical industry aligns with the LS model's expectations. Germany was the first to incorporate scientific research into chemical production, resulting in the synthesis of many artificial

62. Modelski and Thompson 1996, 69; Moe 2007, 426.
63. Ilgen 1983.
64. For example, DuPont did not open its first industrial research facility until 1902 (Bruland and Mowery 2006, 358–66).
65. Reynolds 1986, 700.

dyes before 1880.[66] Overtaking Britain in leadership of the chemical industry, Germany produced 140,000 tons of dyestuffs in 1913, more than 85 percent of the world total.[67]

While Germany's rapid growth trajectory in synthetic dyes was impressive, the greater economic impacts of chemical advances materialized after 1914 through a different pathway: "chemicalization," or the spread of chemical processes across ceramics, food-processing, glass, metallurgy, petroleum refining, and many other industries.[68] Prior to key chemical engineering advances in the 1920s, industrial chemists devoted limited attention to unifying principles across the manufacture of different products. The rapid expansion of chemical-based industries in the twentieth century owed more to these later improvements in chemical engineering than earlier progress in synthetic dyes.[69] Ultimately, these delayed spillovers from chemicalization were substantial, as evidenced by higher growth rates in the German chemical industry during the interwar period than in the two decades before World War I.[70]

Electrification's impact timeframe with respect to US productivity growth mirrored that of chemicalization. Scholarly consensus attributes the US productivity upsurge after 1914 to the delayed impact of the electrification of manufacturing.[71] From 1880 to 1930, power production and distribution systems gradually evolved from shaft and belt drive systems driven by a central steam engine or water wheel to electric unit drive, in which electric motors powered individual machines. Unit drive became the predominant method in the 1920s only after vigorous debates in technical associations over its relative merits, the emergence of large utilities that improved access to cheap electricity, and complementary innovations, like machine tools, that were compatible with electric motors.[72]

Quantitative indicators also verify the long interval between key electrical advances and electrification's productivity boost. Economic geographer Sergio Petralia has investigated the causal relationship between adoption of electrical and electronic (E&E) technologies, operationalized as E&E patenting activity

66. Hull 1996, 195.

67. Drezner 2001, 12; Murmann and Landau 1998, 30.

68. Noble 1977, 18–19.

69. Little 1933, 7; Rosenberg 1998b, 171–76.

70. From 1895 to 1913, German production of chemicals grew by 2.4 times; from 1935 to 1951, the German chemical industry grew by 2.6 times. My calculations are based on statistics compiled in Murmann 2003, 400.

71. David 1990; Devine 1982, 46–47; Field 2003, 92; Rosenberg 1979, 48–49.

72. Devine 1982, 17–45; Devine 1983, 368–71.

in individual American counties and the per-capita growth of those counties over time. One of his main findings is that the effects of E&E technology adoption on growth are not significant prior to 1914.[73] This timeline is confirmed by a range of other metrics, including the energy efficiency of the American economy, electric motors' share of horsepower in manufacturing, and estimates of electricity's total contribution to economic growth.[74]

The diffusion of internal combustion engines across application sectors was also slow. Despite its initial promise, the internal combustion engine never accounted for more than 5 percent of the generation of total horsepower in US manufacturing from 1869 to 1939.[75] In 1900, there were only eight thousand cars in the entire United States, and the U. motor vehicle industry did not overtake its French competitor as the world's largest until 1904.[76] Furthermore, the turning point for the mass production of automobiles, Ford's installation of a moving assembly line for making Model Ts, did not occur until 1913.[77]

KEY TIMINGS: MACHINE TOOLS AND STEEL

When assigning credit to certain technologies for major upheavals in global affairs, awe of the new often overwhelms recognition of the old. Based on the previous analysis, it is unlikely that new breakthroughs in electricity, chemicals, and internal combustion fueled the economic power transition that transpired in this period. Instead, careful tracing reveals the persevering impact of earlier developments in machine tools.[78] During the IR-2, technical advances in machine tools were incremental, continuous improvements that helped disseminate transformative breakthroughs from the mid-nineteenth century, such as the turret lathe and the universal milling machine.[79]

Profiles of key application sectors and quantitative indicators validate the GPT mechanism's expected impact timeframe for machine tools. Marking

---

73. Petralia 2020.

74. Devine 1982; see also Crafts 2002; Rosenberg 1979, 48.

75. Du Boff 1967. On the slow path to ubiquitousness for diesel engines, a specific type of internal combustion engine, see Smil 2010.

76. Smil 2005, 121, 136. In 1912, France exported more automobiles than the United States (Locke 1984, 9n18).

77. Hounshell 1985, 218; Moe 2007, 166–68.

78. Since the development of automobiles and the spread of the internal combustion engine took place so late in the IR-2, I do not specifically trace the effects of this candidate LS and candidate GPT in the two other dimensions.

79. Thomson 2010, 10.

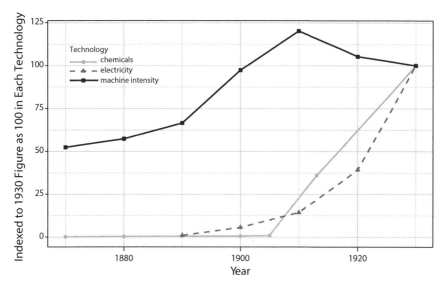

FIGURE 4.3. Technological Impact Timeframes in the IR-2. *Note*: US chemical production, horsepower from electric central stations, and machine intensity over time. *Source*: Murmann 2003; US Census Bureau 1975.

1880 as the date when "the proliferation of new machine tools in American industry had begun to reach torrential proportions," Rosenberg outlines how three application sectors—sewing machines, bicycles, and automobiles—successively adopted improved metal-cutting techniques from 1880 to 1910.[80] As the American system took hold, the number of potential machine tool users multiplied 15-fold, from just 95,000 workers in 1850 to almost 1.5 million in 1910.[81] Patenting data identify the last third of the nineteenth century as the period when extensive technological convergence characterized the machine tool industry and application sectors.[82]

Figure 4.3 depicts the diverging impact timeframes of interchangeable manufacturing methods, electrification, and chemicalization. Machine intensity substantially increased from 1890 to 1910, as measured by horsepower installed per persons employed in manufacturing. By contrast, the United States did not experience significant increases in electrical and chemical production until after 1910.

80. Rosenberg 1963, 433. Singer, one of the largest sewing machine companies, did not fully adopt the American system until the 1870s (Hounshell 1985).
81. Thomson 2010, 9.
82. Ibid., 26.

Of all the candidate leading sectors, the steel industry best fits the expectations of the LS mechanism regarding when industries transformed by radical innovations stimulated growth in the rising powers. Just as the 1780s were a period when the technological conditions for cotton production were transformed, the mid-nineteenth century featured major breakthroughs in the steel industry that allowed for the mass production of steel, such as the Siemens-Martin open-hearth furnace (1867) and Bessemer converter (1856).[83] Over the course of the IR-2 period, the United States and Germany quickly exploited these breakthroughs in steelmaking to massively boost steel production.

The overtaking of Britain by both Germany and the United States in total steel production by the early 1890s matches the timeline of Britain's overall economic decline.[84] Paul Kennedy cites Germany's booming steel output as a key factor driving its industrial rise; by 1914, German steel output was larger than that of Britain, France, and Russia combined.[85] Likewise, US steel output grew from one-fifth of British production in 1871 to almost five times more than British steel output in 1912.[86] Given these impressive figures, the next section investigates the American and German advantages in steel production in further detail.

Phase of Relative Advantage: The American System's Diffusion

The second dimension on which the GPT and LS trajectories differ relates to the phase of technological change that accounted for the relative success of the United States in the IR-2. Cross-country historical evidence on the IR-2's technological drivers illustrates that the United States had true comparative advantages over other advanced economies that were rooted in its absorption and diffusion capabilities.

INNOVATION CLUSTERING IN STEEL, ELECTRICITY, CHEMICALS, AND/OR MOTOR VEHICLES?

In electricity, industrial powers fiercely contested innovation leadership as the United States, Germany, Great Britain, and France all built their first central power stations, electric trams, and alternating current power systems within a

83. Kuznets 1930, 10.
84. Sanderson 1972, 15.
85. Kennedy 1987, 210.
86. My calculations are based on crude steel output figures in Mitchell 1998, 466–67; Mitchell 1993, 356–58.

span of nine years.[87] However, the United States clearly led in diffusing these systems: US electricity production per capita more than doubled that of Germany, the next closest competitor, in 1912. Along this metric of electrification, Britain's level was just 20 percent of the US figure.[88]

To be clear, Britain fell behind in adopting electrification, even though it introduced some of the most significant electrical innovations.[89] In 1884, for example, British inventor Charles Parsons demonstrated the first steam turbine for practical use, an essential step for commercializing electric power, but this technology was more rapidly and widely adopted in other countries.[90] The British Institution of Electrical Engineers aptly captured this phenomenon in an 1892 resolution: "Notwithstanding that our countrymen have been among the first in inventive genius in electrical science, its development in the United Kingdom is in a backward condition, as compared with other countries, in respect of practical application to the industrial and social requirements of the nation."[91]

In chemicals, the achievements of both the US and German chemical industries suggest that no single country monopolized innovation in this sector. Germany's synthetic dye industry excelled not because it generated the initial breakthroughs in aniline-violet dye processes—in fact, those were first pioneered in Britain—but because it had perfected these processes for profitable exploitation.[92] Similar dynamics characterized the US chemical industry.[93]

In most cases, the United States was not the first to introduce major innovations in leading sectors. Many countries introduced major innovations in chemicals, electricity, motor vehicles, and steel during this period (table 4.3).[94] Across the four candidate leading sectors, American firms pioneered less than 30 percent of the innovations. Contrary to the propositions of the LS mechanism, innovations in steel, electricity, chemicals, and motor vehicles were spread across the leading economies.

87. Taylor 2016, 189.
88. My calculations are based on Comin and Hobijn 2009.
89. The London Underground was the first metro line to install an alternating current transformer of significance, but it was the United States that "forged far ahead of Britain in the number of alternating current stations" (Hughes 1962, 36).
90. Field 2008, 23. By 1912, steam turbines provided around 40 percent of the total power to central electric stations in the United States (Bryant and Hunter 1991, 336–51).
91. Quoted in Hughes 1962, 38.
92. Drezner 2001, 12; Hull 1996, 195; Trebilcock 1981, 64.
93. Bruland and Mowery 2006, 362; Murmann 2003, 399.
94. US firms accounted for 45 percent of all major innovations from 1850 to 1914. German firms produced 18 percent of the major innovations over the same period (Modelski and Thompson 1996, 117).

TABLE 4.3. Geographic Distribution of Major Innovations in Leading Sectors, 1850–1914

	Chemicals	Electricity	Motor Vehicles	Steel
France	2	1	1	1
Germany	3	3	3	0
Great Britain	1	3	1	1
United States	2	3	1	0
Various other countries	0	1	0	2
Sole US share	25%	27%	17%	0%

Source: Van Duijn 1983, 176–79 (compilation of 160 innovations introduced during the nineteenth and twentieth centuries).

Moreover, the limited role of electrical and chemical exports in spurring American growth casts further doubt on the significance of monopoly profits from being the first to introduce new advances.[95] The British share of global chemical exports almost doubled the US share in 1913.[96] Overall, the United States derived only 8 percent of its national income from foreign trade in 1913, whereas the corresponding proportion for Britain was 26 percent.[97] Even though the United States was the quickest to electrify its economy, Germany captured around half of the world's exports in electrical products.[98]

If monopoly profits from innovation clustering in any leading sector propelled the industrial rise of the United States and Germany, it would be the steel industry. Both nations made remarkable gains in total steel output over this period, and scholars commonly employ crude steel production as a key indicator of British decline and the shifting balance of industrial power in the decades before World War I.[99] Thus, having established the delayed impact of the electrical, chemical, and automobile industries in this period, the steel industry takes on an especially large burden for the LS mechanism's explanatory power in this period.

Yet Britain capitalized on many major innovations in steelmaking, including the Talbot furnace, which became essential to producing open-hearth

95. Since the automobile industry developed so late in the period, I focus on potential innovation clustering and monopoly profits from the chemical and electrical industries.

96. Murmann 2003, 401.

97. Kennedy 1987, 244.

98. Henderson 1975, 189–90.

99. Kennedy 1987, 199–200; Modelski and Thompson 1996, 87–88; Thompson 1990, 213.

steel.[100] Moreover, trade patterns reveal that Britain still held a comparative advantage in the export of steel between 1899 and 1913.[101] How to square this with Germany's dominance in total steel output?

The prevailing wisdom takes total steel output figures to stand for superior American and German technological know-how and productivity.[102] In truth, new steelmaking processes created two separate steel industries. Britain shifted toward producing open-hearth steel, which was higher in quality and price. According to the British Iron Trade Association, Britain produced about four times more open-hearth steel than Germany in 1890.[103] On the other hand, Germany produced cheap Thomas steel and exported a large amount at dumping prices. In fact, some of Germany's steel exports went to Britain, where they were processed into higher-quality steel and re-exported.[104] In sum, this evidence questions what one scholar deems "the myth of the technological superiority and outstanding productivity of the German steel industry before and after the First World War."[105]

AMERICAN MACHINE TOOLS — GPT DIFFUSION ADVANTAGE

Though new industries like electricity and chemicals hog much of the spotlight, developments in machine tools underpin the most important channel between differential rates of technology adoption and the IR-2's economic power transition. After noting the importance of the electrical and chemical industries during the period, British historian Eric Hobsbawm elevates the

---

100. Hobsbawm (1968, 159) writes, "Every major innovation in the manufacture of steel came from Britain or was developed in Britain." According to George James Snelus, vice president of the Iron and Steel Institute, the Talbot furnace was "the greatest advance that had been made in the manufacture of steel for some years" (Talbot 1900, 62, cited in McCloskey 1973, 71).

101. Crafts 1989, 130.

102. In his particularly influential account, David Landes (1969) highlights Britain's failure to keep up with Germany in steel production (Wengenroth 1994, 393n29). For example, Paul Kennedy's *The Rise and Fall of the Great Powers* cites Landes's work multiple times to argue that declining steel output explains Britain's productivity slowdown (Kennedy 1987, 198n16; 228n110).

103. Wengenroth 1994, 384.

104. Relatedly, the most widely used indicator of national power resources, the Composite Indicator of National Capability (CINC), relies on steel production for the period 1900 to 2012 as one of six key factor variables (Greig and Enterline 2017, 45–46). For criticisms of CINC's usage of steel production as an indicator of industrial power, see Beckley 2018b; Wohlforth 1999, 13.

105. Wengenroth 1994, 390.

importance of machine tools: "Yet nowhere did foreign countries—and again chiefly the USA—leap ahead more decisively than in this field."[106]

In line with the expectations of GPT diffusion theory, comparative estimates confirm a substantial US lead in mechanization in the early twentieth century. In 1907, machine intensity in the United States was more than two times higher than rates in Britain and Germany.[107] In 1930, the earliest year for which data on installed machine tools per employee are available, Germany lagged behind the United States in installed machine tools per employee across manufacturing industries by 10 percent, with a significantly wider gap in the tools most crucial for mass production.[108]

This disparity in mechanization was not rooted in the exclusive access of the United States to special innovations in machine tools. In terms of quality, British machine tools were superior to their American counterparts throughout the IR-2 period.[109] German firms also had advantages in certain fields like sophisticated power technology.[110] Rather, the distinguishing feature of the US machine tool industry was excellence in diffusing innovations across industries.[111] Reports by British and German study trips to the United States provide some of the most detailed, reliable accounts of transatlantic differences in manufacturing methods. German observers traveled to the United States to learn from their American competitors and eventually imitate American interchangeable manufacturing methods.[112] British inspection teams reported that the US competitive edge came from the "adaptation of special apparatus to a single operation in almost all branches of industry"[113] and "the eagerness with which they call in the aid of machinery in almost every department of industry."[114]

106. Hobsbawm 1968, 151.

107. My calculations are based on data in Timmer, Veenstra, and Woltjer 2016. Germany's machine intensity rate is based on 1909 data. For a defense of applied horsepower per hour worked as a useful proxy for American methods of production in this period, see ibid., 879–81. I thank Pieter Woltjer for sharing the link to these data.

108. Ristuccia and Tooze 2013, 959–60.

109. Great Britain Committee on the Machinery of the United States of America 1855, 32, cited in Rosenberg 1963, 420n12; see also Litterer 1961, 467. British machine tools remained superior to those of other European countries in the IR-2 period (Floud 1976, 68).

110. Braun 1984, 16.

111. Rosenberg 1963, 417; Saul 1960, 22.

112. Braun 1984; Nolan 1994; Timmer, Veenstra, and Woltjer 2016, 882–83.

113. Great Britain Committee on the Machinery of the United States of America 1855, 32.

114. Whitworth 1854/1969, 387.

Fittingly, one of the most colorful denunciations of American innovation capacity simultaneously underscored its strong diffusion capacity. In an 1883 address to the American Association for the Advancement of Science, Henry Rowland, the association's vice president, denigrated the state of American science for its skew toward the commercialization of new advances. Rowland expressed his disgust with media representations that upheld the "obscure American who steals the ideas of some great mind of the past, and enriches himself by the application of the same to domestic uses" over "the great originator of the idea, who might have worked out hundreds of such applications, had his mind possessed the necessary element of vulgarity."[115] Yet, it was America's diffusion capacity—in all its obscurity and vulgarity—that sustained its growth to economic preeminence.

Breadth of Growth: The Wide Reach of Interchangeable Manufacture

What were the sources of American productivity growth in the IR-2? The pattern of American economic growth is most pertinent to investigate because the United States overtook Britain in productivity leadership during the IR-2. Regarding the breadth of economic growth, the LS trajectory expects that American productivity growth was concentrated in a narrow set of modernized industries, whereas the GPT trajectory holds that American productivity growth was dispersed across a broad range of industries. Sector-level estimates of total factor productivity (TFP) growth provide useful evidence to assess these diverging propositions.

WIDESPREAD PRODUCTIVITY GROWTH

The historical data support GPT diffusion theory's expectation of pervasive US productivity growth. John Kendrick's detailed study of US productivity growth in this period depicts a relatively balanced distribution. Among the industries studied, nearly 60 percent averaged between 1 and 3 percent increases in output per labor-hour from 1899 to 1909.[116] Broad swathes of the US economy, outside of the leading sectors, experienced technological change. For instance, the service sector, which included segments of the

115. Rowland 1883, 242; Taylor 2016, 9.
116. Kendrick 1961, 163.

construction, transport, wholesale, and retail trade industries, played a key role in the US capacity to narrow the gap with Britain in productivity performance.[117]

R&D-centric sectors were not the primary engines of US growth. In a recent update to Kendrick's estimates, a group of researchers estimated how much of US productivity growth was driven by "great inventions sectors," a designation that roughly corresponds to this chapter's candidate leading sectors.[118] They found that these sectors accounted for only 29 percent of U.S. TFP growth from 1899–1909.[119] Despite employing 40 percent of all research scientists in 1920, the chemical industry was responsible for only 7 percent of US TFP growth throughout the following decade.[120]

MACHINE TOOLS AND BROADLY DISTRIBUTED PRODUCTIVITY GROWTH

Broad-based productivity growth in the US economy does not necessarily mean that a GPT was at work. Macroeconomic factors or the accumulation of various, unconnected sources of TFP growth could produce this outcome. Therefore, if the GPT trajectory captures the breadth of growth in the IR-2, then the historical evidence should connect broadly distributed productivity growth in the United States to developments in machine tools.

The extension of the American system boosted productivity in a wide range of sectors. Applications of this system of special tools reshaped the processes of making firearms, furniture, sewing machines, bicycles, automobiles, cigarettes, clocks, boots and shoes, scientific instruments, typewriters, agricultural implements, locomotives, and naval ordnance.[121] Its influence covered "almost every branch of industry where articles have to be repeated."[122] Per a 1930

---

117. Broadberry 2006.

118. The "great inventions sectors" include chemicals, electric machinery, electric utilities, and transport equipment (Bakker, Crafts, and Woltjer 2019).

119. Bakker, Crafts, and Woltjer 2019, 2285. This figure aggregates various industries' "intensive growth contributions," a measure that is the product of an industry's value-added share and TFP growth.

120. Ibid., 2290.

121. Anderson 1877; Hounshell 1985; Rosenberg 1963; Thomson 2010. Consider the possible spillover effects from sewing machines alone. The percentage increase in value added by manufacture in women's clothing grew by approximately 135 percent in the United States from 1899 to 1909, bringing women's clothing to third highest (only after automobiles and electricity) for industries valued at over $100 million (US Bureau of the Census 1913, 40).

122. Anderson 1877, 235, cited in Rosenberg 1963, 420n12.

inventory of American machine tools, the earliest complete survey, nearly 1.4 million metalworking machines were used across twenty industrial sectors.[123] In his seminal study of American productivity growth during this period, Kendrick identifies progress in "certain types of new products developed by the machinery and other producer industries [that] have broad applications across industry lines" as a key source of the "broad, pervasive forces that promote efficiency throughout the economy."[124]

The breadth of productivity spillovers from machine tools was not boundless. Machine-using industries constituted a minority of the manufacturing industries, which themselves accounted for less than one-quarter of national income.[125] However, users of new machine tools extended beyond just manufacturing industries. Technologically intensive services, such as railroads and steam transportation, also benefited significantly from improved metalworking techniques.[126] In agriculture, specialized machine tools helped advance the introduction of farm machinery such as the reaper, which revolutionized agricultural productivity.[127]

In describing how machine tools served as a transmission center in the US economy, Rosenberg describes the industry as a pool of skills and technical knowledge that replenishes the economy's machine-using sectors—that is, an innovation that addresses one industry's problem gets added to the pool and becomes available, with a few modifications, for all technologically related industries.[128] As sales records from leading machine tool firms show, many application sectors purchased the same type of machine. In 1867, Brown and Sharpe Manufacturing Company sold the universal milling machine, just five years after its invention, not only to machinery firms that made tools for a diverse range of industries but also to twenty-seven other firms that produced everything from ammunition to jewelry.[129] In this way,

123. This is a conservative estimate, as some sectors were omitted from the survey (Thomson 2010, 6).

124. Kendrick 1961, 178, 181.

125. Harley 2003, 827.

126. Rosenberg 1979, 34; Scranton 1997, 290.

127. Beaumont and Higgs 1958; Hounshell 1985.

128. Rosenberg 1963, 426; von Tunzelmann 2000, 132.

129. Brown & Sharpe 1997, 20–23, cited in Thomson 2010, 29. If each industry purchased its own specialized type of machine tool, then broad technological convergence should be questioned. The share of generic patents among a population of lathe patents increased from one-third of all patent types from 1816 to 1865 to 60 percent of all patent types in the period from 1900 to 1921 (Thomson 2010, 14).

the machine tool industry functioned, in Rosenberg's words, as "a center for the acquisition and diffusion of new skills and techniques in a machinofacture type of economy."[130]

Indeed, advances in machine tools had economy-wide effects. The social savings method estimates how much a new technology contributed to economic growth, compared to a counterfactual situation in which the technology had not been invented.[131] Referencing this method to differentiate between the impacts of new technologies in this period, economic historian Joel Mokyr puts forward the American system of manufacturing as the most important:

> From a purely economic point of view, it could be argued that the most important invention was not another chemical dye, a better engine, or even electricity. . . . There is one innovation, however, for which "social savings" calculations from the vantage point of the twentieth century are certain to yield large gains. The so-called American System of manufacturing assembled complex products from mass-produced individual components. Modern manufacturing would be unthinkable without interchangeable parts.[132]

Institutional Complementarities:
GPT Skill Infrastructure in the IR-2

With confirmation that the pattern of technological change in the IR-2 is better characterized by the GPT trajectory, the natural next step is to probe variation among leading economies in adapting to this trajectory. Why was the United States more successful than Britain and Germany in adapting to the demands of interchangeable manufacture? According to GPT diffusion theory, the historical evidence should reveal that the US edge was based on education and training systems that broadened and systematized mechanical engineering skills. These institutional adaptations would have resolved two key bottlenecks in the spread of interchangeable manufacture: a shortage of mechanical engineering talent and ineffective coordination between machine tool producers and users.

130. Rosenberg 1963, 425.

131. In one classic study, Robert Fogel (1964) assessed the contribution of the railroad to the production potential of the US economy by conducting a counterfactual on the possible expansion of the canal system as the next best alternative.

132. Mokyr 1990, 136.

Widening the Base of Mechanical Engineers

Which institutions for skill formation were most central to the ability of the United States to take advantage of new advances in machine tools? Established accounts of economic rivalry among great powers in the IR-2 focus on skills linked to major innovations in new, science-based industries. Emphasizing Germany's advantage in training scientific researchers, these studies attribute Germany's technological success in this period to its investments in R&D facilities and advanced scientific and technical education.[133] Such conclusions echo early-twentieth-century British accounts of Germany's growing commercial prowess, which lauded German higher education for awarding doctorates in engineering and its qualitative superiority in scientific research.[134]

American leadership in the adoption of interchangeable manufacturing methods was beholden to a different set of institutions for skill formation. Progress in this domain did not depend on new scientific frontiers and industrial research laboratories.[135] In fact, the United States trailed both Britain and Germany in scientific achievements and talent.[136] Widespread mechanization in the United States rested instead on a broad base of mechanical engineering skills.

Alongside the development of more automatic and precise machine tools throughout the nineteenth century, this new trajectory of mechanization demanded more of machinists and mechanical engineers. Before 1870, US firms relied on informal apprenticeships at small workshops for training people who would design and use machine tools.[137] At the same time, engineering education at independent technical schools and traditional colleges and universities did not prioritize mechanical engineers but were mostly oriented toward civil engineering.[138] Yet craft-era methods and skills were no longer sufficient to handle advances that enhanced the sophistication of machine tools.[139] Thus, in the mid-eighteenth century, the US potential for mechanization was

133. Drezner 2004, 13; Moe 2009, 216–17.

134. Sanderson 1972, 21–23.

135. Bruland and Mowery 2006, 359–60. In 1921, fewer than seven thousand researchers were employed in American industry, according to the first survey of American industrial laboratories (Chandler 1990, 84).

136. Hughes 1994, 433; Kocka 1980, 95–96; Nelson and Wright 1992, 1940.

137. Monte Calvert (1967) describes this approach as "shop culture." See also Locke 1984, 61; Lundgreen 1990, 55; Scranton 1997, 60.

138. Lundgreen 1990, 55.

139. Thomson 2010, 9.

significantly constrained by the need for more formal technical instruction in mechanical engineering.

Over the next few decades, advances on three main fronts met this need for a wider pool of mechanical engineering expertise: land-grant schools, technical institutes, and standardization efforts. In 1862, the US Congress passed the first Morrill Land-Grant Act, which financed the creation of land-grant colleges dedicated to the agricultural and mechanical arts. Although some of these schools offered low-quality instruction and initially restricted their mission to agricultural concerns, the land-grant funds also supported many important engineering schools, such as the Massachusetts Institute of Technology (MIT) and Cornell University.[140] The number of US engineering schools multiplied from six in 1862, when the Morrill Act was passed, to 126 in 1917.[141] These schools were especially significant in widening the base of professional mechanical engineers. In 1900, out of all students pursuing mechanical engineering at US higher education institutions, 88 percent were enrolled in land-grant colleges.[142]

The establishment of technical institutes also served demands for mechanical engineering training. Pure technical schools like the Worcester Polytechnic Institute, founded in 1868, and the Stevens Institute of Technology, founded in 1870, developed mechanical engineering curricula that would become templates for engineering programs at universities and colleges.[143] Embedded with local and regional businesses, technical institutes developed laboratory exercises that familiarized students with real-world techniques and equipment. In this respect, these institutes and land-grant colleges "shared a common belief in the need to deliver a practice-oriented technical education."[144]

Another significant development in the spread of mechanical engineering knowledge was the emergence of professional engineering societies that created industrial standards. The most prominent of these were the American Society of Mechanical Engineers (ASME), founded in 1880, the American Section of the International Association for Testing Materials, set up in 1898, and the

---

140. Seely 2004, 60. I thank Bruce Seely for providing me with a copy of his chapter on European connections to American engineering education.

141. Noble 1977, 24; see also Maloney and Caicedo 2017, 12–13.

142. Dalby 1903, 39. For these figures, a "land-grant college" refers to a college that received a grant from either the 1862 Morrill Act or the 1890 legislation commonly known as the Second Morrill Act.

143. Calvert 1967, 49; Seely 2004, 61.

144. Seely 2004, 61.

Franklin Institute, which became America's leading technical society around the start of the IR-2.[145] As these associations coordinated to share best practices in mechanical engineering, they improved knowledge flows between the machine tool industry and application sectors.[146] Standardization in various machine processes and components, such as screw threads, helped spread mechanization across disparate markets and communities.[147]

It should be emphasized that these efforts were effective in producing the skills and knowledge necessary for advancing mechanization because they broadened the field of mechanical engineering. Mechanical engineering instruction at land-grant schools and technical institutes and through professional associations allowed for more students to become "average engineers," as opposed to "the perpetuation of a self-recognized elite."[148] Recent research finds that this diffused engineering capacity produced enduring benefits for American industrialization. By collecting granular data on engineering density for the United States at the county level, William Maloney and Felipe Caicedo capture the engineering talent spread across various US counties in 1880 and parse the effect of engineering capacity on industrial outcomes decades later. They find that there is a statistically significant, positive relationship between the level of engineering density in 1880 and the level of industrialization decades later.[149]

The Comparative Advantage of the United States over Britain and Germany in GPT Skill Infrastructure

Both Britain and Germany fell short of the US standard in GPT skill infrastructure. For Britain, the key gap was in the supply of mechanical engineering talent. British educational institutions and professional bodies fiercely guarded the apprenticeship tradition for training mechanical engineers.[150] For instance, the University of Oxford did not establish an engineering professorship

---

145. For the first two decades, the ASME's professionalization activities were mostly limited to holding biannual meetings and publishing an annual volume of papers containing important engineering literature (American Society of Mechanical Engineers 1900). This changed drastically in the early twentieth century as the ASME grew its membership, operated a professional registry for job listings, and endorsed technical standards.

146. Noble 1977, 76; Scranton 1997, 69.

147. Hounshell 1985; Noble 1977.

148. Calvert 1967, 278.

149. Maloney and Caicedo 2017.

150. Locke 1984; Thomson 2010, 40; Wickenden 1929, 35.

until 1908.[151] Meanwhile, American engineers systematically experimented with machine redesigns, benefiting from their training at universities and technical institutes.

These diverging approaches resulted in stark differences in skill formation. In 1901, probably around 2,600 students were enrolled in full-time higher technical education in the United Kingdom.[152] Limiting this population to those in their third or fourth year of full-time study—an important condition because many UK programs, unlike German and American institutions, did not progress beyond two years of study—leaves only about 400 students.[153] By comparison, in mechanical engineering programs *alone*, the United States in 1900 had 4,459 students enrolled in higher technical education.[154] Controlling for population differences, the United States substantially outpaced Britain in engineering density, as measured by the number of university-educated engineers per 100,000 male laborers.[155]

Germany developed a more practical and accessible form of higher technical education than Britain. From 1870 to 1900, enrollments in the German *technische Hochschulen* increased nearly fourfold, from 13,674 to 32,834 students.[156] Alongside the *technische Mittelschulen* (technical intermediate schools comparable to American industrial trade schools and lower-level engineering colleges), the *technische Hochschulen* cultivated a broad base of mechanical engineers.[157] Germany's system of technical education attracted admirers

151. Sanderson 1972, 24–39.

152. "Full-time" excludes students who took evening or weekend classes. For a perspective that disputes the connection between the deficiencies in the United Kingdom's education system and its industrial decline, see Lundgreen 1990, 62–64. Other accounts acknowledge that Britain made remarkable investments in engineering education in the early twentieth century, but they also note that the delay in these actions (relative to industrial rivals) were costly (Wickenden 1929, 43).

153. Wertheimer 1903; Wickenden 1929, 36.

154. Dalby 1903, 39. In 1902, Germany enrolled nearly 15,000 students across all disciplines in the *technische Hochschulen*. Foreigners made up about 2,500 of these enrollments (Rose 1903, 57).

155. Ahlström 1982; Maloney and Caicedo 2017.

156. Rose 1903, 51. Some texts, such as the British consular report cited here, employ "technical high school" as the English translation of *technische Hochschulen*. This is imprecise because the vast majority of students at these institutions were older than eighteen. "Technical universities" is also an imperfect translation because the "university" (*Universität*) was reserved for institutions that conferred doctorates. Following König 1996, I use the German *technische Hochschulen* instead of English translations.

157. Based on data for the machine-building industry in Berlin, in terms of engineers placed in industry, the *technische Mittelschulen* trained almost four times as many engineers as the *technische Hochschulen* (König 1993, 83).

from around the world. Some went there to study in the schools, and others went to study how the school system worked, with the aim of borrowing elements of the German model.[158]

Germany's problems were with weak linkages between mechanical engineering education and industrial applications. Key German standards bodies and technical colleges prioritized scientific and theoretical education at the expense of practical skills—a trend "most pronounced in mechanical engineering."[159] According to an expert on German standard-setting in this period, "no national standards movement was inaugurated in [the machine industry] until after the outbreak of [World War I]."[160] German experts on engineering education, intent on reforming technical instruction to get engineers more experience with factor organization and project management in the field, recommended, for example, that practical training courses be offered in partnerships with engineering associations.[161] Articles in the *Zeitschrift des Vereines Deutscher Ingenieure* (Journal of the Association of German Engineers) lamented that the *technische Hochschulen* and technical universities were not equipping students with practical skills to operate in and manage factories and workshops.[162] These issues slowed Germany's incorporation of interchangeable parts and advanced machine tools.

A report by Professor Alois Riedler of the Technical University of Berlin, who was commissioned by the Prussian Ministry of Education to tour American engineering schools in the 1890s, illustrates the differences in engineering education between the United States and Germany. According to Riedler, extensive practical training and experience with shop and laboratory applications were distinctive features of an American engineering education. To substantiate differences in practical instruction between engineering departments in the two countries, Riedler analyzed the time allocated to theoretical and practical instruction across four-year courses of study.[163] Compared to their German peers, American students spent far more time on exercises in mechanical

---

158. Seely 2004.

159. Gispen 1990, 122.

160. Brady 1933, 149; see also Yates and Murphy 2019, 36.

161. See, for example, Bohmert 1904.

162. US Bureau of Education 1894, 193.

163. Riedler's comparison of engineering schools also included an electrical engineering program at a southern German technical university as well as the Sheffield School at Yale University. In preparing this curricula comparison, I excluded courses of study attached to these two schools because they were not as representative as those of the remaining schools, which accords with Riedler's judgment (US Bureau of Education 1895, 684, 686).

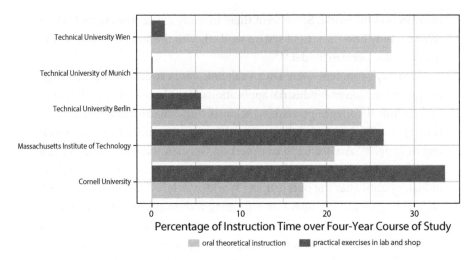

FIGURE 4.4. Comparison of Curricula at German and American Engineering Schools (1893). *Source*: US Bureau of Education (BOE) 1895, 684–86. *Note*: In this BOE report, the German schools are labeled Technological University in Austria, Technological University in Prussia, and Technological University in South Germany. A reasonable assumption, informed by background research, is that these refer to Technical University Wien, Technical University Berlin, and Technical University of Munich, respectively. Though TU Wien is in Austria, it is used to illustrate trends in German engineering education because many German schools saw it as an influential model.

technical laboratories and other types of practical training (figure 4.4). In the Technische Universität Berlin (Technical University Berlin), practical exercises in the laboratory and shop accounted for less than 6 percent of total instruction time over a four-year course of study.[164] In contrast, engineering students at Cornell University spent more than one-third of their course engaged in laboratory study and shopwork. As a consequence of reports by Riedler and others, German institutions began establishing laboratories for mechanical engineering around 1900.[165]

It should be made clear that, in the United States, institutional adaptations to new opportunities presented by interchangeable manufacture were

164. At the Technical University of Munich, the four-year course of study included no time for practical exercises in the laboratory or shop.

165. König 1996, 91–95. According to one historian, Riedler's frank assessment of American engineering education's strengths eventually sparked reforms that "profoundly changed the nature of German engineering in the 20th century" (Zieren 2006, 2).

not rooted in cultivating highly skilled scientific talent. The best and brightest American scientists furthered their education at European universities.[166] Even proponents of American engineering education concluded that "strictly scientific and intellectual education in American technological schools" did not even match "the average of a secondary industrial school" in Germany.[167] According to one study conducted by the National Association of German-American Technologists, an organization that regularly circulated ideas between the two countries, German technical institutes held an edge over their US peers in research on different technologies in mechanical engineering.[168]

The deeper roots of US institutions' greater effectiveness at adapting to the skill formation needs of interchangeable manufacture cannot be fully explored here. The legacy of the Morrill Act certainly looms large, as do the contributions of a diverse set of institutional adaptations unrelated to that groundbreaking federal policy, including independent centers like the Franklin Institute, technical high schools, professional associations, and specialized engineering programs initiated at preexisting universities.[169] Other potential sources for the US advantage in GPT skill infrastructure include its openness to foreign technicians and the unique challenges and culture of the American frontier.[170]

LS-Based Theories and Chemical Engineering

Analyzing the education and training systems for chemical advances provides a secondary test to determine which institutions are most apt to bring national success in technological revolutions.[171] LS accounts typically point to Germany's innovation capacity as the key determinant of its competitiveness in chemicals, especially in the key segment of synthetic dye production.[172] To extend this lead in synthetic dyes, Germany profited from leading industrial research labs and scientific education institutions, which employed the world's

166. Cohen 1976.

167. US Bureau of Education 1895, 676.

168. Braun 1984, 16.

169. Nelson and Wright 1992, 1942; Rosenberg and Steinmueller 2013, 1130; Scranton 1997, 65–71.

170. Braun 1984; Nienkamp 2008.

171. This section draws from Ding 2023, 10–11.

172. Drezner 2001, 12n33; Henderson 1975, 186; Moe 2007, 4, 142.

top academic chemists and produced about two-thirds of the world's chemical research.[173]

By comparison, the US capacity to innovate in chemicals was weak. From 1901 to 1930, only one American researcher received a Nobel Prize in Chemistry, while German and British researchers captured almost three-fourths of the Nobel Prizes in Chemistry in that span.[174] In 1899, German publications accounted for half of all citations in American chemical journals, essentially double the share credited to American publications.[175] At the same time, American scholarship barely registered in Europe-based chemistry journals, where the best research was published. According to one analysis of references in *Annual Reports on the Progress of Chemistry*, an authoritative British review journal, American publications accounted for only 7 percent of the citations in 1904.[176]

As was the case with machine tools, effective adaptation to new chemical technologies in the United States rested on a different set of institutional competencies. Despite trailing Germany in chemical breakthroughs and top chemists, the United States pioneered a chemical engineering discipline that facilitated the gradual chemicalization of many industries. A crucial step in this process was the emergence of unit operations, which broke down chemical processes into a sequence of basic operations (for example, condensing, crystallizing, and electrolyzing) that were useful to many industries, including ceramics, food processing, glass, metallurgy, and petroleum refining.[177] American institutions of higher education, most notably MIT, quickly adopted the unit operations model and helped cultivate a common language and professional community of chemical engineering.[178] As Rosenberg and Steinmueller conclude, "American leadership in introducing a new engineering discipline into the university curriculum, even at a time when the country was far from the frontier of scientific research, was nowhere more conspicuous than in the discipline of chemical engineering early in the 20th century."[179]

In contrast, Germany was slow to develop the infrastructure for supporting chemical engineers. Up through the interwar period, the chemical engineering

173. Throughout the 1890s, there were two times as many academic chemists in Germany as in Britain (Sanderson 1972, 23; see also Locke 1984, 61).

174. Thackray et al. 1985, 161.

175. Ibid., 405–7.

176. Ibid., 157, 402; see also Macleod 1971, 207.

177. Little 1933, 7; Rosenberg 1998b, 176.

178. Guédon 1980, 45–76; Noble 1977, 26–27; Rosenberg 1998b, 171.

179. Rosenberg and Steinmueller 2013, 1145.

profession "failed to coalesce in Germany."[180] Chemical engineering did not become a distinct academic subject area in Germany until after the Second World War.[181] Because German universities did not equip chemists with engineering skills, the burden of training chemists was shifted to firms.[182] Additionally, the German chemical industry maintained a strict division of labor between chemists and mechanical engineers. The lack of skill systematization resulted in more secrecy, less interfirm communication, and a failure to exploit externalities from common chemical processes.[183]

The United States reaped the spoils of technological convergence in chemicalization not just because it trained large numbers of chemical engineers but also because it strengthened university-industry linkages and standardized techniques in chemical engineering.[184] Without the connective tissue that promotes information flows between the chemical sector and application sectors, a large base of chemical engineers was insufficient. Britain, for instance, was relatively successful at training chemical engineers during the interwar period; however, the weak links between British educational institutions and industrial actors limited the dissemination of technical knowledge, and the concept of unit operations did not take hold in Britain to the degree that it did in America.[185] Additionally, professional engineering associations in the United States, including the American Institute of Chemical Engineers, advanced standardization in the chemical industry—an initiative not imitated in Britain until a decade later.[186] Unlike their American peers, it was not until after World War II that British chemical engineers saw themselves as "members of a professional group that shared a broad commonality cutting across the boundary lines of a large number of industries."[187]

Since substantial, economy-wide benefits from these chemical breakthroughs did not materialize until after the end of the IR-2 period, it is important to not overstate these points. Nonetheless, tracing which country best exploited chemical innovations through the interwar period can supplement

180. Divall and Johnston 1998, 204.

181. No chemical engineering departments existed outside of the United States until the 1930s (Rosenberg 1998a, 195).

182. Rosenberg 1998a, 192–99.

183. Guédon 1980.

184. Rosenberg 1998a, 205.

185. Divall and Johnston 1998, 212.

186. Noble 1977, 38, 72; Reynolds 1983, 41–42.

187. Rosenberg and Steinmueller 2013, 1146.

the analysis of institutional complementarities for machine tools.[188] Evidence from the coevolution of chemical technologies and skill formation institutions further illustrates how institutional adaptations suited to GPT trajectories differed from those suited to LS trajectories.

Alternative Factors

Like its predecessor, the IR-2 has been the subject of countless studies. Scholars have thoroughly investigated the decline of Britain and the rise of the United States and Germany, offering explanations ranging from immigration patterns and cultural and generational factors to natural resource endowments and labor relations.[189] My aim is not to sort through all possible causes of British decline. Rather, I am tracing the mechanisms behind an established connection between the IR-2's technological breakthroughs and an economic power transition. Thus, the contextual factors most likely to confound the GPT diffusion explanation are those that provide an alternative explanation of how significant technological changes translated into the United States supplanting Britain in economic leadership. Aside from the LS mechanism, which has been examined in detail, the influence of international security threats and varieties of capitalism deserve further examination.

Threat-Based Explanations

How did external threats influence technological leadership in the IR-2? Scholars have argued that US military investment, mobilized against the threat of a major war, was crucial to the development of many GPTs.[190] US national armories' subsidization of the production of small arms with interchangeable parts in the early nineteenth century was crucial, some studies argue, to the diffusion of the American system to other industries in the second half of the century.[191]

Though firearms production provided an important experimental ground for mechanized production, military support was not necessary to the devel-

---

188. Relatedly, given that chemical engineering tapped into foundational practices from mechanical engineering, one could argue that chemical engineering was an extension of mechanical engineering into chemistry, or "the product of mechanical engineering and chemistry" (Noble 1977, 38).

189. Kennedy 1987, 228.

190. Ruttan 2006.

191. Deyrup 1948; Smith 1985.

opment of the American system of manufacturing. Questioning the necessity of government funding and subsidies for the spread of the American system, one study credits the development of interchangeable manufacture to four civilian industries: clock manufacturing, ax manufacturing, typewriter manufacturing, and watch manufacturing.[192] In particular, the clock industry played a crucial role in diffusing mechanized production practices. More attuned to the dynamics of the civilian economy than the small arms manufacturers, clockmakers demonstrated that interchangeable manufacture could drastically increase sales and cut costs.[193] In his definitive study of the history of American interchangeable parts manufacture, David Hounshell concludes that "the sewing machine and other industries of the second half of the 19th century that borrowed small arms production techniques owed more to the clock industry than to firearms."[194]

Military investment and government contracting did not provide long-term sources of demand for interchangeable manufacturing methods.[195] Over the course of the IR-2, the small arms industry's contribution to American manufacturing declined, totaling less than 0.3 percent of value added in American industry from 1850 to 1940.[196] Thus, arguments centered on military investment neglect that the spread of the American system, not its initial incubation, is the focal point for understanding how the IR-2 catalyzed an economic power transition.[197]

Another threat-based argument posits that countries that face more external threats than internal rivalries will achieve more technological success.[198] In the IR-2 case, however, the United States was relatively isolated from external conflicts, while the United Kingdom and Germany faced many more threats (including each other).[199] Moreover, the United States was threatened

192. Hoke 1990.

193. Hounshell 1985, 50–61. Clockmaking also inspired an earlier generation of machine tool builders in Britain (Musson and Robinson 1969).

194. Hounshell 1985, 51.

195. Federal contracts, including during the Civil War, were only "temporarily sustaining" for American manufacturers (Scranton 1997, 76–77).

196. Deyrup 1948, 6.

197. The military did aid the American system's diffusion through the Navy's investments in mechanical engineering education. Officers from the Naval Engineer Corps played a key role in helping various US educational institutions set up mechanical engineering programs (see Calvert 1967, 50).

198. Taylor 2016.

199. The Spanish-American War in 1898 is an exception, but it lasted one year and occurred late in the period.

more by internal rivalries than by external enemies at the beginning of the IR-2, as it had just experienced a civil war.[200] This argument therefore provides limited leverage in the IR-2 case.

VoC Explanations

What about the connection between America's particular type of capitalism and its economic rise? Rooted in the varieties of capitalism (VoC) tradition, one alternative explanation posits that the United States was especially suited to embrace the radical innovations of the IR-2 because it exhibited the characteristics of a liberal market economy (LME). GPT diffusion theory and VoC-based explanations clash most directly on points about skill formation. The latter's expectation that LMEs like the United States should excel at cultivating general skills could account for US leadership in GPT diffusion during this period.[201]

The empirical evidence casts doubt on this explanation. In the early twentieth century, the leading nations had fairly similar levels of enrollment rates in elementary and post-elementary education. In 1910, enrollment rates for children ages five to nineteen in the United States was about 12 percent lower than Britain's rate and only 3 percent higher than Germany's.[202] Years of education per worker increased by essentially the same proportion in both Britain (by a factor of 2.2) and the United States (by a factor of 2.3) between 1870 and 1929.[203] In terms of higher education expenditures per capita, the two countries were essentially tied.[204] Differences in the formation of general skills cannot account for the technological leadership of the United States in this period.[205]

Moreover, the degree to which the United States fully embraced the characteristics of LMEs is disputed. In the view of studies that position the United

200. Civil wars are categorized as "extreme cases" of high domestic tensions under creative insecurity theory (Taylor 2016, 238).

201. For claims that the United States benefited from a general advantage over Britain in human capital, see Crafts 1989, 35; Greasley and Oxley 1998b; Mankiw, Romer, and Weil 1992, 432.

202. Goldin 2001, 265–66. In 1913, the average years of primary and secondary schooling for the fifteen- to sixty-four-year-old age group was higher in Britain than in the United States (Greasley and Oxley 1998b, 185).

203. Romer 1996, 202.

204. US Bureau of Education 1901, 807–8; US Bureau of Education 1898, 206.

205. In the interwar period, the American "high school movement" would open up a substantial gap in postsecondary and college/university enrollment between the United States and even leading European nations (Goldin 2001, 266–69; Goldin and Katz 2008).

States as a model for managerial capitalism in this period, US industrial governance structures enabled the rise of giant managerialist firms.[206] This approach primarily sees America's rise to industrial preeminence through the most visible actors in the American system of political economy: oligopolies in the automobile, steel, and electrical industries. There was significant diversity, however, in firm structure. Though many giant corporations did grow to take advantage of economies of scale and capital requirements in some mass-produced goods (such as automobiles), networks of medium-sized firms still dominated important segments of these new industries, such as the production of electric motors. One-third of the fifty largest manufacturing plants in the United States made custom and specialty goods.[207] From 1899 to 1909, sectors that relied on batch and custom production, including machine tools, accounted for one-third of value added in manufacturing.[208] No specific brand of capitalism fulfilled the demands of production across all domains.[209]

Case-Specific Factors

Another traditional explanation highlights American natural resource abundance as a key factor in transatlantic differences in mechanization. Compared to its European competitors, the benefits to the United States derived from its endowment of natural resources, such as plentiful supplies of timber, biased its manufacturing processes toward standardized production.[210] "The American turn in the direction of mass production was *natural*," claims one influential study of diverging approaches to mechanization in this period.[211]

The extent to which natural resource endowments determined transatlantic differences in technological trajectories is disputed. Undeterred by natural resource differences, German engineers and industrialists frequently used American machine tools and imitated US production technology.[212] In fact,

---

206. Chandler 1977, 1990. LS accounts in international relations literature adopt this account; see, for example, Kim and Hart 2001.

207. Scranton 1997, 7.

208. US Bureau of the Census 1913, 40–43; see also Scranton 1997, 12.

209. Kitschelt 1991, 472.

210. Ames and Rosenberg 1968; Broadberry 1994; Habakkuk 1962.

211. Piore and Sabel 1984, 41, emphasis mine. A related set of case-specific alternative explanations is rooted in the premise that American demand for products was more homogenous, owing to the spread of transportation networks connecting a larger domestic market (Timmer, Veenstra, and Woltjer 2016, 875). I thank Mike Beckley for bringing this point to my attention.

212. Braun 1984; Nolan 1994; Timmer, Veenstra, and Woltjer 2016, 881–84.

around the early twentieth century, the level of machine intensity in German industries was catching up to the rate in American industries.[213] The US-Germany gap in mechanization was more about Germany's struggles in proficiently using advanced tools, not the choice of methods shaped by natural resource endowments. Crucially, skill formation and embedded knowledge about working with new machinery influenced the efficient utilization of American capital-intensive techniques.[214]

Summary

The standard version of the Second Industrial Revolution's geopolitical aftershocks highlights Germany's challenge to British power. Germany's relative economic rise, according to this account, derived from its advantage in industrial research and scientific infrastructure, which enabled it to capture the gains from new industries such as electricity and chemicals. However, a range of indicators emphasize that it was the United States, not Germany, that surpassed Britain in productivity leadership during this period. The US industrial ascent in the IR-2 illustrates that dominating innovation in leading sectors is not the crucial mechanism in explaining the rise and fall of great powers. Britain's decline was not a failure of innovation but of diffusion. As the renowned economist Sir William Arthur Lewis once mused, "Britain would have done well enough if she merely imitated German and American innovations."[215]

Indeed, the IR-2 case further supports the conclusion that capacity to widely diffuse GPTs is the key driver of long-term growth differentials. The US success in broadening its talent base in mechanical engineering proved critical for its relative advantage in adapting machine tools across a broad range of industries. Like all GPT trajectories, this process was a protracted one, but it aligns better with when the United States surpassed Britain in productive leadership than the more dramatic breakthroughs in chemicals, electricity, and automobiles. To further investigate how the LS mechanism breaks down and why the GPT mechanism holds up, we turn to the high-tech competition in the twentieth century between the United States and Japan—or what some label the Third Industrial Revolution.

213. Ristuccia and Tooze 2013.
214. Timmer, Veenstra, and Woltjer 2016, 896–97.
215. Lewis 1957, 583.

5

Japan's Challenge in the
Third Industrial Revolution

IN THE TWO previous cases, an industrial revolution preceded a shift in global leadership. Britain established its economic dominance in the early nineteenth century, and the United States took the mantle in the late nineteenth century. During the last third of the twentieth century (1960–2000), the technological environment underwent a transformation akin to the First and Second Industrial Revolutions. A cluster of information technologies, connected to fundamental breakthroughs in computers and semiconductors, disrupted the foundations of many industries. The terms "Third Industrial Revolution" (IR-3) and "Information Age" came to refer to an epochal shift from industrial systems to information-based and computerized systems.[1] Amid this upheaval, many thought Japan would follow in the footsteps of Britain and the United States to become the "Number One" technological power.[2]

Of the countries racing to take advantage of the IR-3, Japan's remarkable advances in electronics and information technology garnered a disproportionate share of the spotlight. "The more advanced economies, with Japan taking the lead in one industry after another, [were] restructuring their economies around the computer and other high tech industries of the third industrial

---

1. For a review of work on the history of the IR-3, see Galambos 2013, 2–4. As was the case with drawing temporal bounds around the IR-1 and IR-2, the periodization of the IR-3 is disputed. Rostow (1985, 285), for instance, marks the second half of the 1970s as the start of a new industrial revolution.

2. The most famous example is Vogel 1979. As Drezner (2001, 18) writes, "In 1985, Japan was the only credible challenger to US technological hegemony, and was thought to be an ideal candidate to overtake the United States."

revolution," Gilpin wrote.[3] In the late 1980s and early 1990s, a torrent of works bemoaned the loss of US technological leadership to Japan.[4] In a best-selling book on US-Japan relations, Clyde Prestowitz, a former US trade negotiator, declared, "Japan has . . . become the undisputed world economic champion."[5]

Japan's dominance in the IR-3's leading sectors was perceived as a threat to international security and to US overall leadership of the international system.[6] Former secretary of state Henry Kissinger and other prominent thinkers warned that Japan would convert its economic strength into threatening military power.[7] Per a 1990 *New York Times* poll, 58 percent of Americans believed that Japan's economic power was more of a threat to American security than the Soviet Union's military power.[8]

Historical precedents loomed over these worries. US policymakers feared that falling behind Japan in key technologies would, like relative declines experienced by previous leading powers, culminate in an economic power transition. Paul Kennedy and other historically minded thinkers likened the US position in the 1980s to Britain's backwardness a century earlier: two industrial hegemons on the brink of losing their supremacy.[9] Often alluding to the LS mechanism, these comparisons highlighted Japan's lead in specific industries that were experiencing significant technological disruption, such as consumer electronics and semiconductors. As David Mowery and Nathan Rosenberg wrote in 1991, "Rapidly growing German domination of dyestuffs helped to propel that country into the position of the strongest continental industrial power. The parallels to the Japanese strategy in electronics in recent decades are striking."[10]

3. Gilpin 1991, 15.

4. Dertouzos, Solow, and Lester 1989; Nelson and Wright 1992, 1932. Analyzing the situation from a long-wave perspective, Freeman, Clark, and Soete (1982, 166, 188) believed that Japan would become the leader of a new wave of transformative innovations.

5. Prestowitz 1989, 2.

6. Gilpin 1996, 428; Huntington 1993, 71–82; Rostow 1985. Regarding competition between the United States and Japan in leading sectors, one *International Organization* article concluded, "The fate of systemic leadership, in turn, may well depend on the extent to which there are clear winners and losers within the productive core" (Thompson 1990, 232).

7. In 1987, Kissinger stated that Japan's decision to lift a ceiling on military spending "makes it inevitable that Japan will emerge as a major military power in the not-too-distant future" (Kissinger 1987); see also Gilpin 1996, 428.

8. Oreskes 1990, cited in Mastanduno 1991, 74.

9. Freeman 1987; Kennedy 1987, 529; Nelson and Wright 1992; Piore and Sabel 1984.

10. Mowery and Rosenberg 1991, 80.

Many voices called for the United States to mimic Japan's *keiretsu* system of industrial organization and proactive industrial policy, which they viewed as crucial to the rising power's success with leading sectors.[11] Kennedy's *The Rise and Fall of the Great Powers* attributed Japan's surge in global market shares of high-tech industries to R&D investments and the organizing role of the Ministry of International Trade and Industry (MITI).[12] These claims about the basis of Japan's leadership in the information revolution relied on LS product cycles as the filter for the most important institutional factors.

The feared economic power transition, however, never occurred. To be sure, Japanese firms did take dominant positions in key segments of high-growth industries like semiconductors and consumer electronics. Additionally, the Japanese economy did grow at a remarkable pace, averaging an annual 2.4 percent increase in total factor productivity (TFP) between 1983 and 1991. However, Japan's TFP growth stalled at an average of 0.2 percent per year in the 1990s—a period known as its "lost decade." By 2002, the per capita GDP gap between Japan and the United States was larger than it had been in 1980.[13] Becoming the world's leading producer in high-tech industries did not catalyze Japan's overtaking of the United States as the leading economy.

The IR-3 case is particularly damaging for LS-based explanations. Japan took advantage of the IR-3's opportunities by cornering the market in new, technologically progressive industries, fulfilling the conditions posited by the LS mechanism for Japan to become the foremost economic power. Yet, as the case study evidence will reveal, an economic power transition did not occur, even though all these conditions were present. The Japanese challenge to American technological leadership in the last third of the twentieth century therefore primarily functions as a deviant, or falsifying, case for the LS mechanism.[14]

By contrast, the IR-3 case does not undermine the GPT mechanism. Since Japan did *not* lead the United States in the diffusion of general-purpose information technologies, the conditions for an economic power transition under the GPT mechanism were absent in the IR-3. Since there could be many reasons why an economic power transition does not occur, the absence of a mechanism in a negative case provides limited leverage for explaining how

11. Freeman, Clark, and Soete 1982, 198–99; Johnson 1982; Prestowitz 1989.
12. Kennedy 1987, 462–63, 525.
13. Jin 2016.
14. Beach and Pedersen 2018, 861–63.

technology-driven economic power transitions occur. Still, the IR-3 case evidence will show that LS theory expects an outcome that does not occur—a US-Japan economic power transition—in part because it fails to account for the relative success of the United States in GPT diffusion. This advantage stemmed from its superior ability to cultivate the computer engineering talent necessary to advance computerization. In that regard, this deviant case can help form better mechanism-based explanations.[15]

Surprisingly, few scholars have revisited claims that Japan's leadership in leading sectors meant that it was on its way to economic preeminence.[16] Decades of hindsight bring not just perspective but also more sources to pore over. Revised estimates and the greater availability of data help paint a more granular picture of how the US-Japan productivity gap evolved in this period. To narrow down the crucial technological trajectories, I pieced together histories of semiconductors and other key technologies, comparative histories of technological development in the United States and Japan, and general economic histories of the IR-3. In addition, I leveraged bibliometric techniques to estimate the number of universities in both countries that could supply a baseline quality of software engineering education. Surveys on computer utilization by Japanese agencies, presentations on computer science education by Japanese and American analysts at international meetings, documents from the Edward A. Feigenbaum Papers collection, and back issues of *Nikkei Computer* (日経コンピュータ) at the Stanford University East Asia Library all helped flesh out the state of GPT skill infrastructure in the IR-3.

The evaluation of the GPT and LS mechanisms against historical evidence from the IR-3 proceeds as follows. The chapter first makes clear that a US-Japan economic power transition did not take place. Subsequently, it reviews and organizes the technological breakthroughs of the IR-3 into candidate leading sectors and GPTs. It then examines whether all the components of the GPT or LS mechanism were present. Since the outcome did not occur in this case, it is important to trace where the mechanisms break down. All the aspects of the LS mechanism were present in the IR-3, but the GPT mechanism was not operational because Japan fell behind the United States in diffusing information technologies across a broad range of sectors. Based on this evidence, the next section explains why institutional explanations rooted in LS

15. Beach and Pedersen 2019, 102.
16. One exception is Borrus and Zysman 1997.

trajectories are unconvincing. Before turning to alternative factors and explanations, the chapter analyzes whether GPT skill infrastructure was a factor in sustained US technological leadership.

A Power Transition Unfulfilled: Japan's Rise Stagnates

In a 1983 article for *Parade*, the Pulitzer Prize–winning journalist David Halberstam described Japan's industrial ascent as America's "most difficult challenge for the rest of the century" and "a more intense competition than the previous political-military competition with the Soviet Union."[17] By the end of the century, however, the possibility of Japan displacing the United States as the technological hegemon was barely considered, let alone feared.[18] The economic power transition that accompanied the IR-1 and IR-2 did not materialize in this case. Indeed, most indicators presented a clear trend: Japan's economy catches up in the 1980s, stagnates in the 1990s, and ultimately fails to overtake the US economy in productivity leadership.

GDP PER-CAPITA INDICATORS

During the three decades after 1960, Japan's economy experienced remarkable growth, reaching a GDP per capita in 1990 that was 81 percent of the US mark that year. In the following ten years, known as Japan's "lost decade," Japan's growth in GDP per capita stalled. By 2007, Japan's GDP per capita had dropped back down to 73 percent of that of the United States (figure 5.1).

INDUSTRIALIZATION INDICATORS

Comparative industrialization statistics tell a similar story. In terms of global manufacturing output, Japan gained on the United States through the 1970s and 1980s and nearly matched the United States, at 20 percent of global manufacturing output, in the early 1990s. Japan's share of global manufacturing output subsequently declined to around 10 percent in 2010, while the US share

---

17. Halberstam 1983, 4–5. Though the rivalry between the United States and the Soviet Union also raised concerns about a power transition, the Soviet Union was not at the forefront of advances in electronics and information technologies. Thus, this rivalry is less relevant for tracing the mechanism that connects technological revolutions and economic power transitions.

18. Drezner 2001, 19.

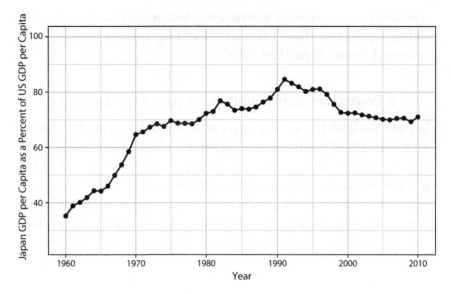

FIGURE 5.1. Japan's Catch-up to the United States in GDP per Capita Stalls in the 1990s. *Note*: Real GDP per capita in 2011$ prices. *Source*: Maddison Project Database, version 2020 (Bolt and van Zanden 2020).

increased in the 1990s and held at 20 percent until 2010.[19] In manufacturing industries, Japan's labor productivity growth from 1995 to 2004 averaged only 3.3 percent, whereas the United States averaged 6.1 percent in the same metric.[20]

PRODUCTIVITY INDICATORS

Productivity statistics also reveal a general trend of convergence without over-taking. From a total factor productivity of just half that of the United States in 1955, Japan's TFP grew steadily. By 1991, the productivity gap between the United States and Japan was only 5 percent. As was the case with the GDP per capita and industrialization figures, Japan's productivity growth then slowed, and the gap between the United States and Japan widened during the 1990s (figure 5.2). Throughout this decade, Japan averaged just 0.2 percent annual

19. R. Baldwin 2016, 87–88.

20. These data come from the OECD Structural Analysis Statistics (STAN) database, which has figures on Japanese productivity growth by industry only from 1995 through 2016 (Baily, Bosworth, and Doshi 2020, 18).

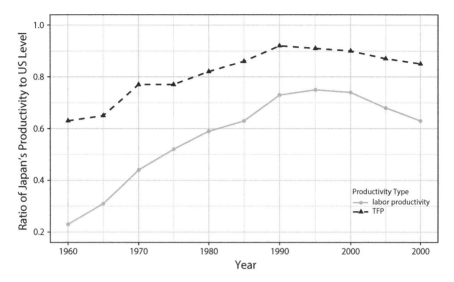

FIGURE 5.2. Japan's Catch-up to the United States in Productivity Stalls in the 1990s. *Source*: Jorgenson, Nomura, and Samuels 2018, 18.

TFP growth.[21] By 2009, Japan's TFP dropped to only 83 percent of the US figure. The US-Japan labor productivity gap followed a similar course.[22]

Key Technological Changes in the IR-3

Parsing through the different trajectories of technological change is a necessary first step to determine whether the LS and GPT mechanisms were operative in this period. This task is complicated by the tremendous technological changes that emerged in the IR-3, such as the first microprocessor (1971), the production of recombinant DNA (1972), the VHS format for video recording (1976), and the first personal computer (1981). Guided by past scholars' efforts to map the key nodes of the information revolution as well as analytic measures for leading sectors and GPTs, this section takes stock of key technological drivers that affected the US-Japan economic power balance.

21. Comin 2010.

22. Jorgenson, Nomura, and Samuels 2018, 18. Japan's average capital productivity did maintain a small lead over US capital productivity, according to the figures of these authors. As outlined earlier, I take TFP and labor productivity as comprehensive measures of productivity growth. Moreover, the capital productivity indicators do not support that Japan overtook the United States during this period, as Japan's capital productivity was already higher than US capital productivity in 1960 and 1970.

Candidate Leading Sectors

Amid a shifting technological landscape, the most likely sources of LS trajectories were information and communications technologies (ICTs). Certainly, scholars have highlighted technological developments in a wide range of industries as possible leading sectors, including lasers and robotics.[23] Nonetheless, Japan's success in the computer, consumer electronics, and semiconductor industries was most relevant for its prospects of overtaking the United States as the foremost economic power. In each of these three leading sectors, Japan dominated the production of key components.[24]

All three relatively new industries achieved extraordinary growth off the back of technological breakthroughs, fulfilling the established criteria for leading sectors. In the US economy during the 1980s, computer and data-processing services ranked as the fastest-growing industries in terms of jobs added.[25] After Japan's MITI identified semiconductors and computers as strategic industries in 1971, both industries experienced extremely high growth rates in the next two decades.[26] The US electronics industry also experienced a remarkable surge during the late twentieth century, growing thirty times faster than other manufacturing industries by some estimates.[27] These trends in computers and electronics held across advanced industrialized countries.[28]

Candidate GPTs

Given that the IR-3 is often known as the "information revolution," clusters of ICT innovations naturally serve as the most likely sources of GPT trajectories. Efforts to map this era's GPTs specifically highlight computers,[29]

23. Modelski and Thompson (1996, 213) compiled leading sectors proposed by eleven technology wave experts during the 1979–1990 period. The resulting list included a diverse range of technologies, including biotechnology, computers, energy, food, or environment technology, lasers, microelectronics, robotics, scientific instruments, telecommunications, and watch industries.

Modelski and Thompson 1996, 213.

24. Inman and Burton 1990; Kennedy 1987, 525; Kitschelt 1991, 480; Mastanduno 1991, 101–2.

25. Plunkert 1990, 10.

26. Calder 1981.

27. Baily and Bosworth 2014, 5–6.

28. Rausch 1998.

29. David 1990; Lipsey, Carlaw, and Bekar 2005.

semiconductors,[30] and the internet.[31] Each of these technological domains exhibited great scope for improvement and complementarities with other technologies.

Because advances in computers, semiconductors, and the internet were all closely connected, I group technological developments in these three domains under "computerization," the process in which computers take over tasks such as the storage and management of information. This is consistent with other studies that identify the general category of ICT as the GPT operative in this period.[32] The growing prevalence of software-intensive systems enabled computers to become more general-purpose. Computerization also benefited from advances in both semiconductors, which reduced costs for investments in IT equipment, and the internet, which connected computers in efficient networks.[33]

Sources of LS and GPT Trajectories

In sum, the IR-3's candidate leading sectors and GPTs all revolved around ICTs (table 5.1). Other technical advances in lasers, new sources of energy, and biotechnology also drew attention as possible sources of LS and GPT trajectories. I do not trace developments in these technologies because their potential was largely unrealized, at least within the context of US-Japan economic competition during the IR-3.

Though candidate leading sectors and GPTs converge on ICTs, they diverge on the key trajectories. The GPT perspective emphasizes the process by which firms transfer tasks and activities to computers. In contrast, LS accounts spotlight the growth of key industry verticals. For example, the consumer electronics industry fits the mold of previous candidate leading sectors like automobiles and cotton textiles, which were large and fast-growing but limited in their linkages to other industries. Taking stock of candidate leading sectors and GPTs merely functions as a preliminary filter. The rest of the chapter will

30. Bresnahan and Trajtenberg 1995.

31. Gordon 2005, 12, 22; Harris 1998; Lipsey, Carlaw, and Bekar 2005.

32. These studies rank ICT alongside electricity as the two most important GPTs in history (David 1990; Jovanovic and Rousseau 2005).

33. The commercialization of the microprocessor, a type of integrated circuit, facilitated the spread of desktop computers across many functions and industries. In 1994 computer applications accounted for 52 percent of end-use demand for commercial sales of integrated circuits (Langlois and Steinmueller 1999, 53). The internet's spectacular expansion in the 1990s also extended networks of computing machines (Langlois 2013, 152).

TABLE 5.1. Key Sources of Technological Trajectories in the IR-3

Candidate Leading Sectors	Candidate GPTs
Computer industry	Computerization
Consumer electronics industry	
Semiconductor industry	

further flesh out the differences between the LS- and GPT-based explanations of how these technologies affected the US-Japan economic rivalry.

GPT vs. LS Mechanisms: The (Non) Spread of ICTs across Japan's Economy

In both the IR-1 and IR-2 cases, a technological revolution sparked a shift in global economic leadership. The case analyses aimed to determine whether the historical evidence fit better with observable implications derived from the GPT or LS mechanism. Revolutionary technological breakthroughs also occurred in the IR-3, but an economic power transition never occurred. Thus, if the case study reveals that Japan dominated innovation in the computer, consumer electronics, and semiconductor industries, then this would provide disconfirming evidence against the LS mechanism. Likewise, if the historical evidence shows that Japan led the way in computerization during this period, this would undermine GPT diffusion theory.

LS Mechanism Present: Japan Dominates the Production of Key ICTs

A bevy of evidence establishes that the LS mechanism was operative during the IR-3. From the mid-twentieth century through the 1980s, Japan captured a growing global market in new industries tied to major technological discoveries in semiconductors, consumer electronics, and computers. In dynamic random-access memory (DRAM) chips, one of the highest-volume verticals in the semiconductor industry, Japanese firms controlled 76 percent of the global market share.[34] By one US federal interagency working group estimate, from 1980 to 1987 the United States lost the lead to Japan in more than 75 percent of critical semiconductor technologies.[35]

34. Vogel 2013, 351; see also Pollack 1982; Kitschelt 1991, 485–86.
35. Herz 1987.

Japanese industry also gained competitive advantages in consumer electronics. From 1984 to 1990, US firms lost global market share in thirty-five of thirty-seven electronics categories as Japanese firms took over the production of many electronic products.[36] Japan occupied dominant shares of global production of color televisions and DVDs.[37] It was also the first economy to commercialize high-definition television (HDTV) systems, a highly touted part of the consumer electronics market.[38]

A similar trend held in computers, especially in computer hardware components like flat panel displays.[39] The US trade balance in computers with Japan turned from a surplus in 1980 into a $6 billion deficit by 1988.[40] According to the *Yearbook of World Electronics Data*, in 1990 Japan's share of global computer production eclipsed the share held by the United States, which had previously led the world.[41]

Comparisons of LS growth rates also indicate that Japan was poised to overtake the United States as the economic leader. In an *International Organization* article published in 1990, Thompson posited that average annual growth rates in leading sectors across major economies heralded shifts in economic leadership. Over the nineteenth century, Britain's growth rate in leading sectors peaked in the 1830s before flattening between 1860 and 1890, a period when the United States and Germany outstripped Britain in LS growth rates.[42] Crucially, Thompson's data showed that Japan outpaced the United States in growth rates within leading sectors from 1960 to 1990.[43] Linking these historical trends, Thompson identified Japan as America's main competitor for "systemic leadership."[44]

Comprehensive assessments of Japan's relative industrial strength support this account of LS growth rates. US government, academic, and industry entities issued a plethora of reports warning of Japan's growing global market share

36. Gover 1993, 61; see also Tyson 1993, 24.

37. Freeman, Clark, and Soete 1982, 105; Vogel 2013, 351.

38. Inman and Burton 1990; Office of Technology Assessment 1990, 27.

39. In 1997, Japan held 100 percent of the global market share in liquid crystal display panels, which are used for computer monitors (Vogel 2013, 351). In the early 1990s Japan also led in producing laptops and other portable computers, which were the fastest-growing markets at the time (Longworth 1992).

40. Ferguson 1990.

41. Kraemer and Dedrick 2001, 9.

42. Thompson 1990, 221, 226.

43. Thompson (1990, 230) calculates LS growth rates based on indicators for production in chemicals, steel, motor vehicles, electricity, electronics, and aerospace. Thompson's measure of electronics is production of semiconductors.

44. Ibid., 232.

and exports in key technologies. One review of six such reports, all published between 1987 and 1991, found a growing consensus that US capabilities in many of these technologies were declining relative to Japan's.[45] A 1990 US Department of Commerce report on trends in twelve emerging technologies, including supercomputers, advanced semiconductor devices, and digital imaging technology, projected that the United States would lag behind Japan in most of these technologies before 2000.[46] The 1989 MIT Commission on Industrial Productivity's *Made in America: Regaining the Productive Edge* serves as a particularly useful barometer of Japan's position in leading sectors.[47] *Made in America* argued that the United States was losing out to Japan in eight manufacturing sectors, including consumer electronics, semiconductors, and computers. As business historian Richard Langlois summarizes, "By the mid-1980s, by most accounts, America had 'lost' consumer electronics and was in imminent danger of losing semiconductors and computers."[48]

Some argued that Japan's advantage in these leading sectors was rooted in certain institutional arrangements. Observers regularly pointed to Japan's *keiretsu* system, which was structured around large, integrated business groups, as the key institutional factor in its success in high-tech industries. The MIT Commission's *Made in America* report, for instance, questioned whether the US system of industrial organization could match up against "much stronger and better organized Japanese competition."[49] This aligned with a common narrative in the mid-1980s that "American firms should become more like Japanese firms."[50]

Others pointed to Japan's industrial policy, coordinated by MITI, as the key institutional competency that explained Japan's success in leading sectors. Academics and policymakers pushed for the United States to imitate Japan's industrial policy approach, which they perceived as effective because of MITI's ability to strategically coordinate R&D investments in key technologies.[51] For instance, scholars regarded the "Fifth Generation Project," a national initiative launched by MITI in 1982, as a stepping-stone to Japan's building of the world's

---

45. Mogee 1991, 24–25.

46. US Department of Commerce 1990.

47. Dertouzos, Solow, and Lester 1989. Organized by a group of leading MIT economists and political scientists, this massive effort drew from 550 interviews and visits to over 200 corporations across the United States, Europe, and Japan, making it arguably the most influential of all the publications about America's industrial decline in this period (Inkster 1991, 159).

48. Langlois 2013, 159.

49. Dertouzos, Solow, and Lester 1989, 20, cited in Langlois and Steinmueller 1999, 20.

50. Langlois 2013, 159.

51. The most influential account is Johnson 1982; see also Inman and Burton 1990.

most advanced computers.[52] The American aversion to industrial policy and a decentralized economic policymaking apparatus, by comparison, was alleged to be detrimental to innovation in the IR-3's new technologies.

By the turn of the millennium, such arguments were no longer being put forward. Despite capturing key LS industries and rapidly catching up to the United States in the 1980s, Japan did not ultimately overtake the United States as the lead economy. Contrary to the expected outcome of the LS mechanism, Japan's control of critical sectors in semiconductors and consumer electronics did not translate into strong, sustained economic growth. This outcome challenges the LS mechanism's validity in the IR-3 case.

An Absent GPT Mechanism: The United States Leads Japan in ICT Diffusion

Does evidence from the IR-3 also discredit the GPT mechanism? If the components of the GPT mechanism, like the LS mechanism, were present during this period, this would weaken the explanatory power of GPT diffusion theory. However, in contrast to its success in key leading sectors, Japan lagged in adopting computerized technologies. Thus, GPT diffusion theory would not expect Japan to have overtaken the United States in the IR-3.

To account for sustained US economic leadership in the IR-3, this section traces the developments of the IR-3 in the United States and Japan across the three dimensions that differentiate GPT from LS trajectories. First, relative to the LS mechanism, the impact timeframes of the IR-3's technological breakthroughs are more elongated. Developments in ICTs did not spread to a wide range of economic applications until the 1990s. Second, though Japan excelled in the production of computers and electronics, it fell behind in the general pace of computerization across the economy. Lastly, Japan's advantages were concentrated in a narrow range of ICT-producing industries, whereas the United States benefited from broad-based productivity growth.

IMPACT TIMEFRAME

The advance of computerization, like past GPT trajectories, demanded a prolonged period of organizational adaptation and complementary innovations. It is reasonable to date the computerization GPT's emergence as the year

52. Kennedy 1987, 462.

1971—the year when Intel introduced the microprocessor, which greatly expanded the functionalities of computers.[53] It was also the year when the share of information technology equipment and software reached 1 percent in the net capital stocks of the median sector in the US economy.[54] Before then, during the 1960s, mainframe computers powered by integrated circuits serviced only a limited range of commercial purposes, such as producing bank statements and managing airline reservations. With the internet's rise in the 1990s, new information and communication networks further spread computerization to different business models, such as e-commerce.[55] Alongside this stream of complementary technical advances, firms needed time to build up their computer capital stock and reorganize their business processes to match the needs of information technology.[56]

Computers traveled a gradual and slow road to widespread use. By the late 1980s, many observers bemoaned the computer revolution's failure to induce a surge of productivity growth. In 1987, the renowned economist Robert Solow distilled this "productivity paradox" in a famous quip: "We see the computers everywhere but in the productivity statistics."[57] A decade later, however, the growing adoption of information technology triggered a remarkable surge in US productivity growth.[58] It took some time, but the American economy did eventually see the computers in the productivity statistics.

The landscape of US-Japan technology competition looks very different when accounting for the elongated lag from computerization's arrival to its widespread diffusion. Japan's control over key segments of ICT production in the 1970s and 1980s did not correspond to an advantage in GPT diffusion. A more patient outlook illuminates that the delayed impact of computerization aligns with when the United States extended its productivity lead over Japan. After 1995, while Japan's economic rise stalled, labor and total factor productivity grew rapidly for a decade in the United States. The difference was that the United States benefited greatly from an ICT-driven productivity acceleration.[59]

---

53. Bruland and Mowery 2006, 369. Langlois (2013, 155) recaps: "By the early 1980s, a microcomputer (personal computer) costing $3,500 could do the work of a $10,000 stand-alone word processor, while at the same time keeping track of the books like a $100,000 minicomputer and amusing the kids with space aliens like a 25-cents-a-game arcade machine."

54. Jovanovic and Rousseau 2005.

55. Gordon 2016, 441–42.

56. Brynjolfsson, Rock, and Syverson 2017, 23–25.

57. David 1990, 355.

58. Crafts 2002; Gordon 2016, 576; Oliner and Sichel 2000.

59. Fueki and Kawamoto 2009, 325; Crafts 2002.

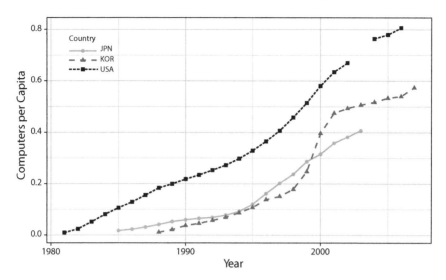

FIGURE 5.3. The US-Japan Computerization Gap Widens in the 1990s.
Source: Milner and Solstad 2021; Comin 2010, 381.

PHASE OF RELATIVE ADVANTAGE

If the GPT mechanism was operative for Japan's rise in the IR-3, Japan should have led the United States in computerization. Though Japan continued to contest US leadership in the production of certain computer architectures and devices, it failed to keep up with the United States in the adoption of computers across industries. As figure 5.3 reveals, the gap between the United States and Japan in computerization widened in the 1990s. In fact, South Korea, which lagged behind Japan in generating new innovations in computer systems, surpassed Japan in its computer usage rate during the 1990s. Taken together, these indicators suggest that Japan's problem was with GPT diffusion, not innovation.

The pathway by which ICTs drove the US-Japan productivity gap is particularly revealing. In sectors that *produced* ICTs, Japan's TFP acceleration was similar to the US trajectory; however, in sectors that intensively *used* IT, Japan's TFP growth lagged far behind that of its rival.[60] In particular, US ICT-using service industries adapted better to computerization. In terms of labor productivity growth in these industries, the United States experienced the strongest improvement out of all OECD countries from the first half of the 1990s

---

60. Fukao and Tsutomu 2007; Jorgenson and Motohashi 2005.

to the second half of the decade.[61] The contribution of ICT-using services to Japan's labor productivity growth, by contrast, declined from the first half to the second half of the decade.[62]

Japan eventually adopted the GPT trajectory associated with ICT. Like all advanced economies at the frontier, Japan could draw from the same technology pool as America. Using a growth accounting framework that accounts for cyclical factors, Takuji Fueki and Takuji Kawamoto trace Japan's post-2000 resurgence in TFP growth to the extension of the ICT revolution to a broader range of IT-using sectors.[63] By then, however, Japan was at least five years behind the United States in taking advantage of computerization.

BREADTH OF GROWTH

Alongside the dispersion of ICTs throughout the US economy, the sources of productivity growth also spread out. In the United States, spillovers from ICT advances, especially in services, contributed to economy-wide TFP growth. Industry-level patterns of TFP growth reveal that US productivity growth became noticeably more broad-based after 1995, a trend that accelerated further after 2000.[64]

In contrast, Japan's advantages in the IR-3 were concentrated in a narrow range of sectors. After 1995, Japanese productivity growth remained localized, only transitioning to a more broad-based pattern after 2000.[65] Michael Porter's exhaustive account of national competitiveness across leading economies describes Japan as a "study in contrasts," with some of the most internationally competitive industries found side by side with some of the most uncompetitive.[66] The hype over Japan's success in leading sectors induced some analysts to generalize from a few exceptional industrial sectors while overlooking developments in struggling sectors.[67]

61. Moe 2009, 219; Pilat, Lee, and van Ark 2002, 60–61. The same comparison could be made between the United States and European countries, which were also able to keep pace with the United States with respect to productivity gains in IT-producing sectors but not in ICT-using sectors (Bloom, Sadun, and Van Reenen 2012).

62. For Japan, this figure declined from just over 0.6 percent to under 0.2 percent. For the United States, the figure increased from just over 0.2 percent to above 1.2 percent (Pilat, Lee, and van Ark 2002, 61).

63. Fueki and Kawamoto 2009.

64. Basu and Fernald 2007; Inklaar and Timmer 2007.

65. Wirkierman 2014.

66. Porter 1990, 394.

67. Kitschelt 1991, 454.

LS Mechanisms and "Wintelism"

Some international political economy scholars divide trends in US competitiveness into a phase of relative decline in the leading sectors of the 1980s (consumer electronics, computer hardware, and parts of the semiconductor industry) and a period of resurgence in the new leading sector of the 1990s (software electronics).[68] This explanation for why Japan's LS advantage did not convert into an economic power transition could conceivably restore credibility to the LS mechanism. However, even this generous interpretation fails to capture the dynamics of the IR-3.[69]

Consider one prominent line of LS-based thinking that emphasizes US advantages in adapting to "Wintelism," a type of industrial structure best suited for new advances in software electronics. Wintelism, a portmanteau of "Windows" and "Intel," refers to the transformation of the computer industry from a vertically integrated oligopoly into a horizontally segmented structure dominated by components providers with controlling architectural standards, such as Intel and Microsoft.[70] Compared to Japan, the US institutional environment was more supportive of horizontal, specialized value-chains in software electronics. It is put forward that Japan's inability to adapt to the Wintelist industrial paradigm explains why it was unable to overtake the United States as the leading economy.[71]

The Wintelism argument falls prey to general issues with the LS mechanism.[72] Like LS accounts of Japan's advantage in semiconductors and consumer electronics in the 1980s, the Wintelism argument still places too much value on ICT-producing industries. Capturing profit shares in the global software electronics industry is not the same as translating new advances in software electronics into economy-wide growth.[73] The pathway from new

68. Hart and Kim 2002. "Software electronics" refers to technologies related to computer architecture, such as computer software and semiconductor chip designs (ibid., 144).

69. The stricter interpretation is that Japan's dominance in the leading sectors of the 1980s, per the propositions of the LS mechanism, should have propelled it to economic leadership. The analysis from earlier sections, however, clearly shows that an economic power transition did not transpire.

70. Borrus and Zysman 1997, 162; Hart and Kim 2002, 1.

71. Borrus and Zysman 1997; Hart and Kim 2002; Kitschelt 1991.

72. To be fair, many discussions of Wintelism were oriented toward the outcome of success in new industries, not an economic power transition (Anchordoguy 1988, 2000). I am primarily critiquing the extension of the Wintelism argument to the latter outcome.

73. Outside of software electronics, Japanese firms still profited greatly from the modular industry architecture of the global electronics industry (Dedrick, Kraemer, and Linden 2010).

technologies to overall productivity growth involves much more than just the success of companies like Microsoft and Intel.

Indeed, as a GPT diffuses more widely, large monopolists may hinder co-ordination between the GPT and application sectors. Both Microsoft and Intel, for instance, often restricted sharing information about their technology roadmaps, thereby hindering complementary innovations and adoption of microelectronics in applications sectors such as automobiles. In fact, regulatory and technological forces were necessary to limit the influence of dominant firms and encourage the development of complementary technologies, which were crucial to widening the GPT trajectory of computerization.[74] It is conceivable that the United States could have achieved a greater rate of computerization if its computer industry had not been dominated by two firms that held key architectural standards.

Overall, hindsight is not kind to LS-based accounts of Japan's institutional advantages in the IR-3. While matching institutional competencies to particularly significant technological trajectories is a sound approach, the LS trajectory fails to capture how technological changes opened opportunities for an economic power transition. Japan's industrial structure and sectoral targeting policies reaped economic gains that were temporary and limited to specific industries.[75] To understand why the United States gained lasting and broad-based advantages from computerization, a different set of institutional complementarities must be explored.

Institutional Complementarities:
GPT Skill Infrastructure in the IR-3

In line with GPT diffusion theory, institutional adaptations that widened the base of computer engineering skills and knowledge proved crucial to the enduring technological leadership of the United States in the IR-3.[76] Comput-

74. Bresnahan and Malerba 2002, 50–52; Bresnahan and Trajtenberg 1995, 102. On the relationship between promoting greater technology diffusion and antitrust actions against Intel and Microsoft, see Wagner 1999.

75. Langlois and Steinmueller 1999, 20. The aforementioned Fifth Generation Project, for instance, oriented Japan's development of computers toward highly specialized machines rather than smaller, general-purpose architectures (Dujarric and Hagiu 2009).

76. To reiterate, evidence that the US advantage in ICT-related skill infrastructure accounted for its accelerated computerization does not necessarily validate the GPT mechanism in the IR-3 case. Strictly speaking, the causal mechanism I am investigating is one that connects significant technological breakthroughs to an economic power transition, not a non-occurrence

erization required not just innovators who created new software architectures but also programmers who undertook more routine software engineering tasks. It was the US ability to tap into a more expansive pool of the latter that fueled a more intensive pace of computerization than in Japan.

Widening the Base of Computer Engineers

GPTs generate an imbalance between the possibility of sweeping changes across many domains and the constraints of existing skills. Historically, engineering disciplines have developed procedures for adapting new GPT-linked knowledge across localized applications and expanded access to such knowledge to a broader set of individuals. Similarly, the key element of the American GPT skill infrastructure in the IR-3 was the development of a computer science discipline—the latest in a line of engineering disciplines that have emerged in the wake of GPTs.[77]

US education effectively adapted to changes in the computerization trajectory. The recognition of computer science as an independent discipline, as evidenced by the early and rapid growth of computer science departments in the United States, helped systematize the knowledge necessary for the spread of computerization.[78] Led by top universities and the Association of Computing Machinery (ACM), US institutions piloted new training programs in computer science. In 1968, the ACM published an influential and forward-looking curriculum that helped colleges organize their computing education.[79] These adaptations converted the practical experience from developers of new computer and software breakthroughs into general, accessible knowledge.[80]

The development of this GPT skill infrastructure met significant hurdles. In the 1970s, the US computer science discipline struggled to meet demands for software engineering education in the midst of conflicts over the right balance between theory-oriented learning and hands-on programming work.[81]

---

of a transition. Still, this case could lend further credence to the GPT mechanism, if one considers the IR-3 case as a close competition between the United States and Japan for economic leadership that resulted in the former establishing a clear edge.

77. Vona and Consoli 2014, 1402–3.

78. Steinmueller 1996, 42.

79. Tedre, Simon, and Malmi 2018.

80. Vona and Consoli 2014, 1404.

81. Tomayko 1998.

Reacting to this situation, the ACM's 1978 curriculum revision directed computer science toward application-based work, stating that programming exercises "provide a philosophy of discipline which pervades all of the course work."[82] Industry pressure and the US Department of Defense's Software Engineering Institute, a partnership established with Carnegie Mellon University in 1984, expanded the number of software engineering specializations at universities.[83] Teaching capacity was another inhibiting factor. Computer science departments had to limit course enrollments because they could not fill the faculty positions to meet exploding student demand, resulting in a decline in computer science enrollments in the mid-1980s.[84]

Though the process was not seamless, overall trends reflect the US success in widening the pool of engineering skills and knowledge for advancing computerization. From 1966 to 1996, the number of undergraduate computer science degrees awarded annually in the United States grew from 89 to about 24,500.[85] In 1986, at its peak during this period, computer science accounted for 12.5 percent of all science and engineering degrees awarded in the United States.[86] According to benchmarking efforts by the Working Group for Software Engineering Education and Training, US institutions accounted for about one-third of the world's bachelor's degree programs in software engineering in 2003.[87] Throughout this period, the United States also benefited from a system open to tapping foreign software engineering talent.[88]

82. Austing et al., 1979, 5.

83. Mead 2009; Tomayko 1998.

84. A big issue was the "eating our seed corn" effect: prospective faculty were taking more lucrative jobs in industry, with detrimental impacts on the supply of talent for industry in the long term (Roberts 2021).

85. National Science Board 2000, A-228.

86. National Research Council 1992, 241.

87. Hislop, Mancoridis, and Shankar 2003.

88. This intersects with my family's story. My dad emigrated from China to the United States in 1995 to study computer science. He has worked as a software engineer for more than twenty years. Compared to Japan, the United States was better able to draw upon a foreign supply of ICT talent through high-skilled immigration and software offshoring. Crucially, imported talent widened the base of software engineering talent in America. As one study concludes, "Relatively few of these imported experts may have been software architects of the highest order, capable of undertaking transformative innovation. However, creating, testing, and implementing software for IT innovation requires both fundamental innovators and programmers undertaking more routine and standardized kinds of software engineering. America's ability to tap into an increasingly abundant (and increasingly foreign) supply of the latter may have raised the productivity of the former and enabled American firms to outpace their rivals" (Arora, Branstetter, and Drev 2013, 772).

The US Comparative Advantage over Japan in GPT Skill Infrastructure

Did GPT skill infrastructure factor decisively in Japan's inability to keep pace with the United States in the diffusion of ICTs? Varying data reporting conventions, especially the fact that Japanese universities subsumed computer science under broader engineering fields, make it difficult to precisely quantify the US-Japan gap in software engineering skills.[89] One narrative that gained momentum in the late 1980s accredited Japan's success in high-tech manufacturing industries to its quantitative advantage in engineers. A National Science Foundation (NSF) report and two State of the Union addresses by President Ronald Reagan endorsed this belief.[90] For example, the NSF's 1997 special report on Japan's scientific and technological capabilities declared, "By 1994, with roughly one-half the population, Japan produced more engineering and computer science degrees at the undergraduate level than the United States."[91] Such statements blended computer science degrees with all categories of engineering education.

Computer science–specific data reveal the US edge in ICT human resources. According to data from Japan's Information Technology Promotion Agency, Japan awarded about 16,300 computer science and mathematics bachelor's degrees in 2009, while the United States awarded 63,300 of these types of degrees that same year.[92] One survey by the Japanese Information Technology Services Industry Association found that only 3.6 percent of college graduates who entered Japan's information service industry in April 1990 received their degree from a computer science department.[93] By counting immigrants entering computer-related professions and total university graduates in ICT software and hardware fields, one study estimated annual inflows into the US and Japanese ICT labor pools. In 1995, these inflows into the US ICT labor pool outpaced those in Japan by 68 percent. By 2001, this gap between

---

89. National Science Foundation 1997.

90. Kinmonth 1991, 328. In most cases, these were not apples-to-apples comparisons. While estimates of Japan's engineering talent included computer science, estimates of US engineering talent excluded a surging population of computer specialists, systems analysts, and programmers owing to different reporting conventions.

91. National Science Foundation 1997, 31.

92. Cole 2013, 9.

93. Baba, Takai, and Mizuta 1996, 111. By 2007, some 20 percent of software engineers in the United States possessed a graduate school degree, compared to just 10 percent in Japan (Nakata and Miyazaki, 2011, 100, cited in Cole 2013, 3).

the two countries' annual inflows of ICT talent had reached almost 300 percent.[94] Therefore, in the years when the US advantage in ICT diffusion was most pertinent, the skill gap between the United States and Japan in computer and software engineering talent grew even wider.[95]

Moreover, a computer science degree in Japan did not provide the same training as one in America. First, Japanese universities were slow to adapt to emerging trends in computer science. In both 1997 and 2007, the Information Processing Society of Japan modeled its computing curriculum revisions on American efforts that had been made six years earlier.[96] The University of Tokyo, Japan's leading university, did not establish a separate department of computer science until 1991, which was twenty-six years later than Stanford.[97] Overly centralized governance of universities also inhibited the development of computer science as an independent discipline in Japan.[98] As Jeffrey Hart and Sangbae Kim concluded in 2002, "The organizational and disciplinary flexibility of US universities in computer science has not been matched in any of the competing economies."[99]

Software engineering presented a particular challenge for Japan. In 1988, the Japanese-language industry journal *Nikkei Computer* surveyed six thousand Japanese firms that used office computers. Situated outside the computer industry, these firms were involved in a broad range of fields, including materials manufacturing, finance, services, government, and education. More than 80 percent of the responding companies disclosed shortages of software programmers and designers.[100] On average, outside firms provided one-quarter

94. Arora, Branstetter, and Drev 2013, 771. These researchers estimate inflows into the ICT talent pool by first aggregating bachelor's, master's, and PhD-level graduates in IT software- and hardware-related disciplines. Then, for the US ICT labor force, they include H1-B immigrants entering computer-related professions. For Japan, they assume that half of all foreign workers newly admitted to Japan as "researchers," "engineers," or "intracompany transferees" are employed in IT industries—a generous assumption that probably overestimates the annual inflows into Japan's ICT talent pool.

95. Many studies attribute Japan's delayed adoption of computerization to its chronic shortages of software engineers (Arora, Branstetter, and Drev 2013; Cole 2013; Cusumano 1991, 52, 130, 464; Moe 2007, 221).

96. Baba, Takai, and Mizuta 1993, 27–28.

97. Cole 2013, 8.

98. Ibid., 9–10; Kitschelt 1991, 482.

99. Hart and Kim 2002, 10.

100. *Nikkei Computer* 1988, 80. For a similar survey conducted by *Nikkei Computer* three years prior, see *Nikkei Computer* 1985, 55–90. I am very grateful to Dr. Regan Kao, head of Stanford University's East Asia Library Special Collections, for assistance with locating back issues of *Nikkei Computer* from 1981 through 1993.

of their information technology personnel, and their reliance on outsourcing was magnified for programmers, system designers, and application managers.[101] A nonprofit foundation for ICT development in Japan reported similar barriers to computer utilization in 1991. The survey found that companies relied heavily on computer personnel, especially software engineers, dispatched temporarily from other organizations.[102] Small and medium-sized software departments, which could not afford to invest in on-the-job training, were especially disadvantaged by the lack of formal software engineering education in Japan.[103]

Bibliometric techniques can help substantiate the gap between the United States and Japan in skill infrastructure for software engineering. I analyzed around seven thousand publications from 1995 in the Web of Science Core Collection's "Computer Science, Software Engineering" category.[104] To gauge the breadth of institutional training in software engineering, I counted the number of Japanese and American universities that employed at least one researcher represented in this dataset. According to my estimates, the United States boasted 1.59 universities per million people that met this baseline quality of software engineering education, while Japan only had 1.17 universities per million people. This amounts to a gap of around 40 percent.

Lastly, weak industry-university linkages in computer science hampered Japan's development of GPT skill infrastructure. Imposing centralized control over universities, the Japanese Ministry of Education, Science, and Culture (MESC) inhibited cooperation between new departments of information science and the corporate labs where much of the computing talent was concentrated.[105] Japanese researchers regularly complained about the size of MESC grants, as well as the ministry's restrictions on their ability to seek alternative funding sources. Japan's overall budget level for university facilities in 1992 remained the same as it was in 1975. Additional government funds went instead to independent centers of excellence, diverting resources away from efforts to broaden the pool of training institutions in software engineering.[106]

101. *Nikkei Computer* 1988, 80.

102. Japan Information Processing Development Center 1992.

103. Baba, Branstetter, and Drev 1993.

104. This methodology is described in more detail in the statistical analysis chapter.

105. Drezner 2001, 20–22. For a contrasting view on Japanese industry-university research links, see Hicks 1993.

106. Anderson and Myers 1992, 565, 569.

Alternative Factors

How do alternative explanations perform in this case? A range of factors beyond GPT skill infrastructure could have influenced diverging rates of ICT diffusion in the United States and Japan. I focus on the role of external threats and varieties of capitalism because they present alternative mechanisms for how states adapted differently to the technological revolution that occurred in the IR-3.

Threat-Based Explanations

Threat-based theories struggle to account for differences in the US and Japanese technological performance in this period. A "cult of vulnerability" permeated Japan's leaders over this period as they coped with tensions in East Asia and the oil crises of the 1970s.[107] Likewise, the growth of the US "national security state," fueled by the dangers of the Cold War, functioned as "the secret to American innovation."[108] Under his creative insecurity framework, Taylor holds up both Japan and the United States as exemplars of the IR-3 period, reasoning that they both partly owed their technological success to the galvanizing effects of a threatening international environment.[109] General threat-based explanations therefore cannot explain differences in technological outcomes between the United States and Japan, namely, why the United States was more successful in ICTs than Japan.

A related argument points to the significance of US military procurement for computerization. As was the case with its influence on the American system of manufacturing in the IR-2, the US military provided the demand for initial investments in computers and semiconductors. In the 1940s and 1950s the US military was a key patron behind computing breakthroughs.[110] Assured by large military procurements, innovative firms undertook risky, fundamental research that produced spillovers to many other industries. For instance, the first all-purpose electronic digital computer, the University of Pennsylvania's electronic numerical integrator and calculator (ENIAC), was developed during World War II. The ENIAC was supported by funding from the Army Bal-

107. Chapman, Drifte, and Gow 1982.
108. Taylor 2016, 357n10.
109. Ibid., 110.
110. Ruttan 2006; Weiss 2014, 78–82.

listics Research Laboratory, and the first program run on the computer was a simulation of the ignition of the hydrogen bomb.[111]

In place of the military, could other entities have served as a large demand source for ICTs? Commercial entities like Bell Labs and IBM also developed fundamental breakthroughs in ICTs. According to Timothy Bresnahan and Manuel Trajtenberg, it was "only a coincidence" that US government demand played such a pivotal role in semiconductor development.[112] Others argue that while commercial advances in semiconductors and computers would likely still have occurred absent the impetus of military funding, they would have emerged after substantial delay.[113]

Resolving this debate depends on one's view of the key stage in computerization. Those who emphasize the importance of military procurement often hold up the importance of first-mover advantages in the American computer industry.[114] However, decades after the military helped develop the first computers and transistors, Japan had cornered the market in many related industries. The significance of military procurement is diminished when a GPT's dissemination, as opposed to its emergence, is taken as the starting point. By 1960, the start of the IR-3 period, ICT development in the United States was already much less reliant on military support. In 1955, the demand for Bell's transistors from two large telephone networks alone was nearly ten times more than from all military projects.[115] In fact, as the commercial sector increasingly drove momentum in ICTs, military involvement arguably hindered continued advances in the commercial sector, as there was tension between the different technical cultures.[116]

On balance, the most significant aspect of the military's involvement in the advance of computerization in the United States was its role in building up GPT skill infrastructure. The US military played a key role in cultivating the computer science discipline in its early years. Beginning in the 1960s, defense agencies supported academic research in computer science, such as the aforementioned Software Engineering Institute, which created centers of excellence

---

111. Ruttan 2006, 92.
112. Bresnahan and Trajtenberg 1995, 95.
113. Edwards 1996, 60–65; Flamm 1988, 251.
114. Flamm 1988.
115. Misa 1985, 177.
116. Alic et al. 1992. In Thomas Misa's (1985) account of the development of semiconductors, he acknowledges the US military's role as an "institutional entrepreneur" (268), but he also notes that military contracting and procurement compromised efficient commercial development of semiconductors later on in the technology's life cycle (277–80, 286–87).

and broadened the base of computer science education.[117] From 1977 through the mid-1980s, defense funding supported more than half of academic computer science R&D.[118] At the same time, military investment in computer science did not come without downsides. Defense funding was concentrated in elite research universities at the cutting edge of the field, such as Carnegie Mellon and Stanford, whereas nondefense government funding supported computer science education across a wider range of US universities.[119] On the effects of military computer science funding, Stanford professor Terry Winograd wrote, "It has resulted in a highly unequal situation in which a few schools have received almost all the resources. Although this may have led to more effective research in the short run, it has also been a factor contributing to the significant long-term shortage of trained computer researchers."[120]

VoC Explanations

The varieties-of-capitalism (VoC) approach provides another possible explanation for why the US economy benefited more than Japan's from the innovations of the IR-3.[121] According to the VoC framework, firms in coordinated market economies (CMEs) provide industry-specific training that is more conducive to incremental innovation, whereas worker training in more general skills in liberal market economies (LMEs) proves more favorable for radical innovations. VoC scholars point to some evidence from the international pattern of innovation during the IR-3 that supports these expectations. Based on patent data from 1983–1984 and 1993–1994, Peter Hall and David Soskice find that Germany, a CME, specialized in technology classes characterized by incremental innovation, whereas the United States, an LME, specialized in domains characterized by radical innovation.[122] Therefore, the VoC perspective

117. National Research Council 1999, 221; Newell 1984.

118. Mowery and Langlois 1996.

119. Ibid., 954.

120. Winograd 1987, 8.

121. This section's claims represent a favorable distillation of the VoC theory's predictions for the IR-3. As detailed earlier, some analysts argued that, in order to meet the challenge of Japanese high-tech competition, American firms needed to imitate parts of Japan's CME structure, including its *keiretsu* system of organization. That the United States sustained its economic lead without reforming its system of industrial governance is disconfirming evidence for this line of thinking. Others dispute whether the United States was an exemplar LME in this period (Weiss 2014, 195–97), as well as Japan's CME status (Witt and Jackson 2016, 794).

122. Hall and Soskice 2001, 41–44.

expects that Japan, a CME like Germany, was unable to keep up with the United States in the IR-3 because high-tech sectors such as computer software and biotechnology demanded radical innovations.[123]

This VoC-derived explanation provides an incomplete account of the IR-3 case. First, comprehensive empirical investigations into the innovative performance of CMEs and LMEs, especially the success of Japan as a radical innovator, undermine the explanatory power of VoC theory for the IR-3 period. Hall and Soskice's initial analysis was based on four years of data on patent counts from only two countries, the United States and Germany. Taylor's more extensive analysis, which covered thirty-six years (1963–1999) of patent counts and forward citations for all LME and CME countries, found that the predictions of VoC theory are not supported by the empirical data.[124] In fact, contrary to the expectations of the VoC explanation, Japan was a leader in radical innovation, ranking second only to the United States in patent counts weighted by forward citations, which are a strong proxy for the radicalness of innovations.[125]

Second, VoC theory does not make distinctions between different types of general skills, which varied in their significance to national success in the IR-3. Regarding general training in terms of foundational schooling, Japan was making substantial improvements in average years of schooling, enrollment ratio, and access to higher education.[126] GPT diffusion theory specifies the key general skills as those that best suited the advance of computerization. Consistent with these expectations, the case study evidence points to the US-Japan gap in software engineering, a set of general skills that permeated sectoral boundaries, as the crucial factor in US success with widespread computerization.

Case-Specific Factors

Other factors unique to the IR-3 case deserve further consideration. Among these alternative explanations, one popular theory was that Japan's *kanji* system (Chinese-based characters) contributed to its slow adoption of

---

123. Ibid., 35.

124. Taylor 2004.

125. Ibid., 621–23. Japan introduced many radical innovations in video games and digital technologies, according to one study that views changes in the meaning of a product as a form of radical innovation (Norman and Verganti 2014).

126. Freeman, Clark, and Soete 1982, 188, 194; Godo 2010.

computers.[127] Marshall Unger, a specialist in the Japanese writing system, highlighted difficulties with representing *kanji* in computerized formats, which resulted in higher costs for storing data and for word-processing functions.[128] American computers had to handle only ninety-five printable characters, whereas Japanese personal computers needed to store six thousand Japanese characters.[129] Not only did language differences increase the cost of Japanese computers, but they also prevented Japanese adopters from using off-the-shelf computers from the United States, as these did not support Japanese language functions.

While particularities of the Japanese language may have initially hindered Japan's computerization, it is important not to overstate the impact of this language barrier. In a review of this theory, another expert on computational linguistics argued that Unger overemphasized the additional overhead and speed costs associated with Japanese writing systems.[130] Moreover, users and companies adapted over time. By the end of the 1980s, advances in processor technology allowed computers to support the greater word-processing demands of Japanese language systems.[131] Therefore, during the critical years when the US-Japan computerization gap widened, the impact of the *kanji* system was less pronounced.

Summary

Through much of the late twentieth century, it was only a matter of time until Japan achieved economic preeminence—at least in the eyes of many analysts and scholars. Invoking the assumptions of the LS mechanism, they expected that this economic power transition would be brought about by Japan's advantages in new sectors such as consumer electronics, semiconductor components, and computer hardware. Today, after Japan's decade-long slowdown in productivity growth, there is virtually no discussion of it overtaking the United States as the leading economic power.

Looking back, one might be tempted to conclude that history has vindicated past critics who labeled the claims of Japan's imminent ascension to

127. Other explanations point to Japan's weak venture capital markets and the asset bubble collapse (Anchordoguy 2000).
128. Unger 1987.
129. West 1996.
130. Somers 1988.
131. West 1996.

technological hegemony as "impressionistic,"[132] as well as the retrospective analyses that called out such projections for being "premature."[133]

This chapter's conclusions suggest a more nuanced interpretation. It is not that the prognoses of LS-based accounts were overeager or overly subjective. The real issue is that they were based on faulty assumptions about the pathway by which technological advances make economic power transitions possible. Indeed, the IR-3 case provides strong negative evidence against the LS mechanism, revealing that the expected outcome of an economic power transition failed to materialize in part because of the US advantage in GPT diffusion. The relative success of the United States in diffusing the trajectory of computerization across many ICT-using sectors, in line with GPT diffusion theory, was due to institutional adaptations to widen the skill base in computer engineering. In sum, the US advantage in GPT diffusion accounts for why the economic power transition expected by the LS account failed to transpire.

132. Huntington 1988, 77.
133. Drezner 2001, 19.

6

A Statistical Analysis of Software Engineering Skill Infrastructure and Computerization

I HAVE ARGUED that the shape of technological change is an overlooked dimension of the rise and fall of great powers. Most researchers point to various institutions to explain why some countries experience more scientific and technological progress than others. A central insight of this book is that the institutional factors most relevant for technological leadership depend on whether key technological trajectories map onto GPT diffusion or LS product cycles. GPT diffusion theory posits that great powers with better GPT skill infrastructure, defined as the ability to broaden the engineering skills and knowledge linked to a GPT, will more effectively adapt to technological revolutions.

This chapter evaluates a key observable implication of GPT diffusion theory. The expectation is that where there is a wider pool of institutions that can train engineering talent related to a GPT, there will be more intensive rates of GPT diffusion. Using data on computerization and a novel approach to estimate the number of universities that provide quality software engineering education in a country, this chapter first tests the theorized connection between GPT skill infrastructure and GPT adoption on time-series cross-sectional data for 19 advanced and emerging economies from 1995 to 2020. I supplement this panel analysis with two additional tests: a duration model of the speed by which 76 countries achieved a certain computerization threshold, as well as a cross-sectional regression of data on 127 countries averaged over the 1995–2020 period. While the historical case studies verified this relationship among great powers, large-*n* quantitative analysis allows us to explore how GPT diffusion applies beyond the chosen case studies.

To preview the findings, the evidence in this chapter backs GPT diffusion theory. Countries better positioned to widen their base of software engineering skills preside over higher rates of computer adoption. This relationship holds even when accounting for other factors that could affect computerization and different specifications of the independent and dependent variables. This chapter proceeds by operationalizing computerization rates and skill infrastructure in software engineering and then statistically testing the relationship between the two variables.

Operationalizing the Independent Variable: GPT Skill Infrastructure in Software Engineering

My key independent variable is skill infrastructure connected to computerization. The computer, a prototypical GPT, represents a natural choice for this type of inquiry, as engineering education data for many past GPTs is nonexistent for many countries.[1] Plus, enough time has passed for us to see the effects of computerization. The statistical analysis focuses on the effects of skill formation institutions in software engineering, the computer science discipline tasked with training generalists in computing technology.[2] Concretely, this chapter's measure of GPT skill infrastructure captures the breadth of a country's pool of software engineering skills and knowledge.

Efforts to measure the GPT skill infrastructure in software engineering face three challenges. First, standardized measures of human capital in computer science across countries are not available. The UNESCO Institute for Statistics (UIS) collects internationally comparable data on technicians and researchers in various fields, but this dataset does not include information specific to computer science and has limited temporal coverage.[3] Second, variation across countries in the format of computer science education undercuts some potential benchmarks, such as undergraduate enrollments in computer science programs. In some countries, computer science education is subsumed under a broad engineering category, not recognized as a separate degree course.[4] Lastly, comparisons of computer science education struggle to account for the

---

1. David 1990; Jovanovic and Rousseau 2005.
2. Mahoney 2004.
3. UIS reports data on the number of researchers in the "engineering and technology" field for thirty-eight countries in 2013, which is the earliest year of data coverage.
4. National Science Foundation 1997.

quality of such training. International rankings of universities for computer science garner media coverage, but they rely on subjective survey responses about reputation and largely concentrate on elite programs.[5]

To the extent possible, my measure of GPT skill infrastructure addresses these obstacles. The goal is to operationalize engineering-oriented computer science education in a way that can be standardized across countries and accounts for differences in the format and quality of computer science education. My novel approach estimates *the number of universities in each country that can be reasonably expected to provide a baseline quality of software engineering education.* To establish this baseline in each country, I count the number of universities that employ at least one researcher who has published in a venue indexed by the Web of Science (WoS) Core Collection's category on "Computer Science, Software Engineering." In this category, the WoS citation database extends back to 1954 and allows for reliable cross-country comparisons based on institutional affiliations for published papers and conference proceedings.[6] This approach is also insulated from distinctions related to whether certain degrees count as "computer science" programs or as "general engineering" courses. A particular university's naming scheme has no bearing; as long as an institution retains at least one researcher who has published in the software engineering field, it counts in the GPT skill infrastructure measure.

To gather data on the number of universities that contribute to software engineering skill formation around the world, I analyze 467,198 papers from the WoS Core Collection's "Computer Science, Software Engineering" category published between the years 1995 and 2020. I use the Bibliometrix opensource software to derive institutional and country affiliations from this corpus.[7] Specifically, I collect the university and country affiliations for the corresponding authors of all 467,198 publications. For each country, I count the number of *distinct* university affiliations. Hypothetically, if country X's researchers were all concentrated at a single center of excellence, it could boast more researchers represented in the corpus than country Y but still score lower on my metric. For making comparisons across countries, the number of distinct university affiliations is a better indicator of a country's access to a broad

5. Loyalka et al. 2019; Marginson 2014.
6. For more on the WoS as an authoritative and widely used database for scientometrics, see Birkle et al. 2010.
7. Aria and Cuccurullo 2017.

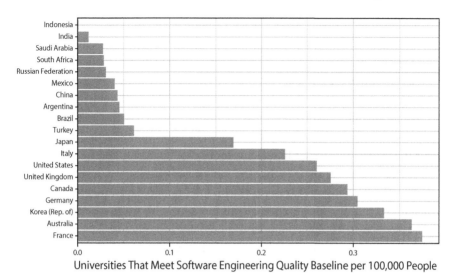

FIGURE 6.1. Software Engineering Skill Infrastructure by Country (2007). *Source*: Author's calculations based on Web of Science Core Collection database.

pool of training institutions for software engineering, which is central to GPT skill infrastructure.

I estimate a country's GPT skill infrastructure in a particular year by averaging its score on this metric in that year along with its scores in the two previous years. This step provides checks against the risk that developments specific to a particular year—a conference cancellation, for example—may muddle the measure. To illustrate country distributions on this metric, figure 6.1 depicts the number of universities that meet my baseline for software engineering skill formation in G20 countries for one of the middle years in the dataset.

As with all bibliometric research, given the bias toward English-language papers in publication datasets, this method could undercount publications from non-English-speaking countries.[8] Fortunately, this linguistic bias found in social science papers is less pronounced in engineering and mathematics papers, which comprise my dataset.[9] Another factor that mitigates this bias is the very low standard for quality engineering education. Even if an institution's researchers publish a substantial portion of their writings in a non-English language, as long as just one publication landed in the WoS "Computer Science,

8. Van Leeuwen et al. 2001. I thank an anonymous reviewer for raising this point.
9. Mongeon and Paul-Hus 2016.

Software Engineering" category, that institution would still count in my definition of GPT skill infrastructure.

I considered other measures of software engineering skills, but none were suitable for this type of analysis. Data on the number of full-time equivalent telecommunication employees, collected by the ITU, shed some light on the distribution of ICT skills in various economies. Concretely, this indicator captures the total number of people employed by telecommunication operators for the provision of fixed-telephone, mobile-cellular, and internet and data services.[10] The rationale is that the number of employees in this critical ICT services industry represents the broader pool of software engineering talent in a country. However, since this measure is biased toward specialists who develop and install computer technologies and other ICTs, it overlooks many engineers who intensively use ICTs in their work, even if they are not involved in developing software and computing tools.[11]

The time coverage of other measures was limited. For instance, the International Telecommunication Union (ITU) database on ICT skills like programming or coding in digital environments only goes back to 2019.[12] In its Global Competitiveness Index, the World Economic Forum surveys business executives on the digital skills of their country's population, but this data series starts in 2017.[13]

Operationalizing the Dependent Variable: Computerization Rates

Divergences among nations in scientific and technological capabilities have attracted a wide range of scholarship. While my focus is on the overall adoption rate of GPTs within economies, many scholars and government bodies have made significant contributions to quantifying national rates of innovation, often based on patenting activity, publications, and R&D investments.[14] Cross-national data on the diffusion of specific technologies, by comparison, has been sparse.[15] The Cross-country Historical Adoption of Technology (CHAT) dataset, which documents the intensity with which countries around

10. International Telecommunication Union 2021.
11. Raja et al. 2013.
12. International Telecommunication Union 2021.
13. Schwab 2017b.
14. Godin 2015; Simmons 2016; Taylor 2016.
15. Comin and Hobijn 2010, 2040.

the world use fifteen historically significant technologies, has helped address this deficiency.[16] Other studies of cross-national technology adoption gaps quantify the diffusion of the internet and government uses of information technology.[17]

My primary measure of computerization is the proportion of households with a computer. These data are sourced from the International Telecommunication Union's World Telecommunication/ICT Indicators (WTI) database.[18] In this dataset, access to a computer includes use of both desktop and portable computers but excludes devices with some computing ability, such as TV sets and mobile phones.[19] By estimating the number of households in a country with access to a computer, this measure elucidates cross-country differences in the intensity of computerization. Though observations for some countries start in 1984, there is limited coverage before 1995, which serves as the initial year for the data collection effort detailed in this chapter.

After the ITU was tasked with supplying indicators for access to ICTs around the world—a crucial target of the United Nations' Millennium Development Goals (MDG) adopted in 2000—the agency started to track the number of personal computers by country.[20] The ITU produces computer usage figures through two methods. First, when available, survey data from national and supranational statistical offices (such as Eurostat) are used. Though the MDG initiative has encouraged national statistical offices to help the ITU in monitoring ICT access, data coverage is still incomplete. If data on the number of households with a computer are unavailable for a country in one year, the ITU makes an estimate based on computer sales and import figures, adjusted to incorporate the average life of a computer as well as other related indicators, such as the number of computer users. For example, the computer usage indicator for Latvia comes from Eurostat in 2013, an ITU estimate in 2014, and the Central Statistical Bureau of Latvia in 2015.

---

16. Comin and Hobijn 2009. For an expanded version of the CHAT dataset, see Milner and Solstad 2021.

17. Bussell 2011; Milner 2006. The diffusion of policy innovations has also been a frequent subject of study in political science; for a review of the related literature, see Graham, Shipan, and Volden 2013.

18. I thank Stanford librarians Ron Nakao and Evan Muzzali for their help with accessing these data.

19. International Telecommunication Union 2021.

20. Minges, Gray, and Magpantay 2003. The ITU also started collecting data on two related indicators: the number of telephone subscribers per 100 inhabitants and internet users per 100 inhabitants.

Despite its limitations, I prefer the ITU's computerization indicator over alternative measures. Francesco Caselli and Wilbur John Coleman examine the determinants of computer adoption across a large sample of countries between 1970 and 1990. To estimate the intensive margin of diffusion, they use the value of a country's computing equipment imports per worker as a proxy for its computer investment per worker.[21] However, imports do not account for a country's computer investments sourced from a domestic computer industry; this is an issue that becomes more salient in the later years of the dataset.[22]

A more optimal indicator would estimate computer access and usage among businesses, since such economic activity is more likely to produce productivity improvements than household use. I examined a few alternatives. The CHAT dataset employs the number of personal computers per capita, which is one of three measures highlighted by the authors as conveying information on GPTs.[23] However, this indicator still does not capture the degree of computerization in productive processes, as opposed to personal use, and has limited temporal coverage compared to the ITU's household computerization measure.[24] The OECD collects some data on ICT access and usage by businesses, but this effort did not start until 2005 and covers only OECD countries.[25]

Fortunately, it stands to reason that a country's household computer adoption can serve as a proxy for its computerization rates in business activities. In the appendix, I provide further support for this claim. Comparing the available data on household and business computerization for twenty-six countries between 2005 and 2014, I find a strong correlation between these two variables (correlation coefficient = 0.8).[26]

21. Caselli and Coleman 2001.

22. Ibid., 329.

23. Comin and Hobijn 2009. The other two are the number of internet users and electricity production.

24. For example, two expanded versions of the original CHAT dataset do not present information on personal computers per capita for the United States between the years 2007 and 2016 (Kenny and Yang 2022; Milner and Solstad 2021).

25. Organization for Economic Cooperation and Development 2018.

26. Another unfortunate limitation is the lack of information on the quality of computing equipment. A country where half the households had access to substandard computers is coded in the same way as a country where half the households used first-rate computers (Chinn and Fairlie 2007). This is a fruitful area for future inquiries built on more granular data collection.

Summary of Main Model Specifications

To review, this chapter tests whether GPTs diffuse more intensively and quickly in countries that have institutional advantages in widening the pool of relevant engineering skills and knowledge. The first hypothesis reads as follows:

H1: Countries with higher levels of GPT skill infrastructure in software engineering will sustain more intensive computerization rates.

With country-years as the unit of analysis, I estimate time-series cross-sectional (TSCS) models of nineteen countries over twenty-six years. Quantitative analysis permits an expansion of scope beyond the great powers covered in the case studies. As outlined in the theory chapter, differences in GPT skill infrastructure are most relevant for economies that possess the absorptive capacity to assimilate new breakthroughs from the global technological frontier.[27] Since less-developed economies are often still striving to build the baseline physical infrastructure and knowledge context to access the technological frontier, variation in GPT skill infrastructure among these countries is less salient. Thus, I limit the sample to nineteen G20 countries (the excluded member is the European Union), which represent most of the world's major industrialized and emerging economies.

Before constructing TSCS regressions, I first probe the relationship between GPT skill infrastructure in software engineering and computerization rates. Prior to the inclusion of any control variables, I plot the independent and dependent variable in aggregate to gauge whether the hypothesized effect of GPT skill infrastructure is plausible. The resulting bivariate plot suggests that there could be a strong, positive relationship between these two variables (figure 6.2).[28]

The basic trend in figure 6.2 provides evidence for the contention that countries better equipped with computer science skill infrastructure experience higher rates of computerization. Although these preliminary results point to a strong relationship between these two variables, further tests are needed to rule out unseen confounders that could create spurious correlations and

---

27. Filippetti, Frenz, and Ietto-Gillies 2017.

28. On transparency-enhancing measures for more credible causal inference with panel data, including tools for data visualization supplied by the PanelView R package, see Mou, Liu, and Xu 2022.

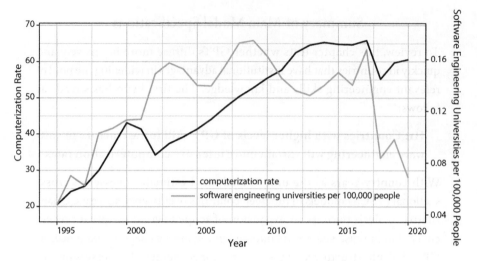

FIGURE 6.2. Software Engineering Skill Infrastructure and Computerization. *Source*: Author's calculations, available at Harvard Dataverse: https://doi.org/10 .7910/DVN/DV6FYS.

influence the strength of this relationship. TSCS regression analysis facilitates a deeper investigation of the relationship between GPT skill infrastructure and computerization.

To control for factors that could distort the relationship between computer-related skill infrastructure and computerization, I incorporate a number of control variables in the baseline model. Rich countries may be able to spend more on computer science education; additionally, they also more easily bear the expenses of adopting new technologies, as exemplified by large disparities between developed and developing countries in information technology investment levels.[29] The inclusion of *GDP per capita* in the model accounts for economic development as a possible confounder. I use expenditure-side real GDP at current purchasing power parities (PPPs), which is best suited to comparing relative living standards across countries. A country's *total population*, another control variable, addresses the possibility that larger countries may be more likely to benefit from network effects and economies of scale, which have been positively linked to technology adoption.[30] I also include the polity score for *regime type*. Research suggests that democratic governments provide

29. Kraemer, Ganley, and Dewan 2005.
30. Hall and Khan 2003.

more favorable environments for technology diffusion, and studies have confirmed this connection in the specific context of internet technologies.[31]

Finally, the baseline model includes two control variables that represent alternative theories of how technological changes differentially advantage advanced economies. First, I include *military spending* as a proportion of GDP in the regressions. The case studies have interrogated the influential view that military procurement is an essential stimulus for GPT adoption.[32] By examining the relationship between military spending and computerization across a large sample of countries, the statistical analysis provides another test of this argument. Moreover, the varieties of capitalism (VoC) scholarship suggests that liberal market economies (LMEs) are especially suited to form the general skills that could aid GPT adoption across sectors. Therefore, the baseline model also controls for whether a country is designated as an LME according to the VoC typology.[33]

In terms of model specification, I employ panel-corrected standard errors with a correction for autocorrelation, a typical method for analyzing TSCS data.[34] Given the presence of both autocorrelation and heteroskedasticity, I estimate linear models on panel data structures using a two-step Prais-Winsten feasible generalized least squares procedure.[35]

Time-Series Cross-Sectional Results

Table 6.1 gives the results of the three initial models, which provide further support for the theoretical expectations.[36] Model 1 incorporates controls that relate to economic size and level of development. Model 2 adds a control variable for regime type. Lastly, model 3 includes a variable that represents a prominent alternative theory for how technological breakthroughs can differentially advantage certain economies. This also functions as the baseline

31. Comin, Dmitriev, and Rossi-Hansberg 2012; Milner 2006. It should be noted that both these claims are disputed (Gerring et al. 2005, 323; Howard et al. 2009; Rød and Weidmann 2015; Taylor 2016, 126–27).

32. See, for example, Ruttan 2006.

33. I follow Taylor (2004) in using the original VoC typology for LMEs (Hall and Soskice 2001).

34. Beck and Katz 1995.

35. Models are estimated using the "PanelAR" package (Kashin 2014).

36. All variables enter the model in logged form, apart from computerization, polity score, and liberal market economies. The data and code to replicate all analyses in this chapter can be found at this Harvard Dataverse link: https://doi.org/10.7910/DVN/DV6FYS.

TABLE 6.1. Results of Time-Series Cross-Sectional Models

	Dependent Variable		
	Computerization		
	(1)	(2)	(3)
GPT skill infrastructure	3.760**	4.064***	4.227**
	(1.643)	(1.676)	(1.666)
GDP per capita	29.754***	29.319***	29.435***
	(3.760)	(3.737)	(3.789)
Total population	6.969***	7.046***	6.781***
	(1.625)	(1.654)	(1.549)
Polity score		−0.456	−0.472*
		(0.295)	(0.277)
Military spending			−0.940
			(2.413)
Liberal market economy			−2.194
			(3.961)
Constant	−374.599***	−368.051***	−361.885***
	(60.452)	(61.173)	(58.374)
Observations	383	370	370

Note: Standard errors in parentheses.
*p < .10; **p < .05; ***p < .01

model. In all three models, the coefficient on the GPT skill infrastructure measure is positive and highly statistically significant ($p < .05$).

The effect of GPT skill infrastructure on GPT adoption is also substantively significant. Given the coefficient of the GPT skill infrastructure measure in the baseline model,[37] a 1 percent increase in the universities per 100,000 people that provide software engineering education results in an increase of the computerization rate by 0.042 percentage points.[38] Though the substantive effect seems small at first glance, its magnitude becomes clear when contextualized by differences in GPT skill infrastructure across the sample. For example, in China over this time period, the average number of universities per 100,000 people that met my baseline for GPT skill infrastructure was 0.040.

37. In models where only the explanatory variable is log-transformed, dividing the estimated coefficient by 100 gives the change in the dependent variable based on a 1 percent increase in the explanatory variable.

38. Since the computerization rate is expressed in the percentage of households with a computer, this represents an increase of 0.042 percentage point units, not a .042 percent increase.

The corresponding figure for the United States was 0.248. According to the coefficient estimate for GPT skill infrastructure, this difference of 520 percent corresponds to a difference of nearly 22 percentage point units in the computerization rate.

It should be noted that only two control variables, economic development and population, came in as statistically significant in the baseline model. As expected, wealthier countries and more populous countries presided over more intensive adoption of computing technologies. The null result for regime type is worth highlighting, as the effects of democracy on technology adoption are disputed.[39] Finally, contrary to the expectations of competing explanations to GPT diffusion theory, the effects of military spending and VoC are insignificant. This is consistent with the findings from the historical case studies.

Quantitative appendix table 1 displays the results after incorporation of three additional controls. First, trade linkages expose countries to advanced techniques and new ideas, opening the door to technology diffusion. A high level of trade openness has been associated with more intensive adoption of information technologies.[40] Relatedly, there is evidence that a country's openness to international trade has a positive and sizable effect on various measures of innovation, including high-technology exports, scientific publications, and patents.[41] Second, higher urban density has been linked to faster diffusion of technologies such as the television and the internet.[42] Model 8 incorporates a trade openness variable and an urbanization variable.

Third, patterns at the regional level could shape how computerization spreads around the world. Scholars have identified such regional effects on the diffusion of ideas, policies, and technologies.[43] In model 9, I assess spatial dynamics with dummy variables for the following regions: East Asia and Pacific; Europe and Central Asia; Latin America and Caribbean; the Middle East and North Africa; North America; South Asia; and sub-Saharan Africa.[44] The positive effect of GPT skill infrastructure on computerization stays strong and highly statistically significant across these two models.

---

39. In model 3, the coefficient for polity score is negative, though this is not statistically significant (p-value $> .05$).

40. Caselli and Coleman 2001; Corrales and Westhoff 2006.

41. Taylor 2007, 246–49.

42. Cava-Ferreruela and Alabau-Muñoz 2006; Milner 2006.

43. Solingen 2012; Vicente and López 2011.

44. These regional groupings come from the World Bank's classification scheme (World Bank 2022). The regression model in quantitative appendix table 1 excludes North America, which serves as the reference group.

To ensure that the results were not determined by my choice of independent variable, I constructed an alternative specification of GPT skill infrastructure. Reanalyzing data on 467,198 software engineering publications, I counted the number of distinct authors for each country, as a proxy for the breadth of researchers who could foster human capital in software engineering. Though I still maintain that the primary specification best captures software engineering skill infrastructure, this alternative construction guards against possible issues with institution-based indicators, such as problems with institutional disambiguation and nonstandardized author affiliations.[45] With this alternative specification, the estimated effect of GPT skill infrastructure on computerization remains positive and significant for the baseline model as well as for models with additional controls.[46]

Duration Analysis

When it comes to whether great powers can harness the potential of GPTs for productivity growth, the speed of adoption—not just the intensity of adoption—is pertinent. In the historical case studies, technological leaders adapted more quickly to industrial revolutions because of their investments in widening the base of engineering knowledge and skills associated with GPTs. This leads to the second hypothesis.

H2: Countries with higher levels of GPT skill infrastructure in software engineering will experience faster levels of computer adoption.

In testing this hypothesis, the dependent variable shifts to the amount of time it takes for a country to reach a particular computerization rate. A critical step is to establish both the specific computerization rate that constitutes successful "adoption" of computers as well as when the process of diffusion begins. Regarding the former, I count the "first adoption" of computerization as when the proportion of households with a computer in a country reaches 25 percent. This approach is in line with Everett Rogers's seminal work on the S-shaped curve for successful diffusion of an innovation, which typically takes off once the innovation reaches a 10 to 25 percent adoption rate.[47] For

45. Donner, Rimmert, and van Eck 2020.
46. See quantitative appendix table 2. As I did with measuring the primary independent variable for a particular year, I averaged a country's count of distinct authors in that year along with its count in the two previous years.
47. Rogers 1995.

the duration analysis, since many of the countries enter the dataset with levels of computer adoption higher than 10 percent, the 25 percent level threshold is more suitable.[48]

I take 1995 as the starting point for the diffusion of computers as a GPT. Though an earlier date may be more historically precise, the 1995 date is more appropriate for modeling purposes, as the data on computerization rates for countries before this time are sparse. In a few cases, a country clearly achieved the 25 percent computerization threshold before 1995.[49] As a practical measure to estimate the duration models, I assume that the time it took for these countries to adopt computers was one year. Right-censoring occurs with the last year of data, 2020, as many countries still had not reached the 25 percent computerization rate.

Using these data, I employ a Cox proportional hazards model to estimate the time it takes for countries to reach a 25 percent computerization rate based on the start date of 1995. Often used by political scientists to study conflict duration or the survival of peace agreements, duration models are also commonly used to investigate the diffusion of new technologies and to determine why some firms take longer to adopt a certain technology than others.[50] Freed from the demands of TSCS analysis for yearly data, the duration analysis expands the county coverage, incorporating all upper-middle-income economies or high-income economies, based on the World Bank's income group classifications.[51] The resulting sample, which excludes countries that never attained the 25 percent computerization threshold, includes seventy-six countries.

Table 6.2 reports the estimated coefficients from the duration analysis. Positive coefficients match with a greater likelihood of reaching the computerization threshold. I use the same explanatory variable and controls as the baseline model from the TSCS analysis. These variables all enter the model with their measures in 1995. Model 4a takes the 25 percent computerization rate as the

48. I also conducted a sensitivity analysis by using 20 percent as an adoption threshold, with similar results (see model 4b).

49. For instance, Iceland entered the dataset with an estimated 50 percent computerization rate in 1995.

50. Hu and Prieger 2010; van Oorschot, Hofman, and Halman 2018.

51. I stratify the dataset by separating economies whose levels of income per capita, averaged throughout the period 1995–2020, are higher than the cutoff for upper-middle-income economies. I establish this threshold using the World Bank's July 2007 classifications of economies by income level (World Bank 2022).

TABLE 6.2. Time to Computerization by Country

	Dependent Variable	
	25% Threshold (4a)	20% Threshold (4b)
GPT skill infrastructure	0.673*** (0.137)	0.517*** (0.119)
GDP per capita	1.186*** (0.335)	1.110*** (0.288)
Total population	0.127 (0.085)	0.062 (0.074)
Polity score	0.022 (0.025)	0.024 (0.023)
Military spending	0.017 (0.218)	−0.042 (0.198)
Liberal market economy	0.760 (0.503)	0.785 (0.493)
N (number of events)	76 (74)	83 (83)
Likelihood ratio test (df = 6)	112.9***	111.2***

Note: Standard errors in parentheses.
*$p < .10$; **$p < .05$; ***$p < .01$

adoption threshold, while model 4b adjusts it to 20 percent to ensure that this designation is not driving results.

As the models demonstrate, the effect of GPT skill infrastructure on the speed by which countries achieve computerization is positive and highly statistically significant, providing support for hypothesis 2. Based on model 4a's hazard ratio for the independent variable (1.96) for a given year, a tenfold increase in software engineering university density doubles the chances of a country reaching the computerization threshold.[52] These results hold up after introducing additional control variables (quantitative appendix table 3).[53]

52. I found minor violations of the proportional hazards assumption in model 4a, so these results should be interpreted with caution.

53. I cannot include all the control variables on top of the baseline model because the relatively small number of events limits the number of iterations. Thus, in quantitative appendix table 3, I remove variables that were not statistically significant from the baseline model before adding the additional predictors.

A Cross-Sectional Approach: Averages across the 1995–2020 Period

As an additional check, I collapse the panel dataset into cross-sectional averages of GPT skill infrastructure and computerization over the 1995–2020 period in a large sample of countries. In certain aspects, cross-sectional evidence could be more appropriate for comprehending the impact of features, like skill formation institutions, that are difficult to capture in yearly intervals because they change gradually.[54] This approach allows for more countries to be included, as the yearly data necessary for TSCS analysis were unavailable for many countries. Limiting the sample based on the same scope conditions as the duration analysis leaves 127 countries.

I also include the same set of controls used in the previous analyses of the panel data: *GDP per capita, total population, regime type, military spending,* and *liberal market economies.* I employ ordinary least squares (OLS) regression to estimate the model. Since both a scale-location plot and a Breausch-Pagan test demonstrate that heteroskedasticity is not present in the data, it is appropriate to use an OLS regression estimator with normal standard errors.

The results of the regression analysis provide further support for the theoretical expectations. To recap, the independent variable is the estimated average skill infrastructure for software engineering between 1995 and 2020, and the dependent variable is the average computerization rate during the same period. Since analyzing bibliographic information on yearly software engineering publications for 127 countries is a demanding exercise, I estimated the average number of universities that nurture software engineering skills based on publications for the two middle years (2007, 2008) in the dataset, instead of deriving this average based on publication data across the entire time range.[55] Table 6.3 displays the results, with the incremental inclusion of control variables, also averaged over the period 1995–2020, across three models.[56] The coefficient on the GPT skill infrastructure measure remains positive and highly statistically significant across all three models ($p < .01$).

54. In considering the cross-section versus panel approach, I benefited greatly from discussions in Simmons 2016 and Stewart 2021.

55. To address concerns that something unique to these two years is driving the results, I also estimate the number of universities that meet the baseline for software engineering skill formation based on publications from 1995, the initial year of the dataset. As illustrated in model 12 of quantitative appendix table 3, the results are robust to this alternative operationalization.

56. All variables enter the model in logged form, except for computerization, polity score, and liberal market economies.

TABLE 6.3. GPT Skill Infrastructure Predicts More Computerization

	Dependent Variable		
	Computerization		
	(5)	(6)	(7)
GPT skill infrastructure	3.211***	3.737***	3.761***
	(0.528)	(0.609)	(0.649)
GDP per capita	16.617***	15.536***	14.977***
	(1.564)	(1.723)	(1.812)
Total population	−1.647***	−0.739	−0.831*
	(0.440)	(0.485)	(0.500)
Polity score		−0.066	−0.070
		(0.147)	(0.180)
Military spending			0.577
			(1.604)
Liberal market economy			5.017
			(4.269)
Constant	−83.099***	−86.165***	−79.773***
	(20.577)	(22.316)	(23.636)
Observations	127	112	110
R^2	0.812	0.833	0.834

Note: Standard errors in parentheses.
*$p < .10$; **$p < .05$; ***$p < .01$

I perform several additional tests to confirm the robustness of the results. I first include the same additional controls used in the preceding TSCS analysis. Quantitative appendix table 4 shows that the main findings are supported. One limitation of models that rely on cross-sectional averages is endogeneity arising from reverse causality. In other words, if greater diffusion of computers throughout the economy spurs more investment in institutions that broaden the pool of software engineers, then this could confound the baseline model's estimates. To account for this possibility, in model 16 in quantitative appendix table 5, I operationalize GPT skill infrastructure using the estimate for the year 1995, the start of the period, instead of its average level over the 1995–2020 period.[57] Thus, this model captures the impact of GPT skill infrastructure in

57. Instrumental variable regression is another option for dealing with endogeneity concerns. I explored adapting instruments used for university education and level of schooling in

1995 on how computerization progressed over the remaining sample years.[58] The effect remains positive and statistically significant.

While this chapter's primary aim is to investigate empirical patterns expected by GPT diffusion theory, the quantitative analysis can also probe whether computerization is positively influenced by institutions that complement LS product cycles. To that end, I add a control variable that stands in for the institutional competencies prioritized by the LS model.[59] Measures of computer exports and ICT patents serve as two ways to capture a country's ability to generate novel innovations in the computer industry.[60] In the resulting analysis, the LS-linked variables do not register as statistically significant.[61]

These results should be interpreted with care. In many cases, measures of institutional capacity to build a strong, innovative computer sector may be highly correlated with measures of GPT skill infrastructure. Because the statistical approach struggles to differentiate between the causal processes that connect these two features and computerization, the historical case studies take on the main burden of comparing the GPT diffusion and LS mechanisms against each other. Still, the inclusion of variables linked with the LS mechanism does suggest that, in the context of computerization, there is ineffectual evidence that the presence of a strong leading sector spills over into other sectors and generates multiplier effects—a key observable implication of LS accounts.[62] Additionally, these models drive home the importance of differentiating between institutions linked to innovative activities (in the sense of introducing new products and processes) and engineering-oriented institutions, like GPT skill infrastructure, which are more connected to adoptive activities.[63]

---

cross-national analysis, but I was unable to find a suitable instrument specific to GPT skill infrastructure. On the difficulty of finding high-quality instruments, see Sovey and Green 2010.

58. On issues related to lagged explanatory variables in time-series analysis, see Bellemare, Masaki, and Pepinsky 2017.

59. See quantitative appendix for details on data collection and analysis procedures.

60. Gaulier and Zignago 2010; Organization for Economic Cooperation and Development 2021; Simoes and Hidalgo 2011.

61. See models 17–18 in quantitative appendix table 6.

62. Thompson 1990.

63. For a similar finding, see Maloney and Caicedo 2017.

Summary

Using a variety of statistical methods, this chapter tested the expectation that countries better equipped to widen the base of engineering talent in a GPT will be more successful at diffusing that GPT throughout their economies. The combination of TSCS models, duration analysis, and cross-sectional regressions lends credence to the strength of the relationship between GPT skill infrastructure and computerization. The results hold across a range of additional tests and robustness checks.

There are two major limitations to this chapter's approach. First, the statistical analysis should be interpreted mainly as an independent evaluation of GPT diffusion theory, not as an additional comparison between GPT diffusion theory and the causal pathway linked to LS product cycles. In the large-scale statistical analysis, indicators linked with the LS mechanism can also be associated with higher computerization rates, making it difficult to weigh the two explanations against each other. The rich historical detail in the case studies therefore provides the prime ground for tracing causal mechanisms.

Second, this chapter evaluates only one aspect of GPT skill infrastructure. A more comprehensive assessment would include not just the capacity to widen the pool of software engineering talent, which was the independent variable in this analysis, but also the strength of information flows between the GPT sector and application sectors. For instance, in the IR-2 case, both the United States and Germany trained large numbers of mechanical engineers, but American technological institutes placed more emphasis on practical training and shop experience, which strengthened connections between the US mechanical engineering education system and industrial application sectors. Building on data collection efforts that are starting to measure these types of linkages, such as the proportion of publications in a technological domain that involve industry-academia collaborations, future research should conduct a more complete assessment of GPT skill infrastructure.[64]

Notwithstanding these limitations, the quantitative analysis backs a key observable implication of GPT diffusion theory: advanced economies' level of GPT skill infrastructure is strongly linked to GPT adoption rates. Not only does this provide some initial support for the generalizability of this book's central argument beyond just great powers, but it also gives further credibility to GPT diffusion theory's relevance to US-China competition today.

64. Zhang et al. 2021.

7

US-China Competition in AI and the Fourth Industrial Revolution

THE FIRST MACHINE to defeat a human Go champion; powerful language models that can understand and generate humanlike text; a computer program that can predict protein structures and enable faster drug discovery—these are just a few of the newest discoveries in AI that have led some to declare the arrival of a Fourth Industrial Revolution (IR-4).[1] As for the latest geopolitical trends, China's rise has been the dominant story of this century as national security establishments grapple with the return of great power competition. Located squarely at the intersection of these two currents, the US-China technological rivalry has become an inescapable topic of debate among those interested in the future of power—and the future itself.

Who will lead the way in the Fourth Industrial Revolution? To answer this question, leading thinkers and policymakers in the United States and China are both drawing lessons from past technology-driven power transitions to grapple with the present landscape. Unfortunately, as this chapter argues, they have learned the wrong lessons. Specifically, the leading-sector perspective holds undue influence over thinking about the relationship between technological change and the possibility of a US-China power transition. Yet careful tracing of historical cases and statistical analysis have revealed that the GPT mechanism provides a better model for how industrial revolutions generate the potential for a power transition. When applied to the IR-4 and the evolving US-China power relationship, GPT diffusion theory produces different insights into the effects of the technological breakthroughs of today on the

---

1. Schwab 2017a.

US-China power balance, as well as on the optimal strategies for the United States and China to pursue.

This chapter sketches out the potential impacts of today's emerging technologies on the US-China power balance. I first describe the current productivity gap between the United States and China, with particular attention to concerns that the size of this gap invalidates analogies to previous rising powers. Next, I review the array of technologies that have drawn consideration as the next GPT or next LS. Acknowledging the speculative nature of technological forecasting, I narrow my focus to developments in AI because of its potential to revitalize growth in ICT industries and transform the development trajectories of other enabling technologies.

The essence of this chapter is a comparison of the implications of the LS and GPT mechanisms for how advances in AI will affect a possible US-China economic power transition. In contrast to prevailing opinion, which hews closely to the LS template, GPT diffusion theory suggests that the effects of AI on China's rise will materialize through the widespread adoption of AI across many sectors in a decades-long process. The institutional factors most pertinent to whether the United States or China will more successfully benefit from AI advances are related to widening the base of AI-related engineering skills and knowledge. I also spell out how the implications of GPT diffusion theory for the US-China power balance differ from those derived from alternative explanations.

The objective here is not to debate whether China will or will not catch up to the United States, or whether technological capabilities are more significant than all other considerations that could affect China's long-term economic growth. Rather, this chapter probes a more limited set of questions: If emerging technologies were to significantly influence the US-China economic power balance, how would this occur? Which country is better positioned to take advantage of the Fourth Industrial Revolution? What would be the key institutional adaptations to track?[2]

A Power Transition in Progress?

Over the past four decades, there has been no greater shift in the global economic balance than China's rise. China is either already the world's largest economy, if measured by purchasing power parity (PPP) exchange rates, or is

2. I thank Steve Brooks for helping me think through this framing.

projected to soon overtake the United States, based on nominal exchange rates.[3] China's impressive economic growth has led many to proclaim that the era of US hegemony is over.[4]

Economic size puts China in contention with the United States as a great power competitor, but China's economic efficiency will determine whether a power transition occurs. Countries like Switzerland outpace the United States on some measures of economic efficiency, but they lack the economic size to contend. Other rising powers, such as India, boast large economies but lag far behind in economic efficiency. Mike Beckley concludes: "If the United States faces a peer competitor in the twenty-first century . . . it will surely be China."[5] For this conditional to be true, China's productivity growth is critical.[6] This is not the first time in history that China has boasted the world's largest economy; after all, it held that distinction even as Britain was taking over economic leadership on the back of the First Industrial Revolution.

Where does China currently stand in comparison to the productivity frontier? Based on 2018 figures, China's real GDP per capita (at 2010 PPPs) is about 30 percent that of the United States.[7] From 2000 to 2017, China's total factor productivity (TFP) never surpassed 43 percent of US TFP (figure 7.1).[8] In 2015, labor productivity in China remained at only 30 percent of that in the United States, though this figure had doubled over the past two decades.[9]

These numbers suggest that China sits much further from the productivity frontier than past rising powers. If the US-China power relationship is fundamentally different from those in previous eras, the relevance of conclusions from previous cases could be limited.[10] For instance, in the early years of the IR-1, Britain was only slightly behind the Netherlands, the productivity leader at the time. The United Kingdom's GDP per capita was 80 percent of Dutch

3. According to data from the International Monetary Fund, China became the world's largest economy in 2014 on a PPP basis (Morrison 2019, 10). The Japan Center for Economic Research projects that China will overtake the United States in nominal GDP in 2029 (Ueharal and Tanaka 2020).

4. For a list of some of the most prominent accounts, see Beckley 2018a, 42n144.

5. Beckley 2018b, 32; see also Brooks and Wohlforth 2016, 32–33.

6. Beckley 2018a, 43–44, 48; Beckley 2021.

7. Guillemette and Turner 2018, 19.

8. Data from Penn World Table, version 9.1, available at http://www.ggdc.net/pwt (Feenstra, Inklaar, and Timmer 2015).

9. International Monetary Fund 2019, 13.

10. Brooks and Wohlforth 2016 (9, 32–36) argue that China, unlike past rising powers, is at a "much lower technological level" relative to the leading state.

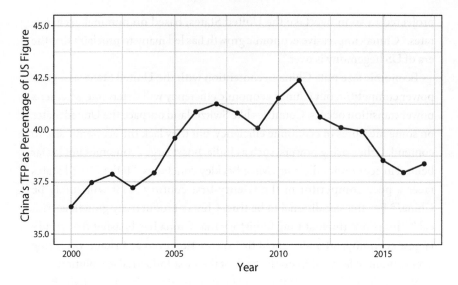

FIGURE 7.1. US-China Productivity Gap (2000–2017). *Source*: Penn World Table version 9.1; Feenstra, Inklaar, and Timmer 2015.

GDP per capita in 1800.[11] Similarly, at the beginning of the IR-2, the United States trailed Britain in productivity by a small margin. In 1870, labor productivity and TFP in the United States were 90 percent and 95 percent, respectively, of labor productivity and TFP in Britain.[12] During the 1870s, average GDP per capita in the United Kingdom was about 15 percent higher than average GDP per capita in the States.[13]

Still, that China *could* surpass the United States in productivity leadership is not outside the realm of possibility.[14] The IR-3 case is a better comparison point for the current productivity gap between the United States and China. In 1960,

11. Bolt and van Zanden 2014, 637. Other productivity comparisons are for the year that marks the start of the case (1870 for the IR-2, 1960 for the IR-3), but this was the earliest available data for the IR-1.

12. Broadberry 2006, 109–10.

13. My calculations are based on the Maddison Project Database, version 2020 (Bolt and van Zanden 2020).

14. According to most projections, this is not a likely scenario. Per the OECD's long-term outlook for the world economy in 2060, China's real GDP per capita will reach only half that of the United States. Its labor efficiency in 2060 will "remain well below those of most OECD countries" (Guillemette and Tuner 2018, 18). The OECD's conception of labor efficiency is closely related to total factor productivity. Still, even though China is unlikely to overtake the United States in productivity leadership, it is still valuable to better understand the pathways by which this transition could occur.

the start of the IR-3 case, Japanese GDP per capita was 35 percent of US GDP.[15] At the time, Japan's TFP was 63 percent of US TFP, and Japan's labor productivity was only 23 percent of US labor productivity, a lower proportion than the China-US ratio at present.[16] Despite the initial chasm, the TFP gap between the United States and Japan narrowed to only 5 percent in 1991.[17]

Indeed, productivity growth is crucial for China to sustain its economic rise in the long term. For the 1978–2007 period, Xiaodong Zhu decomposed the sources of China's economic growth into labor deepening, human capital, capital deepening, and total factor productivity growth. He found that growth in TFP accounted for 78 percent of China's growth in GDP per capita.[18] The burden on TFP improvements will only increase, given the diminishing impact of other drivers of China's growth miracle, such as urbanization and demographic dividends.[19]

Whether China can sustain productivity growth is an open question. Plagued by inefficient infrastructure outlays, China's aggregate TFP growth declined from 2.8 percent in the decade before the global financial crisis to 0.7 percent in the decade after (2009–2018).[20] If calculated using alternative estimates of GDP growth, China's TFP growth was actually negative from 2010 to 2017, averaging −0.5 percent.[21] This productivity slowdown is not unique to China. Even before the 2008 global financial crisis, there was a

---

15. Broadberry and Fukao 2015.

16. Jorgenson, Nomura, and Samuels 2018, 18. By 1970, these percentages were 77 and 44 percent in TFP and labor productivity, respectively.

17. Ibid. This was before Japan's productivity growth slowed in the 1990s. Others compare China to the Soviet Union. Citing the Soviet Union's per capita GDP in 1960, which was 36 percent of US GDP, Brooks and Wohlforth (2016, 42n109) describe the Soviet Union as "richer vis-à-vis the United States during the peak of the Cold War than China is today." However, over the next couple of decades, the Soviet Union, unlike Japan, was unable to sustain its productivity growth (Trachtenberg 2018).

18. Zhu 2012, 108. Applying this approach to the growth of China's GDP per capita relative to the United States, Zhu also found that the shrinking of the US-China GDP per capita gap was "mainly driven by the growth of China's relative total factor productivity" (ibid., 120).

19. Naughton 2018, 178.

20. Brandt et al. 2020, 7.

21. Conference Board 2020, 13. Beckley 2018b, 44. Many of the statistics on China's economic growth draw from Chinese government figures, which some argue should be interpreted differently than statistics for other large economies (see Pettis 2017). For critiques of GDP indicators to measure the economic gap between the United States and China, see Scissors 2016. Chinese economic data should be used with caution, but they can still provide support for general trends. Key elements of China's economic growth, such as fiscal revenues and exports, have been fully verified by independent sources (Naughton 2018, 157–58). Even if China's GDP growth rates were adjusted downward by one to two percentage points per year—the maximum

slowdown in TFP growth among advanced economies due to waning effects from the information and communications technologies (ICTs) boom.[22] China's labor productivity growth also decelerated from 8.1 percent in 2000–2007 to 4.2 percent in 2011–2019, but the later period's slowed growth rate was still six times greater than the US labor productivity growth rate in the same period.[23]

Adaptation to technological advances will be central to China's prospects of maintaining high rates of productivity growth. China's leaders worry about getting stuck in the "middle-income trap," a situation in which an economy is unable to advance to high-income status after it exhausts export-driven, low-cost manufacturing advantages. Many studies have stressed the linkage between China's capacity to develop and absorb emerging technologies and its prospects for escaping the middle-income trap.[24] The Chinese government also increasingly pushes the development and adoption of information technology and other cutting-edge technologies as a way to increase TFP.[25] Thus, tracking China's future productivity growth necessitates a better understanding of specific technological trajectories in the current period.

Key Technological Changes in the IR-4

ICTs, the key technological drivers of the IR-3, are still at the heart of the IR-4. From visionaries and daydreamers to economists and technology forecasters, there is a wide-ranging consensus that AI will breathe new life into the spread of digitization. The World Economic Forum calls AI the "engine that drives the Fourth Industrial Revolution."[26] Kai-Fu Lee, the former head of Google China, boldly asserts, "The AI revolution will be on the scale of the Industrial Revolution but probably larger and definitely faster."[27] To further explore AI's role in the IR-4, I examine this technological domain as a source of both GPT and LS trajectories.

---

plausible adjustment—China's average growth rate over the past three decades "would still be the most sustained period of rapid economic growth in human history" (Naughton 2018, 159).

22. Foda 2016.

23. These figures are based on the Conference Board's Global Productivity Brief, which was published to members in April 2022.

24. Doner and Schneider 2016, 610; Liu et al. 2017; Zhuang, Vandenberg, and Huang 2012.

25. The Economist 2021.

26. Lee 2018, 4.

27. Ibid., 151.

Candidate Leading Sectors

LS accounts forecast that in future waves of technological change ICTs will continue to drive economic transformation. According to one analysis of US-China technological rivalry in the twenty-first century, ICTs are "widely regarded as the current leading sector."[28] I reviewed five key texts that predicted future leading sectors, all written by scholars who study historical cycles of technological change and global leadership transitions.[29] These forecasts also highlight other candidate leading sectors, including lasers and new sources of energy, but they converge on ICTs as the leading sector of the next wave of technological disruption.

Informed by the LS model, AI's effects on global technological competition are often framed through its potential to open up new opportunities for latecomers to catch up and leapfrog advanced countries in key segments like AI chips. China's national AI development plan outlines its ambition to become the world's leading center of innovation in AI by 2030.[30] Scholars analyze China's capacity to develop global intellectual monopolies in certain AI applications and enhance independent innovation in AI so as to guard against other countries leveraging weaponized interdependence.[31] Descriptions of China's AI strategy as aimed toward seizing "the commanding heights" of next-generation technologies reflect the belief that competition in AI will be over global market shares in strategic sectors.[32]

Candidate GPTs

Among the possible GPTs that could significantly impact a US-China economic power transition, AI stands out. Like the literature on leading sectors, the GPT literature also converges on ICTs as a continued driver of technological revolution. Kenneth Carlaw, Richard Lipsey, and Ryan Webb, three pioneers of GPT-based analysis, identify programmable computing networks as the basic GPT

28. Kennedy and Lim 2018, 561.

29. Akaev and Pantin 2014, 868; Goldstein 1988, 353; Modelski and Thompson 1996, 216–22; Rennstich 2002, 159–61; Thompson 1990, 232.

30. Ding 2018.

31. On global intellectual monopolies, see Rikap 2022. On weaponized interdependence, see Xu 2021; Farrell and Newman 2019.

32. Araya 2019; Webster et al. 2017.

that is driving the modern ICT revolution.[33] Crucially, AI could open up a new trajectory for this ICT revolution. Recent breakthroughs in deep learning have improved the ability of machines to learn from data in fundamental ways that can apply across hundreds of domains, including medicine, transportation, and other candidate GPTs like biotechnology and robotics. This is why AI is often called the "new electricity"—a comparison to the prototypical GPT. Economists regard it as the "next GPT"[34] and "the most important general-purpose technology of our era."[35]

Several studies have found evidence for a GPT trajectory in AI. One study, using a novel dataset of preprint papers, finds that articles on deep learning conform with a GPT trajectory.[36] Using patent data from 2005 to 2010 to construct a three-dimensional indicator for the GPT-ness of a technology, Petralia ranks technological classes based on their GPT potential.[37] His analysis finds that image analysis, a field that is closely tied to recent advances in deep learning and AI, ranks among the top technological classes in terms of GPT-ness.[38] Another effort employs online job posting data to differentiate among the GPT-ness of various technological domains, finding that machine learning technologies are more likely to be GPTs than other technologies such as blockchain, nanotechnology, and 3D printing.[39]

To be sure, forecasts of future GPTs call attention to other technological trends as well. Other studies have verified the GPT potential of biotechnology.[40] Robotics, another candidate GPT for the IR-4, could underpin "the next production system" that will boost economy-wide productivity, succeeding the previous one driven by information technology.[41] While my primary rea-

33. Carlaw, Lipsey, and Webb 2007.

34. Trajtenberg 2018.

35. Brynjolfsson and McAfee 2017; see also Teece 2018, 1370.

36. Klinger, Mateos-Garcia, and Stathoulopoulos 2021.

37. The three dimensions correspond to the three characteristics of GPTs: scope for improvement, the variety of applications to products and processes, and complementarity with existing and new technologies. These are measured by patenting growth rates, a text-mining algorithm that looks for patterns in technology-specific vocabulary, and co-occurrence of claims in patents (Petralia 2020, 9–10).

38. Ibid., 2020, 7. Image analysis ranks sixth. The technological classes that rank higher, from highest to lowest, are television, telecommunications, radiant energy, illumination, and electrical communications.

39. Goldfarb, Taska, and Teodoridis 2021.

40. Feldman and Yoon 2012; Ruttan 2001, 368–422.

41. Atkinson 2019; Thurbon and Weiss 2019, 2. Empirical estimates confirm the potential of robots as engines of growth. According to one study of seventeen countries from 1993 to 2007, the increased use of industrial robots accounted for 15 percent of economy-wide productivity

sons for limiting my analysis to AI are based on space constraints as well as on its prominence in the surrounding literature, it is also important to note that developments in both biotechnology and robotics are becoming increasingly dependent on advances in deep learning and big data.[42]

The Limits of Technological Foresight

Unlike exercises to pinpoint key technologies of previous industrial revolutions, which benefited from hindsight, identifying technological drivers in the IR-4 is a more speculative exercise. It is difficult to find true promise amid the hype. The task is made harder by the fact that even experts and technological forecasting bodies regularly miss the next big thing. In 1945, a team led by Dr. Theodore von Kármán, an eminent aerospace engineer, published *Toward New Horizons*, a thirty-two-volume text about the future of aviation. The study failed to foresee major new horizons such as the first human in space, intercontinental ballistic missiles (ICBMs), and solid-state electronics—all of which emerged within fifteen years.[43] In the early 1990s, the US Army conducted a technology forecast assessment to identify the technologies most likely to transform ground warfare in the next century. When the forecast was evaluated in 2008 by the Army's senior scientists and engineers, it graded out at a "C." Among its most significant misses was the development of the internet.[44]

I am no Cassandra. It is very possible that if I were writing this book in 2000, this chapter would focus on the promise of nanotechnology, not AI. At that time, President Bill Clinton had just unveiled the National Nanotechnology Initiative. In a 2003 speech, Philip J. Bond, the undersecretary for technology at the Department of Commerce at the time, declared:

> Nano's potential rises to near Biblical proportions. It is not inconceivable that these technologies could eventually achieve the truly miraculous: enabling the blind to see, the lame to walk, and the deaf to hear; curing AIDS, cancer, diabetes and other afflictions; ending hunger; and even

growth. Based on this figure, the study's authors conclude that the contributions of robots to productivity growth are comparable to those of GPTs in previous historical periods, such as the steam engine (Graetz and Michaels 2018, 765–66).

42. Oliveira 2019; Pierson and Gashler 2017.

43. Hellmeier 1976, 6.

44. Lyons, Chait, and Erchov 2008.

supplementing the power of our minds, enabling us to think great thoughts, create new knowledge, and gain new insights.[45]

Decades later, there is a collective exhaustion around the hype surrounding nanotechnology, a phenomenon one scientist calls "nanofatigue."[46]

One lesson that stands out from mapping the technological landscape in past industrial revolutions is that the most significant GPTs of an era often have humble origins. In the IR-2, new innovations in electricity and chemicals garnered the most attention, but America's economic rise owed more to advances in machine tools that were first introduced decades earlier. In the same way, "old" GPTs like electricity could still shock the world.[47] Today there is still a lot of potential for expanded industrial electrification, which could have a major impact on productivity.[48] Similarly, high-capacity battery technologies could transform productivity on a broad scale.[49] Interestingly, patent data also demonstrate the continued importance of electrical technologies. Among the top ten GPT candidates as ranked by Petralia's indicator of "GPT-ness," there were as many technological classes in the electrical and electronic category as there were in the computers and communications category.[50]

For my purposes, it is reassuring that developments in AI also draw on a long history. In the United States, the legitimization of AI as an important field of research dates back to the 1960s.[51] Thus, though the rest of the chapter takes AI as the most important GPT for the near future, it does so with a humble mindset, acknowledging that looking forward to the future often starts with digging deeper into the past.

The GPT vs. LS Mechanisms in the IR-4

There has been no shortage of speculation about whether the United States or China is better fit for the new AI revolution. Each week it seems there is a new development in the "AI arms race" between the two nations.[52] Many believe that China is an AI superpower on the verge of overtaking the United States

45. Quoted in Kimbrell 2008.
46. Maynard 2016.
47. Edgerton 2011.
48. Burwell 1983.
49. Gross 2014, 32.
50. Petralia 2020, 7.
51. National Research Council 1999, 204.
52. Zwetsloot, Toner, and Ding 2018.

in the key driver of the IR-4.[53] As the following sections will show, these discussions tend to follow the LS template in their assumptions about the trajectory of AI development and key institutional adjustments.

Conversely, GPT diffusion theory provides an alternative model for how AI could affect the US-China power balance, with implications for the optimal institutional adaptations to the AI revolution. I conclude that, if the lessons of past industrial revolutions hold, the key driver of a possible US-China economic power transition will be the relative success of these nations in diffusing AI throughout their economies over many decades. This technological pathway demands institutional adaptations to widen the base of AI engineering skills and knowledge. While recognizing that international competition over AI is still in the early innings, this chapter outlines a preliminary framework for assessing which country's roster is better equipped for success.

Impact Timeframe: The Decisive Years in the US-China AI Competition

If guided by the LS mechanism, one would expect the impacts of AI on US-China power competition to be very significant in the early stages of the technology's trajectory. Indeed, many prominent voices have articulated this perspective. Consider, for example, a report titled "Is China Beating the US to AI Supremacy?," authored by Professor Graham Allison, the director of Harvard Kennedy School's Belfer Center for Science and International Affairs and Eric Schmidt, former CEO of Google and cochair of the National Security Commission on Artificial Intelligence (NSCAI). For Allison and Schmidt, the decisive years in US-China AI competition are just around the corner. Assuming that AI advances will be rapidly adopted across many economic domains, their aim is to "sound an alarm over China's rapid progress and the current prospect of it overtaking the United States in applying AI in the decade ahead."[54] Shaped by a similar framework, other influential texts also predict that China's productivity boost from AI will come to fruition in the 2020s.[55]

53. For assessments that provide a more grounded view of China's AI prowess, see Ding 2018, 2019.

54. Allison and Schmidt 2020, 1.

55. Lee 2018, 25, 154. Allison and Schmidt (2020, 4–5, 12n39) frequently draw on Lee's book in their analysis. The NSCAI (2021, 25) final report warns, "Within the next decade, China could surpass the United States as the world's AI superpower."

If GPT diffusion theory serves as the basis for analysis, these influential texts severely underestimate the time needed for economic payoffs from AI. Historical patterns of GPT advance have borne out that, even in early adopter countries, it takes at least three or four decades for these fundamental technologies to produce a significant productivity boost.[56]

Using this pattern as guidance, we can roughly project AI's impact timeframe, after establishing an initial emergence date for this GPT. In 2012, the AlexNet submission to ImageNet, a competition that evaluates algorithms on large-scale image classification, is widely recognized as spurring this current, deep learning–based paradigm of AI development.[57] If using the metric of when a GPT achieves a 1 percent adoption rate in the median sector, the AI era probably began in the late 2010s.[58] As of 2018, according to the most recent census survey on the extent of AI adoption in the US economy, only 2.75 percent of firms in the median sector reported using AI technologies.[59] Thus, regardless of which arrival date is used, if AI, like previous GPTs, requires a prolonged period of gestation, substantial productivity payoffs should not materialize until the 2040s and 2050s.[60]

Of course, other factors could affect AI's expected impact timeframe, including the possibility that the general process of technological adoption is accelerating. Some evidence indicates that the waiting time for a significant productivity boost from a new GPT has decreased over time.[61] Lee argues that the AI revolution will be faster than previous GPT trajectories owing to the increasingly frictionless distribution of digital algorithms and more mature venture-capital industry.[62] Nevertheless, preliminary evidence suggests that AI will face similar implementation lags as previous GPTs, including bottlenecks in access to computing resources, human capital training, and business process transformations.[63]

---

56. Some scholars argue that the impact of technologies like AI are mismeasured because existing statistics cannot adequately capture the effects of intangible goods and services. On mismeasurement issues related to AI, see Brynjolfsson, Rock, and Syverson 2017, 7–8, 28–33.

57. Gershgorn 2018.

58. Jovanovic and Rousseau 2005, 1184.

59. US Census Bureau 2019.

60. For a similar argument, see Campanella 2018.

61. Brynjolfsson and Petropoulos 2021; Crafts 2004a.

62. Lee 2018, 151–154.

63. Brynjolfsson, Rock, and Syverson 2017, 28–29.

Phase of Relative Advantage: Innovation-centrism and China's AI Capabilities

Debates about China's scientific and technological power reduce complex dynamics to one magic word—"innovation."[64] Whether China can generate novel technologies is often the crux of debates over China's growing scientific and technological capabilities and a potential US-China power transition.[65] For David Rapkin and William Thompson, the prospect of China overtaking the United States as the leading power is dependent on "China's capacity to innovate"—specifically as it relates to revolutionary technological changes that allow challengers to leapfrog the leader in economic competition.[66] "If ... China's innovativeness continues to lag a considerable distance behind that of the US, then China overtaking the US might wait until the twenty-second century," they posit.[67] China's innovation imperative, as Andrew Kennedy and Darren Lim describe it in language common to LS analysis, is motivated by "*monopoly rents* generated by new discoveries."[68]

Innovation-centric views of China's AI capabilities paint an overly optimistic picture of China's challenge to US technological leadership. Allison and Schmidt's Belfer Center paper, for instance, emphasizes China's growing strength in AI-related R&D investments, leading AI start-ups, and valuable internet companies.[69] Likewise, the NSCAI's final report suggests that China is poised to overtake the United States in the capacity to generate new-to-the-world advances in AI, citing shares of top-cited, breakthrough papers in AI and investments in start-ups.[70] These evaluations match up with viewpoints that are bullish on China's overall technological capabilities, which also point to its impressive performance along indicators of innovation capacity, such as R&D expenditures, scientific publications, and patents.[71]

---

64. Historians have decried what Edgerton (2010) labels "innovation-centrism"—the disproportionate attention paid to innovation in studies of technology and politics (Godin 2015).

65. This section derives from Ding 2023, 13–14, 17.

66. Rapkin and Thompson 2003, 333. Ashley Tellis (2013, 112) states that the United States must "sustain its dominance in the new leading sectors of the global economy" to check China's growing power.

67. Rapkin and Thompson 2003, 333.

68. Kennedy and Lim 2018, 555, emphasis mine.

69. Allison and Schmidt 2020.

70. National Security Commission on Artificial Intelligence 2021, 161, 166fn9.

71. Ding 2023, 14; Kennedy 2015, 284.

Some other comparisons of US and Chinese AI capabilities arrive at the opposite conclusion but still rely on the LS template. For instance, two Oxford scholars, Carl Frey and Michael Osborne, have likened claims that China is on the verge of overtaking the United States in AI to overestimates of Japan's technological leadership in computers in the 1980s. In their view, just like Japan, China will fail to overtake the United States as the world's technological leader because of its inability to produce radical innovations in AI. In fact, they claim, the prospects are even bleaker this time around: "China, if anything, looks less likely to overtake the United States in artificial intelligence than Japan looked to dominate in computers in the 1980s."[72]

If analysis of US-China competition in AI was centered on GPT diffusion theory, it would focus more on China's capacity to widely adopt AI advances. In this scenario, it is neither surprising nor particularly alarming that China, like other great power contenders such as Japan in the IR-3, Germany in the IR-2, and France in the IR-1, contributes to fundamental innovations. No one country will corner all breakthroughs in a GPT like AI. The key point of differentiation will be the ability to adapt and spread AI innovations across a wide array of sectors.

A diffusion-centric perspective suggests that China is far from being an AI superpower. Trends in ICT adoption reveal a large gap between the United States and China. China ranks eighty-third in the world on the International Telecommunication Union's ICT development index, a composite measure of a country's level of networked infrastructure, access to ICTs, and adoption of ICTs.[73] By comparison, the United States sits among the world's leaders at fifteenth. Though China has demonstrated a strong diffusion capacity in consumer-facing ICT applications, such as mobile payments and food delivery, Chinese businesses have been slow to embrace digital transformation.[74]

---

72. Frey and Osborne 2020.

73. International Telecommunication Union 2017.

74. Kannan and Thomas 2018. Recently, some analysts have argued that China's rising scientific and technological prowess comes from its strategic advantage in deploying innovations at scale, which benefits from a globalized, open R&D system (see, for example, Breznitz and Murphree 2011; de La Bruyère and Picarsic 2020). These analyses draw from a few examples of Chinese success at large-scale deployment in domains such as high-speed rail and mobile payments. This section's comprehensive evaluation cautions against overestimating China's diffusion capacity.

In fact, it is often Chinese scholars and think tanks that acknowledge these deficiencies. According to an Alibaba Research Institute report, China significantly trails the United States in penetration rates of many digital technologies across industrial applications, including digital factories, industrial robots, smart sensors, key industrial software, and cloud computing.[75] China also significantly trails the United States in an influential index for adoption of cloud computing, which is essential to implementing AI applications.[76] In 2018, US firms averaged a cloud adoption rate of over 85 percent, more than double the comparable rate for Chinese firms.[77]

To be fair, China has achieved some success in adopting robots, a key application sector of AI. China leads the world in total installations of industrial robots. Aided by favorable industry composition and demographic conditions, China added 154,000 industrial robots in 2018, which was more than were installed by the United States and Japan combined.[78] Based on 2021 data from the International Federation of Robotics, China outpaces the United States in robot density as measured by the number of industrial robots per 10,000 manufacturing employees.[79]

However, China's reputed success in robot adoption warrants further scrutiny. The IFR's figures for employees in China's manufacturing sector significantly underestimate China's actual manufacturing workforce. If these figures are revised to be more in line with those from the International Labor Organization (ILO), China's robot density would fall to less than 100 robots per 10,000 manufacturing employees, which would be around one-third of the US figure.[80] On top of that, talent bottlenecks hamper robot diffusion in China, since skilled technicians are required to reprogram robots for specific applications.[81] An unused or ineffective robot counts toward robot density statistics but not toward productivity growth.

75. Alibaba Research Institute 2019. For another Chinese-language report that covers China's struggles to transfer leading technologies from frontier firms to small and medium enterprises, see Synced 2020.

76. BSA Software Alliance 2018.

77. Wang and Chen 2020; see also Kannan and Thomas 2018.

78. Based on statistics from International Federation of Robotics (IFR) 2022. See also Cheng et al. 2019; Rudnik 2022.

79. International Federation of Robotics 2022. The proportional figure is "the most commonly used metric" in comparing nations in terms of robot adoption (Atkinson 2019).

80. Pozzi 2023.

81. Pang 2019.

Breadth of Growth: Picking Winners vs. Horizontal Approaches to AI Development

Divergent perspectives on the breadth of growth in technological revolutions also separate LS-based and GPT-based views of the US-China case. If technological competition in the IR-4 is limited to which country gets a bigger share of the market in new leading industries like AI, then direct sectoral interventions in the mold of China's AI strategy could be successful. However, if the breadth of growth in the IR-4 follows the GPT trajectory of the three previous industrial revolutions, another approach will be more effective.

China's AI strategy has hewed closely to the LS model. This approach builds off a series of directives that prioritize indigenous innovation in select frontier technologies, an emphasis that first appeared in the 2006 "National Medium- and Long-Term Plan for the Development of Science and Technology" and extends through the controversial "Made in China 2025" plan.[82] Since the mid-2000s, the number of sectoral industrial policies issued by the State Council, China's cabinet-level body, has significantly increased.[83] Appropriately, the State Council's 2017 AI development plan outlined China's ambitions to become the world's primary innovation center for AI technology.[84]

On the breadth of growth dimension, tension between GPT diffusion theory and China's application of the LS template is rooted in differing expectations for how the economic boost from revolutionary technologies will unfold. Take, for example, China's 2010 "Strategic Emerging Industries" (SEI) initiative, which targets seven technological sectors based on opportunities for China to leapfrog ahead in new industries.[85] Oriented around assumptions that a limited number of technologically progressive industries will drive China's future growth, the SEI defines success based on the resultant size of these industries, as measured by their value added as a share of GDP.[86]

---

82. "Made in China 2025" has become a key point of contention in US-China trade disputes. Issued in 2015, it aims to further enhance China's self-sufficiency in ten strategic sectors, including biopharmaceuticals, energy-saving and new energy vehicles, and high-performance medical devices (Laskai 2018).

83. Heilmann and Shih 2013.

84. Ding 2018; Webster et al. 2017.

85. In laying out his motivation for this initiative, Chinese premier Wen Jiabao explicitly compared the situation at the time with four previous cases since the 1700s when, in his mind, China had missed a technological revolution and fallen behind as a result (Chen and Naughton 2016, 2148).

86. Chen and Naughton 2016, 2141.

In contrast, GPT diffusion theory expects that, in the country that best capitalizes on the IR-4, productivity growth will be more dispersed. In this view, the AI industry never needs to be one of the largest, provided that AI techniques trigger complementary innovations across a broad range of industries. Relatedly, some Chinese thinkers have pushed back against industrial policies that favor narrow technology sectors. A research center under China's own State Council, in a joint analysis with the World Bank, concluded in 2012: "A better innovation policy in China will begin with a redefinition of government's role in the national innovation system, shifting away from targeted attempts at developing specific new technologies and moving toward institutional development and an enabling environment that supports economy-wide innovation efforts within a competitive market system."[87] The economy-wide transformation enabled by AI, if it lives up to its potential as a GPT, demands a more broad-based response.

When it comes to technology policy, there is always a push and pull between two ends of a spectrum. Vertical industrial policy, or "picking winners," targets certain technologies, often leading to top-down intervention to ensure that the nation's firms are competitive in specific industries. Horizontal industrial policy promotes across-the-board technological development and avoids labeling certain technologies as more significant than others. This book argues that both camps have it partly right, at least when it comes to ensuring long-term economic growth in times of technological revolution. Picking technological winners is needed in that some technologies do matter more than others; however, the "winners" are GPTs, which require horizontal industrial policies to diffuse across many application sectors. Institutions for skill formation in AI engineering, the subject of the next section, split the difference between these two approaches.

Institutional Complementarities: GPT Skill Infrastructure in the IR-4

In 2014, Baidu, one of China's leading tech giants, hired Andrew Ng away from Google, poaching the cofounder of Google's deep learning team. Three years later, Baidu lured Qi Lu away from Microsoft, where he had served as the architect of the company's AI strategy. Their departures were headline news and spurred broader discussions about China's growing AI talent.[88]

87. State Council 2016, cited in Liu et al. 2017, 664.
88. See, for example, Hempel 2017.

When Alibaba, another one of China's tech giants, celebrated its listing on the Hong Kong stock exchange in November 2019, it showcased a different form of AI talent. In one picture of the gong-ringing celebration, Yuan Wenkai, who works for an Alibaba-owned logistics warehouse, stood third from the right. A former tally clerk who graduated from a run-of-the-mill Guangdong vocational school, Yuan holds substantial expertise in automation management. His success with boosting the sorting capacity of a logistics warehouse by twenty thousand orders per hour—responding to elevated demand during the shopping frenzy of Single's Day (November 11)—merited an invite to the ceremony.[89]

Even as AI systems exceed human-level performance at tasks ranging from playing Go to translating news articles, human talent will remain crucial for designing and implementing such systems.[90] According to one global survey of more than three thousand business executives, landing the "right AI talent" ranked as the top barrier to AI adoption for companies at the frontier of incorporating AI into their products, services, and internal processes.[91] But what makes up the "right AI talent"? In its distilled form, GPT diffusion theory suggests that China's chance of leading the AI revolution rests more on the Yuan Wenkais of the world than the Andrew Ngs. The most important institutional adjustments to the IR-4 are those that widen the pool of AI engineering skills and knowledge.

Indeed, alongside the maturation of the AI field, recent reports have emphasized skills linked to implementing theoretical algorithms in practice and in ways suited for large-scale deployment. In early 2022, the China Academy of Information and Communications Technology (CAICT), an influential research institute under the Ministry of Industry and Information Technology, published two reports that identified AI's "engineering-ization" (工程化) as a significant trend that involves addressing challenges in transforming AI-based projects from prototypes to large-scale production.[92] Relatedly, per Burning Glass job postings from 2010 to 2019, the overall increase in demand for "AI-adjacent" positions in the United States far exceeded that for "core AI" positions.[93] Covering skills needed to implement AI throughout many sectors

89. Pang 2019.
90. Kania 2018.
91. Ransbotham et al. 2018.
92. China Academy of Information and Communications Technology 2022a, 2022b.
93. Toney and Flagg 2020a, 3–4. AI-adjacent jobs jumped from about 1 million to 3 million jobs, while core AI jobs increased from 23,000 to 320,000 postings.

and legacy systems, this pool of AI-adjacent jobs includes positions for systems engineers and software development engineers.

GPT Skill Infrastructure for AI: A US-China Comparison

At present, the United States is better positioned than China to develop the skill infrastructure suitable for AI. First, the United States has more favorable conditions for expanding the number of AI engineers. According to three separate projects that mapped out the global AI talent landscape, many more AI engineers work in the United States than in any other country.[94] In 2017, Tencent Research Institute and BOSS Zhipin (a Chinese online job search platform) found that the number of AI "practitioners" (从业者) in the United States far surpassed the corresponding Chinese figure. Figure 7.2 captures this gap across four key AI subdomains: natural language processing (by three times), chips and processors (by fourteen times), machine learning applications (by two times), and computer vision (by three times).[95] Overall, the total number of AI practitioners in the United States was two times greater than the corresponding figure for China.[96] Furthermore, data from two separate reports by LinkedIn and SCMP Research confirm that the United States leads the world in AI engineers.[97]

In addition to statistics on the AI workforce, the quantity and quality of AI education is another consideration for which country is better positioned to develop GPT skill infrastructure for AI. Again, the United States leads China by a significant margin in terms of universities with faculty who are proficient in AI. In 2017, the United States was home to nearly half of the world's 367 universities that provide AI education, operationalized by universities that have at least one faculty member who has published at least

---

94. Many talent comparisons center on elite AI talent, such as PhD graduates in AI from the top universities or researchers who have published in top AI conferences. For example, see Mozur and Metz 2020; Zwetsloot et al. 2019.

95. Tencent Research Institute and BOSS Zhipin 2017, 17. The report measures the number of "AI practitioners" by counting employees at AI companies.

96. Ibid., 9.

97. Though these projects employed different methodologies to measure AI talent, their overall findings were consistent with respect to the US-China gap in AI engineers. Absolute differences actually understate the US edge in AI engineer skills. The most appropriate measures would control for population size or workforce size in order to capture engineering density (LinkedIn 2017; SCMP Research 2020).

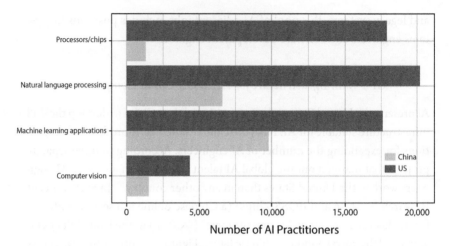

FIGURE 7.2. A US-China Comparison of AI Practitioners in Key Subdomains. *Source*: Tencent Research Institute and BOSS Zhipin 2017.

one paper in a top AI conference.[98] In comparison, China had only 20 universities that met this standard. After replicating this methodology for the years 2020–2021, the US advantage is still pronounced, with 159 universities to China's 29 universities.[99]

These findings contradict prominent views on the present global distribution of AI engineering talent. In his best-selling book *AI Superpowers: China, Silicon Valley, and the New World Order*, Kai-Fu Lee argues that the current AI landscape is shifting from an age of discovery, when the country with the highest-quality AI experts wins out, to an age of implementation, when the country with the largest number of sound AI engineers is advantaged.[100] In an age of implementation, Lee concludes, "China will soon match or even overtake the United States in developing and deploying artificial intelligence."[101] Pitted against the statistics from the previous passages, Lee's evidence for China's lead in AI implementers is meager. His attention is concentrated on anecdotes about the voracious appetite for learning about AI by Chinese entrepreneurs in Beijing.[102] While this analysis benefits from Lee's experience as CEO of

98. Tencent Research Institute and BOSS Zhipin 2017, 12.

99. Author's analysis based on the CSRankings database maintained by Emery Berger and hosted at https://csrankings.org/.

100. Lee 2018, 12–13, 83.

101. Ibid., 18.

102. Ibid., 82–90. Other figures that Lee cites, such as citations in AI journals, are not oriented toward measuring AI engineering talent.

Sinovation Ventures, a venture capital fund that invests in many Chinese AI start-ups, it could also be colored by his personal stake in hyping China's AI capabilities.

Drawing on Lee's book, Allison and Schmidt also assert that China is cultivating a broader pool of AI talent than the United States today. Specifically, they point out that China graduates three times as many computer science students as the United States on an annual basis.[103] Yet the study on which this figure is based finds that computer science graduates in the United States have much higher levels of computer science skills than their Chinese peers. In fact, the average fourth-year computer science undergraduate in the United States scores higher than seniors from the top programs in China.[104] Therefore, estimates of China's pool of AI engineering talent will be misleading if they do not establish some baseline level of education quality. This is another reason to favor the indicators that support an enduring US advantage in AI engineers.[105]

Second, as previous industrial revolutions have demonstrated, strong linkages between entrepreneurs and scientists that systematize the engineering knowledge related to a GPT are essential to GPT skill infrastructure. In the AI domain, an initial evaluation suggests that this connective tissue is especially strong in the United States. Based on 2015–2019 data, it led the world with the highest number of academic-corporate hybrid AI publications—defined as those coauthored by at least one researcher from both industry and academia—more than doubling the number of such publications from China.[106] Xinhua News Agency, China's most influential media organization, has pinpointed the lack of technical exchanges between academia and industry as one of five main shortcomings in China's AI talent ecosystem.[107]

These preliminary indicators align with assessments of the overall state of industry-academia exchanges in China. Barriers to stronger industry-academia linkages include low mobility between institutions, aimless government-sponsored research collaborations, and misguided evaluation incentives for academic researchers.[108] One indicator of this shortcoming

103. Allison and Schmidt 2020, 10.

104. The Belfer report does not explicitly cite this study, but it is very likely the underlying source of the claim (Loyalka et al. 2019).

105. For a good overview of recent changes in AI education in China and the United States, see Peterson, Goode, and Gelhaus 2021.

106. Zhang et al. 2021, 23.

107. Xinhua News Agency 2019.

108. Liu et al. 2017; Tagscherer 2015.

is the share of R&D outsourced by Chinese firms to domestic research institutes: this figure declined from 2.4 percent in 2010 to 1.9 percent in 2020. Over the
same time period, the share of Chinese firms' R&D expenditures performed
by domestic higher education institutions also decreased from 1.2 percent to
0.4 percent.[109]

Moreover, the US approach to AI standard-setting could prove more optimal
for coordinating information flows between labs working on fundamental AI
advances and specific application sectors. Market-mediated, decentralized standardization systems are particularly suited for advancing technological domains
characterized by significant uncertainty about future trajectories, which clearly
applies to AI.[110] In such fields, governments confront a "blind giant's quandary"
when attempting to influence technological development through standards-
setting.[111] The period when government involvement can exert the most influence over the trajectory of an emerging technology coincides with the time
when the government possesses the least technical knowledge about the technology. Government intervention therefore could lock in inferior AI standards
compared with market-driven standardization efforts.

In that light, China's state-led approach to technical standards development
could hinder the sustainable penetration of AI throughout its economy. For
example, the Chinese central government plays a dominant role in China's AI
Industry Alliance, which has pushed to wrest leadership of standards setting
in some AI applications away from industry-led standardization efforts.[112]
Excessive government intervention has been a long-standing weakness of
China's standardization system, producing standards not attuned to market
demands and bureaucratic rivalries that undermine the convergence of standards.[113] Wang Ping, a leading authority on this topic, has argued that China
needs to reform its standardization system to allow private standards development organizations more space to operate, like the Institute of Electrical and
Electronics Engineers in the United States and the European Committee for
Electrotechnical Standardization.[114]

109. See *China Statistical Yearbook on Science and Technology* (Social Science, Technology,
and Cultural Industry Statistics Department, various years).

110. Chan, Jensen, and Zhong 2019; Ding 2020. For an articulation of how the same logic
could apply to AI education policy, see Peterson, Goode, and Gelhaus 2021, 35.

111. David 1987, 1995.

112. Luong and Arnold 2021, 8.

113. Ernst 2011, 85; Breznitz and Murphree 2013.

114. Wang and Zheng 2018; Yates and Murphy 2019, 336.

In sum, the United States is better positioned than China to not only broaden its pool of AI engineering skills but also benefit from academia-industry linkages in AI engineering. In previous industrial revolutions, these types of institutional adaptations proved crucial to technological leadership. Still, much uncertainty remains in forecasts about GPT skill infrastructure for AI, especially with regard to determining the right measures for the right AI talent. Recent studies of market demand for AI- and ICT-related jobs suggest that employers are softening their demands for a four-year degree in computer science as a requirement for such positions.[115] Certificate programs in data science and machine learning that operate under the bachelor-degree level could play an important role in expanding the pool of AI engineering talent.[116] Taking into account these caveats, this section's evaluation of GPT skill infrastructure at the very least calls into question sweeping claims that China is best placed to capitalize on the IR-4.

Reframing National AI Strategies

The preceding conclusions offer a marked contrast with how American and Chinese policymakers devise national AI strategies. Policy proposals for pursuing US leadership in AI consistently call for more AI R&D as the highest priority. For example, the report "Meeting the China Challenge: A New American Strategy for Technology Competition," published in 2020 by a working group of twenty-eight China specialists and experts, provided sixteen policy recommendations for how the United States should ensure its leadership in AI and three other key technological domains. The very first recommendation was for the United States to significantly expand investment in basic research, raising total R&D funding to at least 3 percent of GDP.[117] The Trump administration's "American AI Initiative," launched to maintain US leadership in AI "in a time of global power competition," also listed AI R&D spending as its very first policy recommendation.[118]

The Chinese government also prioritizes investments in R&D, sometimes at the expense of other routes to productivity growth oriented around technology adoption and education.[119] China's five-year plan (2021–2025) aims to

115. Toney and Flagg 2020b.
116. Mason, Rincon-Aznar, and Venturini 2020.
117. Working Group on Science and Technology in US-China Relations 2020, 8.
118. White House Office of Science and Technology Policy 2020.
119. Brandt et al. 2020, 20.

raise basic research spending by over 10 percent in 2021, targeting AI and six other key technological domains.[120] China consistently sets and meets ambitious targets for R&D spending, but that same commitment has not extended to education funding. While China's R&D spending as a percentage of GDP in 2018 was higher than that of Brazil, Malaysia, Mexico, or South Africa (other middle-income countries that industrialized on a similar timeline), China's public expenditure on education as a percentage of GDP was lower than the figure in those countries.[121] According to a group of experts on China's science and technology policy, one possible explanation for this disparity between attention to R&D versus education is the longer time required for efforts in the latter to yield tangible progress in technological development.[122]

As both the United States and China transition from initiating a new GPT trajectory to diffusing one across varied application sectors, investing in the broader AI-adjacent skill base will become more crucial than cornering the best and the brightest AI experts. Policies directed at widening the AI talent base, such as enhancing the role of community colleges in developing the AI workforce, deserve more attention.[123] Applied technology centers, dedicated field services, and other technology diffusion institutions can incentivize and aid adoption of AI techniques by small and medium-sized enterprises.[124] Reorienting engineering education toward maintaining and overseeing AI systems, not solely inventing new ones, also fits this frame.[125]

A strategy oriented around GPT diffusion does not necessarily exclude support for the exciting research progress in a country's leading labs and universities. R&D spending undoubtedly will not just help cultivate novel AI breakthroughs but also contribute to widening the GPT skill infrastructure in AI. All too often, however, boosting R&D spending seems to be the boilerplate

120. Horwitz, Yang, and Sun 2021.

121. This trend has stayed consistent since at least 2010, which is the last year of available data to compare across all five countries. See the UNESCO Institute for Statistics database at http://data.uis.unesco.org/.

122. Liu et al. 2017, 663.

123. See West 2018, 112–13; National Security Commission on Artificial Intelligence 2021, 175.

124. Shapira and Youtie 2017.

125. Russell and Vinsel 2019, 249–58. Using the "AI Education Catalog" compiled by CSET and the AI Education Project (Perkins et al. 2021), I downloaded details on ninety education initiatives targeted at postsecondary students. The vast majority were oriented around supporting the development of new prototypes and moving forward the state of the art in a field; very few were targeted at building up capabilities for maintaining systems. One exception was the DARPA Cyber Grand Challenge, which tasks participants with deploying automatic defensive systems on a network in real time.

recommendation for any strategic technology.[126] GPTs like AI are not like other technologies, and they demand a different toolkit of strategies.

Alternative Factors

In exploring how the IR-4 could bring about an economic power transition, it is important to compare the implications derived from the GPT diffusion mechanism to those that follow from explanations stressing other factors. Consistent with the previous chapters, I first consider threat-based explanations and the varieties of capitalism (VoC) approach. I then address how US-China competition over emerging technologies could be shaped by differences in regime type, a factor that is particularly salient in this case.

Threat-Based Explanations

One potentially dangerous implication of threat-based explanations is that war, or manufacturing the threat of war, is necessary for economic leadership in the IR-4. Crediting the US military's key role in spurring advances in GPTs during the twentieth century, Ruttan doubts that the United States could initiate the development of GPTs "in the absence of at least a *threat* of major war."[127] Extending Ruttan's line of thinking to the US strategic context in 2014, Linda Weiss expressed concerns that the end of the Cold War, along with the lack of an existential threat, removed the impetus for continued scientific and technological innovation. Specifically, she questioned "why China has not yet metamorphosed into a rival that spurs innovation like the Soviet Union and Japan."[128] Weiss only needed a little more patience. A few years later, the narrative of a US-China "Tech Cold War" gained momentum as both sides of the bilateral relationship trumped up threats to push national scientific and technological priorities.[129]

GPT diffusion theory strongly refutes the notion that manufacturing external threats is necessary for the United States or China to prevail in the IR-4. An external menace did not drive the rise of the United States in the IR-2.

---

126. For an analysis of the concept of strategic technologies, see Ding and Dafoe 2021.

127. Ruttan 2006, 184.

128. Weiss 2014, 204.

129. See, for example, Segal 2019; Zhong and Mozur 2018. Taylor (2016, 290–92) warns against this cynical application of threat-based theories. Instead, he argues, policymakers should emphasize nonstate, external threats, such as climate change, to spur innovation.

Across all cases, military actors were involved in but not indispensable to spurring the development of GPTs, as many civilian entities also fulfilled the purported role of military investment in providing a large initial demand for incubating GPTs. Furthermore, threat-based interpretations extend only to the moment when one country stimulates the first breakthroughs in a GPT. Even if stoking fears can galvanize support for grand moonshot projects, these do not determine which country is able to benefit most from the widespread adoption of advances in GPTs like AI. That hinges on the more low-key toil of broadening the engineering skill base and advancing interoperability standards in GPTs—not fearmongering.

VoC Explanations

Applying the VoC framework to US-China competition in AI gives more ambiguous results. The VoC approach states that liberal market economies (LME)—prototypically represented by the United States—are more conducive to radical innovation than coordinated market economies (CME).[130] It is unclear, however, whether China fits into the VoC framework as a CME or LME. While some label China a CME, others characterize it as an LME.[131] This disputed status speaks to the substantial hybridity of China's economy.[132] China has been treated as a "white space on the map" of VoC scholarship, which was originally developed to classify different forms of advanced capitalist economies.[133] This makes it difficult to derive strong conclusions from VoC scholarship about China's ability to adapt to the IR-4's radical innovations.

The same holds if we focus on the skill formation aspect of the VoC framework. China's education system emphasizes training for general skills over vocational skills.[134] In this respect, it is similar to LMEs like the United States, which means VoC theory provides limited leverage for explaining how the IR-4 could differentially advantage the United States or China. On this topic, GPT diffusion theory points to differences in AI engineering education as more significant than distinctions based on the CME-LME models.

---

130. Hall and Soskice 2001.
131. For the former, see Fligstein and Zhang 2011; for the latter, see Witt 2010.
132. Witt and Redding 2014; Zhang and Peck 2016.
133. Peck and Zhang 2013, 358.
134. Ibid., 363; Witt and Redding 2014.

Case-Specific Factors: Regime Type

What is the effect of regime type on technological leadership in the IR-4? The distinction between authoritarian China and the democratic United States takes center stage in arguments about the future of great power rivalry.[135] Regime type could also influence the specific aspect of great power competition that GPT diffusion tackles—whether one great power is able to sustain productivity growth at greater rates than its rivals by taking advantage of emerging technologies. Some evidence suggests that, owing to investments in inclusive economic institutions, democracies produce more favorable conditions for growth than autocracies.[136] Additionally, empirical work shows that democracies outgrow autocracies in the long run because they are more open to absorbing and diffusing new techniques.[137] Other studies find, more specifically, that internet technologies diffuse faster in democracies, possibly because nondemocracies are threatened by the internet's potential to empower anti-government movements.[138]

On the other hand, the impact of democracy on technological progress and economic growth is disputed. Drawing on data from fifty countries over the 1970–2010 period, Taylor finds that regime type does not have a strong relationship with national innovation rates, as measured by patenting rates.[139] One review of the econometric evidence on democracy and growth concludes that "the *net* effect of democracy on growth performance cross-nationally over the last five decades is negative or null."[140] Moreover, China's rapid economic growth and adoption of internet technologies stands out as an exception to general claims about a democratic advantage when it comes to leveraging new technologies as sources of productivity growth. Contrary to initial expectations, incentives to control online spaces have made some autocratic regimes like China more inclined to spread internet technologies.[141] Other scholars point out that the stability of China's authoritarian regime has encouraged substantial contributions to R&D and technical education,

135. See, for example, Kroenig 2020.
136. Acemoglu and Robinson 2012; Acemoglu et al. 2018.
137. Knutsen 2015; Milner and Solstad 2021.
138. Milner 2006; Howard et al. 2009.
139. Taylor 2016, 126–27.
140. Gerring et al. 2005, 323, emphasis in original.
141. Howard et al. 2009; Rød and Weidmann 2015.

the type of investments in sustained productivity growth typically associated with democracies.[142]

It is not within the scope of this chapter to settle these debates.[143] Still, the juxtaposition of the GPT and LS mechanisms does speak to *how* regime type could shape US-China competition in the IR-4. Though the conventional wisdom links democracy to freewheeling thought and capacity for innovation, the most important effects of regime type in US-China technological competition during the IR-4, under the GPT diffusion framework, may materialize through changes in GPT skill infrastructure. Democracies tend to be more politically decentralized than autocracies, and decentralized states could be more responsive to the new demands for engineering skills and knowledge in a particular GPT. This accords with evidence that new technologies consistently diffuse more quickly in decentralized states.[144]

Summary

How far can we take GPT diffusion theory's implications for the US-China case? I have presented support for the GPT mechanism across a range of historical case studies, each of which covers at least four decades and two countries. At the same time, it is necessary to acknowledge limitations in translating lessons from past industrial revolutions and power transitions to the present.

To begin, it is important to clarify that my findings directly address the mechanism by which technological breakthroughs enable China to surpass the United States in economic productivity.[145] The scenario in which China overtakes the United States as the most powerful economy is different from one in which the US-China power gap narrows but does not fully disappear. Scholars have rightly noted that the latter scenario—"posing problems without catching up," in the words of Thomas Christensen—still significantly bears

142. Doner and Schneider 2016. At the same time, the excessive influence of the Chinese Communist Party may hamper the ability of Chinese universities and state-owned enterprises to adapt to new innovations (Abrami, Kirby, and McFarlan 2014).

143. The quantitative analysis includes regime type as a control variable in analyzing the relationship between GPT skill infrastructure and computerization. It is not statistically significant in the baseline time-series cross-section model.

144. Taylor 2016, 133–36.

145. For a piece that explores the effects of AI on global politics beyond a race for technological dominance, in particular the relationship between AI and informational feedback loops, see Farrell, Newman, and Wallace 2022.

on issues such as Taiwan's sovereignty.[146] Even so, the possibility of China fully closing the power gap with the United States is especially crucial to study. When rising and established powers are close to parity, according to power transition theory, the risk of hegemonic war is the greatest.[147] China's ability to sustain economic growth also affects its willingness and ability to exert influence in the international arena.

Next, GPT diffusion theory speaks to only one pathway to productivity leadership. The historical case studies have demonstrated that institutional responses to disruptive technological breakthroughs play a key part in economic power transitions. However, China's prospects for long-term economic growth could also hinge on demographic and geographic drivers.[148]

A number of factors could affect whether lessons from the past three industrial revolutions extend to the implications of present-day technological advances for a US-China power transition. The most plausible transferability issues can be grouped into those that relate to the nature of great power competition and those that relate to the nature of technological change.

First, as put forward by Stephen Brooks and William Wohlforth, China's rise in the twenty-first century could face structural barriers that did not exist in previous eras.[149] Relying in part on data from 2005–2006, they argue that the present gap between the United States and China in military capabilities, as captured in long-term investments in military R&D, is much larger than past gaps between rising powers and established powers.[150] Arguably, the US-China gap in military expenditures has narrowed to the extent that comparisons to historical distributions of military capabilities are more viable. In 2021, China accounted for 14 percent of global military expenditures. This updated figure, albeit still much lower than the US share (38 percent), reflects China's military modernization efforts over the past two decades during a time of declining US military spending.[151] This ratio is more comparable to

---

146. Shifrinson and Beckley 2012; Christensen 2001.

147. Organski 1968, 372–73.

148. For studies that comprehensively assess key drivers of long-term economic growth in relation to the US-China power balance, see Beckley 2018a, 2021.

149. Brooks and Wohlforth 2016.

150. Ibid., 22–59, esp. 29–30 (for unpacking military capability data). Many of Brooks and Wohlforth's other points still stand, in particular regarding US command of the commons.

151. My calculations are based on the Stockholm International Peace Research Institute database on military expenditures (https://www.sipri.org/databases/milex).

distributions of military capabilities in the historical periods analyzed in the case studies.[152]

Another structural barrier China faces is that the growing complexity of developing and deploying advanced military systems now makes it more difficult for rising powers to convert economic capacity into military capacity than it was in the past.[153] There are a few reasons why it is still relevant to study China's ability to convert the technological breakthroughs of the IR-4 into sustained productivity growth. To start, rising states could still benefit from the steady diffusion of some complex military technologies connected to advances in the commercial domain, such as armed uninhabited vehicles.[154] In addition, military effectiveness does not solely derive from extremely complex systems like the F-22 stealth fighter. Converting production capacity to military strength could be more relevant for China's investments in asymmetric capabilities and those suited for specific regional conflicts, such as ground-based air defense systems and the rapid replacement of naval forces.[155] Lastly, there remains a strong connection between economic development and countries' capabilities to "produce, maintain, and coordinate complex military systems."[156]

As for the second set of transferability issues, the technological landscape itself is changing. Accelerated globalization of scientific and technological activities may reduce the likelihood of adoption gaps between advanced economies when it comes to emerging technologies.[157] Despite these considerations, there are also compelling reasons to think that the nature of technological change in this current period only magnifies the importance of GPT diffusion theory. Cross-country studies indicate that while new technologies are spreading between countries faster than ever, they are spreading to all firms within a country at increasingly slower rates. Networks of multinational firms at the global technology frontiers have reduced cross-national lags in the initial adoption of new technologies, but the cross-national lags in the "intensive adoption" of new technologies, as measured by the time between the technologies' initial adoption to intensive penetration throughout

152. Brooks and Wohlforth 2008, 30.
153. Brooks 2005, 234–40; Brooks and Wohlforth 2016, 9, 40–41; Gilli and Gilli 2019.
154. Horowitz et al. 2019.
155. Ibid.; Pickrell 2020.
156. Beckley 2010, 75. Further, many of the arguments against economic-to-military capability conversion focus on economic size rather than economic productivity.
157. Archibugi and Michie 1997; Xie and Killewald 2012, 27–29.

a country, has only grown.[158] These trends give more weight to the GPT mechanism.

Finally, even if the rise and fall of great technologies and powers is fundamentally different in the twenty-first century, previous industrial revolutions still exert substantial influence in the minds of academics and policymakers.[159] To justify and sustain their agendas, influential figures in both the United States and China still draw on these historical episodes. At the very least, this chapter submits different lessons to be learned from these guiding precedents.

When some of the leading thinkers of our era declare that the AI revolution will be more significant than the industrial revolution, it is difficult to not get caught up in their excitement. Somehow, every generation winds up believing that their lives coincide with a uniquely important period in history. But our present moment might not be so unprecedented. Unpacking how AI could influence a possible US-China power transition in the twenty-first century requires first learning the lessons of GPT diffusion from past industrial revolutions.

158. Andrews, Criscuolo, and Gal 2015; Comin and Mestieri 2014. The shrinking gap in initial adoption is especially relevant for GPTs, as one study finds that innovation in these technologies is more internationalized than in non-GPT fields (Qiu and Cantwell 2018).

159. Doshi 2021; Li 2018; Qiushi 2018.

8

Conclusion

STUDIES OF HOW TECHNOLOGY interacts with the international landscape often fixate on the most dramatic aspect of technological change—the eureka moment. Consistent with this frame, the standard explanation for the technological causes of economic power transitions emphasizes a rising power's ability to dominate profits in leading sectors by generating the first implementation of radical inventions. This book draws attention, in contrast, to the often unassuming process by which an innovation spreads throughout an economy. The rate and scope of diffusion is particularly relevant for GPTs—fundamental advances like electricity or AI that have the potential to drive pervasive transformation across many economic sectors.

Based on the process of GPT diffusion, this book puts forward an alternative theory of how and when significant technological breakthroughs generate differential rates of economic growth among great powers. When evaluating how technological revolutions affect economic power transitions, GPTs stand out as historical engines of growth that can provide major boosts to national productivity. Though each is different, GPTs tend to follow a common pattern: after multiple decades of complementary innovations and institutional adaptations, they gradually diffuse across a broad range of industries. Everything, everywhere, but not all at once.

This impact pathway markedly diverges from existing theories based on leading sectors. Akin to a sprint on a narrow lane, great power competition over leading sectors is framed as a race to dominate initial breakthroughs in the early growth periods of new industries. In contrast, GPT diffusion theory proposes that by more effectively adopting GPTs across many application sectors, some great powers can sustain higher levels of productivity growth than their competitors. Like a marathon on a wide road, great power competition over GPTs is a test of endurance.

Disruptive technological advances can bring about economic power transitions because some countries are more successful at GPT diffusion than others. A nation's effectiveness at adapting to emerging technologies is determined by the fit between its institutions and the demands of those technologies. Thus, if economic power transitions are driven by the GPT trajectory, as opposed to LS product cycles, the institutional adaptations that matter most are those that facilitate information exchanges between the GPT sector and application sectors, in particular the ability of nations to widen the engineering skill base linked to a new GPT.

Three historical case studies, designed and conducted in a way to assess the explanatory power of the GPT mechanism against the LS mechanism, provide support for GPT diffusion theory. The case studies cover periods characterized by both remarkable technological change—the "three great industrial revolutions" in the eyes of some scholars—and major fluctuations in the global balance of economic power.[1] Overall, the case study evidence underscores the significance of GPT diffusion as the key pathway by which the technological changes associated with each industrial revolution translated into differential rates of economic growth among the great powers.

In the case of Britain's rise to economic preeminence during the First Industrial Revolution, expanded uses of iron in machine-making spurred mechanization, the key GPT trajectory. The gradual progression of mechanization aligned with the period when Britain's productivity growth outpaced that of France and the Netherlands. Britain's proficiency in adopting iron machinery across a wide range of economic activities, rather than export advantages from dominating innovation in leading sectors such as cotton textiles, proved more central to its industrial ascent. Though its industrial rivals boasted superior systems of higher technical education for training expert scientists and top-flight engineers, Britain benefited from mechanics' institutes, educational centers like the Manchester College of Arts and Sciences, and other associations that expanded access to technical literacy and applied mechanics knowledge.

The Second Industrial Revolution case also favors the GPT mechanism's explanation of why certain great powers better adapt to periods of remarkable technological change. The LS mechanism focuses on Germany's discoveries in new science-based industries, such as chemicals, as the driving force behind its catching up to Britain before World War I. However, the United States, emerging as the preeminent economic power during this period, was more

1. Von Tunzelmann 1997, 2.

successful than Germany in exploiting the technological opportunities of
the Second Industrial Revolution. Enabled by innovations in machine tools, the
extension of interchangeable manufacturing techniques across many American industries functioned as the key GPT trajectory that fueled the rise of the
United States. Scientific infrastructure or industrial R&D capabilities, areas in
which the United States lagged behind its industrial rivals, cannot account for
its advantage in adopting special-purpose machinery across nearly all branches
of industry. Rather, the United States gained from institutional adaptations to
widen the base of mechanical engineering talent, including through the expansion of technical higher education schools and the professionalization of
mechanical engineering.

Evidence from the US-Japan rivalry amid the information revolution exposes more gaps in the LS account. During the late twentieth century Japan
captured global market shares in new fast-growing sectors such as consumer
electronics and semiconductor components, prompting many to predict that
it would overtake the United States as the leading economic power. Yet such
an economic power transition, an inevitability based on the expectations of
the LS mechanism, never occurred. Instead, the United States sustained higher
rates of economic growth than Japan owing, in part, to greater spread of computerization across many economic sectors. Japan's productivity growth kept
up with the US rate in sectors that produced information technology but
lagged far behind in sectors that intensively used information technology.
Once again, differences in institutional adaptations to widen the GPT skill
base turned out to be significant. While Japanese universities were very slow
to adapt their training to the demand for more software engineers, US institutions effectively broadened the pool of such skills by cultivating a separate
discipline of computer science.

As a supplement to the case studies, I conducted a large-n statistical analysis
to test whether countries with superior GPT skill infrastructure preside over
higher rates of GPT diffusion. Leveraging time-series cross-sectional data on
software engineering education and computerization rates in nineteen countries (the G20 economies) across twenty-five years, the quantitative analysis
confirmed this crucial expectation derived from GPT diffusion theory. I found
less support for other factors often assumed to have a positive effect on an
economy's broader technological transformation, including institutional
factors linked to securing LS product cycles. This empirical test validates a core
component of GPT diffusion theory across a sample of the world's major
emerging and developed economies.

Main Contributions

First, at its core, *Technology and the Rise of Great Powers* introduces and defends GPT diffusion theory as a novel explanation for how and when technological change can lead to a power transition. Historical case studies and statistical analysis substantiate the explanatory power of GPT diffusion theory over the standard explanation of technology-driven power transitions based on leading sectors, which exerts enduring influence in policy and academic circles.[2] In doing so, the book answers the call by scholars such as Michael Beckley and Matthew Kroenig for the international relations field to devote more attention to the causes of power transitions, not just their consequences.[3]

By expounding on the significance of GPT skill infrastructure, the book points toward next steps to better understanding the politics behind some of the most significant technological advances in human history. To investigate why some countries are more successful in cultivating GPT skill infrastructure, promising avenues of research could tap into existing work that concentrates on centralization, inclusiveness of political institutions, government capacity to adopt long time horizons, and industrial organization.[4] In these efforts, being careful to differentiate between various pathways by which technological changes make their mark, as this book does with the GPT and LS mechanisms, will be especially important when underlying political factors that satisfy the demands of one type of technological trajectory run counter to the demands of another.

Future work should also probe other institutional factors beyond GPT skill infrastructure that contribute to cross-national differences in GPT adoption. This opens up a universe of institutions that are often ignored in innovation-centered accounts of technological leadership, including gender gaps in engineering education,[5] transnational ethnic networks that facilitate technology transfer,[6] and "technology diffusion institutions," such as standard-setting organizations and applied technology centers.[7]

---

2. Drezner 2019, 289; Kennedy 2018; Tellis et al. 2000.

3. Beckley 2021; Kroenig 2020.

4. Acemoglu and Robinson 2006, 2012; Doner and Schneider 2016; Simmons 2016.

5. On changing gender norms and mechanics' education in the First Industrial Revolution, see Jacob 1997, 211.

6. Taylor 2016; Saxenian and Hsu 2001.

7. Shapira and Youtie 2017.

In positioning the LS mechanism as the main foil to the GPT mechanism, my intention is to use this clash between theories to productively advance our understanding of the rise and fall of great technologies and powers. Contestation should not be misread as disparagement. In one sense, GPT diffusion theory builds on previous scholarship about leading sectors, which first identified the need to flesh out more specific linkages between certain technological advances and more highly aggregated economic changes in the context of power transitions.[8] Testing, revising, and improving upon established theories is essential to gradual yet impactful scientific progress—not so unlike the incremental, protracted advance of a GPT.

Second, the book's central argument also suggests revisions to assessments of power in international politics. Recognizing that scientific and technological capabilities are becoming increasingly central to a nation's overall power, researchers tend to equate technological leadership with a country's ability to initiate "key 'leading sectors' that are most likely to dominate the world economy into the twenty-first century."[9] For instance, an influential RAND report, "Measuring National Power in the Postindustrial Age," proposes a template for measuring national power based on a country's capacity to dominate innovation cycles in "leading sectors."[10] In this effort, the authors draw directly from LS-based scholarship: "The conceptual underpinnings of this template are inspired by the work of Schumpeter, Rostow, Gilpin, Kennedy, and Modelski and Thompson."[11] This study has gained considerable traction in academic and policymaking circles, inspired further workshops on national power, and has been called "the definitive US study on CNP [Comprehensive National Power]."[12]

Contrary to these approaches, this book submits that evaluations of scientific and technological power should take diffusion seriously. Assessments that solely rely on indicators of innovation capacity in leading sectors will be misleading, especially if a state lags behind in its ability to spread and embed innovations across productive processes. A more balanced judgement of a state's potential for technological leadership requires looking beyond multinational corporations, innovation clusters like Silicon Valley, and eye-popping R&D

8. Thompson 1990, 221.
9. Wohlforth 1999, 17.
10. Tellis et al. 2000, 37.
11. Ibid., 36. In the order cited in the quote, see Schumpeter 1934, 1939; Rostow 1960; Gilpin 1981; Kennedy 1987; and Modelski and Thompson 1996.
12. Singh, Gera, and Dewan 2013, 60; Treverton and Jones 2005.

numbers to the humble undertaking of diffusion. It shines the spotlight on a different cast of characters: medium-sized firms in small towns, engineers who tweak and implement new methods, and channels that connect the technological frontier with the rest of the economy.

In an article published in the *Review of International Political Economy* journal, I illustrated the value of this diffusion-oriented approach in gauging China's scientific and technological capabilities.[13] Preoccupied with China's growing strength in developing new-to-the-world advances, existing scholarship warns that China is poised to overtake the United States in technological leadership. This is mistaken. There is still a large gap between the United States and China when it comes to the countries' readiness to effectively spread and utilize cutting-edge technologies, as measured by penetration rates of digital technologies such as cloud computing, smart sensors, and key industrial software. When the focus shifts away from impressive and flashy R&D achievements and highly cited publications, China's "diffusion deficit" comes to light. Indeed, a diffusion-centric assessment indicates that China is much less likely to become a scientific and technological superpower than innovation-centric assessments predict.

Relatedly, the GPT diffusion framework can be fruitfully applied to debates about the effects of emerging technologies on military power. Major theories of military innovation focus on relatively narrow technological developments, such as aircraft carriers, but the most consequential military implications of technological change might come from more fundamental advances like GPTs. In an article that employs evidence from electricity's impact on military effectiveness to analyze how AI could affect the future of warfare, Allan Dafoe and I challenge studies that predict AI will rapidly spread to militaries around the world and narrow gaps in capabilities.[14]

Third, as chapter 7 spells out in detail, GPT diffusion theory provides an alternative model for how revolutionary technologies, in particular AI, could affect the US-China power balance. This, in turn, implies different optimal policies for securing technological advantage. Drawing on the LS template, influential thinkers and policymakers in both the United States and China place undue emphasis on three points: the rapid timeframe of economic payoffs from AI and other emerging technologies; where the initial, fundamental innovations in such technologies cluster; and growth driven by a narrow range of economic sectors.

13. Ding 2023.
14. Ding and Dafoe 2023.

GPT diffusion theory suggests diverging conclusions on all three dimensions. The key technological trajectory is the relative success of the United States and China in adopting AI advances across many industries in a gradual process that will play out over multiple decades. It will be infeasible for one side to cut the other off from foundational innovations in GPTs. The most important institutional factors, therefore, are not R&D infrastructure or training grounds for elite AI scientists but rather those factors that widen the skill base in AI and enmesh AI engineers in cross-cutting networks with entrepreneurs and scientists.[15]

Yet, the United States is fixated on dominating innovation cycles in leading sectors. When it comes to their grand AI strategy, US policymakers are engrossed in ensuring that leading-edge innovations do not leak to China, whether by restricting the immigration of Chinese graduate students in advanced technical fields or by imposing export controls on high-end chips for training large models like GPT-3 and ChatGPT.[16] A strategy informed by GPT diffusion theory would, instead, prioritize improving and sustaining the rate at which AI becomes embedded in a wide range of productive processes. For instance, in their analysis of almost 900,000 associate's degree programs, Center for Security and Emerging Technology researchers Diana Gehlhaus and Luke Koslosky identified investment in community and technical colleges as a way to unlock "latent potential" in the US AI talent pipeline.[17] This recommendation accords with an OECD working paper on the beneficial effects of a wider ICT skills pool on digital adoption rates across twenty-five European countries. The study finds that "the marginal benefit of training for adoption is found to be twice as large for low-skilled than for high-skilled workers, suggesting that measures that encourage the training of low-skilled workers are likely to entail a double dividend for productivity and inclusiveness."[18]

At the broadest level, this book demonstrates a method to unpack the causal effects of technological change on international politics. International relations scholars persistently appeal for the discipline to better anticipate the

---

15. I am not arguing that policies and institutional adaptations that nurture cutting-edge innovations are counterproductive. After all, R&D investments have been referred to as "diffusion policies in disguise" because they can also have a positive impact on diffusion, even if that is not their main goal. But why go for the disguise when you can have the real thing? (Stoneman and Diederen 1994; see also Fagerberg 1987; Howitt and Mayer-Foulkes 2002).

16. Hua 2021; Palmer 2023.

17. Gelhaus and Koslosky 2022.

18. Nicoletti, von Rueden, and Andrews 2020.

consequences of scientific and technological change, yet these demands remain unmet. By one measure, between 1990 and 2007, only 0.7 percent of the twenty-one thousand articles published in major international relations journals explicitly dealt with the topic of science and technology.[19] One bottleneck to researching this topic, which Harold Sprout articulated back in 1963, is that most theories either grossly underestimate the implications of technological advances or assume that technological advance is the "master variable" of international politics.[20]

This book shows that the middle ground can be a place for fruitful inquiry. Technology does not determine the rise and fall of great powers, but some technological trends, like the diffusion of GPTs, do seem to possess momentum of their own. Social and political factors, as represented by GPT skill infrastructure, shape the pace and direction of these technological trajectories. This approach is particularly useful for understanding the effects of technological change across larger scales of time and space.[21]

19. Mayer, Carpes, and Knoblich 2014, 14.
20. Sprout 1963, 187.
21. Dafoe 2015; Herrera 2006; Mayer, Carpes, and Knoblich 2014.

Case Analysis Procedures

Each of the case studies follows a very similar structure to assess whether the expected implications of the LS and GPT mechanisms are present. First, I observe whether emerging technologies generate growth differentials among leading economies through GPT diffusion or LS product cycles. In terms of impact timeframe, evidence that leading sectors had a disproportionate impact on growth in the early stages of their development would support the LS account. Under the GPT diffusion pathway, there should be an extended lag between initial technological breakthroughs and their ultimate impact on economic productivity.

Assessing whether the historical timeline matches up with what mechanisms postulate is a crucial endeavor. Theda Skocpol's classic study on social revolutions, for instance, found that ideologically motivated vanguard movements cannot be important causes of social revolutions because these movements emerged only *after* major revolts had occurred.[1] In the same way, the historical case analysis finds that some technological changes had a significant impact on productivity growth only after an economic power transition had occurred.

Second, according to GPT diffusion theory, the state that most effectively takes advantage of a technological revolution should lead in the diffusion of GPTs across its entire economy. Highlighting a different phase of technological change, the LS mechanism expects that the nation that rises to industrial preeminence gains its edge through monopoly profits from innovation in leading sectors. Notably, the predictions of the two mechanisms are not mutually exclusive in this dimension. It is possible for a state to both monopolize innovation in leading sectors and outpace rivals in widespread adoption of

1. Skocpol 1979.

GPTs.[2] Stronger evidence for GPT diffusion theory therefore would include evidence that the eventual economic leader was not superior to its rivals at LS innovation. By the same logic, stronger evidence for the LS product cycle pathway would include evidence that the eventual economic leader did not outpace its rivals in adopting GPTs at scale.

I evaluate the key phase of relative advantage by compiling export statistics, cross-national technology adoption rates, and sectoral contributions to overall industrial production. Evaluations of this dimension are further informed by assessments of relative industrial advantages by contemporary observers. Geographical distributions of historically significant innovations also enable a specific test of whether the principal source of innovation in leading sectors is concentrated in a single economy, which is one of the key implications of the LS mechanism.[3] It is easier to identify the introduction of a new technological breakthrough than to track the adoption of new technologies across industries and countries.[4] Fortunately, recent efforts to improve data on historical technology adoption have helped with measuring GPT diffusion.[5]

Third, the LS and GPT mechanisms present different perspectives on the breadth of economic growth in a particular period. Under the LS mechanism, we should observe a few key sectors advancing the aggregate rate of growth in the lead state, and technological advances should be concentrated in these sectors. According to the GPT mechanism, a wide range of industries should contribute to the lead state's productivity growth. Since complementary innovations in application sectors are necessary to advance GPTs, technological advances should be relatively dispersed across sectors.

I determine the breadth of economic growth in a particular lead state by using data on the backward and forward linkages associated with various technologies, the distribution of patents, and estimated contributions to productivity growth by sector. Given the differences in data availability, the specific evidence for all three dimensions will vary in each case.

Next, I assess whether the fit between technological developments and institutional adaptations can account for certain countries' success in exploiting

2. In these cases, we can still assess GPT diffusion against LS product cycles by tracing which advantage was more crucial to that state's sustained productivity growth.
3. Reuveny and Thompson 2001, 696.
4. Most diffusion studies present information on how a single technology spreads through one or a limited number of industries and countries (Griliches 1957; Skinner and Staiger 2007).
5. Comin and Hobijn 2009.

GPT diffusion or LS product cycles. If GPT diffusion holds, the state that gains or sustains economic leadership should have an advantage over its rivals in GPT skill infrastructure. Evidence of this advantage would materialize in a wider pool of engineering skills linked to GPTs, more standardization activities in the relevant engineering field, and stronger linkages between those advancing the GPT's frontier and the implementers applying the GPT across various domains. In some periods, my evaluation relies on qualitative comparisons of engineering education. For other cases, I can bring to bear data on engineering graduates in certain subjects, the proportion of engineering education devoted to practical exercises, and bibliometric indicators, such as the number of universities with faculty who publish in a particular engineering field, or the number of publications coauthored by at least one researcher from industry and one from academia.

If effective adaptation to technological revolutions is determined by LS product cycles, institutional adjustments in the most successful state should enable it to dominate innovation in new industries. These institutions include sectoral governance structures suited to a leading sector, as well as scientific research infrastructure and education organizations that produce top-end experts. Investments in R&D, the number of graduates with advanced degrees, and a country's share of research publications and citations in a leading sector can help measure cross-national differences in the institutional competencies that support radical breakthroughs and innovations.

Careful interpretation of the case study evidence is key to fairly assessing these competing mechanisms. As typically happens when evaluating mechanisms cast at higher levels of abstraction, some of my tests leave room for subjective interpretation and investigator bias. Determining whether the historical evidence supports the LS or GPT mechanism's expectations regarding impact timeframe, for instance, may require subjective interpretations of relatively fuzzy notions of whether leading sectors or GPTs stimulate an industrial power shift after a prolonged period as compared to early on in their development. Relatedly, the problem of selecting the "facts" that favor a particular theory is especially pressing given my aim of testing competing theories. In comparing these two mechanisms, I limit the potential for overly subjective judgments by grounding the assessments of the diverging propositions in a consistent set of measures and drawing on a wide variety of sources.[6]

---

6. Thies 2002.

Case Selection Strategy

In developing my case selection strategy, I considered three main factors. First and foremost, the case studies should facilitate tracing mechanisms that connect technological breakthroughs to the rise and fall of industrial powers. Second, I selected the most relevant and crucial cases in a way that avoided favoritism toward my proposed theory of GPT diffusion. Lastly, my case selection strategy allows for my findings about the LS and GPT mechanisms to be generalizable within certain bounds, directly bearing on the current case of China's challenge to American technological leadership. Considering these factors, I chose the following three case studies: the First Industrial Revolution (IR-1, 1780–1840), the Second Industrial Revolution (IR-2, 1870–1914), and the Third Industrial Revolution (IR-3, 1960–2000).

Typical Cases and Deviant Cases

The IR-1 and IR-2 stand out among a limited number of potential typical cases, since a shift in the predominant economic power in the international system, my outcome of interest, is a relatively rare occurrence. I also considered the role of technological change in the seventeenth-century rise of the Dutch Republic, which many historians and theorists regard as a hegemonic power.[7] Ultimately, I coded pre-industrial revolution cases like the Dutch Republic's rise as ones where the cause of interest was not present, since the industrial revolution marked a fundamental shift in the extent to which technological changes affected the productive power of nations.[8]

To supplement the typical cases, I also selected Japan's challenge to American technological leadership in the IR-3 as a deviant case. Useful for disconfirming causal mechanisms when the cause is present but the outcome is not, deviant case analysis can aid theory development by pointing to other variables that can explain why a mechanism breaks down.[9] Specifically, the US-Japan case is an important deviant case with respect to the LS mechanism, in which all the components of the mechanism are present but the outcome does not materialize. Based on Japan's success in key leading sectors, such as

7. Chase-Dunn 1989; Modelski and Thompson 1996, 69; Wallerstein 1984.

8. The IR-1 was a "unique break" in history that separated pre-industrial periods of extremely slow technological advance and modern times characterized by rapid rates of technological advance (Clark 2014, 220).

9. Beach and Pedersen 2018, 861–63; Goertz 2017, 66; Ripsman and Levy 2007, 33–34.

semiconductors and electronics, many scholars predicted that Japan would overtake the United States during this period, yet an economic power transition never occurred.[10] In addition, the case also serves as a check on the GPT mechanism. If the empirical information shows that all the components of the GPT mechanism were also present in this case, this would weaken the credibility of GPT diffusion theory.[11]

I also considered the Cold War competition between the United States and the Soviet Union as a possible deviant case.[12] The Soviet economy was perceived as gaining on the United States but the Soviet Union never overtook the United States in economic leadership; in fact, the Soviet Union experienced negative productivity growth in the 1970s and 1980s.[13] However, compared to US-Japan competition in the IR-3, the US-Soviet case provides less leverage to test GPT diffusion theory against the LS explanation, because the Soviet Union did not have an advantage in any of the candidate leading sectors or GPTs of this time period.[14] From the population of potential cases, qualitative appendix table 1 depicts four types of cases based on whether they score positively or negatively on the cause and outcome.[15] In sum, the three selected cases provide the best leverage for tracing the causal processes that connect technological revolutions to economic power transitions.

---

10. As Gilpin (1996, 428) writes, "The appreciation of Japan's increasing strength in one high-tech industry after another has led many American and European observers to fear that Japan will acquire a monopoly of the commanding technologies of the third industrial revolution."

11. With respect to the GPT mechanism, this case is less relevant, since the empirical analysis reveals that the causal mechanism and outcome are not present ($X = 0, Y = 0$). One could think that this case shows that if the GPT mechanism is not present, then a shift in productivity leadership is less likely. However, while we have a relatively clear notion of what causes economic power transitions, there are countless explanations for nonshifts in economic leadership, which makes these types of cases conceptually problematic (Mahoney and Goertz 2004).

12. I thank Duncan Snidal for pointing out this possible case.

13. Beckley 2018, 34.

14. Graham 2013.

15. The Thucydides's Trap Case File (https://www.belfercenter.org/thucydides-trap/case-file), a project at the Harvard Belfer Center that tracks power transitions, is another source for possible cases. Some of these power shifts are closely linked to technological changes. For instance, after undergoing technological modernization following the Meiji Restoration in the late nineteenth century, Japan surpassed China and Russia in industrial power. Since neither China nor Russia were the leading economic power in that period, however, this case does not qualify.

QUALITATIVE APPENDIX TABLE 1. A Typology of Cases

	Outcome absent (−)	Outcome present (+)
Cause absent (−)	*Irrelevant* Dutch Republic (mid-seventeenth century)	*Deviant coverage case* Portugal–Dutch Republic transition (early seventeenth century)
Cause present (+)	*Deviant consistency case* Third Industrial Revolution	*Typical case* First Industrial Revolution; Second Industrial Revolution

Source: Terminology adapted from Beach and Pedersen 2019, 96–97.
Note: Cause = technological revolution; outcome = economic power transition; shaded = selected.

Crucialness, Relevance, and Selection Bias

This array of cases has strong theoretical relevance for testing the LS and GPT mechanisms. Early in each of the cases, significant technological breakthroughs sparked the growth of new leading sectors. The LS mechanism is the dominant lens through which scholars analyze how technological change affected economic power balances in all three periods. Existing scholarship holds up the IR-1 and IR-2 as the classic cases of power transitions driven by LS product cycles.[16] Many scholars also point to the IR-3 case as evidence of the LS mechanism.[17] Thus, these are all "most likely" cases for the LS mechanism.[18]

I take a cautious approach in characterizing the likeliness of the cases for GPT diffusion theory. The normal expectations of GPT diffusion theory for each case are more unsettled, as it is not as established as the LS interpretation. One could argue that the conditions were ripe for the GPT mechanism in the IR-1 and IR-2 because two prototypical GPTs, the steam engine and electricity, gained traction in the two eventual leaders of the IR-1 and IR-2. At the same time, the predictions of the GPT diffusion mechanism regarding the steam engine and electricity, derived from the background factors within the cases, are that they diffused too slowly to meaningfully affect the economic power transitions associated with the IR-1 and IR-2. Ultimately, I categorize these as

16. Gilpin 1981, 1987; Kennedy 2018, 51; Modelski and Thompson 1996.
17. Freeman, Clark, and Soete 1982; Kim and Hart 2001.
18. George and Bennett 2005, 91.

"likeliness unclear" cases for the GPT mechanism.[19] The IR-3 case is a "least likely" case for the GPT mechanism, since the surrounding literature and background contextual factors establish that the rising power, Japan, lagged behind the United States in adapting to computerization, the period's representative GPT trajectory.

According to one scheme that grades case designs based on their possible impact on undermining dominant theories and strengthening new theories, the IR-1 and IR-2 cases each rank as the second-best of sixteen possible options.[20] Of course, this potential for modifying existing theories is realized only if the empirical results confirm the GPT mechanism and disconfirm the LS mechanism across all three cases.

The case selection also helps account for rival explanations. Similarities in the external pressures faced by great powers help control for alternative explanations that stress external threats and military procurement as a mobilizing factor for technological leadership. Since Britain and France fought against each other in the Napoleonic Wars during the period covered by the IR-1 case, external security threats cannot explain why Britain was more successful than France in adapting to the IR-1's technological breakthroughs. Inevitably, since the selected cases involve long timeframes and macro-level processes, it is infeasible to isolate the GPT and LS mechanisms from all potentially confounding factors at the case selection step. Therefore, accounting for alternative explanations also occurs at the level of analyzing mechanistic evidence within the case analysis itself.[21]

One natural source of concern with my case selection strategy is selection on both the explanatory and dependent variables, which has been described as the "most egregious error" of case selection.[22] This criticism applies only if my intention is to calculate the average treatment effect of one unit of technological change on the likelihood of an economic power transition. In variance-based interpretations of causality, the mean effect of causes is derived from evidence of covariation between values of the explanatory and

19. This phrasing comes from Blatter and Haverland 2012, 198–99.
20. To qualify as a case set up with the strongest impact for assessing novel theories against established ones, the IR-1 or IR-2 case would have to be considered a "least likely" case for the GPT mechanism (Blatter and Haverland 2012, 198).
21. Beach and Pedersen 2013, 100; Gerring 2006, 122. I further discuss my approach to dealing with alternative causes later in this appendix.
22. King, Keohane, and Verba 1994, 142. For a critique of selection on the dependent variable, see Achen and Snidal 1989.

dependent variables across a range of cases. Since representativeness is the key criterion for case selection, selecting cases that vary on both the independent and dependent variables is encouraged.[23] Some scholars advocate for random selection.[24]

I am not studying the average treatment effect of one unit of technological change on the likelihood of an economic power transition. My interest is in the causal mechanisms that link major technological revolutions with the rise and fall of great powers. Since this is an infrequent outcome, there are not many (1,1) cases. Random selection would lead to studying many cases without a technological revolution and hegemonic transition. Rooted in a mechanism-based approach to causality, I choose instead to prioritize typical cases where the cause and outcome are present.[25] This approach is consistent with recent discussions of case selection for studying causal mechanisms in small-N research, which have moved toward favoring the selection of cases that are positive on the main independent variable of interest and the dependent variable.[26]

Scope Conditions and Generalizability

How generalizable are the findings from these case studies? Addressing this question demands clarifying the scope conditions of the causal mechanisms. First, there are spatial bounds. Empirical information from these case studies is restricted to dynamics that affect great powers at the technological frontier because the GPT and LS mechanisms may operate differently in this context. Causal pathways that facilitate "catching up" may be very different from the ones that enable "forging ahead."[27] Drezner's analysis, for instance, shows that the very institutions that are crucial for technological catch-up in developing countries may constrain innovation at the technological frontier.[28] Additionally, recent empirical research has found that variables such as openness to trade and higher education are more growth-enhancing in countries closer to the technological frontier.[29] Lastly, the contextual differences between great powers and minor powers, including even small states that are technologically

---

23. For a critique of representativeness as a criterion for case selection, see Goertz 2017, 247–52.

24. Fearon and Laitin 2008; Herron and Quinn 2016.

25. Beach and Pedersen 2019, 97–98; Mahoney 2010.

26. Goertz and Mahoney 2012, 177–91; Rohlfing and Schneider 2013.

27. Abramovitz 1986.

28. Drezner 2001, 18.

29. Aghion, Akcigit, and Howitt 2014.

advanced, could confound the GPT and LS mechanisms, since a nation with a larger overall economy and population may be better equipped to diversify its industrial specializations.[30]

Second, temporal bounds should also be specified. It is not a coincidence that the three periods I study correspond to what some scholars have deemed the "three great industrial revolutions," with Britain as the archetypal leader of the first in the late eighteenth century, the United States taking on that role in the second from the late nineteenth century, and Japan as the leader of the third in the latter part of the twentieth century.[31] Although not without qualifications, this characterization reflects a consensus that certain periods feature particularly significant technological changes, which serves as an initial condition for both the GPT and LS mechanisms. Therefore, care should be exercised when applying the findings of this study to periods that do not feature a technological revolution. Nevertheless, if those who claim we are in the midst of a Fourth Industrial Revolution today are to be taken seriously, then it would be a mistake to undervalue the relevance of my results.[32]

The scope conditions establish the external validity of my conclusions. The findings extend to all contexts in which great powers grapple with a technological revolution. These scenarios may be limited, but they are substantively significant owing to the potential consequences of hegemonic power transitions.[33] Moreover, limiting the spatial scope conditions to great powers represents a conservative approach. Some LS accounts have argued that causal mechanisms related to shifts in industrial leadership among great powers can be extended to smaller powers.[34] Viewed in this light, studying the extreme cases of technological revolutions and the competitiveness of great powers could function as a building block for more general theories about technological change and the power of nations. As exemplified by how studies of the European Union have shaped broader thinking about supranational political institutions, in-depth investigation of extreme examples can be foundational for further research.[35]

30. Kitschelt 1991, 469.

31. Von Tunzelmann 1997, 2. In the case study of the Third Industrial Revolution, I challenge the notion that Japan was the technological leader in that period.

32. See, for example, Schwab 2017a. I discuss the possibility of a Fourth Industrial Revolution in chapter 7.

33. Tellis et al. 2000, 36.

34. See, for example, Moe 2009, 223.

35. Blatter and Haverland 2012, 84.

QUALITATIVE APPENDIX TABLE 2. Classifications of Leading Sectors across Industrial Revolutions

Proposed Leading Sectors	Gilpin 1987	Modelski and Thompson 1996	Kim and Hart 2001	Moe 2009	Akaev and Pantin 2014
First Industrial Revolution (1780–1840)					
Cotton textiles	x	x	x	x	x
Iron	x	x		x	
Steam power	x				x
Consumer goods			x		
Light machine tools			x		
Second Industrial Revolution (1870–1914)					
Chemicals	x	x	x	x	x
Electricity	x	x	x		x
Steel	x	x			
Automobiles			x	x	
Consumer durables			x		
Third Industrial Revolution (1960–2000)					
Information and communications technology	x	x		x	
Computers	x		x		x
Electronics	x		x		
Internet					x
Semiconductors					x

GPT and LS Identification

The book's research methodology section describes how I chose the leading sectors and GPTs to trace in the empirical analysis. As part of this process, I surveyed five key texts that pinpointed leading sectors as drivers of economic power transitions. I also examined five key texts that identified GPTs across multiple historical periods. Qualitative appendix table 2 and qualitative appendix table 3 collect these classification schemes for leading sectors and GPTs, respectively.

One issue with narrowing down technological drivers in each case is that the focus on GPTs could exclude other types of technological trajectories that have a profound impact on economic growth. The focus on GPTs, for instance, may neglect many single-purpose innovations, such as the cotton gin and the Haber-Bosch process for synthesizing ammonia, which produced transforma-

QUALITATIVE APPENDIX TABLE 3. Classifications of GPTs across Industrial Revolutions

Proposed GPTs	Nelson and Winter 1982	Bresnahan and Trajtenberg 1995	Wright 2000	Jovanovic and Rousseau 2005	Lipsey, Carlaw, and Bekar 2005
First Industrial Revolution (1780–1840)					
Steam engine		x	x	x	x
Mechanization	x				x
Factory system		x			x
Railroad			x		x
Iron steamship					x
Second Industrial Revolution (1870–1914)					
Electricity	x	x	x	x	x
American system of manufactures	x				x
Chemicalization	x		x		
Internal combustion engine			x	x	x
Third Industrial Revolution (1960–2000)					
Information and communications technology		x	x	x	x
Computers			x		x
Semiconductors		x			
Internet					x
Lean production					x

tive effects despite not qualifying as a GPT.[36] Since I trace leading sectors, in addition to GPTs, I also consider other non-GPT innovations for each period that scholars identify as particularly transformative. In fact, many of these single-purpose technologies feature heavily in leading-sector accounts of shifts in industrial power among great powers, such as breakthroughs in textile machinery in the First Industrial Revolution. Therefore, testing my mechanism against the LS mechanism across all cases should go a long way toward alleviating concerns related to excluding important technological trajectories in my selection of GPTs.[37]

36. Field 2008. The Haber-Bosch process revolutionized agriculture by making nitrogen fertilizer more accessible.

37. Moreover, since single-purpose innovations offer "relatively complete, immediately usable solutions to a readily apparent problem" (Field 2008, 13), they are less likely to generate adoption differentials among countries at the technological frontier, at least compared to the difficulties and delays associated with GPT diffusion.

Two other practical considerations affect LS and GPT selection. First, some technologies are characterized as candidates for both trajectories. For instance, GPT and LS scholarship both classify the steam engine as a critical technological breakthrough in the IR-1. However, the LS and GPT approaches make very different predictions about how the steam engine shaped differential growth rates among great powers. The former concentrates on early advantages from the British steam engine–producing industry's monopoly over innovation, while the latter stresses the delayed effects of Britain's widespread adoption of steam engines across many different sectors. In such situations, I categorize these technologies as both candidate GPTs and leading sectors, leaving it for the empirical analysis to reveal whether the GPT or LS trajectory more accurately captures that technology's development.

Second, there may be multiple leading sectors and GPTs that overlap in a time period. When it comes to GPTs, Cristiano Ristuccia and Solomos Solomou rightly note that various GPTs at different stages of their life cycles could affect the economic growth rate.[38] I take care, therefore, to track when GPTs made their key contributions to economic growth differentials. For instance, in the IR-2 case, I find that electrification and chemicalization—two of the period's most recognizable GPT trajectories—were still in the early stages of their diffusion at the turn of the twentieth century, so they could not have been the main drivers of the industrial rise of the United States.[39]

---

38. Ristuccia and Solomou 2014, 229.
39. Instead, the IR-2 case analysis points to the significance of a GPT trajectory linked to machine tools.

Replication data and code for the quantitative analysis is hosted on Harvard Dataverse at: https://doi.org/10.7910/DVN/DV6FYS.

Robustness Tests for Time-Series Cross-Sectional Analysis

QUANTITATIVE APPENDIX TABLE 1. Additional Controls for Time-Series Cross-Sectional Models

	Dependent Variable	
	Computerization	
	(8)	(9)
GPT skill infrastructure	5.710***	4.041**
	(1.830)	(1.679)
GDP per capita	25.282***	33.265***
	(6.645)	(4.186)
Total population	6.645***	−5.465***
	(1.619)	(2.057)
Polity score	−.590	−.064**
	(0.315)	(0.305)
Military spending	−2.212	0.970
	(2.430)	(3.168)
Liberal market economies	−2.446	−1.874
	(1.934)	(6.211)
Trade openness	0.0887	
	(0.076)	
Urbanization	0.112	
	(0.127)	
East Asia/Pacific		8.164*
		(4.458)

(continued)

| | Dependent Variable | |
| | Computerization | |
	(8)	(9)
Europe/Central Asia		0.091
		(6.487)
Latin America/Caribbean		12.237*
		(6.926)
Middle East/North Africa		−6.144
		(15.126)
South Asia		16.966**
		(8.201)
Sub-Saharan Africa		8.957
		(7.388)
Constant	−326.811***	−381.623***
	(66.138)	(62.207)
Observations	226	370

Note: Standard errors in parentheses.
*p < .10; **p < .05; ***p < .01

QUANTITATIVE APPENDIX TABLE 2. Alternative Specification of Independent Variable (Time-Series Cross-Sectional Models)

	Dependent Variable		
	Computerization		
	(10)	(11)	(12)
Alt GPT skill infrastructure	5.389**	7.023***	5.792**
	(1.840)	(1.827)	(1.747)
GDP per capita	27.737***	23.059***	31.211***
	(3.860)	(4.189)	(4.118)
Total population	6.312***	6.333***	5.311**
	(1.544)	(1.579)	(2.036)
Polity score	−.485*	−.616*	−.647*
	(0.275)	(0.304)	(0.308)
Military spending	−1.445	−2.853	0.649
	(2.356)	(2.356)	(3.110)
Liberal market economy	−4.923	−3.821	−4.176
	(4.169)	(2.281)	(6.266)
Trade openness		0.084	
		(0.073)	
Urbanization		0.139	
		(0.123)	
East Asia/Pacific			7.894
			(4.331)
Europe/Central Asia			6.371
			(0.575)
Latin America/Caribbean			15.498*
			(6.543)
Middle East/North Africa			−3.050
			(15.095)
South Asia			18.358*
			(7.875)
Sub-Saharan Africa			11.529
			(7.457)
Constant	−339.414***	−304.478***	−361.033***
	(58.917)	(64.942)	(60.355)
Observations	370	226	370

Note: Standard errors in parentheses. All logged except polity, LME, and regions.
*p < .05; **p < .01; ***p < .001

Additional Controls for Duration Analysis

QUANTITATIVE APPENDIX TABLE 3. Time to Computerization (Additional Controls)

	Dependent Variable
	25% Threshold (13)
GPT skill infrastructure	0.447***
	(0.092)
GDP per capita	1.124***
	(0.189)
Trade openness	−0.190
	(0.211)
Urbanization	0.700
	(0.510)
East Asia/Pacific	−0.393
	(0.836)
Europe/Central Asia	−1.039
	(0.813)
Latin America/Caribbean	−0.990
	(0.851)
Middle East/North Africa	−1.204
	(0.839)
South Asia	0.554
	(1.361)
Sub-Saharan Africa	−1.680*
	(0.962)
N (number of events)	103 (101)
Likelihood ratio test (df = 10)	127.3***

Note: Standard errors in parentheses. All logged except regional dummies.
*$p < .10$; **$p < .05$; ***$p < .01$

Robustness Tests for Cross-Sectional Analysis

QUANTITATIVE APPENDIX TABLE 4. Additional Controls for Cross-Sectional Models

	Dependent Variable	
	Computerization	
	(14)	(15)
GPT skill infrastructure	3.703***	2.995***
	(0.661)	(0.781)
GDP per capita	15.122***	14.544***
	(1.829)	(1.842)
Total population	−0.467	−0.753
	(0.771)	(0.519)
Polity score	−0.060	0.044
	(0.187)	(0.222)
Military spending	0.276	0.460
	(1.643)	(1.683)
Liberal market economies	4.375	3.897
	(4.343)	(5.030)
Trade openness	−0.213	
	(2.676)	
logavgurbanization	1.040	
	(1.027)	
East Asia/Pacific		−2.620
		(8.184)
Europe/Central Asia		−2.490
		(8.236)
Latin America/Caribbean		−5.233
		(8.610)
Middle East/North Africa		−1.763
		(8.874)
South Asia		−13.155
		(9.854)
Sub-Saharan Africa		−13.362
		(8.792)
Constant	−90.549***	−75.458***
	(33.028)	(26.353)
Observations	110	110
R^2	0.836	0.853

Note: Standard errors in parentheses.
*$p < .10$; **$p < .05$; ***$p < .01$

QUANTITATIVE APPENDIX TABLE 5. GPT Skill Infrastructure and Lagged Computerization

	Dependent Variable
	Computerization (16)
GPT skill infrastructure (1995)	2.059***
	(0.676)
GDP per capita	19.527***
	(1.720)
Total population	−0.276
	(0.538)
Polity score	0.111
	(0.197)
Military spending	1.972
	(1.744)
Liberal market economies	0.937
	(4.726)
Constant	−137.066***
	(23.171)
Observations	110
R^2	0.798

Note: Standard errors in parentheses.
*$p < .10$; **$p < .05$; ***$p < .01$

QUANTITATIVE APPENDIX TABLE 6. LS Model and Computerization

	Dependent Variable	
	Computerization	
	(17)	(18)
GPT skill infrastructure	2.011***	1.363*
	(0.709)	(0.756)
GDP per capita	17.430***	17.334***
	(1.922)	(2.706)
Total population	−0.741	−2.168**
	(0.595)	(1.079)
Polity score	0.006	−0.189
	(0.200)	(0.238)
Military spending	2.193	1.487
	(1.735)	(1.846)
Liberal market economies	1.627	2.675
	(4.617)	(4.410)
Computer exports	0.702*	
	(0.356)	

QUANTITATIVE APPENDIX TABLE 6. (*continued*)

	Dependent Variable	
	Computerization	
	(17)	(18)
ICT patents		0.438
		(0.377)
Constant	−120.464***	−83.258*
	(24.102)	(42.679)
Observations	106	80
R^2	0.808	0.803

Note: Standard errors in parentheses.
*$p < .10$; **$p < .05$; ***$p < .01$

Note: The computer exports variable uses data from 1996, which is the earliest year covered for bilateral trade flows in computers in a dataset on international trade flows at the product level.[1] The ICT patents variable is based on patent applications granted by the US Patent and Trademark Office from 1995, which is the first year in the period covered by the baseline model.

Correlation between Household and Business Computerization

Quantitative appendix figure 1 shows the strong, positive correlation between household and business computerization rates for twenty-six countries. The indicator for household computerization is the same as the dependent variable in the main analysis: the proportion of households with a computer. This comes from the International Telecommunication Union's WTI dataset. The indicator for business computerization is the percentage of businesses with employees who use a computer in work settings. This figure comes from an OECD database on ICT access and use by businesses.[2] Both computerization rates are averages for the period between 2005 and 2014, limited to years when both measures are available. As the figure shows, these two computerization measures are strongly correlated (Pearson correlation coefficient = 0.79).[3]

1. Gaulier and Zignago 2010.
2. Organization for Economic Cooperation and Development 2018.
3. In almost all cases, household computerization outpaced business computerization. One exception was Colombia, where computers diffused more slowly across households than businesses over this period.

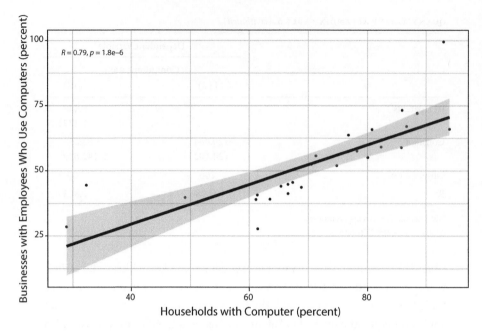

QUANTITATIVE APPENDIX FIGURE 1. Correlation between Household and Business Computerization. *Source*: ICT Access and Usage by Businesses database (Organization for Economic Cooperation and Development 2018).

The distinction between household computerization and business computerization can explain some notable discrepancies in the main analysis. For instance, based on averages of household computer adoption across the period between 1995 and 2014, Japan (64.9 percent) led the United States (64.2 percent) by a small margin.[4] This runs counter to the findings from the IR-3 case, in which Japan lagged behind the United States in the spread of computers across industries. A detailed look at business computerization data helps account for this inconsistency.[5] Compared to their US counterparts, Japanese businesses adopted computers at much slower rates than Japanese households. In 2007, for instance, only 35 percent of Japanese companies were placing orders over computer networks, as compared to 63 percent of US businesses.[6]

4. International Telecommunication Union 2021.
5. OECD data on the percentage of businesses with employees who use a computer in work settings is not available for Japan, so I use a different indicator of ICT usage by businesses to compare the United States and Japan.
6. Organization for Economic Cooperation and Development 2018.

REFERENCES

Abrami, Regina M., William C. Kirby, and F. Warren McFarlan. "Why China Can't Innovate."
Harvard Business Review, March 1, 2014. https://hbr.org/2014/03/why-china-cant-innovate.

Abramovitz, Moses. "Catching Up, Forging Ahead, and Falling Behind." *Journal of Economic History* 46, no. 2 (1986): 385–406.

Acemoglu, Daron, Simon Johnson, and James A. Robinson. "Reversal of Fortune: Geography and Institutions in the Making of the Modern World Income Distribution." *Quarterly Journal of Economics* 117, no. 4 (November 1, 2002): 1231–94. https://doi.org/10.1162/003355302320935025.

———. "Institutions as a Fundamental Cause of Long-Run Growth." In *Handbook of Economic Growth*, edited by Philippe Aghion and Steven N. Durlauf, 1:385–472. Amsterdam: Elsevier/North-Holland, 2005.

Acemoglu, Daron, Suresh Naidu, Pascual Restrepo, and James A. Robinson. "Democracy Does Cause Growth." *Journal of Political Economy* 127, no. 1 (September 27, 2018): 47–100. https://doi.org/10.1086/700936.

Acemoglu, Daron, and James A. Robinson. "Economic Backwardness in Political Perspective." *American Political Science Review* 100, no. 1 (February 2006): 115–31. https://doi.org/10.1017/S0003055406062046.

———. *Why Nations Fail: The Origins of Power, Prosperity, and Poverty*. New York: Crown Publishers, 2012.

Achen, Christopher H., and Duncan Snidal. "Rational Deterrence Theory and Comparative Case Studies." *World Politics* 41, no. 2 (January 1989): 143–69. https://doi.org/10.2307/2010405.

Aghion, Philippe, Ufuk Akcigit, and Peter Howitt. "What Do We Learn from Schumpeterian Growth Theory?" In *Handbook of Economic Growth*, edited by Philippe Aghion and Steven N. Durlauf, 2:515–63. Amsterdam: Elsevier, 2014.

Aghion, Philippe, and Peter Howitt. *Endogenous Growth Theory*. Cambridge, MA: MIT Press, 1998.

———. "Wage Inequality and the New Economy." *Oxford Review of Economic Policy* 18, no. 3 (2002): 306–23.

Ahlström, Göran. *Engineers and Industrial Growth: Higher Technical Education and the Engineering Profession during the Nineteenth and Early Twentieth Centuries: France, Germany, Sweden, and England*. Kent, UK: Croom Helm, 1982.

Akaev, Askar, and Vladimir Pantin. "Technological Innovations and Future Shifts in International Politics." *International Studies Quarterly* 58, no. 4 (December 1, 2014): 867–72. https://doi.org/10.1111/isqu.12124.

Alibaba Research Institute. "From Connected to Empowered: Smart+ Assisting the High-Quality Development of China's Economy (从连接到赋能:'智能+'助力中国经济高质量发展)." March 11, 2019. http://www.cbdio.com/BigData/2019-03/18/content_6049452.htm.

Alic, John A., Lewis M. Branscomb, and Harvey Brooks. *Beyond Spinoff: Military and Commercial Technologies in a Changing World.* Boston: Harvard Business Press, 1992.

Allen, Robert C. "Progress and Poverty in Early Modern Europe." *Economic History Review* 56, no. 3 (2003): 403–43.

———. "Why the Industrial Revolution Was British: Commerce, Induced Invention, and the Scientific Revolution." *Economic History Review* 64, no. 2 (2011): 357–84. https://doi.org/10.1111/j.1468-0289.2010.00532.x.

Allison, Graham. *Destined for War: Can America and China Escape Thucydides's Trap?* Boston: Houghton Mifflin Harcourt, 2017.

Allison, Graham, and Eric Schmidt. "Is China Beating the US to AI Supremacy?" Cambridge, MA: Harvard Kennedy School, Belfer Center for Science and International Affairs, August 2020.

Alphen, Marc van, Jan Hoffenaar, Alan Lemmers, and Christiaan van der Spek. *Military Power and the Dutch Republic: War, Trade, and the Balance of Power in Europe, 1648–1813,* vol. 2. Leiden: Leiden University Press, 2021.

American Society of Mechanical Engineers. *The American Society of Mechanical Engineers: History of the Society.* New York and London: Press of the Cassier magazine co., 1900. https://www.loc.gov/item/43019873/.

Ames, Edward, and Nathan Rosenberg. "The Enfield Arsenal in Theory and History." *Economic Journal* 78, no. 312 (December 1, 1968): 827–42. https://doi.org/10.2307/2229180.

Anchordoguy, Marie. "Mastering the Market: Japanese Government Targeting of the Computer Industry." *International Organization* 42, no. 3 (1988): 509–43.

———. "Japan's Software Industry: A Failure of Institutions?" *Research Policy* 29, no. 3 (March 1, 2000): 391–408. https://doi.org/10.1016/S0048-7333(99)00039-6.

Anders, Therese, Christopher J. Fariss, and Jonathan N. Markowitz. "Bread before Guns or Butter: Introducing Surplus Domestic Product (SDP)." *International Studies Quarterly* 64, no. 2 (June 1, 2020): 392–405. https://doi.org/10.1093/isq/sqaa013.

Anderson, Alun, and Fred Myers. "Japanese Academics Bemoan the Cost of Years of Neglect." *Science* 258, no. 5082 (October 23, 1992): 564–70.

Anderson, John. "Machines and Tools for Working Metals, Wood, and Stone." In *Reports on the Philadelphia International Exhibition of 1876,* vol. 1, presented to both Houses of Parliament by Command of Her Majesty. London: printed by George E. Eyre and William Spottiswoode, 1877.

Andrews, Dan, Chiara Criscuolo, and Peter N. Gal. "Frontier Firms, Technology Diffusion, and Public Policy: Micro Evidence from OECD Countries." Paris: Organization for Economic Cooperation and Development, 2015.

Araya, Daniel. "Who Will Lead in the Age of Artificial Intelligence?" *Forbes,* January 1, 2019. https://www.forbes.com/sites/danielaraya/2019/01/01/who-will-lead-in-the-age-of-artificial-intelligence/.

Archibugi, Daniele, and Jonathan Michie. "Technological Globalisation or National Systems of Innovation?" *Futures* 29, no. 2 (March 1, 1997): 121–37. https://doi.org/10.1016/S0016 -3287(96)00072-9.

Aria, Massimo, and Corrado Cuccurullo. "Bibliometrix: An R-Tool for Comprehensive Science Mapping Analysis." *Journal of Informetrics* 11, no. 4 (November 1, 2017): 959–75. https://doi .org/10.1016/j.joi.2017.08.007.

Armytage, W.H.G. *A Social History of Engineering.* London: Faber & Faber, 1961.

Arora, Ashish, Lee G. Branstetter, and Matej Drev. "Going Soft: How the Rise of Software-Based Innovation Led to the Decline of Japan's IT Industry and the Resurgence of Silicon Valley." *Review of Economics and Statistics* 95, no. 3 (July 1, 2013): 757–75. https://doi.org/10.1162 /REST_a_00286.

Ashton, Thomas Southcliffe. *Iron and Steel in the Industrial Revolution* [1924], 3rd ed. Manchester, UK: Manchester University Press, 1963.

Atkinson, Robert D. "Robotics and the Future of Production and Work." Information Technology and Innovation Foundation, October 15, 2019. https://itif.org/publications/2019/10 /15/robotics-and-future-production-and-work.

Austing, Richard H., Bruce H. Barnes, Della T. Bonnette, Gerald L. Engel, and Gordon Stokes. "Curriculum Recommendations for the Undergraduate Program in Computer Science: A Working Report of the ACM Committee on Curriculum in Computer Sciences." *ACM SIGCSE Bulletin* 9, no. 2 (1977): 16.

Baba, Yasunori, Shinji Takai, and Yuji Mizuta. "The Evolution of Software Industry in Japan: A Comprehensive Analysis." Unpublished paper, 1993.

———. "The User-Driven Evolution of the Japanese Software Industry: The Case of Customized Software for Mainframes." In *The International Computer Software Industry: A Comparative Study of Industry Evolution and Structure*, edited by David C. Mowery, 104–30. New York: Oxford University Press, 1996.

Baily, Martin Neil, and Barry P. Bosworth. "US Manufacturing: Understanding Its Past and Its Potential Future." *Journal of Economic Perspectives* 28, no. 1 (February 2014): 3–26. https://doi .org/10.1257/jep.28.1.3.

Baily, Martin Neil, Barry Bosworth, and Siddhi Doshi. "Productivity Comparisons: Lessons from Japan, the United States, and Germany." Washington, DC: Brookings Institute, January 22, 2020. https://www.brookings.edu/wp-content/uploads/2020/01/ES-1.30.20 -BailyBosworthDoshi.pdf.

Bairoch, Paul. "International Industrialization Levels from 1750 to 1980." *Journal of European Economic History* 11, no. 2 (Fall 1982): 269–333.

Bakker, Gerben, Nicholas Crafts, and Pieter Woltjer. "The Sources of Growth in a Technologically Progressive Economy: The United States, 1899–1941." *Economic Journal* 129, no. 622 (August 1, 2019): 2267–94. https://doi.org/10.1093/ej/uez002.

Baldwin, David A. "Power and International Relations." In *Handbook of International Relations*, edited by Walter Carlsnaes, Thomas Risse, and Beth A. Simmons, 273–96. Thousand Oaks, CA: SAGE Publications, 2012.

———. *Power and International Relations: A Conceptual Approach.* Princeton, NJ: Princeton University Press, 2016.

Baldwin, Richard. *The Great Convergence: Information Technology and the New Globalization*. Cambridge, MA: Harvard University Press, 2016.

Barker, Theo. "Consular Reports: A Rich but Neglected Historical Source." *Business History* 23, no. 3 (November 1, 1981): 265–66. https://doi.org/10.1080/00076798100000048.

Baron, Justus, and Julia Schmidt. "Technological Standardization, Endogenous Productivity, and Transitory Dynamics." SSRN Scholarly Paper. Rochester, NY: Social Science Research Network, August 1, 2014. https://doi.org/10.2139/ssrn.2478707.

Basu, Susanto, and John Fernald. "Information and Communications Technology as a General-Purpose Technology: Evidence from US Industry Data." *German Economic Review* 8, no. 2 (2007): 146–73.

Baten, Joerg, and Jan Luiten van Zanden. "Book Production and the Onset of Modern Economic Growth." *Journal of Economic Growth* 13, no. 3 (September 1, 2008): 217–35. https://doi.org/10.1007/s10887-008-9031-9.

Battke, Benedikt, and Tobias S. Schmidt. "Cost-Efficient Demand-Pull Policies for Multi-Purpose Technologies—The Case of Stationary Electricity Storage." *Applied Energy* 155 (October 1, 2015): 334–48. https://doi.org/10.1016/j.apenergy.2015.06.010.

Beach, Derek, and Rasmus Brun Pedersen. *Process-Tracing Methods: Foundations and Guidelines*. Ann Arbor: University of Michigan Press, 2013.

———. "Selecting Appropriate Cases When Tracing Causal Mechanisms." *Sociological Methods and Research* 47, no. 4 (November 1, 2018): 837–71. https://doi.org/10.1177/0049124115622510.

———. *Process-Tracing Methods: Foundations and Guidelines*, 2nd ed. Ann Arbor: University of Michigan Press, 2019.

Beaumont, Olga, and J.W.Y. Higgs. "Part I, Agriculture: Farm Implements." In *A History of Technology*, vol. 4, *The Industrial Revolution, 1750–1850*, edited by Charles Singer, E. J. Holmyard, A. R. Hall, and Trevor I. Williams. New York: Oxford University Press, 1958.

Beck, Nathaniel, and Jonathan N. Katz. "What to Do (and Not to Do) with Time-Series Cross-Section Data." *American Political Science Review* 89, no. 3 (1995): 634–47.

Beckley, Michael. "Economic Development and Military Effectiveness." *Journal of Strategic Studies* 33, no. 1 (February 1, 2010): 43–79. https://doi.org/10.1080/01402390003603581.

———. "China's Century? Why America's Edge Will Endure." *International Security* 36, no. 3 (2011): 41–78.

———. *Unrivaled: Why America Will Remain the World's Sole Superpower*. Ithaca, NY: Cornell University Press, 2018a.

———. "The Power of Nations: Measuring What Matters." *International Security* 43, no. 2 (November 1, 2018b): 7–44. https://doi.org/10.1162/isec_a_00328.

———. "Conditional Convergence and the Rise of China: A Political Economy Approach to Understanding Global Power Transitions." *Journal of Global Security Studies* 6, no. 1 (March 1, 2021): ogaa010. https://doi.org/10.1093/jogss/ogaa010.

Bellemare, Marc F., Takaaki Masaki, and Thomas B. Pepinsky. "Lagged Explanatory Variables and the Estimation of Causal Effect." *Journal of Politics* 79, no. 3 (July 2017): 949–63. https://doi.org/10.1086/690946.

Bénétrix, Agustín S., Kevin Hjortshøj O'Rourke, and Jeffrey G. Williamson. "The Spread of Manufacturing to the Poor Periphery 1870–2007." *Open Economies Review* 26, no. 1 (February 1, 2015): 1–37. https://doi.org/10.1007/s11079-014-9324-x.

Bennett, Andrew, and Jeffrey T. Checkel. *Process Tracing: From Metaphor to Analytic Tool*. Cambridge: Cambridge University Press, 2015.

Berg, Maxine. *The Age of Manufactures 1700–1820*. London: Fontana, 1985.

Berg, Maxine, and Pat Hudson. "Rehabilitating the Industrial Revolution." *Economic History Review* 45, no. 1 (1992): 24–50. https://doi.org/10.2307/2598327.

Birkle, Caroline, David A. Pendlebury, Joshua Schnell, and Jonathan Adams. "Web of Science as a Data Source for Research on Scientific and Scholarly Activity." *Quantitative Science Studies* 1, no. 1 (February 1, 2020): 363–76. https://doi.org/10.1162/qss_a_00018.

Birse, Ronald M. *Engineering at Edinburgh University: A Short History, 1673–1983*. Edinburgh: University of Edinburgh, School of Engineering, 1983.

Blatter, Joachim, and Markus Haverland. *Designing Case Studies: Explanatory Approaches in Small-N Research*. Basingstoke, UK: Palgrave Macmillan, 2012.

Bloom, Nicholas, Raffaella Sadun, and John Van Reenen. "Americans Do IT Better: US Multinationals and the Productivity Miracle." *American Economic Review* 102, no. 1 (2012): 167–201.

Bohmert, O. V. "Recht, Wirtschaft und Technik: Ein Beitrag zur Frage der Ingenieurausbildung" (Law, Economy and Technology: A Contribution to the Question of Engineering Education). 1904. Estate of Karl Bücher, Leipzig University Library.

Bolt, Jutta, and Jan Luiten van Zanden. "The Maddison Project: Collaborative Research on Historical National Accounts." *Economic History Review* 67, no. 3 (2014): 627–51. https://doi.org/10.1111/1468-0289.12032.

———. "Maddison Style Estimates of the Evolution of the World Economy: A New 2020 Update." Working Paper 15. Groningen: University of Groningen, Maddison Project, October 2020. https://www.rug.nl/ggdc/historicaldevelopment/maddison/publications/wp15.pdf.

Borrus, Michael, and John Zysman. "Globalization with Borders." *Industry and Innovation* 4, no. 2 (December 1, 1997): 141–66. https://doi.org/10.1080/13662719700000008.

Brady, Robert A. *The Rationalization Movement in German Industry: A Study in the Evolution of Economic Planning*. Berkeley: University of California Press, 1933.

Brandt, Loren, John Litwack, Elitza Mileva, Luhang Wang, Yifan Zhang, and Luan Zhao. "China's Productivity Slowdown and Future Growth Potential." Policy Research Working Paper. Washington, DC: World Bank Group, June 2020.

Braun, Hans-Joachim. "The National Association of German-American Technologists and Technology Transfer between Germany and the United States, 1884–1930." In *History of Technology*, edited by Norman Smith, 15–38. London: Mansell Publishing Ltd., 1984.

Bresnahan, Timothy. "General Purpose Technologies." In *Handbook of the Economics of Innovation*, edited by Bronwyn H. Hall and Nathan Rosenberg, 2:761–91. Amsterdam: Elsevier/North-Holland, 2010.

Bresnahan, Timothy F., and Franco Malerba. "The Value of Competitive Innovation and US Policy toward the Computer Industry." In *Technology and the New Economy*, edited by Chong-En Bai and Chia-Wa Yuen, 49–94. Cambridge, MA: MIT Press, 2003.

Bresnahan, Timothy F., and Manuel Trajtenberg. "General Purpose Technologies 'Engines of Growth'?" *Journal of Econometrics* 65, no. 1 (January 1, 1995): 83–108. https://doi.org/10.1016/0304-4076(94)01598-T.

Breznitz, Dan. "National Institutions and the Globalized Political Economy of Technological Change: An Introduction." *Review of Policy Research* 26, nos. 1/2 (2009): 1–11. https://doi .org/10.1111/j.1541-1338.2008.00388.x.

Breznitz, Dan, and Michael Murphree. *Run of the Red Queen: Government, Innovation, Globalization, and Economic Growth in China.* New Haven, CT: Yale University Press, 2011.

———. "The Rise of China in Technology Standards: New Norms in Old Institutions." Washington, DC: US-China Economic and Security Review Commission, January 16, 2013. https://www.uscc.gov/sites/default/files/Research/RiseofChinainTechnologyStandards .pdf.

Broadberry, Stephen N. "Technological Leadership and Productivity Leadership in Manufacturing since the Industrial Revolution: Implications for the Convergence Debate." *Economic Journal* 104, no. 423 (1994): 291–302. https://doi.org/10.2307/2234750.

———. *The Productivity Race: British Manufacturing in International Perspective, 1850–1990.* Cambridge: Cambridge University Press, 1997.

———. *Market Services and the Productivity Race, 1850–2000: British Performance in International Perspective.* Cambridge: Cambridge University Press, 2006.

Broadberry, Stephen, Bruce M. S. Campbell, Alexander Klein, Mark Overton, and Bas van Leeuwen. *British Economic Growth, 1270–1870.* Cambridge: Cambridge University Press, 2015.

Broadberry, Stephen N., and Kyoji Fukao. "How Did Japan Catch-Up on the West? A Sectoral Analysis of Anglo-Japanese Productivity Differences, 1885–2000." Discussion Paper 10570. London: Centre for Economic Policy Research, May 3, 2015. https://cepr.org/publications /dp10570.

Brooks, Harvey. "Technology, Evolution, and Purpose." *Daedalus* 109, no. 1 (1980): 65–81.

Brooks, Stephen G. *Producing Security: Multinational Corporations, Globalization, and the Changing Calculus of Conflict.* Princeton, NJ: Princeton University Press, 2005.

Brooks, Stephen G., and William C. Wohlforth. "World Out of Balance." In Brooks and Wohlforth, *World Out of Balance: International Relations and the Challenge of American Primacy.* Princeton, NJ: Princeton University Press, 2008.

———. "The Rise and Fall of the Great Powers in the Twenty-First Century: China's Rise and the Fate of America's Global Position." *International Security* 40, no. 3 (January 1, 2016): 7–53. https://doi.org/10.1162/ISEC_a_00225.

Brown & Sharpe. *A Brown & Sharpe Catalogue Collection, 1868 to 1899.* Mendham, NJ: Astragal Press, 1997.

Bruland, Kristine. "Industrialisation and Technological Change." In *The Cambridge Economic History of Modern Britain*, vol. 1, *Industrialisation, 1700–1860*, edited by Paul Johnson and Roderick Floud, 1:117–46. Cambridge: Cambridge University Press, 2004.

Bruland, Kristine, and David C. Mowery. "Innovation through Time." In *The Oxford Handbook of Innovation*, edited by Jan Fagerberg and David C. Mowery, 350–77. Oxford: Oxford University Press, 2006. xfordhb-9780199286805-e-13.

Bruland, Kristine, and Keith Smith. "Assessing the Role of Steam Power in the First Industrial Revolution: The Early Work of Nick von Tunzelmann." *Research Policy* 42, no. 10 (December 1, 2013): 1716–23. https://doi.org/10.1016/j.respol.2012.12.008.

Bryant, Lynwood. "The Role of Thermodynamics in the Evolution of the Heat Engine." *Technology and Culture* 14, no. 2, part 1 (April): 152–65.

Bryant, Lynwood, and Louis C. Hunter. *A History of Industrial Power in the US, 1780–1930,* vol. 3, *The Transmission of Power.* Cambridge, MA: MIT Press, 1991.

Brynjolfsson, Erik, and Andrew McAfee. "The Business of Artificial Intelligence." *Harvard Business Review,* July 18, 2017. https://hbr.org/2017/07/the-business-of-artificial-intelligence.

Brynjolfsson, Erik, and Georgios Petropoulos. "The Coming Productivity Boom." *MIT Technology Review,* June 10, 2021. https://www.technologyreview.com/2021/06/10/1026008/the-coming-productivity-boom/.

Brynjolfsson, Erik, Daniel Rock, and Chad Syverson. "Artificial Intelligence and the Modern Productivity Paradox: A Clash of Expectations and Statistics." Cambridge, MA: National Bureau of Economic Research, November 6, 2017. https://doi.org/10.3386/w24001.

BSA Software Alliance. "2018 BSA Global Cloud Computing Scorecard." Washington, DC, 2018.

Buchanan, Robertson. *Practical Essays on Mill Work and Other Machinery.* London: J. Weale, 1841.

Bureau of the Census. "Census of Manufactures, 1914." Volume 2, "Reports for Selected Industries," 1918.

———. "Manufactures, 1905: Special Reports in Selected Industries," 1908.

———. "Thirteenth Census of the United States, Vol. 8, Manufactures—1909." Washington, DC, 1913.

Burwell, Calvin C. "Industrial Electrification: Current Trends." Oak Ridge, TN: Oak Ridge Associated Universities, 1983.

Bussell, Jennifer. "Explaining Cross-National Variation in Government Adoption of New Technologies." *International Studies Quarterly* 55, no. 1 (March 1, 2011): 267–80. https://doi.org/10.1111/j.1468-2478.2010.00644.x.

Calder, Kent E. "High-Technology Electronics Trade and the US-Japan Relationship." *Fletcher Forum* 5, no. 1 (1981): 27–48.

Calvert, Professor Monte A. *The Mechanical Engineer in America, 1830–1910: Professional Cultures in Conflict.* Baltimore: Johns Hopkins University Press, 1967.

Cameron, Rondo E. *A Concise Economic History of the World: From Paleolithic Times to the Present.* New York: Oxford University Press, 1989.

Campanella, Edoardo. "The Real Payoff from Artificial Intelligence Is Still a Decade Off." *Foreign Policy,* August 9, 2018. https://foreignpolicy.com/2018/08/09/the-solution-to-the-productivity-puzzle-is-simple-robots-ai/.

Cantner, Uwe, and Simone Vannuccini. "A New View of General Purpose Technologies." Jena Economic Research Papers 2012-054. Jena: Friedrich Schiller University Jena and Max Planck Institute of Economics 2012.

Cardwell, Donald S. *The Fontana History of Technology.* London: Harper & Collins/Fontana, 1994.

Carlaw, Kenneth, Richard G. Lipsey, and Ryan Webb. "The Past, Present, and Future of the GPT-Driven Modern ICT Revolution." *Industry Canada,* March 27, 2007.

Caselli, Francesco, and Wilbur John Coleman. "Cross-Country Technology Diffusion: The Case of Computers." *American Economic Review* 91, no. 2 (2001): 328–35.

Cava-Ferreruela, Inmaculada, and Antonio Alabau-Muñoz. "Broadband Policy Assessment: A Cross-National Empirical Analysis." *Telecommunications Policy* 30, no. 8 (September 1, 2006): 445–63. https://doi.org/10.1016/j.telpol.2005.12.002.

Cerny, Philip G. *The Changing Architecture of Politics: Structure, Agency, and the Future of the State.* Thousand Oaks, CA: SAGE Publications, 1990.

Chan, Julian Tszkin, Matthew H. Jensen, and Weifeng Zhong. "Federal Agencies Should Stay in the Back Seat for AI Standard Setting" (comment). Gaithersburg, MD: US Department of Commerce, National Institute of Standards and Technology, May 31, 2019. https://www.nist.gov/system/files/documents/2021/10/14/nist-ai-rfi-jtchan_mhjensen_wzhong_001.pdf.

Chan, Steve. *China, the US, and the Power-Transition Theory: A Critique.* New York: Routledge, 2007.

Chandler, Alfred Dupont. *The Visible Hand: The Managerial Revolution in American Business.* Cambridge, MA: Harvard University Press, 1977.

———. *Scale and Scope: The Dynamics of Industrial Capitalism.* Cambridge, MA: Harvard University Press, 1990.

Chapman, J.W.M., Reinhard Drifte, and I.T.M. Gow. *Japan's Quest for Comprehensive Security: Defence—Diplomacy—Dependence.* London: Frances Pinter, 1982.

Chase-Dunn, Christopher K. *Global Formation: Structures of the World-Economy.* Oxford: Oxford: Basil Blackwell, 1989.

Chen, Ling, and Barry Naughton. "An Institutionalized Policy-Making Mechanism: China's Return to Techno-Industrial Policy." *Research Policy* 45, no. 10 (December 1, 2016): 2138–52. https://doi.org/10.1016/j.respol.2016.09.014.

Cheng, Hong, Ruixue Jia, Dandan Li, and Hongbin Li. "The Rise of Robots in China." *Journal of Economic Perspectives* 33, no. 2 (May 2019): 71–88. https://doi.org/10.1257/jep.33.2.71.

China Academy of Information and Communication Technology (CAICT). "AI Frameworks Development White Paper (AI 框架发展白皮书)." February 2022a. http://www.caict.ac.cn/kxyj/qwfb/bps/202202/P020220226369908606520.pdf.

———. "AI White Paper (2022) (人工智能白皮书 [2022 年]." April 2022b. http://www.caict.ac.cn/kxyj/qwfb/bps/202204/t20220412_399752.htm.

Chinn, Menzie D., and Robert W. Fairlie. "The Determinants of the Global Digital Divide: A Cross-Country Analysis of Computer and Internet Penetration." *Oxford Economic Papers* 59, no. 1 (January 1, 2007): 16–44. https://doi.org/10.1093/oep/gpl024.

Christensen, Thomas J. "Posing Problems without Catching Up: China's Rise and Challenges for US Security Policy." *International Security* 25, no. 4 (2001): 5–40.

Cipolla, Carlo M. *The Economic History of World Population.* Harmondsworth, UK: Penguin, 1962.

Clark, Gregory. "What Made Britannia Great? How Much of the Rise of Britain to World Dominance by 1850 Does the Industrial Revolution Explain?" In *The New Comparative Economic History: Essays in Honor of Jeffrey G. Williamson,* edited by T. J. Hatton, Kevin H. O'Rourke, and Alan M. Taylor, 33–57. Cambridge, MA: MIT Press, 2007.

———. "The Industrial Revolution." In *Handbook of Economic Growth,* edited by Philippe Aghion and Steven N. Durlauf, 2:217–62. Amsterdam: Elsevier, 2014.

Coccia, Mario. "The Source and Nature of General Purpose Technologies for Supporting Next K-Waves: Global Leadership and the Case Study of the US Navy's Mobile User Objective System." *Technological Forecasting and Social Change* 116 (March 1, 2017): 331–39. https://doi.org/10.1016/j.techfore.2016.05.019.

Cohen, I. Bernard. "Science and the Growth of the American Republic." *Review of Politics* 38, no. 3 (1976): 359–98.

Cohen, Wesley M., and Daniel A. Levinthal. "Innovation and Learning: The Two Faces of R&D." *Economic Journal* 99, no. 397 (1989): 569–96. https://doi.org/10.2307/2233763.

Cole, Robert. "Academic Entrepreneurship: A Comparison of US and Japanese Promotion of Information Technology and Computer Science." Working paper. New York: Columbia Business School, Center on Japanese Economy and Business, 2013.

Collier, David. "Understanding Process Tracing." *PS: Political Science and Politics* 44, no. 4 (2011): 823–30.

Comin, Diego A. "An Exploration of the Japanese Slowdown during the 1990s." In *Japan's Bubble, Deflation, and Long-term Stagnation,* edited by Koichi Hamada, Anil Kashyap, and David Weinstein. Cambridge, MA: MIT Press, 2010.

Comin, Diego A., Mikhail Dmitriev, and Esteban Rossi-Hansberg. "The Spatial Diffusion of Technology." Working Paper 18534. Cambridge, MA: National Bureau of Economic Research, November 2012. https://www.nber.org/papers/w18534.

Comin, Diego, and Bart Hobijn. "Cross-Country Technology Adoption: Making the Theories Face the Facts." *Journal of Monetary Economics* 51, no. 1 (January 1, 2004): 39–83. https://doi.org/10.1016/j.jmoneco.2003.07.003.

———. "The CHAT Dataset." Working Paper 15319. Cambridge, MA: National Bureau of Economic Research, September 2009. https://doi.org/10.3386/w15319.

———. "An Exploration of Technology Diffusion." *American Economic Review* 100, no. 5 (December 2010): 2031–59. https://doi.org/10.1257/aer.100.5.2031.

Comin, Diego, and Martí Mestieri. "Technology Diffusion: Measurement, Causes, and Consequences." In *Handbook of Economic Growth,* edited by Philippe Aghion and Steven N. Durlauf, 2:565–622. Amsterdam: Elsevier, 2014.

Conference Board. "Total Economy Database Summary Tables," July 2020. https://www.conference-board.org/retrievefile.cfm?filename=TED_SummaryTables_Charts_july20201.pdf&type=subsite.

Cookson, Gillian. *The Age of Machinery: Engineering the Industrial Revolution, 1770–1850.* Woodbridge, UK: Boydell and Brewer, 2018.

Copeland, Adam M., and Adam Hale Shapiro. "The Impact of Competition on Technology Adoption: An Apples-to-PCs Analysis." *Federal Reserve Bank of New York Staff Report* 462 (2010).

Corrales, Javier, and Frank Westhoff. "Information Technology Adoption and Political Regimes." *International Studies Quarterly* 50, no. 4 (December 1, 2006): 911–33. https://doi.org/10.1111/j.1468-2478.2006.00431.x.

Crafts, Nicholas F. R. *British Economic Growth during the Industrial Revolution.* New York: Oxford University Press, 1985.

———. "Revealed Comparative Advantage in Manufacturing, 1899–1950." *Journal of European Economic History* 18, no. 1 (Spring 1989): 127–37.

———. "Exogenous or Endogenous Growth? The Industrial Revolution Reconsidered." *Journal of Economic History* 55, no. 4 (1995): 745–72.

———. "The First Industrial Revolution: A Guided Tour for Growth Economists." *American Economic Review* 86, no. 2 (1996): 197–201.

Crafts, Nicholas F. R. "Forging Ahead and Falling Behind: The Rise and Relative Decline of the First Industrial Nation." *Journal of Economic Perspectives* 12, no. 2 (1998): 193–210.

———. "Historical Perspectives on Development." In *Frontiers of Development Economics*, edited by Gerald M. Meier and Joseph E. Stiglitz, 301–34. Washington, DC: World Bank Publications, 2001.

———. "The Solow Productivity Paradox in Historical Perspective." SSRN Scholarly Paper. Rochester, NY: Social Science Research Network, January 1, 2002. https://papers.ssrn.com /abstract=298444.

———. "Productivity Growth in the Industrial Revolution: A New Growth Accounting Perspective." *Journal of Economic History* 64, no. 2 (2004a): 521–35.

———. "Steam as a General Purpose Technology: A Growth Accounting Perspective." *Economic Journal* 114, no. 495 (2004b): 338–51. https://doi.org/10.1111/j.1468-0297.2003.00200.x.

———. "Industrialization: Why Britain Got There First." Working Paper 214. Coventry, UK: University of Warwick, Center for Competitive Advantage in the Global Economy, November 26, 2014.

Crafts, N.F.R., and C. K. Harley. "Output Growth and the British Industrial Revolution: A Restatement of the Crafts-Harley View." *Economic History Review* 45, no. 4 (1992): 703–30. https://doi.org/10.2307/2597415.

Crouch, Colin, David Finefold, and Mari Sako. *Are Skills the Answer? The Political Economy of Skill Creation in Advanced Industrial Countries.* Oxford, New York: Oxford University Press, 1999.

Crouzet, François. "England and France in the Eighteenth Century: A Comparative Analysis of Two Economic Growths." In *The Causes of the Industrial Revolution in England*, edited by R. M. Hartwell, 139–74. London: Methuen, 1967.

———. *Britain Ascendant: Comparative Studies in Franco-British Economic History.* New York: Cambridge University Press, 1990.

Culpepper, Pepper D., and David Finegold. *The German Skills Machine: Sustaining Comparative Advantage in a Global Economy*, vol. 3. Oxford: Berghahn Books, 1999.

Cusumano, Michael A. *Japan's Software Factories: A Challenge to US Management.* New York: Oxford University Press, 1991.

Dafoe, Allan. "On Technological Determinism: A Typology, Scope Conditions, and a Mechanism." *Science, Technology, and Human Values* 40, no. 6 (November 1, 2015): 1047–76. https:// doi.org/10.1177/0162243915579283.

Dalby, W. E. "The Training of Engineers in the United States." *Proceedings of the Institute of Naval Architects* 45 (1903).

Dale, Robert. "GPT-3: What's It Good For?" *Natural Language Engineering* 27, no. 1 (January 2021): 113–18. https://doi.org/10.1017/S1351324920000601.

David, Paul A. *Technical Choice Innovation and Economic Growth: Essays on American and British Experience in the Nineteenth Century.* Cambridge: Cambridge University Press, 1975.

———. "Some New Standards for the Economics of Standardization in the Information Age." In *Economic Policy and Technological Performance*, edited by Partha Dasgupta and Paul Stoneman, 206–39. Cambridge: Cambridge University Press, 1987.

———. "The Dynamo and the Computer: An Historical Perspective on the Modern Productivity Paradox." *American Economic Review* 80, no. 2 (1990): 355–61.

————. "Standardization Policies for Network Technologies: The Flux between Freedom and Order Revisited." In *Standards, Innovation, and Competitiveness: The Politics and Economics of Standards in Natural and Technical Environments*, edited by R. Hawkins, R. Mansell, and J. Skea, 15–35. Aldershot, UK: Edward Elgar, 1995.

David, Paul A., and Gavin Wright. "General Purpose Technologies and Surges in Productivity: Historical Reflections on the Future of the ICT Revolution." Oxford Economic and Social History Working Paper 31. University of Oxford, Department of Economics, 1999.

————. "General Purpose Technologies and Surges in Productivity: Historical Reflections on the Future of the ICT Revolution." In *The Economic Future in Historical Perspective*, edited by Paul A. David and Mark Thomas, 135–66. Oxford: Oxford University Press, 2006.

Davids, Karel. "Shifts of Technological Leadership in Early Modern Europe." In *A Miracle Mirrored: The Dutch Republic in European Perspective*, edited by Karel Davids and Jan Lucassen, 338–66. Cambridge: Cambridge University Press, 1995.

————. *The Rise and Decline of Dutch Technological Leadership* (2 vols.), vol. 1, *Technology, Economy, and Culture in the Netherlands, 1350–1800*. Leiden: Brill, 2008.

Davis, Ralph. *The Industrial Revolution and British Overseas Trade*. Leicester, UK: Leicester University Press, 1979.

Day, C. R. "The Making of Mechanical Engineers in France: The Écoles d'arts et métiers, 1803–1914." *French Historical Studies* 10, no. 3 (1978): 439–60. https://doi.org/10.2307/286339.

Deane, Phyllis M. *The First Industrial Revolution*. New York: Cambridge University Press, 1965.

Debs, Alexandre, and Nuno P. Monteiro. "Known Unknowns: Power Shifts, Uncertainty, and War." *International Organization* 68, no. 1 (January 2014): 1–31. https://doi.org/10.1017/S0020818313000192.

Dedrick, Jason, Kenneth L. Kraemer, and Greg Linden. "Who Profits from Innovation in Global Value Chains? A Study of the iPod and Notebook PCs." *Industrial and Corporate Change* 19, no. 1 (2010): 81–116.

DeLong, J. Bradford. *Slouching Towards Utopia: An Economic History of the Twentieth Century*. New York: Basic Books, 2022.

Dertouzos, Michael, Robert M. Solow, and Richard K. Lester. *Made in America: Regaining the Productive Edge*. Cambridge, MA: MIT Press, 1989.

Devine, Warren D. "Historical Perspective on the Value of Electricity in American Manufacturing." Oak Ridge, TN: Oak Ridge Associated Universities, Institute for Energy Analysis, September 1, 1982. https://doi.org/10.2172/6774921.

————. "From Shafts to Wires: Historical Perspective on Electrification." *Journal of Economic History* 43, no. 2 (June 1983): 347–72. https://doi.org/10.1017/S0022050700029673.

Deyrup, Felicia Johnson. *Arms Makers of the Connecticut Valley: A Regional Study of the Economic Development of the Small Arms Industry, 1798–1870*. Northampton, MA: Smith College Studies in History Series, 1948.

Diamond, Jared M. *Guns, Germs, and Steel: The Fates of Human Societies*. New York: W. W. Norton & Co., 1997.

Dickson, Ben. "What It Takes to Create a GPT-3 Product." *VentureBeat*, January 26, 2021. https://venturebeat.com/2021/01/26/what-it-takes-to-create-a-gpt-3-product/.

Ding, Jeffrey. "Deciphering China's AI Dream." Technical report. Oxford: Future of Humanity Institute, March 2018.

Ding, Jeffrey. "China's Current Capabilities, Policies, and Industrial Ecosystem in AI." Testimony before the US-China Economic and Security Review Commission hearing on "Technology, Trade, and Military-Civil Fusion: China's Pursuit of Artificial Intelligence, New Materials, and New Energy," June 7, 2019. https://www.uscc.gov/sites/default/files /June%207%20Hearing_Panel%201_Jeffrey%20Ding_China%27s%20Current%20 Capabilities%2C%20Policies%2C%20and%20Industrial%20Ecosystem%20in%20AI.pdf.

———. "Balancing Standards: US and Chinese Strategies for Developing Technical Standards in AI." Washington, DC: National Bureau of Asian Research, July 1, 2020. https://www.nbr .org/publication/balancing-standards-u-s-and-chinese-strategies-for-developing-technical -standards-in-ai/.

———. "The Diffusion Deficit in Scientific and Technological Power: Re-assessing China's Rise." *Review of International Political Economy* (March 13, 2023): 1–26. https://doi.org/10 .1080/09692290.2023.2173633.

———. "The Rise and Fall of Technological Leadership: General-Purpose Technology Diffusion and Economic Power Transitions." *International Studies Quarterly* (2024).

Ding, Jeffrey, and Allan Dafoe. "The Logic of Strategic Assets: From Oil to AI." *Security Studies* 30, no. 2 (March 15, 2021): 182–212. https://doi.org/10.1080/09636412.2021.1915583.

———. "Engines of Power: Electricity, AI, and General-Purpose, Military Transformations." *European Journal of International Security* 8, no. 3 (August 2023): 377–94. https://doi.org/10 .1017/eis.2023.1.

Divall, Colin, and Sean Johnston. "Scaling Up: The Evolution of Intellectual Apparatus Associated with the Manufacture of Heavy Chemicals in Britain, 1900–1939." In *Determinants in the Evolution of the European Chemical Industry, 1900–1939: New Technologies, Political Frameworks, Markets, and Companies*, edited by Anthony S. Travis, Harm G. Schröter, Ernst Homburg, and Peter J. T. Morris, 199–214. Dordrecht: Springer Netherlands, 1998.

Doner, Richard F., Allen Hicken, and Bryan K. Ritchie. "Political Challenges of Innovation in the Developing World." *Review of Policy Research* 26, nos. 1/2 (2009): 151–71. https://doi.org /10.1111/j.1541-1338.2008.00373.x.

Doner, Richard F., Bryan K. Ritchie, and Dan Slater. "Systemic Vulnerability and the Origins of Developmental States: Northeast and Southeast Asia in Comparative Perspective." *International Organization* 59, no. 2 (2005): 327–61.

Doner, Richard F., and Ben Ross Schneider. "The Middle-Income Trap: More Politics than Economics." *World Politics* 68, no. 4 (October 2016): 608–44. https://doi.org/10.1017 /S0043887116000095.

Donner, Paul, Christine Rimmert, and Nees Jan van Eck. "Comparing Institutional-Level Bibliometric Research Performance Indicator Values Based on Different Affiliation Disambiguation Systems." *Quantitative Science Studies* 1, no. 1 (February 1, 2020): 150–70. https://doi .org/10.1162/qss_a_00013.

Doshi, Rush. *The Long Game: China's Grand Strategy to Displace American Order*. New York: Oxford University Press, 2021.

Drezner, Daniel W. "State Structure, Technological Leadership, and the Maintenance of Hegemony." *Review of International Studies* 27, no. 1 (January 2001): 3–25. https://doi.org/10.1017 /S0260210501000031.

———. "Technological Change and International Relations." *International Relations* 33, no. 2 (June 2019): 286–303. https://doi.org/10.1177/0047117819834629.

Du Boff, Richard B. "The Introduction of Electric Power in American Manufacturing." *Economic History Review* 20, no. 3 (1967): 509–18. https://doi.org/10.1111/j.1468-0289.1967.tb00151.x.

Dujarric, Robert, and Andrei Hagiu. "Capitalizing on Innovation: The Case of Japan." Working Paper 09-114. Boston: Harvard Business School, April 2009.

Durham Chronicle. "Durham Mechanics' Institute," May 21, 1825. British Newspaper Archive.

Dutton, H. I. *The Patent System and Inventive Activity during the Industrial Revolution, 1750–1852.* Manchester, UK: Manchester University Press, 1984.

The Economist. "China's Future Economic Potential Hinges on Its Productivity." *The Economist,* August 14, 2021. https://www.economist.com/briefing/2021/08/14/chinas-future-economic-potential-hinges-on-its-productivity.

Edgerton, David. "Innovation, Technology, or History: What Is the Historiography of Technology About?" *Technology and Culture* 51, no. 3 (2010): 680–97.

———. *The Shock of the Old: Technology in Global History since 1900.* London: Profile Books Ltd., 2011.

Edquist, Harald, and Magnus Henrekson. "Technological Breakthroughs and Productivity Growth." In *Research in Economic History,* edited by Alexander J. Field, Gregory Clark, and William A. Sundstrom, 24:1–53. Leeds, UK: Emerald Group Publishing Ltd., 2006.

Edwards, Paul N. *The Closed World: Computers and the Politics of Discourse in Cold War America.* Cambridge, MA: MIT Press, 1996.

Engerman, Stanley L., and Patrick K. O'Brien. "The Industrial Revolution in Global Perspective." In *The Cambridge Economic History of Modern Britain,* edited by Roderick Floud and Paul Johnson, 1:451–64. Cambridge: Cambridge University Press, 2004.

Ernst, Dieter. "Toward Greater Pragmatism? China's Approach to Innovation and Standardization." Policy Brief 18. San Diego: University of California, Institute on Global Conflict and Cooperation, August 2011. https://escholarship.org/uc/item/5bk9533c.

Fagerberg, Jan. "A Technology Gap Approach to Why Growth Rates Differ." *Research Policy* 16, no. 2 (August 1, 1987): 87–99. https://doi.org/10.1016/0048-7333(87)90025-4.

Falleti, Tulia G., and Julia F. Lynch. "Context and Causal Mechanisms in Political Analysis." *Comparative Political Studies* 42, no. 9 (September 1, 2009): 1143–66. https://doi.org/10.1177/0010414009331724.

Farnie, Douglas. "Cotton, 1780–1914." In *The Cambridge History of Western Textiles,* edited by David Trevor Jenkins, 1:721–60. Cambridge: Cambridge University Press, 2003.

Farrell, Henry, and Abraham L. Newman. "Weaponized Interdependence: How Global Economic Networks Shape State Coercion." *International Security* 44, no. 1 (July 1, 2019): 42–79. https://doi.org/10.1162/isec_a_00351.

Farrell, Henry, Abraham Newman, and Jeremy Wallace. "Spirals of Delusion: How AI Distorts Decision-Making and Makes Dictators More Dangerous." *Foreign Affairs* (October 2022).

Fearon, James D., and David D. Laitin. "Integrating Qualitative and Quantitative Methods: Putting It Together Again." In *The Oxford Handbook of Political Science,* edited by Robert Goodin, 1166–86. Oxford: Oxford University Press, 2008.

Feenstra, Robert C., Robert Inklaar, and Marcel P. Timmer. "The Next Generation of the Penn World Table." *American Economic Review* 105, no. 10 (October 2015): 3150–82. https://doi.org /10.1257/aer.20130954.

Feldman, Maryann P., and Ji Woong Yoon. "An Empirical Test for General Purpose Technology: An Examination of the Cohen-Boyer RDNA Technology." *Industrial and Corporate Change* 21, no. 2 (April 1, 2012): 249–75. https://doi.org/10.1093/icc/dtr040.

Ferguson, Charles H. "Computers and the Coming of the US Keiretsu." *Harvard Business Review*, July 1, 1990. https://hbr.org/1990/07/computers-and-the-coming-of-the-us-keiretsu.

Ferguson, Eugene S. *Bibliography of the History of Technology*. London and Cambridge, MA: Society for the History of Technology and MIT Press, 1968.

Fernihough, Alan, and Kevin Hjortshøj O'Rourke. "Coal and the European Industrial Revolution." *Economic Journal* 131, no. 635 (April 1, 2021): 1135–49. https://doi.org/10.1093/ej /ueaa117.

Field, Alexander J. "Telegraph." In *The Oxford Encyclopedia of Economic History*, edited by Joel Mokyr, 90–92. Oxford: Oxford University Press, 2003.

———. "Does Economic History Need GPTs?" SSRN Scholarly Paper. Rochester, NY: Social Science Research Network, September 28, 2008. https://papers.ssrn.com/abstract =1275023.

Filippetti, Andrea, Marion Frenz, and Grazia Ietto-Gillies. "The Impact of Internationalization on Innovation at Countries' Level: The Role of Absorptive Capacity." *Cambridge Journal of Economics* 41, no. 2 (March 1, 2017): 413–39. https://doi.org/10.1093/cje/bew032.

Findlay, Ronald, and Kevin H. O'Rourke. *Power and Plenty: Trade, War, and the World Economy in the Second Millennium*. Princeton, NJ: Princeton University Press, 2007.

Finnemore, Martha, and Kathryn Sikkink. "International Norm Dynamics and Political Change." *International Organization* 52, no. 4 (1998): 887–917.

Fishlow, Albert. "Productivity and Technological Change in the Railroad Sector, 1840–1910." In National Bureau of Economic Research, *Output, Employment, and Productivity in the United States after 1800*, 583–646. New York: National Bureau of Economic Research and Columbia University Press, 1966.

Flamm, Kenneth S. *Creating the Computer: Government Support and International Competition*. Washington, DC: Brookings Institution, 1988.

Fligstein, Neil, and Jianjun Zhang. "A New Agenda for Research on the Trajectory of Chinese Capitalism." *Management and Organization Review* 7, no. 1 (March 2011): 39–62. https://doi .org/10.1111/j.1740-8784.2009.00169.x.

Floud, Roderick. *The British Machine Tool Industry, 1850–1914*. Cambridge: Cambridge University Press, 1976.

Foda, Karim. "The Productivity Slump: A Summary of the Evidence." Brookings Institution, August 26, 2016. https://www.brookings.edu/research/the-productivity-slump-a-summary -of-the-evidence/.

Fogel, Robert William. *Railroads and American Economic Growth: Essays in Econometric History*. Baltimore: Johns Hopkin University Press, 1964.

Fouquin, Michel, and Jules Hugot. "Two Centuries of Bilateral Trade and Gravity Data: 1827–2014." Bogotá: Universidad Javeriana-Bogotá, 2016.

Fox, Robert, and Anna Guagnini. "Sites of Innovation in Electrical Technology, 1880–1914." *Annales historiques de l'électricité* 2, no. 1 (2004): 159–72.

Freeman, Christopher. *Technology Policy and Economic Performance: Lessons from Japan*. London: UNKNO, 1987.

Freeman, Christopher, John Clark, and Luc Soete. *Unemployment and Technical Innovation: A Study of Long Waves and Economic Development*. London: Frances Pinter Publishers, 1982.

Freeman, Christopher, and Francisco Louca. *As Time Goes By: From the Industrial Revolutions to the Information Revolution*. Oxford: Oxford University Press, 2001.

Frey, Carl Benedikt, and Michael Osborne. "China Won't Win the Race for AI Dominance." *Foreign Affairs*, October 7, 2020. https://www.foreignaffairs.com/articles/united-states/2020-06-19/china-wont-win-race-ai-dominance.

Fu, Xiaolan. "Foreign Direct Investment, Absorptive Capacity, and Regional Innovation Capabilities: Evidence from China." *Oxford Development Studies* 36, no. 1 (March 1, 2008): 89–110. https://doi.org/10.1080/13600810701848193.

Fueki, Takuji, and Takuji Kawamoto. "Does Information Technology Raise Japan's Productivity?" *Japan and the World Economy* 21, no. 4 (December 1, 2009): 325–36. https://doi.org/10.1016/j.japwor.2009.02.001.

Fukao, Kyoji, and Miyagawa Tsutomu. "Productivity in Japan, the US, and Major EU Economies: Is Japan Falling Behind?" RIETI Discussion Paper 07-E-046. Tokyo: Research Institute of Economy, Trade, and Industry, 2007.

Galambos, Louis. "Introduction." In *The Third Industrial Revolution in Global Business*, edited by Alfonso Gambardella, Giovanni Dosi, Louis Galambos, and Luigi Orsanigo, 1–9. Cambridge: Cambridge University Press, 2013.

Gallup, John Luke, Jeffrey D. Sachs, and Andrew D. Mellinger. "Geography and Economic Development." *International Regional Science Review* 22, no. 2 (August 1, 1999): 179–232. https://doi.org/10.1177/016001799761012334.

Gambardella, Alfonso, Sohvi Heaton, Elena Novelli, and David J. Teece. "Profiting from Enabling Technologies?" *Strategy Science* 6, no. 1 (March 2021): 75–90. https://doi.org/10.1287/stsc.2020.0119.

Gaulier, Guillaume, and Soledad Zignago. "BACI: International Trade Database at the Product-Level. The 1994–2007 Version." CEPII Working Paper 2010–23, Paris: CEPII, 2010. http://www.cepii.fr/CEPII/fr/publications/wp/abstract.asp?NoDoc=2726.

Gelhaus, Diana, and Luke Koslosky. "Training Tomorrow's AI Workforce: The Latent Potential of Community and Technical Colleges." Washington, DC: Center for Security and Emerging Technology, April 2022. https://cset.georgetown.edu/publication/training-tomorrows-ai-workforce/.

George, Alexander L. "Case Studies and Theory Development: The Method of Structured, Focused Comparison." In *Diplomacy: New Approaches in History, Theory, and Policy*, edited by Paul Gordon Lauren, 43–68. New York: Free Press, 1979.

George, Alexander L., and Andrew Bennett. *Case Studies and Theory Development in the Social Sciences*. Cambridge, MA: MIT Press, 2005.

Gerring, John. *Case Study Research: Principles and Practices*. Cambridge: Cambridge University Press, 2006.

Gerring, John, Philip Bond, William T. Barndt, and Carola Moreno. "Democracy and Economic Growth: A Historical Perspective." *World Politics* 57, no. 3 (2005): 323–64.

Gerschenkron, Alexander. "Economic Backwardness in Historical Perspective" [1962]. In *The Political Economy Reader: Markets as Institutions*, edited by Naazneen Barma and Steven K. Vogel, 211–28. New York: Routledge, 2008.

Gershgorn, Dave. "The Inside Story of How AI Got Good Enough to Dominate Silicon Valley." *Quartz*, June 18, 2018. https://qz.com/1307091/the-inside-story-of-how-ai-got-good-enough-to-dominate-silicon-valley/.

Gilboy, Elizabeth Waterman. "Demand as a Factor in the Industrial Revolution." In *Facts and Factors in Economic History*, edited by Arthur H. Cole. Cambridge, MA: Harvard University Press, 1932.

Gilli, Andrea, and Mauro Gilli. "Why China Has Not Caught Up Yet: Military-Technological Superiority and the Limits of Imitation, Reverse Engineering, and Cyber Espionage." *International Security* 43, no. 3 (February 1, 2019): 141–89. https://doi.org/10.1162/isec_a_00337.

Gilpin, Robert. *US Power and the Multinational Corporation*. London: Palgrave Macmillan UK, 1975.

———. *War and Change in World Politics*. Cambridge: Cambridge University Press, 1981.

———. *The Political Economy of International Relations*. Princeton, NJ Princeton University Press, 1987.

———. "The Transformation of the International Political Economy." Jean Monnet Chair Papers. Fiesole, Italy: European University Institute, 1991.

———. "Economic Evolution of National Systems." *International Studies Quarterly* 40, no. 3 (September 1, 1996): 411–31. https://doi.org/10.2307/2600718.

Gispen, Kees. *New Profession, Old Order: Engineers and German Society, 1815–1914*. Cambridge: Cambridge University Press, 1990.

Godin, Benoît. *Innovation Contested: The Idea of Innovation over the Centuries*. Abingdon, UK: Routledge Taylor & Francis Group, 2015.

Godo, Yoshihisa. "The Human Capital Basis of the Japanese Miracle: A Historical Perspective." In *Community, Market, and State in Development*, edited by Keijiro Otsuka and Kaliappa Kalirajan, 103–20. London: Palgrave Macmillan UK, 2010.

Goertz, Gary. *Multimethod Research, Causal Mechanisms, and Case Studies: An Integrated Approach*. Princeton, NJ: Princeton University Press, 2017.

Goertz, Gary, and James Mahoney. *A Tale of Two Cultures: Qualitative and Quantitative Research in the Social Sciences*. Princeton, NJ: Princeton University Press, 2012.

Goldfarb, Avi, Bledi Taska, and Florenta Teodoridis. "Could Machine Learning Be a General Purpose Technology? A Comparison of Emerging Technologies Using Data from Online Job Postings." SSRN Scholarly Paper. Rochester, NY: Social Science Research Network, May 8, 2021. https://doi.org/10.2139/ssrn.3468822.

Goldin, Claudia. "The Human-Capital Century and American Leadership: Virtues of the Past." *Journal of Economic History* 61, no. 2 (2001): 263–92.

Goldin, Claudia, and Lawrence F. Katz. *The Race between Education and Technology*. Cambridge, MA: Belknap Press of Harvard University Press, 2008.

Goldman, Emily O., and Richard B. Andres. "Systemic Effects of Military Innovation and Diffusion." *Security Studies* 8, no. 4 (June 1999): 79–125. https://doi.org/10.1080/09636419908429387.

Goldstein, Joshua S. *Long Cycles: Prosperity and War in the Modern Age*. New Haven, CT: Yale University Press, 1988.

Gordon, Robert J. "The 1920s and the 1990s in Mutual Reflection." Working Paper 11778. Cambridge, MA: National Bureau of Economic Research, November 2005. https://doi.org/10.3386/w11778.

———. *The Rise and Fall of American Growth: The US Standard of Living since the Civil War*. Princeton, NJ: Princeton University Press, 2016.

Gover, James E. "Review of the Competitive Status of the United States Electronics Industry." In *Technological Competitiveness: Contemporary and Historical Perspectives on Electrical, Electronics, and Computer Industries*, edited by William Aspray, 57–74. Piscataway, NJ: IEEE Press, 1993.

GPT-3. "A Robot Wrote This Entire Article. Are You Scared Yet, Human?" *Guardian*, September 8, 2020. https://www.theguardian.com/commentisfree/2020/sep/08/robot-wrote-this -article-gpt-3.

Graetz, Georg, and Guy Michaels. "Robots at Work." *Review of Economics and Statistics* 100, no. 5 (December 1, 2018): 753–68. https://doi.org/10.1162/rest_a_00754.

Graham, Erin R., Charles R. Shipan, and Craig Volden. "The Diffusion of Policy Diffusion Research in Political Science." *British Journal of Political Science* 43, no. 3 (July 2013): 673–701. https://doi.org/10.1017/S0007123412000415.

Graham, Loren. *Lonely Ideas: Can Russia Compete?* Cambridge, MA: MIT Press, 2013.

Greasley, David, and Les Oxley. "Causality and the First Industrial Revolution." *Industrial and Corporate Change* 7, no. 1 (March 1, 1998a): 33–47. https://doi.org/10.1093/icc/7.1.33.

———. "Comparing British and American Economic and Industrial Performance 1860–1993: A Time Series Perspective." *Explorations in Economic History* 35, no. 2 (April 1, 1998b): 171–95. https://doi.org/10.1006/exeh.1997.0688.

———. "British Industrialization, 1815–1860: A Disaggregate Time-Series Perspective." *Explorations in Economic History* 37, no. 1 (January 1, 2000): 98–119. https://doi.org/10.1006/exeh .1999.0735.

Great Britain Committee on the Machinery of the United States of America. "Report of the Committee on Machinery of US," 1855.

Greenberg, Dolores. "Reassessing the Power Patterns of the Industrial Revolution: An Anglo-American Comparison." *American Historical Review* 87, no. 5 (December 1, 1982): 1237–61. https://doi.org/10.1086/ahr/87.5.1237.

Greig, J. Michael, and Andrew J. Enterline. "National Material Capabilities (NMC) Data Documentation Version 5.0." Correlates of War Project, February 1, 2017.

Griliches, Zvi. "Hybrid Corn: An Exploration in the Economics of Technological Change." *Econometrica* 25, no. 4 (1957): 501–22. https://doi.org/10.2307/1905380.

Gross, Daniel P. "Hiding in Plain Sight: The Identification and (Humble) Origins of General Purpose Technologies," University of California, Berkeley, April 8, 2014. https://allucgroup .ucdavis.edu/uploads/5/6/8/7/56877229/hips_20140408.hbs.pdf.

Grübler, Arnulf. *Technology and Global Change*. Cambridge: Cambridge University Press, 1998.

Guédon, Jean-Claude. "Conceptual and Institutional Obstacles to the Emergence of Unit Operations in Europe." In *History of Chemical Engineering*, edited by William F. Furter, 45–75. Washington, DC: American Chemical Society, 1980.

Guillemette, Yvan, and David Turner. "The Long View: Scenarios for the World Economy to 2060." OECD Economic Policy Papers. Paris: OECD Publishing, 2018.

Gutmann, Myron P. *Toward the Modern Economy: Early Industry in Europe, 1500–1800*. Philadelphia: Temple University Press, 1988.

Guzdial, Mark, Barbara Ericson, Tom McKlin, and Shelly Engelman. "Georgia Computes! An Intervention in a US State, with Formal and Informal Education in a Policy Context." *ACM Transactions on Computing Education* 14, no. 2 (June 1, 2014): 13:1–29. https://doi.org/10.1145/2602488.

Habakkuk, H. J. *American and British Technology in the Nineteenth Century: The Search for Labour Saving Inventions*. Cambridge: Cambridge University Press, 1962.

Habakkuk, H. J., and Phyllis Deane. "The Take-off in Britain." In *The Economics of Take-off into Sustained Growth*, edited by Walt W. Rostow. London: Macmillan, 1963.

Haber, Ludwig Fritz. *The Chemical Industry during the Nineteenth Century: A Study of the Economic Aspect of Applied Chemistry in Europe and North America*. Oxford: Clarendon Press, 1958.

Halberstam, David. "Can We Rise to the Japanese Challenge?" *Parade*, October 9, 1983.

Hall, Bronwyn H., and Beethika Khan. "Adoption of New Technology." Working Paper 9730. Cambridge, MA: National Bureau of Economic Research, May 2003. https://doi.org/10.3386/w9730.

Hall, Peter A., and David Soskice. "Introduction." In *Varieties of Capitalism: The Institutional Foundations of Comparative Advantage*, edited by Peter A. Hall and David Soskice, 1–68. New York: Oxford University Press, 2001.

Hampshire Advertiser. "Annual Soiree of the Southampton Polytechnic Institution," January 20, 1849. British Newspaper Archive.

Hannah, Leslie. "Delusions of Durable Dominance, or the Invisible Hand Strikes Back: A Critique of the New Orthodoxy in Internationally Comparative Business History." Unpublished paper. 1994.

Hanson, Victor Davis. *The Second World Wars: How the First Global Conflict Was Fought and Won*. Illustrated edition. New York: Basic Books, 2017.

Harberger, Arnold C. "A Vision of the Growth Process." *American Economic Review* 88, no. 1 (1998): 1–32.

Harley, C. Knick. "British Industrialization before 1841: Evidence of Slower Growth during the Industrial Revolution." *Journal of Economic History* 42, no. 2 (1982): 267–89.

———. "Growth Theory and Industrial Revolutions in Britain and America." *Revue canadienne d'économique* (*Canadian Journal of Economics*) 36, no. 4 (2003): 809–31.

Harris, John R. "Movements of Technology between Britain and Europe in the Eighteenth Century." In *International Technology Transfer: Europe, Japan, and the USA, 1700–1914*, edited by David J. Jeremy, 9–30. Cheltenham, UK: Edward Elgar Publishing, 1991.

Harris, Richard G. "The Internet as a GPT: Factor Market Implications." In *General Purpose Technologies and Economic Growth*, edited by Elhanan Helpman, 145–66. Cambridge, MA: MIT Press, 1998.

Harrison, Lawrence E., and Samuel P. Huntington. *Culture Matters: How Values Shape Human Progress*. New York: Basic Books, 2000.

Hart, Jeffrey A. *Rival Capitalists: International Competitiveness in the United States, Japan, and Western Europe*. Ithaca, NY: Cornell University Press, 1992.

Hart, Jeffrey A., and Sangbae Kim. "Explaining the Resurgence of US Competitiveness: The Rise of Wintelism." *The Information Society* 18, no. 1 (January 1, 2002): 1–12. https://doi.org /10.1080/01972240252818180.

Hartwell, R. M. "The Causes of the Industrial Revolution: An Essay in Methodology." *Economic History Review* 18, no. 1 (1965): 164–82. https://doi.org/10.2307/2591880.

Heilmann, Sebastian, and Lea Shih. "The Rise of Industrial Policy in China, 1978–2012." Working paper. Cambridge, MA: Harvard-Yenching Institute, 2013.

Hellmeier, George. "Guarding against Technological Surprise." *Air University Review* 27, no. 6 (October 1976): 2–8.

Helpman, Elhanan, and Manuel Trajtenberg. "A Time to Sow and a Time to Reap: Growth Based on General Purpose Technologies." Working Paper 4854. Cambridge, MA: National Bureau of Economic Research, September 1994. https://doi.org/10.3386/w4854.

Hempel, Jessi. "Inside Baidu's Bid to Lead the AI Revolution." *Wired*, December 6, 2017. https:// www.wired.com/story/inside-baidu-artificial-intelligence/.

Henderson, W. O. *The Rise of German Industrial Power, 1834–1914*. Berkeley: University of California Press, 1975.

Herrera, Geoffrey Lucas. *Technology and International Transformation: The Railroad, the Atom Bomb, and the Politics of Technological Change*. Albany: State University of New York Press, 2006.

Herron, Michael C., and Kevin M. Quinn. "A Careful Look at Modern Case Selection Methods." *Sociological Methods and Research* 45, no. 3 (August 1, 2016): 458–92. https://doi.org/10.1177 /0049124114547053.

Herz, Charles H. *The Semiconductor Industry: Report of a Federal Interagency Staff Working Group*. Alexandria, VA: National Science Foundation, 1987.

Hicks, Diana. "University-Industry Research Links in Japan." *Policy Sciences* 26, no. 4 (December 1, 1993): 361–95. https://doi.org/10.1007/BF00999478.

Hislop, Gregory W., Spiros Mancoridis, and P. M. Shankar. "A Collaborative Bachelor's Degree in Software Engineering." Paper presented at 33rd ASEE/IEEE Frontiers in Education Conference, Westminster, CO, November 5–8, 2003. https://www.cs.drexel.edu/~mancors /papers/bsse.pdf.

Hobsbawm, Eric J. *Industry and Empire: An Economic History of Britain since 1750*. London: Pantheon Books, 1968.

Hoke, Donald R. *Ingenious Yankees: The Rise of the American System of Manufactures in the Private Sector*. New York: Columbia University Press, 1990.

Horowitz, Michael. "Artificial Intelligence, International Competition, and the Balance of Power." *Texas National Security Review* 1, no. 3 (2018): 36–57. https://doi.org/10.15781 /T2639KP49.

Horowitz, Michael C., Shahryar Pasandideh, Andrea Gilli, and Mauro Gilli. "Correspondence: Military-Technological Imitation and Rising Powers." *International Security* 44, no. 2 (October 1, 2019): 185–92. https://doi.org/10.1162/isec_c_00363.

Horrell, Sara, Jane Humphries, and Martin Weale. "An Input-Output Table for 1841." *Economic History Review* 47, no. 3 (1994): 545–66. https://doi.org/10.2307/2597593.

Horwitz, Josh, Yingzhi Yang, and Yilei Sun. "China Ramps Up Tech Commitment in 5-Year Plan, Eyes 7% Boost in R&D Spend." *Reuters*, March 5, 2021. https://www.reuters.com /article/us-china-parliament-technology-idUSKBN2AX055.

Hounshell, David. *From the American System to Mass Production, 1800–1932: The Development of Manufacturing Technology in the United States*. Baltimore: Johns Hopkins University Press, 1985.

Howard, Philip N., Ken Anderson, Laura Busch, and Dawn Nafus. "Sizing Up Information Societies: Toward a Better Metric for the Cultures of ICT Adoption." *The Information Society* 25, no. 3 (May 12, 2009): 208–19. https://doi.org/10.1080/01972240902848948.

Howitt, Peter, and David Mayer-Foulkes. "R&D, Implementation, and Stagnation: A Schumpeterian Theory of Convergence Clubs." *Journal of Money, Credit, and Banking* 37, no. 1 (2005): 147–77.

Hu, Krystal. "ChatGPT Sets Record for Fastest-Growing User Base—Analyst Note." *Reuters*, February 2, 2023. https://www.reuters.com/technology/chatgpt-sets-record-fastest-growing-user-base-analyst-note-2023-02-01/.

Hu, Wei-Min, and James E. Prieger. "The Empirics of the Digital Divide: Can Duration Analysis Help?" In *Handbook of Research on Overcoming Digital Divides: Constructing an Equitable and Competitive Information Society*, edited by Enrico Ferro, Yogesh K. Dwivedi, J. Ramon Gil-Garcia, and Michael D. Williams, 645–65. Hershey, PA: IGI Global, 2010.

Hua, Sha. "Visa Restrictions on Chinese Students Endanger US Innovation Edge, Universities Say." *Wall Street Journal*, November 2, 2021. https://www.wsj.com/articles/visa-restrictions-on-chinese-students-endanger-u-s-innovation-edge-universities-say-11635856001.

Huang, Jinhong. "'Firmly Grasp the Opportunity of the New Round of Industrial Revolution' (牢牢把握新一轮工业革命的机遇)." *Red Flag Manuscript* (红旗文稿), October 26, 2018. http://www.qstheory.cn/dukan/hqwg/2018-10/26/c_1123616939.htm.

Hueckel, Glenn. "War and the British Economy, 1793–1815: A General Equilibrium Analysis." *Explorations in Economic History* 10, no. 4 (Summer 1973): 365–96.

Hughes, Thomas Parke. "British Electrical Industry Lag: 1882–1888." *Technology and Culture* 3, no. 1 (1962): 27–44. https://doi.org/10.2307/3100799.

———. "Beyond the Economics of Technology: Summary Remarks 2." In *Economics of Technology*, edited by Ove Granstrand, 425–37. Amsterdam: North-Holland, 1994.

Hull, James P. "From Rostow to Chandler to You: How Revolutionary Was the Second Industrial Revolution?" *Journal of European Economic History* 25 (1996).

Huntington, Samuel P. "The US: Decline or Renewal?" *Foreign Affairs* 67, no. 2 (1988): 76–96. https://doi.org/10.2307/20043774.

———. "Why International Primacy Matters." *International Security* 17, no. 4 (1993): 68–83.

Huo, Jingjing. *How Nations Innovate: The Political Economy of Technological Innovation in Affluent Capitalist Economies*. Oxford: Oxford University Press, 2015.

Hyde, Charles K. *Technological Change and the British Iron Industry, 1700–1870*. Princeton, NJ: Princeton University Press, 1977.

Ikenberry, G. John. *After Victory: Institutions, Strategic Restraint, and the Rebuilding of Order after Major Wars*. Princeton, NJ: Princeton University Press, 2001.

Ilgen, Thomas L. "'Better Living through Chemistry': The Chemical Industry in the World Economy." *International Organization* 37, no. 4 (1983): 647–80. https://doi.org/10.1017/S0020818300034809.

Inklaar, Robert, Harmen de Jong, Jutta Bolt, and Jan van Zanden. "Rebasing 'Maddison': New Income Comparisons and the Shape of Long-Run Economic Development." GGDC Research Memorandum. Groningen: University of Groningen, Groningen Growth and Development Centre, 2018. https://econpapers.repec.org/paper/gruruggd/gd-174.htm.

Inklaar, Robert, and Marcel P. Timmer. "Of Yeast and Mushrooms: Patterns of Industry-Level Productivity Growth." *German Economic Review* 8, no. 2 (2007): 174–87. https://doi.org/10.1111/j.1468-0475.2007.00403.x.

Inkster, Ian. "Made in America but Lost to Japan: Science, Technology and Economic Performance in the Two Capitalist Superpowers." *Social Studies of Science* 21, no. 1 (1991): 157–78.

Inman, B. R., and Daniel F. Burton Jr. "Technology and Competitiveness: The New Policy Frontier." *Foreign Affairs* (Spring 1990). https://www.foreignaffairs.com/articles/united-states/1990-03-01/technology-and-competitiveness-new-policy-frontier.

International Federation of Robotics. "China Overtakes USA in Robot Density." *IFR Press Room*, December 5, 2022. https://ifr.org/ifr-press-releases/news/china-overtakes-usa-in-robot-density.

International Monetary Fund. "Staff Report for the 2019 Article IV Consultation." IMF Country Report, July 12, 2019.

International Telecommunication Union. *Measuring the Information Society: 2017*, vol. 1. Geneva, 2017. https://www.itu.int/en/ITU-D/Statistics/Documents/publications/misr2017/MISR2017_Volume1.pdf.

———. "World Telecommunication/ICT Indicators Database 2021 (25th Edition)," 2021. https://www.itu.int/en/ITU-D/Statistics/Pages/publications/wtid.aspx.

Iqbal, Badar Alam. "BRICS as a Driver of Global Economic Growth and Development." *Global Journal of Emerging Market Economies* 14, no. 1 (January 1, 2022): 7–8. https://doi.org/10.1177/09749101211067096.

Jacob, Margaret C. *Scientific Culture and the Making of the Industrial West*. Oxford: Oxford University Press, 1997.

Japan Information Processing Development Center. "Informatization White Paper." Box 6, folder 44, 1992. Edward A. Feigenbaum Papers, Stanford University.

Jefferys, James. *The Story of the Engineers*. London: Lawrence and Wishart, 1945.

Jin, Canrong. "Jin Canrong: The Fourth Industrial Revolution Is Mainly a Competition between China and the United States, and China Has a Greater Chance of Winning (金灿荣：第四次工业革命主要是中美之间的竞争，且中国胜算更大)." *The Forum of Leadership Science* (领导科学论坛), July 29, 2019. https://www.guancha.cn/JinCanRong/2019_07_29_511347_s.shtml.

Jin, Keyu. "No, China Is Not the 'Next Japan.'" World Economic Forum, October 13, 2016. https://www.weforum.org/agenda/2016/10/no-china-is-not-the-next-japan/.

Johnson, Chalmers. *MITI and the Japanese Miracle: The Growth of Industrial Policy, 1925–1975*. Stanford, CA: Stanford University Press, 1982.

Johnson, George E. "Changes in Earnings Inequality: The Role of Demand Shifts." *Journal of Economic Perspectives* 11, no. 2 (June 1997): 41–54. https://doi.org/10.1257/jep.11.2.41.

Jones, S.R.H. "Technology, Transaction Costs, and the Transition to Factory Production in the British Silk Industry, 1700–1870." *Journal of Economic History* 47, no. 1 (1987): 71–96.

Jorgenson, Dale W., and Kazuyuki Motohashi. "Information Technology and the Japanese Economy." *Journal of the Japanese and International Economies* 19, no. 4 (special conference issue, "Enhancing Productivity") (December 1, 2005): 460–81. https://doi.org/10.1016/j.jjie.2005.05.001.

Jorgenson, Dale W., Koji Nomura, and Jon D. Samuels. "Progress on Measuring the Industry Origins of the Japan-US Productivity Gap." Paper presented at the Fifth World KLEMS Conference, Cambridge, MA, June 4–5, 2018.

Jovanovic, Boyan, and Peter Rousseau. "General Purpose Technologies." In *Handbook of Economic Growth*, edited by Philippe Anghion and Steven Durlauf, 1:1181–24. Amsterdam: Elsevier/North-Holland, 2005.

Juhász, Réka. "Temporary Protection and Technology Adoption: Evidence from the Napoleonic Blockade." *American Economic Review* 108, no. 11 (2018): 3339–76.

Kaempffert, Waldemar. "War and Technology." *American Journal of Sociology* 46, no. 4 (1941): 431–44.

Kaiser, David. Review of *The Rise and Fall of the Great Powers: Economic Change and Military Conflict from 1500 to 2000* by Paul Kennedy. *Journal of Modern History* 61, no. 4 (1989): 736–42.

Kania, Elsa B. "China's AI Talent 'Arms Race.'" *The Strategist*, April 23, 2018. https://www.aspistrategist.org.au/chinas-ai-talent-arms-race/.

Kannan, Hari, and Christopher Thomas. "Public Cloud in China: Big Challenges, Big Upside." McKinsey & Company, July 6, 2018. https://www.mckinsey.com/industries/technology-media-and-telecommunications/our-insights/public-cloud-in-china-big-challenges-big-upside#.

Kashin, Konstantin. "Package 'PanelAR.'" *Estimation of Linear AR(1) Panel Data Models with Cross-Sectional Heteroskedasticity and/or Correlation (Version 0.1)*, 2014.

Katzenstein, Peter J. *Small States in World Markets: Industrial Policy in Europe*. Ithaca, NY: Cornell University Press, 1985.

Kelly, Kevin. "The Three Breakthroughs That Have Finally Unleashed AI on the World." *WIRED*, October 27, 2014. https://www.wired.com/2014/10/future-of-artificial-intelligence/.

Kelly, Morgan, Joel Mokyr, and Cormac Ó Gráda. "The Mechanics of the Industrial Revolution." Discussion Paper 14884. Washington, DC: Center for Economic and Policy Research, June 2020. https://ideas.repec.org/p/cpr/ceprdp/14884.html.

Kelly, Thomas. "The Origin of Mechanics' Institutes." *British Journal of Educational Studies* 1, no. 1 (1952): 17–27. https://doi.org/10.2307/3119430.

Kendrick, John W. *Productivity Trends in the United States*. Princeton, NJ: Princeton University Press, 1961.

Kennedy, Andrew B. "Powerhouses or Pretenders? Debating China's and India's Emergence as Technological Powers." *Pacific Review* 28, no. 2 (March 15, 2015): 281–302. https://doi.org/10.1080/09512748.2014.995126.

———. *The Conflicted Superpower America's Collaboration with China and India in Global Innovation*. New York: Columbia University Press, 2018.

Kennedy, Andrew B., and Darren J. Lim. "The Innovation Imperative: Technology and US-China Rivalry in the Twenty-First Century." *International Affairs* 94, no. 3 (May 1, 2018): 553–72. https://doi.org/10.1093/ia/iiy044.

Kennedy, Paul M. *The Rise and Fall of British Naval Mastery*. London: Penguin Press, 1976.

———. *The Rise and Fall of the Great Powers: Economic Change and Military Conflict from 1500 to 2000*. New York: Random House, 1987.

Kenny, Charles, and George Yang. "Technology and Development: An Exploration of the Data." Working Paper 617. Washington, DC: Center for Global Development, 2022. https://www.cgdev.org/publication/technology-and-development-exploration-data.

Keohane, Robert O. *After Hegemony: Cooperation and Discord in the World Political Economy.* Princeton, NJ: Princeton University Press, 1984.

Kim, Dong Jung. "Making Geoeconomics an IR Research Program." *International Studies Perspectives*, no. ekaa018 (November 12, 2020). https://doi.org/10.1093/isp/ekaa018.

Kim, Sangbae, and Jeffrey A. Hart. "Technological Capacity as Fitness: An Evolutionary Model of Change in the International Political Economy." In *Evolutionary Interpretations of World Politics*, edited by William R. Thompson, 285–314. New York: Routledge, 2001.

Kim, Woosang, and James D. Morrow. "When Do Power Shifts Lead to War?" *American Journal of Political Science* 36, no. 4 (1992): 896–922. https://doi.org/10.2307/2111353.

Kimbrell, George. "Don't, Don't, Don't Believe the Hype." *Los Angeles Times*, February 27, 2008.

Kindleberger, Charles. "Technical Education and the French Entrepreneur." In *Enterprise And Entrepreneurs in Nineteenth- and Twentieth-Century France*, edited by Edward C. Carter II, Robert Forster, and Joseph N. Moody, 3–39. Baltimore: Johns Hopkins University Press, 1976.

King, Gary, Robert O. Keohane, and Sidney Verba. *Designing Social Inquiry: Scientific Inference in Qualitative Research.* Princeton, NJ: Princeton University Press, 1994.

Kinmonth, Earl H. "Japanese Engineers and American Myth Makers." *Pacific Affairs* 64, no. 3 (1991): 328–50. https://doi.org/10.2307/2759467.

Kirshner, Jonathan. "Political Economy in Security Studies after the Cold War." *Review of International Political Economy* 5, no. 1 (January 1, 1998): 64–91. https://doi.org/10.1080/096922998347651.

Kissinger, Henry. "The Rearming of Japan and the Rest of Asia." *Washington Post*, January 29, 1987. https://www.washingtonpost.com/archive/opinions/1987/01/29/the-rearming-of-japan_and-the-rest-of-asia/786911cb-8515-435b-a729-471d126cd76a/.

Kitschelt, Herbert. "Industrial Governance Structures, Innovation Strategies, and the Case of Japan: Sectoral or Cross-National Comparative Analysis?" *International Organization* 45, no. 4 (1991): 453–93. https://doi.org/10.1017/S002081830003318X.

Klinger, Joel, Juan Mateos-Garcia, and Konstantinos Stathoulopoulos. "Deep Learning, Deep Change? Mapping the Evolution and Geography of a General Purpose Technology." *Scientometrics*, March 26, 2021. https://doi.org/10.1007/s11192-021-03936-9.

Knutsen, Carl Henrik. "Why Democracies Outgrow Autocracies in the Long Run: Civil Liberties, Information Flows, and Technological Change." *Kyklos* 68, no. 3 (2015): 357–84. https://doi.org/10.1111/kykl.12087.

Kocka, Jurgen. "The Rise of the Modern Industrial Enterprise in Germany." In *Managerial Hierarchies: Comparative Perspectives on the Rise of the Modern Industrial Enterprise*, edited by Alfred Dupont Chandler, 77–116. Cambridge, MA: Harvard University Press, 1980.

König, Wolfgang. "Technical Education and Industrial Performance in Germany: A Triumph of Heterogeneity." In *Education, Technology and Industrial Performance in Europe, 1850–1939*, edited by Robert Fox and Anna Guagnini. Cambridge: Cambridge University Press, 1993.

———. "Science-Based Industry or Industry-Based Science? Electrical Engineering in Germany before World War I." *Technology and Culture* 37, no. 1 (1996): 70–101. https://doi.org/10.2307/3107202.

Kraemer, Kenneth L., and Jason Dedrick. "Creating a Computer Industry Giant: China's Industrial Policies and Outcomes in the 1990s." Irvine: University of California, Center for Research on Information Technology and Organizations, 2001.

Kraemer, Kenneth, Dale Ganley, and Sanjeev Dewan. "Across the Digital Divide: A Cross-Country Multi-Technology Analysis of the Determinants of IT Penetration." *Journal of the Association for Information Systems* 6, no. 12 (December 1, 2005). https://doi.org/10.17705/1jais.00071.

Kreps, Sarah R., Miles McCain, and Miles Brundage. "All the News That's Fit to Fabricate: AI-Generated Text as a Tool of Media Misinformation." *Journal of Experimental Political Science* 9, no. 1 (2022): 104–17. https://doi.org/10.1017/XPS.2020.37.

Kroenig, Matthew. *The Return of Great Power Rivalry: Democracy versus Autocracy from the Ancient World to the US and China*. New York: Oxford University Press, 2020.

Krueger, Alan B. "How Computers Have Changed the Wage Structure: Evidence from Microdata, 1984–1989." *Quarterly Journal of Economics* 108, no. 1 (1993): 33–60. https://doi.org/10.2307/2118494.

Krugman, Paul. "Competitiveness: A Dangerous Obsession," *Foreign Affairs* (March/April 1994). https://www.foreignaffairs.com/articles/1994-03-01/competitiveness-dangerous-obsession.

———. *The Age of Diminished Expectations: US Economic Policy in the 1990s*, 3rd ed. Cambridge, MA: MIT Press, 1997.

Kugler, Jacek, and Douglas Lemke. *Parity and War: Evaluations and Extensions of the War Ledger*. Ann Arbor: University of Michigan Press, 1996.

Kurth, James R. "The Political Consequences of the Product Cycle: Industrial History and Political Outcomes." *International Organization* 33, no. 1 (1979): 1–34.

Kuznets, Simon. *Secular Movements in Production and Prices: Their Nature and Their Bearing upon Cyclical Fluctuations*. Boston: Houghton Mifflin, 1930.

La Bruyère, Emily de, and Nathan Picarsic. "Beijing's Innovation Strategy: Threat-Informed Acquisition for an Era of Great Power Competition." Proceedings of the 17th Annual Acquisition Research Symposium, April 28, 2020. https://calhoun.nps.edu/bitstream/handle/10945/66005/Beijings_Innovation_Strategy_SYM-AM-20-091_Panel.pdf?sequence=1&isAllowed=y.

Landau, Ralph, and Nathan Rosenberg. "Successful Commercialization in the Chemical Process Industries." In *Technology and the Wealth of Nations*, edited by Ralph Landau, David C. Mowery, and Nathan Rosenberg. Stanford, CA: Stanford University Press, 1992.

Landes, David S. *The Unbound Prometheus: Technological Change and Industrial Development in Western Europe from 1750 to the Present*. London: Cambridge University Press, 1969.

———. *Revolution in Time: Clocks and the Making of the Modern World*. Cambridge, MA: Harvard University Press, 1983.

Langlois, Richard N. "Organizing the Electronic Century." In *The Third Industrial Revolution in Global Business*, edited by Alfonso Gambardella, Giovanni Dosi, Louis Galambos, and Luigi Orsanigo, 119–67. Cambridge: Cambridge University Press, 2013.

Langlois, Richard N., and W. Edward Steinmueller. "The Evolution of Competitive Advantage in the Worldwide Semiconductor Industry, 1947–1996." In *Sources of Industrial Leadership:*

Studies of Seven Industries, edited by David C. Mowery and Richard R. Nelson, 19–78. Cambridge: Cambridge University Press, 1999.

Laskai, Lorand. "Why Does Everyone Hate Made in China 2025?" Council on Foreign Relations, March 28, 2018. https://www.cfr.org/blog/why-does-everyone-hate-made-china-2025.

Lee, Kai-Fu. *AI Superpowers: China, Silicon Valley, and the New World Order*. Boston: Houghton Mifflin Harcourt, 2018.

Lehrer, Mark. "Science-Driven vs. Market-Pioneering High Tech: Comparative German Technology Sectors in the Late Nineteenth and Late Twentieth Centuries." *Industrial and Corporate Change* 14, no. 2 (April 1, 2005): 251–78. https://doi.org/10.1093/icc/dth052.

Leunig, Tim, Chris Minns, and Patrick Wallis. "Networks in the Premodern Economy: The Market for London Apprenticeships, 1600–1749." *Journal of Economic History* 71, no. 2 (2011): 413–43.

Lewis, W. Arthur. "International Competition in Manufacturers." *American Economic Review* 47, no. 2 (1957): 578–87.

Li, Jie. "Deeply Understand and Grasp the World's 'Big Changes Unseen in a Century' (深刻理解把握世界'百年未有之大变局')." *Study Times* (学习时报), September 3, 2018. https://web.archive.org/web/20200624172344/http://www.qstheory.cn/llwx/2018-09/03/c_1123369881.htm.

Lilley, Samuel. "Technological Progress and the Industrial Revolution, 1700–1914." In *The Fontana Economic History of Europe*, edited by Cario M. Cipolla, 187–254. London: Collins, 1971.

Lind, Jennifer. "Half-Vicious: China's Rise, Authoritarian Adaptation, and the Balance of Power." Unpublished paper, 2023.

LinkedIn. "Global AI Talent Report (全球AI领域人才报告)." LinkedIn, 2017. https://business.linkedin.com/content/dam/me/business/zh-cn/talent-solutions/Event/july/lts-ai-report/%E9%A2%86%E8%8B%B1%E3%80%8A%E5%85%A8%E7%90%83AI%E9%A2%86%E5%9F%9F%E4%BA%BA%E6%89%8D%E6%8A%A5%E5%91%8A%E3%80%8B.pdf.

Lipsey, Richard G., Cliff Bekar, and Kenneth Carlaw. "What Requires Explanation." In *General Purpose Technologies and Economic Growth*, edited by Elhanan Helpman, 2:15–54. Cambridge, MA: MIT Press, 1998.

Lipsey, Richard G., Kenneth Carlaw, and Clifford Bekar. *Economic Transformations: General Purpose Technologies and Long-Term Economic Growth*. Oxford: Oxford University Press, 2005.

Litterer, Joseph A. "Systematic Management: The Search for Order and Integration." *Business History Review* 35, no. 4 (1961): 461–76. https://doi.org/10.2307/3111754.

Little, Arthur D. *Twenty-Five Years of Chemical Engineering Progress*, silver anniversary edition. New York: American Institute of Chemical Engineers, 1933.

Liu, Xielin, Sylvia Schwaag Serger, Ulrike Tagscherer, and Amber Y. Chang. "Beyond Catchup—Can a New Innovation Policy Help China Overcome the Middle Income Trap?" *Science and Public Policy* 44, no. 5 (October 1, 2017): 656–69. https://doi.org/10.1093/scipol/scw092.

Locke, Robert R. *The End of the Practical Man: Entrepreneurship and Higher Education in Germany, France, and Great Britain, 1880–1940*. Greenwich, CT: JAI Press, 1984.

Longworth, R. C. "US Losing Computer Dominance to Japan." *Chicago Tribune*, May 17, 1992. https://www.chicagotribune.com/news/ct-xpm-1992-05-17-9202140315-story.html.

Loyalka, Prashant, Ou Lydia Liu, Guirong Li, Igor Chirikov, Elena Kardanova, Lin Gu, Guangming Ling, et al. "Computer Science Skills across China, India, Russia, and the United States." *Proceedings of the National Academy of Sciences* 116, no. 14 (April 2, 2019): 6732–36. https://doi.org/10.1073/pnas.1814646116.

Lundgreen, Peter. "Engineering Education in Europe and the USA, 1750–1930: The Rise to Dominance of School Culture and the Engineering Professions." *Annals of Science* 47, no. 1 (January 1, 1990): 33–75. https://doi.org/10.1080/00033799000200111.

Luong, Ngor, and Zachary Arnold. "China's Artificial Intelligence Industry Alliance: Understanding China's AI Strategy through Industry Alliances." Washington, DC: Center for Security and Emerging Technology, May 2021. https://cset.georgetown.edu/publication/chinas-artificial-intelligence-industry-alliance/.

Luttwak, Edward. *The Endangered American Dream: How to Stop the United States from Becoming a Third World Country and How to Win the Geo-Economic Struggle for Industrial Supremacy.* New York: Simon & Schuster, 1993.

Lyme Regis Mechanics Institute. "Letter from the Joint Secretaries of the Lyme Regis Mechanics Institute to the Poor Law Commission," February 14, 1844. National Archives (United Kingdom).

Lyons, John, Richard Chait, and Simone Erchov. "An Assessment of the Science and Technology Predictions in the Army's STAR21 Report." Washington, DC: National Defense University, Center for Technology and National Security Policy, July 2008.

MacLeod, Christine. *Inventing the Industrial Revolution: The English Patent System, 1660–1800.* Cambridge: Cambridge University Press, 1988.

MacLeod, Christine, and Alessandro Nuvolari. "'Glorious Times': The Emergence of Mechanical Engineering in Early Industrial Britain, c. 1700–1850." *Brussels Economic Review* 52, nos. 3/4 (2009): 215–37.

Macleod, Roy M. "The Support of Victorian Science: The Endowment of Research Movement in Great Britain, 1868–1900." *Minerva* 9, no. 2 (1971): 197–230.

Macpherson, David. *Annals of Commerce, Manufactures, Fisheries, and Navigation with Brief Notices of the Arts and Sciences Connected with Them: Containing the Commercial Transactions of the British Empire and Other Countries: With a Large Appendix; in Four Volumes.* Nichols and Son, 1805.

Maddison, Angus. *Monitoring the World Economy, 1820–1992.* Paris: Organization for Economic Cooperation and Development (OECD), Development Centre, 1995.

———. *Contours of the World Economy 1–2030 AD: Essays in Macro-Economic History.* Oxford: Oxford University Press, 2007.

———. "Statistics on World Population, GDP and per Capita GDP, 1–2008 AD." *Historical Statistics* 3 (2010): 1–36.

Mahoney, James. "Tentative Answers to Questions about Causal Mechanisms." Paper presented at the American Political Science Association meetings, Philadelphia, August 29, 2003.

———. "After KKV: The New Methodology of Qualitative Research." *World Politics* 62, no. 1 (January 2010): 120–47. https://doi.org/10.1017/S0043887109990220.

Mahoney, James, and Gary Goertz. "The Possibility Principle: Choosing Negative Cases in Comparative Research." *American Political Science Review* 98, no. 4 (2004): 653–69.

Mahoney, Michael S. "Finding a History for Software Engineering." *IEEE Annals of the History of Computing* 26, no. 1 (January 2004): 8–19. https://doi.org/10.1109/MAHC.2004.1278847.

Maloney, William F., and Felipe Valencia Caicedo. "Engineering Growth: Innovative Capacity and Development in the Americas." Working Paper 6339. Munich: CESifo GmbH, 2017. https://ideas.repec.org/p/ces/ceswps/_6339.html.

Mankiw, N. G., David Romer, and David Weil. "A Contribution to the Empirics of Economic Growth." *Quarterly Journal of Economics* 107 (May 1992): 407–37.

Manning, Robert A. "Emerging Technologies: New Challenges to Global Stability." Issue Brief. Washington, DC: Atlantic Council, Scowcroft Center for Strategy and Security, May 2020. https://www.atlanticcouncil.org/wp-content/uploads/2020/06/Emerging-Technologies-New-Challenges-To-Global-Stability-May-2020.pdf.

Mantoux, Paul. *The Industrial Revolution in the Eighteenth Century: An Outline of the Beginnings of the Modern Factory System in England.* Abingdon, UK: Taylor & Francis, 2006.

Marginson, Simon. "University Rankings and Social Science." *European Journal of Education* 49, no. 1 (2014): 45–59. https://doi.org/10.1111/ejed.12061.

Marsden, Ben. "'The Progeny of These Two "Fellows"': Robert Willis, William Whewell and the Sciences of Mechanism, Mechanics, and Machinery in Early Victorian Britain." *British Journal for the History of Science* 37, no. 4 (December 2004): 401–34. https://doi.org/10.1017/S0007087404006144.

Mason, Geoff, Ana Rincon-Aznar, and Francesco Venturini. "Which Skills Contribute Most to Absorptive Capacity, Innovation, and Productivity Performance? Evidence from the US and Western Europe." *Economics of Innovation and New Technology* 29, no. 3 (April 2, 2020): 223–41. https://doi.org/10.1080/10438599.2019.1610547.

Mastanduno, Michael. "Do Relative Gains Matter? America's Response to Japanese Industrial Policy." *International Security* 16, no. 1 (1991): 73–113.

Mathias, Peter. *The First Industrial Nation: An Economic History of Britain 1700–1914.* London: Methuen, 1969.

———. "Skills and the Diffusion of Innovations from Britain in the Eighteenth Century." *Transactions of the Royal Historical Society* 25 (1975): 93–113. https://doi.org/10.2307/3679088.

Mayer, Maximilian, Mariana Carpes, and Ruth Knoblich, eds. *The Global Politics of Science and Technology,* vol. 1, *Concepts from International Relations and Other Disciplines.* Berlin Heidelberg: Springer-Verlag, 2014.

Maynard, Andrew. "Why I'm Suffering from Nanotechnology Fatigue." *Slate,* September 27, 2016. https://slate.com/technology/2016/09/why-im-suffering-from-nanotechnology-fatigue.html.

Mayntz, Renate. "Mechanisms in the Analysis of Social Macro-Phenomena." *Philosophy of the Social Sciences* 34, no. 2 (June 1, 2004): 237–59. https://doi.org/10.1177/0048393103262552.

McCloskey, Deirdre Nansen. *Bourgeois Dignity: Why Economics Can't Explain the Modern World.* Chicago: University of Chicago Press, 2010.

———. *Economic Maturity and Entrepreneurial Decline: British Iron and Steel, 1870–1913.* Cambridge, MA: Harvard University Press, 1973.

McCloskey, Deirdre Nansen. "The Industrial Revolution, 1780–1860: A Survey." In *The Economic History of Britain since 1700*, edited by Roderick Floud and Deirdre Nansen McCloskey. Cambridge: Cambridge University Press, 1981.

Mead, Nancy R. "Software Engineering Education: How Far We've Come and How Far We Have to Go." *Journal of Systems and Software* (special issue, "Selected Papers from the 2008 IEEE Conference on Software Engineering Education and Training [CSEET08]"), 82, no. 4 (April 1, 2009): 571–75. https://doi.org/10.1016/j.jss.2008.12.038.

Mearsheimer, John J. *The Tragedy of Great Power Politics*, updated edition. New York: W. W. Norton & Co., 2014.

Meisenzahl, Ralf R., and Joel Mokyr. "The Rate and Direction of Invention in the British Industrial Revolution: Incentives and Institutions." In *The Rate and Direction of Inventive Activity Revisited*, edited by Josh Lerner and Scott Stern, 443–79. Chicago: University of Chicago Press, 2011.

Milner, Helen V. "The Digital Divide: The Role of Political Institutions in Technology Diffusion." *Comparative Political Studies* 39, no. 2 (March 1, 2006): 176–99. https://doi.org/10.1177/0010414005282983.

Milner, Helen V., and Sondre Ulvund Solstad. "Technological Change and the International System." *World Politics* 73, no. 3 (July 2021): 545–89. https://doi.org/10.1017/S0043887121000010.

Minges, M., V. Gray, and E. Magpantay. *World Telecommunication Development Report 2003: Access Indicators for the Information Society*, 7th ed. Geneva: International Telecommunication Union, 2003.

Misa, Thomas J. "Military Needs, Commercial Realities, and the Development of the Transistor, 1948–1958." In *Military Enterprise and Technological Change*, edited by Merritt Roe Smith, 253–87. Cambridge, MA: MIT Press, 1985.

Mitch, David. "The Role of Education and Skill in the British Industrial Revolution." In *The British Industrial Revolution: An Economic Perspective*, 2nd ed., edited by Joel Mokyr, 1–127. Boulder, CO: Westview Press, 1999.

Mitchell, Brian R. *International Historical Statistics: The Americas 1750–2000*. London: Palgrave Macmillan, 1993.

———. *International Historical Statistics: Europe 1750–1993*. London: Palgrave Macmillan, 1998.

Modelski, George, and William R. Thompson. *Leading Sectors and World Powers: The Coevolution of Global Politics and Economics*. Columbia: University of South Carolina Press, 1996.

Moe, Espen. "Governance and Growth: The Role of the State in Technological Progress and Industrial Leadership." University of California, Los Angeles, 2004.

———. *Governance, Growth, and Global Leadership: The Role of the State in Technological Progress, 1750–2000*. Burlington, VT: Ashgate, 2007.

———. "Mancur Olson and Structural Economic Change: Vested Interests and the Industrial Rise and Fall of the Great Powers." *Review of International Political Economy* 16, no. 2 (June 26, 2009): 202–30. https://doi.org/10.1080/09692290802408865.

Mogee, Mary Ellen. *Technology Policy and Critical Technologies: A Summary of Recent Reports*. Washington, DC: National Academies Press, 1991.

Mokyr, Joel. *The Lever of Riches: Technological Creativity and Economic Progress*. New York: Oxford University Press, 1990.

————. "The Second Industrial Revolution, 1870–1914." In *Storia Dell'economia Mondiale*, edited by Valerio Castronovo, 219–45. Bari, Italy: Editori Laterza, 1998.

————. "Editor's Introduction: The New Economic History and the Industrial Revolution." In *The British Industrial Revolution: An Economic Perspective*, 2nd ed., edited by Joel Mokyr, 1–127. Boulder, CO: Westview Press, 1999.

————. "The Industrial Revolution and the Netherlands: Why Did It Not Happen?" *De Economist* 148, no. 4 (October 1, 2000): 503–20. https://doi.org/10.1023/A:1004134217178.

————. "The Rise and Fall of the Factory System: Technology, Firms, and Households since the Industrial Revolution." *Carnegie-Rochester Conference Series on Public Policy* 55, no. 1 (December 1, 2001): 1–45. https://doi.org/10.1016/S0167-2231(01)00050-1.

————. *The Gifts of Athena: Historical Origins of the Knowledge Economy*. Princeton, NJ: Princeton University Press, 2002.

————. "The Intellectual Origins of Modern Economic Growth." *Journal of Economic History* 65, no. 2 (2005): 285–351.

————. "Economic Transformations." *Journal of Economic History* 66, no. 4 (2006): 1072–75.

————. *The Enlightened Economy: An Economic History of Britain 1700–1850*. New Haven, CT: Yale University Press, 2010.

Mokyr, Joel, and Hans-Joachim Voth. "Understanding Growth in Europe, 1700–1870: Theory and Evidence." In *The Cambridge Economic History of Modern Europe*, vol. 1, edited by Stephen Broadberry and Kevin H. O'Rourke, 7–42. Cambridge: Cambridge University Press, 2010.

Mongeon, Philippe, and Adèle Paul-Hus. "The Journal Coverage of Web of Science and Scopus: A Comparative Analysis." *Scientometrics* 106, no. 1 (January 1, 2016): 213–28. https://doi.org/10.1007/s11192-015-1765-5.

Monteiro, Nuno P. *Theory of Unipolar Politics*. New York: Cambridge University Press, 2014.

Morrison, Wayne M. "China's Economic Rise: History, Trends, Challenges, Implications for the United States." Congressional Research Service, June 25, 2019. https://crsreports.congress.gov/product/pdf/RL/RL33534.

Moser, Petra, and Tom Nicholas. "Was Electricity a General Purpose Technology? Evidence from Historical Patent Citations." *American Economic Review* 94, no. 2 (2004): 388–94.

Mosk, Carl. "The American System of Manufactures: Factor Bias or the Democratization of Invention?" SSRN Scholarly Paper. Rochester, NY: Social Science Research Network, November 1, 2010. https://doi.org/10.2139/ssrn.1803615.

Mou, Hongyu, Licheng Liu, and Yiqing Xu. "PanelView: Panel Data Visualization in R and Stata." SSRN Scholarly Paper. Rochester, NY, August 27, 2022. https://doi.org/10.2139/ssrn.4202154.

Mowery, David C., and Richard N. Langlois. "Spinning Off and Spinning On(?): The Federal Government Role in the Development of the US Computer Software Industry." *Research Policy* 25, no. 6 (September 1, 1996): 947–66. https://doi.org/10.1016/0048-7333(96)00888-8.

Mowery, David C., and Nathan Rosenberg. *Technology and the Pursuit of Economic Growth*. Cambridge: Cambridge University Press, 1991.

Mozur, Paul, and Cade Metz. "A US Secret Weapon in AI: Chinese Talent." *New York Times*, June 9, 2020. https://www.nytimes.com/2020/06/09/technology/china-ai-research-education.html.

Murmann, Peter. "Chemical Industries after 1850." In *Oxford Encyclopedia of Economic History*, edited by Joel Mokyr, 398–406. Oxford: Oxford University Press, 2003.

Murmann, Peter, and Ralph Landau. "On the Making of Competitive Advantage: The Development of the Chemical Industries in Britain and Germany since 1850." In *Chemicals and Long-Term Economic Growth*, edited by Ashish Arora, Ralph Landau, and Nathan Rosenberg. New York: Wiley, 1998.

Musson, Albert E. "The Engineering Industry." In *The Dynamics of Victorian Business*, edited by Roy Church, 87–106. London: Allen and Unwin, 1980.

———. "British Origins." In *Yankee Enterprise: The Rise of the American System of Manufactures: A Symposium*, edited by Otto Mayr and Robert C. Post, sponsored by the US Chamber of Commerce, and held at the Dibner Rare Book Library. Washington, DC: Smithsonian Institution, National Museum of American History, 1981.

Musson, Albert E., and Eric Robinson. "Science and Industry in the Late Eighteenth Century." *The Economic History Review* 13, no. 2 (1960): 222–44.

———. *Science and Technology in the Industrial Revolution*. Manchester, UK: Manchester University Press, 1969.

Nakata, Yoshifumi, and Satoru Miyazaki. "The Labor Market for Japanese Scientists and Engineers: Is the Labor Market Externalized? What Has Happened at Their Workplace?" *Japan Labor Review* 8, no. 3 (2011).

National Research Council. *Computing the Future: A Broader Agenda for Computer Science and Engineering*. Washington, DC: National Academies Press, 1992.

———. *Funding a Revolution: Government Support for Computing Research*. Washington, DC: National Academies Press, 1999.

National Science Board. "Science & Engineering Indicators—2000." Alexandria, VA: National Science Foundation, 2000.

National Science Foundation. "The Science & Technology Resources of Japan: A Comparison with the United States." NSF Special Report 88-318. Arlington, VA: National Science Foundation, 1997.

National Security Commission on Artificial Intelligence. "The Final Report." Washington, DC: NSCAI, March 2021. https://www.nscai.gov/2021-final-report/.

Naughton, Barry J. *The Chinese Economy: Adaptation and Growth*, 2nd ed. Cambridge, MA: MIT Press, 2018.

Nelson, Richard R. *National Innovation Systems: A Comparative Analysis*. Oxford: Oxford University Press, 1993.

Nelson, Richard R., and Edmund S. Phelps. "Investment in Humans, Technological Diffusion, and Economic Growth." *American Economic Review* 56, nos. 1/2 (1966): 69–75.

Nelson, Richard R., and Sidney G. Winter. *An Evolutionary Theory of Economic Change*. Cambridge, MA: Belknap Press of Harvard University Press, 1982.

Nelson, Richard R., and Gavin Wright. "The Rise and Fall of American Technological Leadership: The Postwar Era in Historical Perspective." *Journal of Economic Literature* 30, no. 4 (1992): 1931–64.

Newell, Allen. "Introduction to the COMTEX Microfiche Edition of Reports on Artificial Intelligence from Carnegie-Mellon University." *AI Magazine*, September 15, 1984.

Newman, Abraham, and John Zysman. "Transforming Politics in the Digital Era." In *How Revolutionary Was the Digital Revolution? National Responses, Market Transitions, and Global Tech-*

nology, edited by John Zysman and Abraham Newman, 391–411. Stanford, CA: Stanford University Press, 2006.

Nicoletti, Giuseppe, Christina von Rueden, and Dan Andrews. "Digital Technology Diffusion: A Matter of Capabilities, Incentives or Both?" *European Economic Review* 128 (September 2020): 103513. https://doi.org/10.1016/j.euroecorev.2020.103513.

Nienkamp, Paul. "A Culture of Technical Knowledge: Professionalizing Science and Engineering Education in Late-Nineteenth Century America." PhD diss., Iowa State University (accessed April 15, 2022). https://www.proquest.com/docview/194021966/abstract/6D87B9A67DC14D0BPQ/1.

Nikkei Computer. "User Adjustments: Actual Condition of SE Services (ユーザー調査:SE サービスの実態)." *Nikkei Computer*, March 4, 1985.

———. "The Second Survey Related to SE Services" (第2回SE サービス関連調査)." *Nikkei Computer*, March 14, 1988.

Noble, David F. *America by Design: Science, Technology, and the Rise of Corporate Capitalism*. New York: Alfred A. Knopf, 1977.

Nolan, Mary. *Visions of Modernity: American Business and the Modernization of Germany*. Oxford: Oxford University Press, 1994.

Norman, Donald A., and Roberto Verganti. "Incremental and Radical Innovation: Design Research vs. Technology and Meaning Change." *Design Issues* 30, no. 1 (2014): 78–96.

North, Douglass Cecil. *Structure and Change in Economic History*. New York: W. W. Norton & Co., 1981.

———. *Institutions, Institutional Change, and Economic Performance*. Cambridge: Cambridge University Press, 1990.

Nuvolari, Alessandro. "Collective Invention during the British Industrial Revolution: The Case of the Cornish Pumping Engine." *Cambridge Journal of Economics* 28, no. 3 (May 1, 2004): 347–63. https://doi.org/10.1093/cje/28.3.347.

Nuvolari, Alessandro, Bart Verspagen, and Nick von Tunzelmann. "The Early Diffusion of the Steam Engine in Britain, 1700–1800: A Reappraisal." *Cliometrica* 5, no. 3 (October 1, 2011): 291–321. https://doi.org/10.1007/s11698-011-0063-6.

Nye, Joseph S. "The Myth of Free-Trade Britain and Fortress France: Tariffs and Trade in the Nineteenth Century." *Journal of Economic History* 51, no. 1 (1991): 23–46.

O'Brien, Patrick. "The Contributions of Warfare with Revolutionary and Napoleonic France to the Consolidation and Progress of the British Industrial Revolution." Department of Economic History Working Paper 264. London: London School of Economics and Political Science, June 2017. http://eprints.lse.ac.uk/82411/1/WP264.pdf.

Organization for Economic Cooperation and Development. "ICT Access and Use by Businesses (Edition 2017)." OECD Telecommunications and Internet Statistics (database), 2018. https://doi.org/10.1787/58897a61-en.

———. "Patents by Main Technology and by International Patent Classification (IPC) (Edition 2020)." OECD Patent Statistics (database), 2021. https://doi.org/10.1787/e92e7be0-en.

Ogburn, William F. *Technology and International Relations*. Chicago: University of Chicago Press, 1949a.

———. "The Process of Adjustment to New Inventions." In Ogburn, *Technology and International Relations*. Chicago: University of Chicago Press, 1949b.

Oliner, Stephen D., and Daniel E. Sichel. "The Resurgence of Growth in the Late 1990s: Is Information Technology the Story?" *Journal of Economic Perspectives* 14, no. 4 (December 2000): 3–22. https://doi.org/10.1257/jep.14.4.3.

Oliveira, Arlindo L. "Biotechnology, Big Data, and Artificial Intelligence." *Biotechnology Journal* 14, no. 8 (August 2019): e1800613. https://doi.org/10.1002/biot.201800613.

Olson, Mancur. *The Rise and Decline of Nations: Economic Growth, Stagflation, and Social Rigidities.* New Haven, CT: Yale University Press, 1982.

Oorschot, Johannes A.W.H. van, Erwin Hofman, and Johannes I. M. Halman. "A Bibliometric Review of the Innovation Adoption Literature." *Technological Forecasting and Social Change* 134 (September 1, 2018): 1–21. https://doi.org/10.1016/j.techfore.2018.04.032.

Oreskes, Michael. "Americans Express Worry on Japan, as Feelings in Tokyo Seem to Soften." *New York Times*, July 10, 1990.

Organski, A.F.K. *World Politics.* New York: Alfred A. Knopf, 1958.

———. *World Politics*, 2nd ed., revised. New York: Alfred A. Knopf, 1968.

Ostry, Sylvia, and Richard R. Nelson. *Techno-Nationalism and Techno-Globalism: Conflict and Cooperation.* Washington, DC: Brookings Institution Press, 1995.

Office of Technology Assessment. "The Big Picture: HDTV and High-Resolution Systems." Washington, DC: US Government Printing Office, 1990.

Palmer, Alex W. "'An Act of War': Inside America's Silicon Blockade against China." *New York Times Magazine*, July 12, 2023. https://www.nytimes.com/2023/07/12/magazine/semiconductor-chips-us-china.html.

Pang, Wei. "China Has a Shortage of as Many as 20 Million Senior Technicians. Who Will Make China into a Manufacturing Power? (中国高级技工缺口高达两千万，大国智造谁来造?)." *Jiqizhineng* (机器之能), December 11, 2019.

Paulinyi, Akos. "Revolution and Technology." In *Revolution in History*, edited by Roy Porter and Mikulas Teich, 261–89. Cambridge: Cambridge University Press, 1986.

Pavitt, Keith, and Luc Soete. "International Differences in Economic Growth and the International Location of Innovation." In *Emerging Technologies: Consequences for Economic Growth, Structural Change, and Employment*, edited by Herbert Giersch, 105–33. Tuebingen: Mohr, 1982.

Peck, Jamie, and Jun Zhang. "A Variety of Capitalism . . . with Chinese Characteristics?" *Journal of Economic Geography* 13, no. 3 (May 1, 2013): 357–96. https://doi.org/10.1093/jeg/lbs058.

Perez, Carlota. "Structural Change and Assimilation of New Technologies in the Economic and Social Systems." *Futures* 15, no. 5 (October 1, 1983): 357–75. https://doi.org/10.1016/0016-3287(83)90050-2.

———. *Technological Revolutions and Financial Capital: The Dynamics of Bubbles and Golden Ages.* Illustrated edition. Cheltenham, UK: Edward Elgar Publishing, 2002.

Perkins, Claire, Diana Gehlhaus, Kayla Goode, Jennifer Melot, Ehrik Aldana, Grace Doerfler, and Gayani Gamage. "AI Education Catalog." Center for Security and Emerging Technology and the AI Education Project, October 19, 2021. https://cset.georgetown.edu/publication/ai-education-catalog/.

Peterson, Dahlia, Kayla Goode, and Diana Gelhaus. "AI Education in China and the United States: A Comparative Assessment." Issue brief. Washington, DC: Center for Security and

Emerging Technology, September 2021. https://cset.georgetown.edu/publication/ai
-education-in-china-and-the-united-states/.

Petralia, Sergio. "Mapping General Purpose Technologies with Patent Data." *Research Policy* 49, no. 7 (September 1, 2020): 104013. https://doi.org/10.1016/j.respol.2020.104013.

Pettis, Michael. "Is China's Economy Growing as Fast as China's GDP?" Carnegie Endowment for International Peace, September 5, 2017. https://carnegieendowment.org/chinafinancial markets/72997.

Pickrell, Ryan. "China Is the World's Biggest Shipbuilder, and Its Ability to Rapidly Produce New Warships Would Be a 'Huge Advantage' in a Long Fight with the US, Experts Say." *Business Insider*, September 8, 2020. https://www.businessinsider.com/china-has-advantage -over-the-us-in-shipbuilding-2020-9.

Pierson, Harry A., and Michael S. Gashler. "Deep Learning in Robotics: A Review of Recent Research." *Advanced Robotics* 31, no. 16 (2017): 821–35.

Pilat, Dirk, Franck Lee, and Bart van Ark. "Production and Use of ICT: A Sectoral Perspective on Productivity Growth in the OECD Area." *OECD Economic Studies* 2002, no. 2 (2002): 47–78.

Piore, Michael J., and Charles F. Sabel. *The Second Industrial Divide: Possibilities for Prosperity*. New York: Basic Books, 1984.

Pleijt, Alexandra M. de. "Human Capital Formation in the Long Run: Evidence from Average Years of Schooling in England, 1300–1900." *Cliometrica* 12, no. 1 (January 1, 2018): 99–126. https://doi.org/10.1007/s11698-016-0156-3.

Plunkert, Lois M. "The 1980s: A Decade of Job Growth and Industry Shifts." *Monthly Labor Review* (September 1990).

Pollack, Andrew. "Japan's Big Lead in Memory Chips." *New York Times*, February 28, 1982. https://www.nytimes.com/1982/02/28/business/japan-s-big-lead-in-memory-chips.html.

Pollard, Sidney. *The Genesis of Modern Management: A Study of the Industrial Revolution in Great Britain*. Cambridge, MA: Harvard University Press, 1965.

Pomeranz, Kenneth. *The Great Divergence: China, Europe, and the Making of the Modern World Economy*. Princeton, NJ: Princeton University Press, 2000.

Porter, Michael E. *The Competitive Advantage of Nations*. New York: Free Press, 1990.

Pozzi, Simone. "The Long March of the Machines in China." *Robeco*, July 16, 2023. https://www .robeco.com/en-za/insights/2023/07/the-long-march-of-the-machines-in-china.

Prestowitz, Clyde, Jr. *Trading Places: How We Are Giving Our Future to Japan and How to Reclaim It*. New York: Basic Books, 1989.

Qiu, Ranfeng, and John Cantwell. "The International Geography of General Purpose Technologies (GPTs) and Internationalisation of Corporate Technological Innovation." *Industry and Innovation* 25, no. 1 (January 2, 2018): 1–24. https://doi.org/10.1080/13662716.2016 .1264065.

Qiushi. "What Is the Fourth Industrial Revolution? Xi Jinping Described the Blueprint Like This! (第四次工业革命什么样？习近平这样描绘蓝图！)." *Qiushi* (求是网), July 27, 2018. http://www.qstheory.cn/zhuanqu/2018-07/27/c_1123186013.htm.

Raja, Siddhartha, Saori Imaizumi, Tim Kelly, Junko Narimatsu, and Cecilia Paradi-Guilford. "Connecting to Work: How Information and Communication Technologies Could Help Expand Employment Opportunities." Washington, DC: World Bank, 2013.

Ransbotham, Sam, Philipp Gerbert, Martin Reeves, David Kiron, and Michael Spira. "Artificial Intelligence in Business Gets Real." *MIT Sloan Management Review*, July 24, 2018. https://sloanreview.mit.edu/article/global-competition-of-ai-in-business-how-china-differs/.

Rapkin, David, and William Thompson. "Power Transition, Challenge, and the (Re)Emergence of China." *International Interactions* 29, no. 4 (October 1, 2003): 315–42. https://doi.org/10.1080/714950652.

Rasler, Karen A., and William R. Thompson. *The Great Powers and Global Struggle, 1490–1990.* Lexington: University Press of Kentucky, 1994.

Rausch, Lawrence M. "High-Tech Industries Drive Global Economic Activity." National Science Foundation, July 20, 1998.

Rennstich, Joachim K. "The New Economy, the Leadership Long Cycle, and the Nineteenth K-Wave." *Review of International Political Economy* 9, no. 1 (2002): 150–82.

Reuveny, Rafael, and William R. Thompson. "Leading Sectors, Lead Economies, and Economic Growth." *Review of International Political Economy* 8, no. 4 (January 1, 2001): 689–719. https://doi.org/10.1080/09692290110077629.

Reynolds, Terry S. *75 Years of Progress: A History of the American Institute of Chemical Engineers, 1908–1983.* New York: American Institute of Chemical Engineers, 1983.

———. "Defining Professional Boundaries: Chemical Engineering in the Early 20th Century." *Technology and Culture* 27, no. 4 (1986): 694–716. https://doi.org/10.2307/3105325.

Ridolfi, Leonardo. "The French Economy in the Longue Durée: A Study on Real Wages, Working Days, and Economic Performance from Louis IX to the Revolution (1250–1789)." *European Review of Economic History* 21, no. 4 (2017): 437–38.

Rikap, Cecilia. "Becoming an Intellectual Monopoly by Relying on the National Innovation System: The State Grid Corporation of China's Experience." *Research Policy* 51, no. 4 (May 1, 2022): 104472. https://doi.org/10.1016/j.respol.2021.104472.

Rincon-Aznar, Ana, John Forth, Geoff Mason, Mary O'Mahony, and Michele Bernini. *UK Skills and Productivity in an International Context.* Department for Business, Innovation, and Skills Research Paper 262. London: National Institute of Economic and Social Research, December 2015. https://assets.publishing.service.gov.uk/media/5a807a4ded915d74e33faa79/BIS-15-704-UK-skills-and-productivity-in-an-international_context.pdf

Ripsman, Norrin M., and Jack S. Levy. "The Preventive War That Never Happened: Britain, France, and the Rise of Germany in the 1930s." *Security Studies* 16, no. 1 (April 16, 2007): 32–67. https://doi.org/10.1080/09636410701304549.

Ristuccia, Cristiano Andrea, and Solomos Solomou. "Can General Purpose Technology Theory Explain Economic Growth? Electrical Power as a Case Study." *European Review of Economic History* 18, no. 3 (August 1, 2014): 227–47. https://doi.org/10.1093/ereh/heu008.

Ristuccia, Cristiano Andrea, and Adam Tooze. "Machine Tools and Mass Production in the Armaments Boom: Germany and the United States, 1929–44." *Economic History Review* 66, no. 4 (2013): 953–74.

Roberts, Eric. "Resources for the CS Capacity Crisis." Eric Roberts's Personal Website, July 24, 2021. https://cs.stanford.edu/people/eroberts/ResourcesForTheCSCapacityCrisis/.

Robson, R. *The Cotton Industry in Britain.* London: Macmillan & Co. Ltd., 1957.

Rød, Espen Geelmuyden, and Nils B. Weidmann. "Empowering Activists or Autocrats? The Internet in Authoritarian Regimes." *Journal of Peace Research* 52, no. 3 (May 1, 2015): 338–51. https://doi.org/10.1177/0022343314555782.

Rogers, Everett M. *Diffusion of Innovations*, 4th ed. New York: Free Press, 1995.

Rohlfing, Ingo, and Carsten Q. Schneider. "Improving Research on Necessary Conditions: Formalized Case Selection for Process Tracing after QCA." *Political Research Quarterly* 66, no. 1 (2013): 220–35.

Romeo, Anthony A. "Interindustry and Interfirm Differences in the Rate of Diffusion of an Innovation." *Review of Economics and Statistics* 57, no. 3 (1975): 311–19. https://doi.org/10.2307/1923915.

Romer, Paul M. "Why, Indeed, in America? Theory, History, and the Origins of Modern Economic Growth." *American Economic Review* 86, no. 2 (1996): 202–6.

Rose, Frederick. "Report on the German Technical High Schools." Miscellaneous Series of Diplomatic and Consular Reports. Stuttgart, April 29, 1903.

Rosecrance, Richard N. *The Rise of the Virtual State: Wealth and Power in the Coming Century.* New York: Basic Books, 2000.

Rosenberg, Nathan. "Technological Change in the Machine Tool Industry, 1840–1910." *Journal of Economic History* 23, no. 4 (1963): 414–43.

———. "Economic Development and the Transfer of Technology: Some Historical Perspectives." *Technology and Culture* 11, no. 4 (1970): 550–75. https://doi.org/10.2307/3102691.

———. *Technology and American Economic Growth.* New York: Harper & Row, 1972.

———. "Technological Interdependence in the American Economy." *Technology and Culture* 20, no. 1 (1979): 25–50. https://doi.org/10.2307/3103110.

———. *Inside the Black Box: Technology and Economics.* Cambridge: Cambridge University Press, 1982.

———. "Technological Change in Chemicals: The Role of University-Industry Relations." In *Chemicals and Long-Term Economic Growth: Insights from the Chemical Industry.* New York: Wiley, 1998a.

———. "Chemical Engineering as a General Purpose Technology." In *Chemical Engineering as a General Purpose Technology*, edited by Elhanan Helpman, 167–92. Cambridge, MA: MIT Press, 1998b.

Rosenberg, Nathan, and W. Edward Steinmueller. "Engineering Knowledge." *Industrial and Corporate Change* 22, no. 5 (October 1, 2013): 1129–58. https://doi.org/10.1093/icc/dts053.

Rostow, Walt W. "The Take-off into Self-Sustained Growth." *Economic Journal* 66, no. 261 (1956): 25–48. https://doi.org/10.2307/2227401.

———. *The Stages of Economic Growth: A Non-Communist Manifesto.* Cambridge: Cambridge University Press, 1960.

———. *The World Economy: History and Prospect.* Austin: University of Texas Press, 1978.

———. "Is There Need for Economic Leadership? Japanese or US?" *American Economic Review* 75, no. 2 (1985): 285–91.

———. *The Stages of Economic Growth: A Non-Communist Manifesto*, 3rd ed. Cambridge University Press, 1991.

Rowland, Henry A. "A Plea for Pure Science." *Science* 2, no. 29 (1883): 242–50.

Rudnik, Rita. "Machines Rising Slowly: Robot Adoption Hasn't Kicked into High Gear . . . Yet." MacroPolo, August 10, 2022. https://macropolo.org/analysis/machines-rising-robot-adoption/.

Russell, Andrew L. *Open Standards and the Digital Age*. New York: Cambridge University Press, 2014.

Russell, Andrew L., and Lee Vinsel. *Make Maintainers: Engineering Education and an Ethics of Care*. Cambridge, MA: MIT Press, 2019.

Ruttan, Vernon W. *Technology, Growth, and Development: An Induced Innovation Perspective*. Oxford: Oxford University Press, 2001.

———. *Is War Necessary for Economic Growth? Military Procurement and Technology Development*. Oxford: Oxford University Press, 2006.

Samuels, Richard J. *"Rich Nation, Strong Army": National Security and the Technological Transformation of Japan*. Ithaca, NY: Cornell University Press, 1994.

Sanderson, Michael. *The Universities and British Industry, 1850–1970*. London: Routledge and Kegan Paul, 1972.

Sarid, Assaf, Joel Mokyr, and Karine van der Beek. "The Wheels of Change: Human Capital, Millwrights, and Industrialization in Eighteenth-Century England." Discussion Paper 14138. Washington, DC: Center for Economic and Policy Research, November 2019. https://econpapers.repec.org/paper/cprceprdp/14138.htm.

Satia, Priya. *Empire of Guns: The Violent Making of the Industrial Revolution*. New York: Penguin, 2018.

Saul, S. B. "The American Impact on British Industry 1895–1914." *Business History* 3, no. 1 (December 1, 1960): 19–38. https://doi.org/10.1080/00076796000000014.

Saxenian, Annalee, and Jinn-Yuh Hsu. "The Silicon Valley–Hsinchu Connection: Technical Communities and Industrial Upgrading." *Industrial and Corporate Change* 10, no. 4 (December 1, 2001): 893–920. https://doi.org/10.1093/icc/10.4.893.

Schumpeter, Joseph A. *The Theory of Economic Development: An Inquiry into Profits, Capital, Credit, Interest, and the Business Cycle*. Cambridge, MA: Harvard University Press, 1934.

———. *Business Cycles*. New York: McGraw-Hill, 1939.

———. *Capitalism, Socialism, and Democracy*. London: Routledge, 1994.

Schwab, Klaus. *The Fourth Industrial Revolution*. New York: Crown Business, 2017a.

———, ed. "The Global Competitiveness Report 2017–2018." Geneva: World Economic Forum, 2017b. https://www3.weforum.org/docs/GCR2017-2018/05FullReport/TheGlobalCompetitivenessReport2017%E2%80%932018.pdf.

Scissors, Derek. "The Surest Measure of How China's Economy Is Losing." RealClearWorld, November 29, 2016. https://www.realclearworld.com/articles/2016/11/29/the_surest_measure_of_how_chinas_economy_is_losing_112131.html.

SCMP Research. "China AI Report 2020." SCMP Research, February 2020.

Scranton, Philip. *Endless Novelty: Specialty Production and American Industrialization, 1865–1925*. Princeton, NJ: Princeton University Press, 1997.

Seely, Bruce E. "European Connections to American Engineering Education, 1800–1990." In *La formation des ingénieurs en perspective: modèles de référence et réseaux de médiation, XIXe et XXe Siècles*, edited by Irina Gouzévitch, André Grelon, and Anousheh Karvar, 53–69. Rennes: Presses de l'Université de Rennes, 2004.

Segal, Adam. "Year in Review 2019: The US-China Tech Cold War Deepens and Expands." Council on Foreign Relations, December 18, 2019. https://www.cfr.org/blog/year-review -2019-us-china-tech-cold-war-deepens-and-expands.

Shapira, Philip, and Jan Youtie. "The Next Production Revolution and Institutions for Technology Diffusion." In *The Next Production Revolution: Implications for Governments and Business.* Paris: Organization for Economic Cooperation and Development, 2017.

Shapley, Deborah, and Rustum Roy. *Lost at the Frontier: US Science and Technology Policy Adrift.* Philadelphia: ISI Press, 1985.

Shifrinson, Joshua R. Itzkowitz, and Michael Beckley. "Debating China's Rise and US Decline." *International Security* 37, no. 3 (2012): 172–81.

Simmons, Beth A., and Zachary Elkins. "The Globalization of Liberalization: Policy Diffusion in the International Political Economy." *American Political Science Review* 98, no. 1 (February 2004): 171–89. https://doi.org/10.1017/S0003055404001078.

Simmons, Joel W. *The Politics of Technological Progress.* Cambridge: Cambridge University Press, 2016.

Simoes, Alexander James Gaspar, and César A. Hidalgo. "The Economic Complexity Observatory: An Analytical Tool for Understanding the Dynamics of Economic Development." Paper presented at a 25th AAAI Conference on Artificial Intelligence workshop, San Francisco, August 7–11, 2011.

Singh, P. K., Y. K. Gera, and Sandeep Dewan, eds. *Comprehensive National Power: A Model for India.* New Delhi: Vij Books India, 2013.

Skinner, Jonathan, and Douglas Staiger. "Technology Adoption from Hybrid Corn to Beta-Blockers." In *Hard-to-Measure Goods and Services: Essays in Honor of Zvi Griliches,* edited by Ernst R. Berndt and Charles R. Hulten, 545–70. Cambridge, MA, and Chicago: National Bureau of Economic Research and University of Chicago Press, 2007.

Skocpol, Theda. *States and Social Revolutions: A Comparative Analysis of France, Russia, and China.* Cambridge: Cambridge University Press, 1979.

———, ed. *Vision and Method in Historical Sociology.* Cambridge: Cambridge University Press, 1984.

Skolnikoff, Eugene B. *The Elusive Transformation: Science, Technology, and the Evolution of International Politics.* Princeton, NJ: Princeton University Press, 1993.

Smil, Vaclav. *Creating the Twentieth Century: Technical Innovations of 1867–1914 and Their Lasting Impact.* Oxford: Oxford University Press, 2005.

———. *Prime Movers of Globalization: The History and Impact of Diesel Engines and Gas Turbines.* Cambridge, MA: MIT Press, 2010.

Smith, Merritt Roe. *Military Enterprise and Technological Change: Perspectives on the American Experience.* Cambridge, MA: MIT Press, 1985.

Smits, Jan-Pieter, Edwin Horlings, and Jan Luiten van Zanden. "Dutch GNP and Its Components, 1800–1913." Monograph 5. Groningen: Groningen Growth and Development Centre, 2000.

Snidal, Duncan. "The Limits of Hegemonic Stability Theory." *International Organization* 39, no. 4 (1985): 579–614.

Social Science, Technology, and Cultural Industry Statistics Department. *China Statistical Yearbook on Science and Technology.* China Statistics Press, various years.

Solingen, Etel. "Of Dominoes and Firewalls: The Domestic, Regional, and Global Politics of International Diffusion." *International Studies Quarterly* 56, no. 4 (December 1, 2012): 631–44. https://doi.org/10.1111/isqu.12034.

Somers, Harold. "Book Reviews: The Fifth Generation Fallacy: Why Japan Is Betting Its Future on Artificial Intelligence." *Computational Linguistics* 14, no. 4 (1988). https://aclanthology.org/J88-4009.

Sovey, Allison J., and Donald P. Green. "Instrumental Variables Estimation in Political Science: A Readers' Guide." *American Journal of Political Science* 55, no. 1 (2010): 188–200. https://doi.org/10.1111/j.1540-5907.2010.00477.x.

Sprout, Harold. "Geopolitical Hypotheses in Technological Perspective." *World Politics* 15, no. 2 (1963): 187–212. https://doi.org/10.2307/2009373.

Starrs, Sean. "American Economic Power Hasn't Declined—It Globalized! Summoning the Data and Taking Globalization Seriously." *International Studies Quarterly* 57, no. 4 (December 1, 2013): 817–30. https://doi.org/10.1111/isqu.12053.

State Council. "Plan for Promoting the Development of SMEs 2016–2020 (促进中小企业发展规划年 2016–2020)." 2016. http://www.gov.cn/xinwen/2016-07/05/content_5088531.htm.

Steinmueller, W. Edward. "The US Software Industry: An Analysis and Interpretive History." In *The International Computer Software Industry: A Comparative Study of Industry Evolution and Structure*, edited by David C. Mowery, 15–52. New York: Oxford University Press, 1996.

Stewart, Megan A. *Governing for Revolution: Social Transformation in Civil War*. Cambridge: Cambridge University Press, 2021.

Stoneman, Paul, and Paul Diederen. "Technology Diffusion and Public Policy." *Economic Journal* 104, no. 425 (1994): 918–30. https://doi.org/10.2307/2234987.

Streeck, Wolfgang. *Social Institutions and Economic Performance: Studies of Industrial Relations in Advanced Capitalist Economies*. Thousand Oaks, CA: SAGE Publications, 1992.

Sullivan, Richard J. "The Revolution of Ideas: Widespread Patenting and Invention during the English Industrial Revolution." *Journal of Economic History* 50, no. 2 (1990): 349–62.

Synced (机器之心). "Market Research Report on Supply and Demand for Digital Intelligentization Solutions for China's Small and Medium Enterprises (中国中小企业数智化解决方案供应市场研究报告 2020)." October 2020.

Tagscherer, Ulrike. "Science-Industry Linkages in China: Motivation, Models, and Success Factors for Collaborations of MNCs with Chinese Academia." Discussion Paper 47. Karlsruhe: Fraunhofer Institute for Systems and Innovation Research (ISI), 2015. https://ideas.repec.org/p/zbw/fisidp/47.html.

Talbot, Benjamin. "The Open-Hearth Continuous Steel Process." *Journal of the Iron and Steel Institute* 55, no. 1 (1900): 33–108.

Tammen, Ronald L. "The Organski Legacy: A Fifty-Year Research Program." *International Interactions* 34, no. 4 (December 11, 2008): 314–32. https://doi.org/10.1080/03050620802561769.

Tann, Jennifer, and M. J. Breckin. "The International Diffusion of the Watt Engine, 1775–1825." *Economic History Review* 31, no. 4 (1978): 541–64. https://doi.org/10.1111/j.1468-0289.1978.tb00304.x.

Taylor, Mark Zachary. "Empirical Evidence against Varieties of Capitalism's Theory of Technological Innovation." *International Organization* 58, no. 3 (2004): 601–31.

———. "Political Decentralization and Technological Innovation: Testing the Innovative Advantages of Decentralized States." *Review of Policy Research* 24, no. 3 (2007): 231–57. https://doi.org/10.1111/j.1541-1338.2007.00279.x.

———. "Conclusion: International Political Economy—The Reverse Salient of Innovation Theory." *Review of Policy Research* 26, nos. 1/2 (2009): 219–23. https://doi.org/10.1111/j.1541-1338.2008.00376.x.

———. "Toward an International Relations Theory of National Innovation Rates." *Security Studies* 21, no. 1 (January 1, 2012): 113–52. https://doi.org/10.1080/09636412.2012.650596.

———. *The Politics of Innovation: Why Some Countries Are Better than Others at Science and Technology*. New York: Oxford University Press, 2016.

Tedre, Matti, Simon, and Lauri Malmi. "Changing Aims of Computing Education: A Historical Survey." *Computer Science Education* 28, no. 2 (2018): 158–86.

Teece, David J. "Profiting from Innovation in the Digital Economy: Enabling Technologies, Standards, and Licensing Models in the Wireless World." *Research Policy* 47, no. 8 (October 1, 2018): 1367–87. https://doi.org/10.1016/j.respol.2017.01.015.

Tellis, Ashley J. "Balancing without Containment: A US Strategy for Confronting China's Rise." *Washington Quarterly* 36, no. 4 (October 1, 2013): 109–24. https://doi.org/10.1080/0163660X.2013.861717.

Tellis, Ashley J., Janice Bially, Christopher Layne, and Melissa McPherson. *Measuring National Power in the Postindustrial Age*. Santa Monica, CA: RAND Corporation, 2000.

Temin, Peter. "Two Views of the British Industrial Revolution." *Journal of Economic History* 57, no. 1 (1997): 63–82.

Tencent Research Institute and BOSS Zhipin. "2017 Global AI Talent White Paper (2017 全球人工智能人才白皮书)." Shenzen: Tencent Research Institute, 2017. https://www.tisi.org/Public/Uploads/file/20171201/20171201151555_24517.pdf.

Thackray, Arnold, Jeffrey L. Sturchio, P. Thomas Carroll, and Robert F. Bud. *Chemistry in America 1876–1976: Historical Indicators*. Dordrecht and Hingham, MA: Springer, 1985.

Thelen, Kathleen. *How Institutions Evolve: The Political Economy of Skills in Germany, Britain, the United States, and Japan*. Cambridge: Cambridge University Press, 2004.

Thies, Cameron G. "A Pragmatic Guide to Qualitative Historical Analysis in the Study of International Relations." *International Studies Perspectives* 3, no. 4 (2002): 351–72. https://doi.org/10.1111/1528-3577.t01-1-00099.

Thoma, Grid. "Striving for a Large Market: Evidence from a General Purpose Technology in Action." *Industrial and Corporate Change* 18, no. 1 (February 1, 2009): 107–38. https://doi.org/10.1093/icc/dtn050.

Thompson, Silvanus P. "The Apprenticeship of the Future." *Contemporary Review, 1866–1900* 38 (1880): 472–85.

Thompson, William R. "Long Waves, Technological Innovation, and Relative Decline." *International Organization* 44, no. 2 (1990): 201–33. https://doi.org/10.1017/S0020818300035256.

———. *American Global Pre-Eminence: The Development and Erosion of Systemic Leadership*. Oxford: Oxford University Press, 2022.

Thompson, William R., and Leila Zakhirova. *Racing to the Top: How Energy Fuels System Leadership in World Politics*. New York: Oxford University Press, 2018.

Thomson, Ross. "Eras of Technological Convergence: Machine Tools and Mechanization in the United States, 1820–1929." Paper presented at the Economic History Association meetings, San Jose, CA, September 2010.

Thurbon, Elizabeth, and Linda Weiss. "Economic Statecraft at the Frontier: Korea's Drive for Intelligent Robotics." *Review of International Political Economy* 28, no. 1 (September 12, 2019): 103–27. https://doi.org/10.1080/09692290.2019.1655084.

Thurow, Lester C. "Microchips, Not Potato Chips," *Foreign Affairs* (July/August 1994). https://www.foreignaffairs.com/articles/1994-07-01/microchips-not-potato-chips.

Tilly, Charles. "Mechanisms in Political Processes." *Annual Review of Political Science* 4, no. 1 (2001): 21–41. https://doi.org/10.1146/annurev.polisci.4.1.21.

Timmer, Marcel P., Joost Veenstra, and Pieter J. Woltjer. "The Yankees of Europe? A New View on Technology and Productivity in German Manufacturing in the Early Twentieth Century." *Journal of Economic History* 76, no. 3 (September 2016): 874–908. https://doi.org/10.1017/S0022050716000760.

Tomayko, James E. "Forging a Discipline: An Outline History of Software Engineering Education." *Annals of Software Engineering* 6, no. 1 (March 1, 1998): 3–18. https://doi.org/10.1023/A:1018953214201.

Tomory, Leslie. "Technology in the British Industrial Revolution." *History Compass* 14, no. 4 (2016): 152–67. https://doi.org/10.1111/hic3.12306.

Toney, Autumn, and Melissa Flagg. "US Demand for AI-Related Talent." Data brief. Washington, DC: Center for Security and Emerging Technology, August 2020a. https://cset.georgetown.edu/publication/u-s-demand-for-ai-related-talent/.

———. "US Demand for AI-Related Talent, Part II: Degree Majors and Skills Assessment." Data brief. Washington, DC: Center for Security and Emerging Technology, September 2020b. https://cset.georgetown.edu/wp-content/uploads/CSET-U.S.-Demand-for-AI-Related-Talent-Part-II-1.pdf.

Trachtenberg, Marc. "Assessing Soviet Economic Performance during the Cold War: A Failure of Intelligence?" *Texas National Security Review* 1, no. 2 (February 2018): 76–101.

Trajtenberg, Manuel. "AI as the Next GPT: A Political-Economy Perspective." Working Paper 24245. Cambridge, MA: National Bureau of Economic Research, January 2018. https://www.nber.org/papers/w24245.

Trebilcock, Clive. "'Spin-Off' in British Economic History: Armaments and Industry, 1760–1914." *Economic History Review* 22, no. 3 (1969): 474–90. https://doi.org/10.1111/j.1468-0289.1969.tb00184.x.

———. *The Industrialization of the Continental Powers, 1780–1914.* London: Longman, 1981.

Treverton, Gregory F., and Seth G. Jones. "Measuring National Power." Product Page, 2005. https://www.rand.org/pubs/conf_proceedings/CF215.html.

Tsebelis, George. *Veto Players: How Political Institutions Work.* Princeton, NJ: Princeton University Press, 2002.

Tunzelmann, G. Nick von. *Steam Power and British Industrialization to 1860.* Oxford: Clarendon Press, 1978.

———. *Technology and Industrial Progress: The Foundations of Economic Growth.* Aldershot, UK: Edward Elgar Publishing, 1995.

———. "Innovation and Industrialization: A Long-Term Comparison." *Technological Forecasting and Social Change* 56, no. 1 (September 1, 1997): 1–23. https://doi.org/10.1016/S0040-1625(97)00027-9.

———. "Technology Generation, Technology Use, and Economic Growth." *European Review of Economic History* 4, no. 2 (August 1, 2000): 121–46. https://doi.org/10.1017/S136149 1600000022.

Tyson, Laura. *Who's Bashing Whom? Trade Conflict in High Technology Industries.* Washington, DC: Institute for International Economics, 1993.

Ueharal, Masashi, and Akira Tanaka. "China to Overtake US Economy by 2028–29 in COVID's Wake: JCER." *Nikkei Asia*, December 10, 2020. https://asia.nikkei.com/Economy/China-to-overtake-US-economy-by-2028-29-in-COVID-s-wake-JCER.

Unger, J. Marshall. *The Fifth Generation Fallacy: Why Japan Is Betting Its Future on Artificial Intelligence.* Oxford: Oxford University Press, 1987.

US Bureau of Education. *Report of the Commissioner of Education for the Year 1890–'91.* Washington, DC: US Government Printing Office, 1894. https://babel.hathitrust.org/cgi/pt?id=coo.31924067337554&view=1up&seq=5&skin=2021.

———. *Report of the Commissioner of Education for the Year 1892–93.* Washington, DC: US Government Printing Office, 1895. https://catalog.hathitrust.org/Record/009164574.

———. *Report of the Commissioner of Education for the Year 1896–1897.* Washington, DC: US Government Printing Office, 1898. https://babel.hathitrust.org/cgi/pt?id=coo.31924067337562&view=1up&seq=7&skin=2021.

———. *Report of the Commissioner of Education for the Year 1899–1900.* Washington, DC: US Government Printing Office, 1901. https://babel.hathitrust.org/cgi/pt?id=coo.31924067337562&view=1up&seq=7&skin=2021.

US Bureau of the Census. "Thirteenth Census of the United States," vol. 8, "Manufactures—1909." Washington, DC, 1913.

US Census Bureau. *Historical Statistics of the United States, Colonial Times to 1970.* Washington, DC: US Department of Commerce, US Census Bureau, 1975.

———. "2019 Annual Business Survey (ABS)—Technology Characteristics of Businesses." Washington, DC: US Census Bureau, 2019. https://www.census.gov/data/tables/2019/econ/abs/2019-abs-automation-technology-module.html.

US Department of Commerce. "Emerging Technologies: A Survey of Technical and Economic Opportunities." Washington, DC: US Department of Commerce, 1990.

Van Duijn, Jacob J. *The Long Wave in Economic Life.* London: Allen and Unwin, 1983.

Van Evera, Stephen. *Guide to Methods for Students of Political Science.* Ithaca, NY: Cornell University Press, 1997.

Van Leeuwen, Thed N., Henk F. Moed, Robert J. W. Tijssen, Martijn S. Visser, and Anthony F. J. Van Raan. "Language Biases in the Coverage of the Science Citation Index and Its Consequences for International Comparisons of National Research Performance." *Scientometrics* 51 (2001): 335–46.

Väyrynen, Raimo. "Economic Cycles, Power Transitions, Political Management, and Wars between Major Powers." *International Studies Quarterly* 27, no. 4 (December 1, 1983): 389–418. https://doi.org/10.2307/2600554.

Vazquez, John A. "When Are Power Transitions Dangerous? An Appraisal and Reformulation of Power Transition Theory." In *Parity and War: Evaluations and Extensions of the War Ledger*, edited by Jacek Kugler and Douglas Lemke, 35–56. Ann Arbor: University of Michigan Press, 1996.

Vernon, Raymond. *Sovereignty at Bay: The Multinational Spread of US Enterprises*. New York: Basic Books, 1971.

Vicente, María Rosalía, and Ana Jesús López. "Assessing the Regional Digital Divide across the European Union." *Telecommunications Policy* 35, no. 3 (April 1, 2011): 220–37. https://doi.org /10.1016/j.telpol.2010.12.013.

Vincent, James. "OpenAI's Latest Breakthrough Is Astonishingly Powerful, but Still Fighting Its Flaws." *The Verge*, July 30, 2020. https://www.theverge.com/21346343/gpt-3-explainer -openai-examples-errors-agi-potential.

Vogel, Ezra F. *Japan as Number One: Lessons for America*. Cambridge, MA: Harvard University Press, 1979.

Vogel, Steven K. "Japan's Information Technology Challenge." In *The Third Globalization: Can Wealthy Nations Stay Rich in the Twenty-First Century?*, edited by Dan Breznitz and John Zysman, chap. 13. Oxford: Oxford University Press, 2013.

Vona, Francesco, and Davide Consoli. "Innovation and Skill Dynamics: A Life-Cycle Approach." *Industrial and Corporate Change* 24, no. 6 (2014): 1393–1415. https://doi.org/10 .1093/icc/dtu028.

Vries, Jan de, and Ad van der Woude. *The First Modern Economy: Success, Failure, and Perseverance of the Dutch Economy, 1500–1815*. Cambridge: Cambridge University Press, 1997.

Vries, Peer. *Escaping Poverty: The Origins of Modern Economic Growth*. Vienna: Vienna University Press, 2013.

Wadsworth, Alfred P., and Julia De Lacy Mann. *The Cotton Trade and Industrial Lancashire 1600–1780*. Manchester, UK: Manchester University Press, 1931.

Wagner, Dana R. "The Keepers of the Gates: Intellectual Property, Antitrust, and the Regulatory Implications of Systems Technology." *Hastings Law Journal* 51 (1999): 1073.

Waldner, David. "What Makes Process Tracing Good? Causal Mechanisms, Causal Inference, and the Completeness Standard in Comparative Politics." In *Process Tracing: From Metaphor to Analytic Tool*, edited by Andrew Bennett and Jeffrey T. Checkel, 126–52. Cambridge: Cambridge University Press, 2015.https://doi.org/10.1017/CBO9781139858472.008.

Wallerstein, Immanuel. *The Politics of the World-Economy: The States, the Movements, and the Civilizations*. Cambridge: Cambridge University Press, 1984.

Waltz, Kenneth N. *Theory of International Politics*. New York: McGraw-Hill, 1979.

Wang, Jianhui, and Xiaobo Chen. "Information Security: A Comparative Study on Cloud Security in China and the United States: What Gaps Exist in Chinese Cloud Security? (信息 安全：中美云安全产业对比研究，国内云安全公司空间几何?)." *DongXing Securities*, June 29, 2020. http://www.xcf.cn/article/2a6265f3bc2f11eabf3cd4c9efcfdeca.html.

Wang, Ping, and Liang Zheng. "Beyond Government Control of China's Standardization System—History, Current Status, and Reform Suggestions." In *Megaregionalism 2.0*, edited by Dieter Ernst and Michael Plummer, 311–39. World Scientific, 2018.

Weber, Max. *The Protestant Ethic and the Spirit of Capitalism*. London: Allen and Unwin, 1930.

Webster, Graham, Rogier Creemers, Paul Triolo, and Elsa Kania. "China's Plan to 'Lead' in AI: Purpose, Prospects, and Problems." *New America*, August 1, 2017. http://newamerica.org /cybersecurity-initiative/blog/chinas-plan-lead-ai-purpose-prospects-and-problems/.

Weiss, Linda. *States in the Global Economy: Bringing Domestic Institutions Back In.* Cambridge: Cambridge University Press, 2003.

———. *America Inc.? Innovation and Enterprise in the National Security State.* Ithaca, NY: Cornell University Press, 2014.

Wengenroth, Ulrich. "The Steel Industries of Western Europe Compared, 1870–1914." In *Economics of Technology*, edited by Ove Granstrand. Amsterdam: North-Holland, 1994.

Wertheimer, J. "Higher Technical Education in Great Britain and Germany." *Nature* 68, no. 1760 (1903): 274–76.

West, Darrell M. *The Future of Work: Robots, AI, and Automation.* Washington, DC: Brookings Institution Press, 2018.

West, Joel. "Moderators of the Diffusion of Technological Innovation: Growth of the Japanese PC Industry." Paper presented at the 56th annual meeting of the Academy of Management, Cincinnati, OH, 1996.

The White House. "Remarks by President Biden in Press Conference," March 25, 2021. https:// www.whitehouse.gov/briefing-room/speeches-remarks/2021/03/25/remarks-by-president -biden-in-press-conference/.

White House Office of Science and Technology Policy. "American Artificial Intelligence Initiative: Year One Annual Report." February 2020. https://trumpwhitehouse.archives.gov/wp -content/uploads/2020/02/American-AI-Initiative-One-Year-Annual-Report.pdf.

Whitworth, Joseph. "Special Report of Joseph Whitworth" [1854]. In *The American System of Manufactures*, edited by Nathan Rosenberg, 329–87. Edinburgh: Edinburgh University Press, 1969.

Wickenden, William E. *A Comparative Study of Engineering Education in the United States and in Europe: Bulletin 16 of the Investigation of Engineering Education.* Lancaster, PA: Lancaster Press, June 1929. https://catalog.hathitrust.org/Record/005762499.

Williams, Eric. *Capitalism and Slavery.* Chapel Hill: University of North Carolina Press, 1944.

Winograd, Terry A. "Strategic Computing Research and the Universities." Working Paper 7. San Jose, CA: Silicon Valley Research Group, 1987.

Wirkierman, Ariel Luis. "Yeasty vs. Mushroom-Like Patterns of Hyper-Integrated Productivity Growth: An Analysis of Six Advanced Industrial Economies," 22nd International Input-Output Conference, Lisbon, July 14–18, 2014. https://www.iioa.org/conferences/22nd /papers/files/1777_20140514011_alw-iioa-vhiptvty-ym.pdf.

Witt, Michael A. "China: What Variety of Capitalism?" SSRN Scholarly Paper. Rochester, NY: Social Science Research Network, October 22, 2010. https://doi.org/10.2139/ssrn.1695940.

Witt, Michael A., and Gregory Jackson. "Varieties of Capitalism and Institutional Comparative Advantage: A Test and Reinterpretation." *Journal of International Business Studies* 47, no. 7 (September 1, 2016): 778–806. https://doi.org/10.1057/s41267-016-0001-8.

Witt, Michael A., and Gordon Redding. "China: Authoritarian Capitalism." In *The Oxford Handbook of Asian Business Systems*, edited by Michael A. Witt and Gordon Redding, 11–32. Oxford: Oxford University Press, 2014.

Wohlforth, William C. "The Stability of a Unipolar World." *International Security* 24, no. 1 (1999): 5–41.

Working Group on Science and Technology in US-China Relations. "Meeting the China Challenge: A New American Strategy for Technology Competition." San Diego: University of California, School of Global Policy and Strategy, November 16, 2020. https://china.ucsd.edu /_files/meeting-the-china-challenge_2020_report.pdf.

World Bank. "World Bank Country and Lending Groups." 2022. https://datahelpdesk .worldbank.org/knowledgebase/articles/906519-world-bank-country-and-lending-groups.

Wright, Gavin. "The Origins of American Industrial Success, 1879–1940." *American Economic Review* 80, no. 4 (1990): 651–68.

———. "General Purpose Technologies and Economic Growth." *Journal of Economic Literature* 38, no. 1 (March 2000): 161–62.

Wrigley, E. A. *Continuity, Chance, and Change: The Character of the Industrial Revolution in England*. Cambridge: Cambridge University Press, 1988.

———. "The Divergence of England: The Growth of the English Economy in the Seventeenth and Eighteenth Centuries: The Prothero Lecture." *Transactions of the Royal Historical Society* 10 (2000): 117–41.

Xi, Jinping. "Strive to Become the World's Primary Center for Science and High Ground for Innovation (努力成为世界主要科学中心和创新高地)." *Qiushi* (求是网), June 2021. http:// www.qstheory.cn/zhuanqu/2018-07/27/c_1123186013.htm.

Xie, Yu, and Alexandra A. Killewald. *Is American Science in Decline?* Cambridge, MA: Harvard University Press, 2012.

Xinhua News Agency. "News Analysis: Examining the Five Shortcomings of China's AI Talent System (新闻分析: 透视中国人工智能人才体系五大短板)." Xinhua News Agency, August 28, 2019. http://www.gov.cn/xinwen/2019-08/28/content_5425310.htm.

Xu, Xiujun. "The International Environment and Countermeasures of Network Governance during the 14th Five-Year Plan Period (十四五'时期网络安全治理的国际环境与应对策略)." *China Information Security*, February 27, 2021.

Yates, JoAnne, and Craig N. Murphy. *Engineering Rules: Global Standard Setting since 1880*. Baltimore: Johns Hopkins University Press, 2019.

Zanden, Jan Luiten van, and Bas van Leeuwen. "Persistent but Not Consistent: The Growth of National Income in Holland 1347–1807." *Explorations in Economic History* 49, no. 2 (2012): 119–30.

Zanden, Jan Luiten van, and Arthur van Riel. *The Strictures of Inheritance: The Dutch Economy in the Nineteenth Century*. Princeton, NJ: Princeton University Press, 2004.

Zeev, Nadav Ben, Joel Mokyr, and Karine van der Beek. "Flexible Supply of Apprenticeship in the British Industrial Revolution." *Journal of Economic History* 77, no. 1 (March 2017): 208–50. https://doi.org/10.1017/S0022050717000043.

Zhang, Daniel, Saurabh Mishra, Erik Brynjolfsson, John Etchemendy, Deep Ganguli, Barbara Grosz, Terah Lyons, et al. "The AI Index 2021 Annual Report." Stanford, CA: Stanford Human-Centered Artificial Intelligence Institute, 2021.

Zhang, Jun, and Jamie Peck. "Variegated Capitalism, Chinese Style: Regional Models, Multi-Scalar Constructions." *Regional Studies* 50, no. 1 (January 2, 2016): 52–78. https://doi.org/10 .1080/00343404.2013.856514.

Zhong, Raymond, and Paul Mozur. "For the US and China, a Technology Cold War That's Freezing Over." *New York Times*, March 23, 2018. https://www.nytimes.com/2018/03/23/technology/trump-china-tariffs-tech-cold-war.html.

Zhu, Xiaodong. "Understanding China's Growth: Past, Present, and Future." *Journal of Economic Perspectives* 26, no. 4 (2012): 103–24.

Zhuang, Juzhong, Paul Vandenberg, and Yiping Huang. *Growing beyond the Low-Cost Advantage: How the People's Republic of China Can Avoid the Middle-Income Trap*. Manila: Asian Development Bank, 2012.

Zieren, Gregory. "American Engineering Education in International Perspective: Alois Riedler and the Reform of German Engineering, 1893 1914." American Society for Engineering Education, 2006, 11.169.1–11.169.10. https://peer.asee.org/american-engineering-education-in-international-perspective-alois-riedler-and-the-reform-of-german-engineering-1893-1914.

Zwetsloot, Remco, James Dunham, Zachary Arnold, and Tina Huang. "Keeping Top AI Talent in the United States: Findings and Policy Options for International Graduate Student Retention." Washington, DC: Center for Security and Emerging Technology, December 2019. https://cset.georgetown.edu/wp-content/uploads/Keeping-Top-AI-Talent-in-the-United-States.pdf.

Zwetsloot, Remco, Helen Toner, and Jeffrey Ding. "Beyond the AI Arms Race." *Foreign Affairs*, November 16, 2018. https://www.foreignaffairs.com/reviews/review-essay/2018-11-16/beyond-ai-arms-race.

INDEX

Brooks, Harvey, 45

Brown and Sharpe Manufacturing Company, 115

Bruland, Kristine, 74

Burning Glass Institute, 196

Caicedo, Felipe, 119

Cambridge, 81

capitalism: Britain and, 84–85; China and, 203; First Industrial Revolution and, 84–85; Fourth Industrial Revolution and, 203; GPT diffusion theory and, 11, 29n75, 39–40; Japan and, 154, 156–57; Second Industrial Revolution and, 126, 128–29; skill infrastructure and, 169; Third Industrial Revolution and, 154, 156–57; United States and, 126, 128–29, 203; varieties of (VoC), 39–40, 84–85, 128–29, 156–57, 169, 203

Carlaw, Kenneth, 185, 229

Carnegie Mellon University, 150

Caselli, Francesco, 166

Center for Security and Emerging Technology (CSET), 202n125, 216

chatbots, 6

ChatGPT, 6, 216

chemical industry: American Institute of Chemical Engineers and, 104, 125; *Annual Reports on the Progress of Chemistry* and, 124; Britain and, 3, 10, 68, 89, 104–5, 109–10, 125, 130, 211; dyes and, 9, 17, 35, 88, 96, 101, 104–5, 109, 116, 123, 132; First Industrial Revolution and, 68; Germany and, 3–4, 8–10, 17, 34–35, 88–89, 96n34, 97–111, 114, 116, 123–26, 130, 211; GPT diffusion theory and, 17, 26, 33–35, 188, 211; Haber-Bosch process and, 228; innovation clustering in, 108–11; leading-sector (LS) theory and, 123–26; qualitative analysis and, 228–29, 230; Second Industrial Revolution and, 88–89, 96n34, 97–111, 114, 116, 123–26, 130; skill infrastructure and, 8, 35, 123–26; United States and, 9, 17, 35, 88–89, 96n34, 97–111, 114, 116, 123–26, 130, 211

China: artificial intelligence (AI) and, 2, 179–209; BRICS and, 1–2, 5, 13; capitalism and, 203; competition and, 2–3, 13, 178–209; complementary innovations and, 195; computers and, 179, 188, 192, 197–201, 206n143; diffusion deficit of, 215; economic size of, 180–81; education and, 196–206; electricity and, 186–88; electronics and, 187–88, 200; engineering and, 4n20, 150, 170, 180, 186–206; First Industrial Revolution and, 52; Fourth Industrial Revolution and, 1, 3, 179–209, 215–16; Google and, 184, 189, 195; GPT diffusion theory and, 20–21, 44, 179–209, 216; growth and, 1, 3, 52, 180–84, 193–94, 201, 205–8, 215; human capital and, 190; ICT talent and, 150n88; impact timeframe and, 189–90; information and communications technologies (ICTs) and, 180, 184–86, 188, 192, 196, 200–201, 206n145; institutional complementarities and, 195–203; internet and, 187, 191, 205; investment and, 191, 201, 204–8; *kanji* characters and, 157–58; key technologies and, 184–88, 201–2; labor and, 181–84; leading-sector (LS) theory and, 180, 184–85, 188–94, 206; linkages and, 184, 199, 201; Made in China 2025 plan and, 194; market issues and, 185, 194–95, 200–201, 204; military and, 203–4, 207–8; modernization and, 207, 223n15; monopolies and, 185; National Medium- and Long-Term Plan for the Development of Science and Technology, 194; policymakers and, 11, 13, 21, 179, 201, 203n129, 209, 215–16; power transitions and, 2–3, 179–81, 185, 189, 191, 203, 206–9; production and, 186, 196, 208; productivity and, 2, 20, 52, 150n88, 181–84, 189, 193, 201, 205–8; qualitative analysis and, 222, 223n15; regime type and, 205–6; relative advantage and, 191–93; research and, 181n3, 188, 191–202, 205–7; Second Industrial Revolution and, 89; security and, 179, 189, 216; skill

Fourth Industrial Revolution: BRICS conference on, 1; Britain and, 181–82; capitalism and, 203; China and, 1, 3, 179–209, 215–16; complementary innovations and, 195; computers and, 179, 188, 192, 197–201, 206n143; education and, 197–206; electricity and, 186–88; engineering and, 180, 187, 189, 195–206; France and, 192; GDP and, 181–83, 194, 201–2; Germany and, 192, 211–12; human capital and, 190; impact timeframe and, 189–90; India and, 181; information and communications technologies (ICTs) and, 180, 184–86, 192, 196, 201; institutional complementarities and, 195–203; internet and, 187, 191, 205; investment and, 191, 201, 204–8; Japan and, 181n3, 183, 192–93, 203; key technologies and, 184–88, 201–2; labor and, 181–84; leading-sector (LS) theory and, 180, 184–85, 188–94, 206; linkages and, 184, 199, 201; market issues and, 185, 194–95, 200–201, 204; Mexico and, 202; military and, 203–4, 207–8; monopolies and, 185; power transitions and, 179–81, 185, 189, 191, 203, 206–9; production and, 186, 196, 208; productivity and, 180–90, 193, 195, 201, 205–8; relative advantage and, 191–93; research and, 191, 192n74, 200–202, 205–7; software and, 193, 197; South Africa and, 202; Thompson and, 191; threat-based arguments and, 203–4; United States and, 1–3, 186–88, 215–16
Fox, Robert, 25
France: comparative advantage and, 79–82; education and, 50, 80–81, 85, 211; First Industrial Revolution and, 49–55, 68–72, 79–82, 84–85, 211; Fourth Industrial Revolution and, 192; GPT diffusion theory and, 26; innovation clustering in, 108–11; iron and, 70–71; market issues and, 85; Napoleonic Wars and, 82–84; qualitative analysis and, 225; scientists and, 81; Second Industrial Revolution and, 106n76, 108, 110; skill infrastructure and, 163, 166; steel and, 108

Franklin Institute, 118–19
Frey, Carl, 192
Fueki, Takuji, 146

G20 (Group of 20), 163, 167, 212
GDP: BRICS and, 1; Britain and, 52–55, 92–93; First Industrial Revolution and, 52–55; Fourth Industrial Revolution and, 181–83, 194, 201–2; Germany and, 92–93; GPT diffusion theory and, 20–21; lost decade and, 133, 135; quantitative analysis and, 231–36; Second Industrial Revolution and, 92–95; skill infrastructure and, 168–69, 170, 174, 175, 176; Third Industrial Revolution and, 133, 135–36
Gehlhaus, Diana, 216
genetics, 137
Germany: chemical industry and, 3–4, 8–10, 17, 34–35, 88–89, 96n34, 97–111, 114, 116, 123–26, 130, 211; comparative advantage and, 119–21; competition and, 91; as coordinated market economy (CME), 156–57; cultural issues and, 126; dyes and, 9, 17, 35, 88, 96, 101, 104–5, 109, 116, 123, 132; education and, 4, 10, 90, 116–24, 128, 178; engineering and, 9–10, 17, 35, 39, 116–25, 178; First Industrial Revolution and, 68n70; Fourth Industrial Revolution and, 192, 211–12; GDP and, 92–93; GPT diffusion theory and, 17, 26, 34–35, 39; growth and, 91–97, 104–5, 141; innovation clustering in, 108–11; inventors and, 17; investment and, 4, 8, 17, 35, 117; leading-sector (LS) theory and, 3–4, 8, 10, 35, 97, 110, 130, 141; market issues and, 10, 39, 89, 156; mechanics and, 10, 39, 116–23, 178; military and, 92n18; productivity and, 90–96, 104, 111, 130; profit and, 102, 110, 123; research and, 4, 8–10, 35, 104, 117, 122–23, 130; Second Industrial Revolution and, 10, 88–97, 102–5, 108–12, 116–30; skill infrastructure and, 8, 35, 163, 178; steel and, 89, 96–97, 102, 108–11; Third Industrial Revolution and, 141, 156–57

innovation clustering in, 108–11; institutional complementarities and, 116–26; internal combustion engine and, 88, 96–106, 229; internet and, 139, 144, 187, 191, 205; inventors and, 109, 115; investment and, 117, 120n152, 126–27, 191, 201, 204–8; key technologies and, 91, 96–100, 184–88, 201–2; labor and, 92, 94, 95, 113, 125–26, 181–84; leading-sector (LS) theory and, 88–92, 96–110, 113, 123, 126, 129–30, 180, 184–85, 188–94, 206; linkages and, 121, 125; machine tools and, 88–90, 99–108, 111–21, 124–30; market issues and, 39, 89, 97, 100, 119, 128, 129n211, 140, 155–56, 200–201, 204, 212; mechanics and, 10, 14, 90, 116–20, 178, 212; military and, 126–27, 203–4, 207–8; modernization and, 102, 113; monopolies and, 89, 109; Morrill Land-Grant Act and, 118, 123; policymakers and, 2, 4, 11, 13, 132, 179, 201, 203n129, 209, 215–16; power transitions and, 2, 88–96, 100–103, 106, 111, 126–27, 179–81, 185, 189, 191, 203, 206–9; product cycles and, 89, 97–101; production and, 89, 90n13, 94, 98–99, 102–12, 116n131, 123, 126–29, 186, 196, 208; productivity and, 2, 11, 21, 89–96, 102–4, 113–14, 130, 134–37, 140n88, 142–46, 150, 180–83, 189, 205–6, 212, 223; profit and, 102, 109–10, 123; qualitative analysis and, 223, 225, 227, 230; quantitative analysis and, 238; relative advantage and, 91, 102–3, 108, 130; research and, 9, 35, 89–90, 104, 114, 117, 119, 122, 123–24, 130, 153, 155, 181n3, 188, 193, 196–201; Revolutionary War and, 82–83; Rostow and, 97–98; scientists and, 114, 123, 142n47, 187–88, 199; Second Industrial Revolution and, 2, 14, 88–97, 101–30, 211–12; semiconductor industry and, 39; skill infrastructure and, 123, 163, 166n24, 171, 178; software and, 193, 197; source material for, 90; steam engines and, 98, 105, 109, 115; steel and, 88–89, 96–111, 129; as superpower, 4, 188, 189n55,

192, 198; Tech Cold War and, 203; telecommunications industry and, 39; Third Industrial Revolution and, 131–59; threat-based arguments and, 126–28; World War I and, 89–96, 101, 104–5, 110–11, 121; World War II and, 125, 154
University of Leipzig, 90
University of Nottingham, 45, 51
US Army, 187
US Commissioner of Education, 90
US Congress, 118
US Council of Economic Advisers, 36
US Department of Commerce, 142
US Department of Defense, 150

varieties of capitalism (VoC), 39–40; First Industrial Revolution and, 84–85; Fourth Industrial Revolution and, 203; Second Industrial Revolution and, 128–29; skill infrastructure and, 169; Third Industrial Revolution and, 156–57
Vernon, Raymond, 26
VHS format, 137
von Kármán, Theodore, 187

Wang Ping, 200
water frames, 49, 56, 60n43, 68–69
Watt, James: Boulton and, 65, 72; First Industrial Revolution and, 34, 50, 56, 64–65, 68, 72, 76, 83; steam engine and, 50, 56, 64–65, 68, 72, 83; Wilkinson and, 83
Weale, Martin, 75
Webb, Ryan, 185
Web of Science, 153, 162–64
Weiss, Linda, 203
Wilkinson, John, 63, 83
Windows (Microsoft), 147
Winograd, Terry, 150, 155–56
Wintelism, 147–48
WIRED (magazine), 6
Working Group for Software Engineering Education and Training, 150